Contents KT-497-792

SECTION I — LIVING IN FRANCE

GENERAL INTRODUCTION

RESIDENCE AND ENTRY REGULATIONS

SETTING UP HOME

DAILY LIFE

RETIREMENT

Live&Work
— IN —
FRANCE

THIRD
Completely revised and updated
EDITION

Victoria Pybus

Published by Vacation Work, 9 Park End Street, Oxford

LIVE AND WORK IN FRANCE

First edition 1991 Mark Hempshell
Second edition 1994 Victoria Pybus
Third edition 1998 Victoria Pybus

Copyright © Vacation Work 1998

ISBN 1 85458 180-5 (softback)

ISBN 1 85458 181-3 (hardback)

Publicity: Roger Musker

Cover design by
Miller Craig & Cocking Design Partnership

Imageset and Printed by **Unwin Brothers Ltd.** , Old Woking, Surrey

SECTION II — WORKING IN FRANCE

EMPLOYMENT

STARTING A BUSINESS

MAPS AND CHARTS

CASE HISTORIES

Foreword

This is the third edition of *Live and Work in France* to be published. The first edition in 1991 was also the first in our current series of books on living and working in different countries around the world. Since the last edition of this book, France has been through a severe recession which resulted in unemployment exceeding 12%, and in which the under 25s seemed most affected; one in five of them was without work. The French electorate, evidently concerned at the expanding welfare bill, voted in a right wing government partly on a ticket of welfare reform, (i.e. reduction) to try to protect the economy from further strain. But the electorate obviously found the stringent economy measures and the government plans to restrict immigration, too much against the grain of France's liberal traditions, and in 1997 the socialists were resoundingly returned to power. In the meantime signs of an economic turn around, had been growing and at the time of press France is shaping up economically to meet the EMU deadline of 1 January 1999. The major crisis of confidence and uncharacteristic pessimism that was uppermost in 1996 and early 1997 seems to be resolving itself as France continues her economic recovery.

The continuing popularity of this book confirms that there is a growing demand for information on the opportunities for work, buying and setting up a home, starting a business, or retiring in France. Even though the Single European Market has been up and running for five years and Europe's single currency, the Euro will be with us from 1999, there still remain many differences in procedures between the UK and France. This means a comprehensive base of information on the many and various regulations and practicalities still involved in relocating from the UK to France is still needed. Buying a house and starting a new job are both upheavals; doing them in another country which has a different language, laws and practices is liable to increase the apprehension felt, so the more advance information you have, the less helpless you are going to feel. Once you decide to make the cross-channel move, this book will act as a reference manual to help you steer a smoother and more informed path through the essential preparations. It provides the information needed before, during and after a move — from dealing with the residency regulations to finding a job or home, or handling the many routine day-to-day matters of existence.

The book is divided into two sections *Living in France* and *Working in France* which between them cover all areas of such a venture, including French banking, how to arrange a mortgage for French property, employment regulations and advice and ideas for setting up a small business. Social and cultural aspects are also covered with sections on the aesthetics of French social life, language, education and culture.

It is estimated that approximately 200,000 Britons have purchased property in France. This grand figure, owes less however to permanent emigrants than to inveterate Francophiles and those affluent enough to have second homes (*résidences secondaires*) in that country. A newer phenomenon is the Euro-commuter who may for instance live and work in London or the south coast during the week and spend the weekends in France, usually in the Pas de Calais or Normandy; or even the reverse. Of the French themselves, it is estimated that one in ten owns some kind of second home — within France.

From an employment perspective, the full realization of the freedom of movement of people, goods, services and capital within the EU should result in more French employers recruiting internationally for suitably qualified staff and the generally higher salary levels on the continent should attract UK nationals to these and other positions. Such conditions should tempt not only the above-mentioned groups but also professional people, the skilled, semi-skilled and unskilled, as well as those planning retirement.

L'Hexagone (as the French call their country), has much to recommend it to the British professional. In a survey taken on the factors that proved the main inducements to move to France, the majority perceived the advantages to be career prospects, earnings and lifestyle, in that order. Improved career prospects are often inseparable from the financial advantages of living overseas and it may well be that, in France, your particular field of work is better remunerated than in the UK. You may find your particular trade or profession is in greater demand in France, or it may be held in higher regard or offer better chances of promotion or responsibility. In short, the whole package offers greater potential.

For some, an better lifestyle may be a sufficient attraction. This does not necessarily mean better weather as the benefit of warm summers and mild winters is limited to the far south and the south-west of France. Brittany, Normandy and Nord-Pas-de-Calais on the other hand, have very similar meteorological conditions to the UK. Food is very high on the list of priorities. If, as Napoleon claimed *'L'Angleterre est une nation de boutiquiers'* (England is a nation of shopkeepers) then France is a nation of restaurateurs. Fortunately, the cost of dining out in France is, on the whole, approximately one third of the cost for the equivalent in Britain.

The existence of modern cities alongside medieval villages, the contrast between the industrial north and the Mediterranean south of France and the variety of the many uncrowded, untrammelled, and in some cases deserted, places in between offer a choice and quality of life which seems to have all but disappeared from overcrowded Britain. This ambience and quality of life has lured many people to uproot themselves and their families to go to some unknown corner of France. Additionally, the decentralization of industry presently occuring in France, means that more and more jobs are becoming available in quite small towns in lovely parts of the country, thus providing an alternative to the frenetic metropolitan area around Paris.

There exists a stereotype image of the unfriendly and xenophobic Gallic personality, but if you allow yourself to be deterred by this perception, you may come to regret it later when others have snapped up the cheap property still available in most areas of France (except Provence and Paris). Moreover, once out there, do not create a 'Little England' but delve deep into the initally strange but eventually fruitful and rewarding experience of living and working in a foreign culture.

Victoria Pybus
January 1998

Acknowledgments

Vacation Work is indebted to the following in no particular order for their invaluable help in compiling this book: Keith Baker of John Venn & Sons Notaries Public & Translators, Christophe Aerts of AGF Insurance, Monsieur Philippe Galy, L'Attaché des Douanes in London, Agnes Crompton, Chris Pengelly of VNU Business Information Europe, the French Chamber of Commerce in Great Britain, the Franco-British Chamber in Paris, the heroic Press and Information service of the French Embassy and Jackie and Barry Devereux and Moira Evans and Paul Player for recounting to us their experiences of living and work in France.

SECTION I

Living in France

General Introduction

Residence and Entry Regulations

Setting Up Home

Daily Life

Retirement

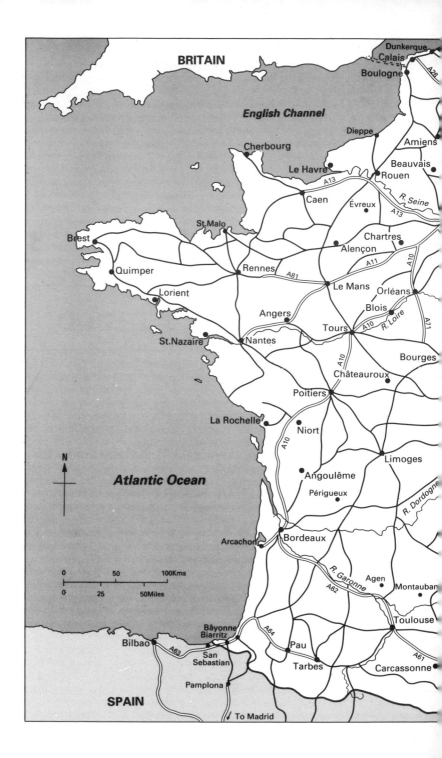

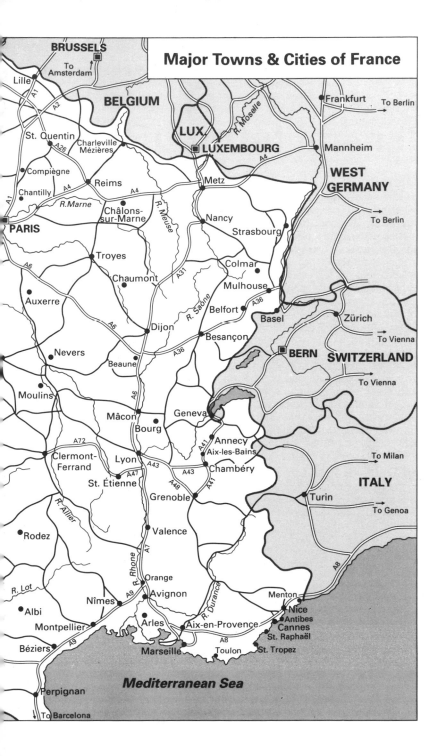

Major Towns & Cities of France

General Introduction

Destination France

In the past, the destinations most often considered for emigration by the British tended to be the countries of the 'New World' (i.e. the USA and Canada), and Australia and New Zealand. In the last fifteen years this has changed, principally because these countries now have much more restrictive immigration policies and in addition offer far fewer work opportunities than used to be the case.

The drawing together of the countries of western Europe into the European Union has led (some say forced) Britain to be part of a consolidated Europe at the expense of particular historic relationships with the North American continent and Australasia. The inevitable result is a stronger focus on European countries by those from Britain wishing to live and work abroad.

Not only are immigration procedures within the EU relatively simple for any of its citizens, compared with North America, but European countries, unswamped by anglophone expatriates offer the British a more rewarding, grass roots experience from living and working in another country.

As the UK's nearest neighbour, France is a logical choice for those considering working, retiring or buying a holiday home abroad. Additionally, the physical link of the Channel Tunnel has made France seem even closer to Britain. The likely result of this easier access is that many UK citizens, who had previously never thought of it, will become aware of the new opportunities being offered by the EU for work and business and will seriously consider moving abroad.

Pros and Cons of Moving to France

Those seeking employment will find France is home to many major national and international companies which offer a full range of career opportunities in which pay, conditions and career opportunities are very favourable. The quaint old France of vineyards, village cafés and rickety 2CVs, or *deuches* (pronounced dersh — from deux chevaux) as they are known in France still exists, but alongside are some of the most modern cities and up-to-date, high technology industries in the world. Some French industries are generally acknowledged as being more dynamic than in the UK and therefore offer far better career opportunities; these include most scientific and technological companies. However, other industries fare less well and whether you stand to gain or lose on this count will depend on the specific trade or profession that you ply.

Overall, French wages and salaries tend to be higher than in the UK and most people undertaking similar work in France to that in the UK will find that they are paid more for it. However, a much greater differential exists in France between the best paid jobs and the worst ones: a particular skill could be sought after and well paid, or it may be much less well regarded by French employers.

Although living costs vary between the UK and France, generally property is cheaper in France than in the UK. As a result a French resident can usually enjoy a higher disposable income than his or her UK counterpart; this can benefit retirement and holiday home buyers as well as working residents. However other living costs, particularly food and utilities are more expensive than in the UK.

French income tax tends to be lower than in the UK, with the tax rate for the lowest earners starting at 5%. However, social security contributions tend to be higher in the UK. Total deductions from the typical French salary range between about 22% and 32%, whereas deductions from the average UK salary are rarely less than 32%.

France has always been seen as offering a stylish way of living. In many parts of the country the weather is warm and sunny, but more temperate than Spain. Most parts of the country have beautiful scenery and some like the volcanic Auvergne and the majestic Alps are outstanding. There is probably more scenic variation in France than almost any other country in Europe. Rural France has an unhurried pace of life; food, drink and social life are regarded as priorities. Conversely, some parts of France like Picardy are wet and cold, with relatively dull scenery. Some of the big cities and industrial belts surrounding them can be congested and polluted and suffer from chronic unemployment and all the social problems associated with similar deprived areas in Britain.

Moving to the continent involves an obvious language hurdle. French is not considered difficult to learn, and it would certainly be impractical to attempt taking up residence in France without a reasonable degree of linguistic competence. While the French are not renowned for welcoming foreigners unreservedly, they are rarely hostile to attempts, however faltering, to converse in their language; nevertheless, they will probably not resist the temptation to correct your pronunciation (just repeat it until you get it right). However, the process of integration will take time and effort; more so in some parts of France where people are considered foreign even if they come from another part of the country.

The following is a summary of the main pros and cons of living in France from the British point of view:

Pros: France is the nearest EU country to the UK.
Rates of pay are as high or higher than in the UK.
Land and property prices are lower than in the UK.
Scientific and technology industries are very advanced and successful.
Dining out costs much less than in the UK.
Most regions have a better climate than the UK.
France is an interesting country with a rich culture.

Cons: Knowledge of French necessary.
Some jobs in France do not have same prestige or pay as in the UK.
The French are not always receptive to foreign employees.
Locals can initially be suspicious of strangers.
Some regions are remote and rather backward.
Higher costs of living exist for some items e.g. electrical and telephone, plumbing and renovation services.
French culture and lifestyle are sometimes totally at odds with the British way of life.
Despite the relaxed pace of life, the French can be both more formal and more officious than the British.

Political and Economic Structure

Government and Politics

The French republican system of government was set up in 1792, three years after the storming of the Bastille and the outbreak of the Revolution. As such France was one of the earliest modern republics and over the years, this has been refined to an efficient and well-balanced form of government with its own peculiarities. The current republic is the fifth and was established in 1958. It has a few similarities to the system by which the UK is governed, but unlike the UK it is based upon a written constitution.

The President is Head of State and Head of the Government: He (there has as yet been no woman President) must abide by the rules of the constitution but has limited powers to amend it. Thus the President is an active politician, not merely an official figurehead; a constitutional council ensures that the constitution is followed properly. The President is elected by popular vote every seven years and the presidency cannot be transferred to another person. The President appoints a Prime Minister, and through him or her, other ministers, to head the various ministries and government departments. The current President is the Gaullist, Jacques Chirac who was appointed in May 1995, and the the Prime Minister is the leftist Lionel Jospin (appointed in May 1977). There are 42 ministers.

The choice of ministers (42 of them) is determined by the political make-up of the elected Parliament; a deputy appointed to ministership automatically gives up his or her seat in the assembly to a previously selected stand-in (*adjoint*).

Owing to the power vested in the Presidential office, the parliament has slightly less importance than in other countries. It introduces and reviews legislation, but much of this has been formulated beforehand and will be approved as a matter of course. The President is usually bound by the decisions of Parliament but can, in certain circumstances overrule them. Parliament consists of two houses: the Assemblée Nationale with 577 MP's (*députés*) who must be elected every five years by the people; and the Sénat (a.k.a. *Haute Assemblée*), consisting of 321 members elected every nine years (one third of the seats being contested every three years) by local town councillors (*conseillers généraux*).

The National Assembly (lower house) deputies are elected in districts of varying sizes which works out roughly at one deputy per 100,000 inhabitants of France. The term of the legislature is five years but it can be abridged if the President of the Republic decides to dissolve the Assembly as Chirac did in 1997 when he dissolved the Assembly nine months early in an attempt to give his Gaullist-led government a clear mandate for the move to a single European currency.

The long term of office of the senators in the upper house promotes political stability, which is further strengthened by the fact that, unlike the National Assembly, the Senate cannot be dissolved. The Constitution also confers on the President of the Senate the job of taking over the Presidency of the Republic should the office suddenly be vacated as in a resignation or (as happened with President Pompidou), the President dies in office. The Sénat reviews the legislation of the Assemblée Nationale but, in effect, cannot overrule it.

Elections

All French elections have an unusual double-ballot system. The first election includes all nominees, the second only the two candidates who receive the two highest numbers of votes. In the case of governmental elections, the two ballots are held about a week apart. Proportional representation is used in some elections.

It is not unusual for the President to be of a different political persuasion to the government. This was the case in the during the last term of the late President Mitterand. Such an anomaly (i.e. a president and a government of different political colours) can arise in France where the balance of power tends to be held by a coalition of parties and because the presidential and the parliamentary elections are out of sync.

Women in Politics
It used to be said that women governed France from the bedroom. Historically, there was no alternative as The Salic Law excluded women from succession to the French crown; so, there was no tradition or role models after Jeanne d'Arc until Edith Cresson became the first woman Prime Minister. However, there is still a long way to go. France has always been late in promoting women to power. French women did not get the vote or the right to stand as political candidates until 1945 (compared with 1929 in the UK). At the time of press France still has a smaller number of women in national government than any other EU nation and is 72 in the world league of female representation in politics, behind many developing countries. In the 1997 French parliamentary elections the Socialists agreed by party edict, to field a quota of at least 30% women candidates which has considerably increased the number of women deputies with seats in *L'Assemblée Nationale*. Some well-known French female politicians are: Martine Aubry, Employment Minister and the daughter of Jacques Delors, Cathcrine Trautmann, mayor of Strasbourg and the only women to hold such a position in a main French city, Simone Veil (a former health minister) and Edith Cresson who was France's first female Prime Minister.

For a further insight into why French women lag behind their Scandinavian and other European counterparts in politics, read Elizabeth Guigou's book *Etre Femme et Politique*. Guigou was the former Socialist minister for European Affairs (of the political kind).

Administration — Région, Département and Commune
The other layers of political administration in France are the Région, The Départment and the Commune. The Région is the newest administrative unit and was established in 1982. There are 26 regions in France, 22 of them are in Metropolitan France and the remaining four are overseas. Since the mid 1980's each region has had its own executive and elected assembly — the Assemblée Régional, whose members aer elected for six years through a system of proportional representation.

The Département was first instituted in 1789 and was the administrative district of the Republic. France comprises 100 departements, 96 of which are in Metropolitan France and four overseas (Martinique, Guadeloupe, Réunion and French Guiana). From 1800 to 1982 the executive power of the departement was invested in the Prefect. Since 1982 the Prefect has been replaced by a Chairman of the General Council who is elected from among the general council members for a period of three years. The General Councillors are elected for six years in a two-round majority voting election. Half the members of the general council come up for re-election every three years.

The *commune* or municipality is the smallest and oldest administrative unit instituted in 1789 and is the ground level administrative unit of France. There are almost 37,000 communes — a large number by European nation standards. The reason for this is that the term applies to communities regardless of size: 80% of municipalities have fewer than 1000 inhabitants. Because of this, the government brought in a new law in 1992 to encourage the very small communes to band together into urban communities or associations of several communities known as *syndicats* to develop their shared local interests. The executive of the *commune* is the mayor. He or she, is elected for six years by the municipal council and is chosen from its ranks. The mayor has a dual role as both an official of the municipality and the representative of the state in the municipality. In the latter function, he or she performs marriages, keeps the civil register of births, marriages and deaths and is an officer of the *police judiciare*. He or she is also responsible for administrative functions such as publishing laws and regulations, establishing the electoral role, and the draft roll of those eligible for national military service.

Each commune has an elected council, the number of its members being proportional to the population of the commune. Municipal councillors are elected for six years by direct universal suffrage and they shape local policies, define the administrative operations of the municipality, vote the budget and manage the property and facilities of the commune.

The commune and mayoral elections are the only ones that foreigners resident in France can vote in. Holders of the *carte de séjour* can also stand for local election to the council, but not for mayor.

Political Parties

The French political system hosts a wide range of political parties and the balance of power depends on coalition (known in France as 'cohabitation'). The main parties include the Parti Socialiste (PS), and the Rassemblement pour la République (RPR), which follows the ideals of de Gaulle and the Union pour la Démocratie Française (UDF) which formed the RPR-UDF alliance in 1988. There is also the declining Parti Communiste Francais (PCF). The Front National (FN), founded in 1972 manifests extreme Right tendencies mixed with Roman Catholic fundamentalism and, is gaining support though it lost its single seat in the 1993 elections. This caused its splenetic founder, Jean-Marie Le Pen to complain indignantly since his party's support has extended around the country and amounted to 12% of the plebiscite in the 1993 elections. The FN campaigns mainly on immigration, in particular, non-European immigration which it would like not only to end but to reverse. Finally, like most European countries, France has its ecology parties: the Green Party (Les Verts) was founded in 1984 and is a confederation of several ecological groups including Génération Ecologie.

Issues like the Maastricht treaty and the French decision to join the European single currency in January 1999, have made the French more politically aware than usual. However, membership of political parties is generally quite low compared to other countries.

The Economy

Often the economic importance of France is underestimated when compared to other major world powers. In general, the economy has been successful since the end of the Second World War and at times in the 1960's France had a rate of growth comparable to that of the USA. France is rated the fourth strongest capitalist economy in the world after the USA, Japan and Germany. However, in France as in other European countries, the long, worldwide recession of recent years affected most major industries and escalated unemployment to 12.8% (nearly four million people), one of the highest totals in the EU. The French franc is coupled to the Deutsche Mark in the ERM, and this has led to French economic policy being dictated by the Bundesbank (i.e. interest rates have been kept high). This is known as the *franc fort* (strong franc) policy. At the time of press all economic efforts in France are geared to ensuring that France stays economically on course for the Franco-German goal of European Monetary Union (EMU) which will come into effect from midnight on 1 January 1999. Britain is not joining then, although British businesses will almost certainly be dealing in Euros from that date. The French people probably have their own doubts about the single currency which partly explains why barely half the French electorate voted in favour of Maastricht and total European integration, in the national referendum.

The cliff-hanger Yes vote (51%) in favour of the Maastricht treaty and the currency crisis in the autumn of 1992 spawned a wave of industrial protests. Like the UK, France experienced heavy redundancies during 1992 and 1993. The tax-paying electorate decided they could no longer afford the cost of social support and welfare and chose a rightest government which was faced with taking unpopular austerity measures such as reducing benefits and pensions to bring down the massive 350 billion franc budget deficit. Deciding after all, that the government's various belt-tightening tactics were insupportable, the electorate voted the socialists back into power in 1997. The socialist government is also however, comitted to reducing spending on welfare, particularly child welfare for better off families.

In the past, economical setbacks have been seen as temporary and France has remained optimistic about its future. Even in the 1970's when economic prospects were poor, both government and business seemed keen to invest money and effort in research and technology projects for the future; investments which paid off by putting France at the forefront in generating technological progress in everything from nuclear power to satellite launchers.

At the time of press, all economic signals coming from France signify that the recession is largely over and inflation is down to under 2% again. However, the last few years of recession have had a significant effect on economic growth and this and a perception that France's role in the world has receded have produced a national state of mind which is uncharacteristically gloomy. One factor likely to be significant in the recovery of the French economy is the gradual evolution from state-controlled or state-partnership industries to private companies. The list of enterprises sold or being sold off in France is expected to help her maintain a strong economic position both by keeping abreast of new technology and international markets and through the government's continued support of French companies and products, especially in export markets. Such a situation obviously bodes well for those considering employment with French companies.

France is one of the leading countries within Europe to encourage regional development, with the state agency DATAR to oversee this. Unlike the UK, in France there is no north-south or capital-provinces divide although, as in the UK, the south is one of the most prosperous areas.

France was a founder member of the European Community in 1957 and, although placed second to Germany in economic terms, is generally acknowledged to be the joint leader of the community. Critics say that France has set up many self-interested EU procedures and policies; either way, there is no doubt that France sees the EU as being an excellent way of promoting its own interests. French business and industry were well prepared to take full advantage of the single market, being both competitive and technologically minded. The central position of the country within the EU is of great importance. The Channel Tunnel link with the UK is valuable to both countries and unlike neighbouring Belgium or the Netherlands there is plenty of space in France for industrial development.

Less optimistically, economic drawbacks that France will have to overcome in the future include the fact that its financial markets are not well developed.

Additionally, some industries lack good financial management and planning, both of which are, relatively speaking, strong points within the UK economy. Finally, France has little involvement in the potentially lucrative economies of Eastern Europe which other EU countries are much better positioned to take advantage of.

For background information on French government, politics, society and the economy *France Today* by John Ardagh (Penguin, 1990) is recommended; and for information on trends generally *Francoscopie*, the annual Larousse publication that provides information for an in-depth analysis of France based on thousands of statistics.

Geographical Information

Area and Main Physical Features

France is the largest country of the EU and has a surface area of 544,500 square kilometres. However, with an average population density of approximately 49 people per square kilometre (compared to 361 people per square kilometre in the UK) it is markedly less populated than the UK, Belgium, Germany, the Netherlands or Italy. The borders of France are largely defined by physical barriers; the Channel (la Manche), Atlantic Ocean, Pyrenees, Mediterranean Sea, Alps and the River Rhine. France is generally a lowland country, with most of its surface less than 200 metres above sea level. There are only three mountainous areas: the French Alps, the Pyrenees and the rather less mountainous Massif Central in central southern France. The country's most important rivers are the Loire, the Rhône, the Seine and the Garonne.

Neighbouring Countries

France shares a land border with five other EU countries — Spain, Italy, Luxembourg, Germany and Belgium — as well as with Switzerland. The Channel Tunnel is not only the first artificial link between England and France but an umbilical cord between the rest of Europe and Britain from which France is bound to benefit.

Internal Organisation

France was divided into 22 official regions in the 1980's in order to provide a modern working framework for the economic development of the provinces and and also to assist in the effective decentralization of industry. This move has served both to reintroduce several historic, provincial titles, such as Languedoc, Provence, etc., (lost after the 1789 Revolution) and to encourage a resurgence of local feeling within the newly-delimited regions. The 96 *départements* which make up the Metropolitan regions date from immediately after the Revolution in 1790. They were formed for administrative purposes after the old feudal territories had been swept away, along with the vestiges of the *ancien régime*. Each department has a directly elected *conseil général* (council). Finally, there are the smallest internal administrative divisions within France, the *communes*, of which there are some 37,500 each with a council and a mayor elected every six years. Mayors are far more influential figures in France than in the UK being both a servant of the local people and responsible to the state. Additionally, the island of Corsica (annexed by revolutionary France in 1789) is officially an integrated part of France and forms two départements.

SECTION II — WORKING IN FRANCE

EMPLOYMENT

STARTING A BUSINESS

MAPS AND CHARTS

CASE HISTORIES

Foreword

This is the third edition of *Live and Work in France* to be published. The first edition in 1991 was also the first in our current series of books on living and working in different countries around the world. Since the last edition of this book, France has been through a severe recession which resulted in unemployment exceeding 12%, and in which the under 25s seemed most affected; one in five of them was without work. The French electorate, evidently concerned at the expanding welfare bill, voted in a right wing government partly on a ticket of welfare reform, (i.e. reduction) to try to protect the economy from further strain. But the electorate obviously found the stringent economy measures and the government plans to restrict immigration, too much against the grain of France's liberal traditions, and in 1997 the socialists were resoundingly returned to power. In the meantime signs of an economic turn around, had been growing and at the time of press France is shaping up economically to meet the EMU deadline of 1 January 1999. The major crisis of confidence and uncharacteristic pessimism that was uppermost in 1996 and early 1997 seems to be resolving itself as France continues her economic recovery.

The continuing popularity of this book confirms that there is a growing demand for information on the opportunities for work, buying and setting up a home, starting a business, or retiring in France. Even though the Single European Market has been up and running for five years and Europe's single currency, the Euro will be with us from 1999, there still remain many differences in procedures between the UK and France. This means a comprehensive base of information on the many and various regulations and practicalities still involved in relocating from the UK to France is still needed. Buying a house and starting a new job are both upheavals; doing them in another country which has a different language, laws and practices is liable to increase the apprehension felt, so the more advance information you have, the less helpless you are going to feel. Once you decide to make the cross-channel move, this book will act as a reference manual to help you steer a smoother and more informed path through the essential preparations. It provides the information needed before, during and after a move — from dealing with the residency regulations to finding a job or home, or handling the many routine day-to-day matters of existence.

The book is divided into two sections *Living in France* and *Working in France* which between them cover all areas of such a venture, including French banking, how to arrange a mortgage for French property, employment regulations and advice and ideas for setting up a small business. Social and cultural aspects are also covered with sections on the aesthetics of French social life, language, education and culture.

It is estimated that approximately 200,000 Britons have purchased property in France. This grand figure, owes less however to permanent emigrants than to inveterate Francophiles and those affluent enough to have second homes (*résidences secondaires*) in that country. A newer phenomenon is the Euro-commuter who may for instance live and work in London or the south coast during the week and spend the weekends in France, usually in the Pas de Calais or Normandy; or even the reverse. Of the French themselves, it is estimated that one in ten owns some kind of second home — within France.

From an employment perspective, the full realization of the freedom of movement of people, goods, services and capital within the EU should result in more French employers recruiting internationally for suitably qualified staff and the generally higher salary levels on the continent should attract UK nationals to these and other positions. Such conditions should tempt not only the above-mentioned

Population

The current population of France comprises approximately 56.9 million people. This includes almost one million immigrants from the former French colony of Algeria and just over two million from other EU countries, of which nearly half are from Portugal and the remainder from Italy, Spain, Morocco, Tunisia, former Yugoslavia and Poland. It is not known how many illegal immigrants from Africa and Eastern Europe are in France, but some estimates put it as high as three million. The population of Paris itself is two and a half million while that of the whole Paris region is approximately ten million.

The populations of the largest cities of France are:
Lyon — 1,222,000; Rouen — 448,000; Lille — 1,050,000; Bordeaux — 645,000; Marseille — 1,111,000; Toulouse — 543,000

Other Territories

In addition to mainland France there are the overseas territories of French Polynesia (including Tahiti) and New Caledonia, the French Southern & Antarctic Territories and the Wallis and Futuna islands, and the overseas départements (*départements d'outre-mer*) of French Guiana, Guadeloupe, Martinique, Mayotte and Réunion. The latter have a greater degree of autonomy than internal regions, but are still départements of France.

Monaco has the status of a principality and is not a French département.

Climatic Zones

As a very large country France experiences a wide variation in weather. Unlike the UK these variations are not gradual but are very sharply defined in different parts of the country.

Continental Zone: Continental weather affects the north eastern quarter of France; this features warm summers, but with fairly high rainfall and consistently cold winters. Continental weather also characterises the Auvergne, Burgundy and the Rhône Valley.

Mediterranean Zone: Mediterranean weather affects the south and south eastern corner of France: Roussillon, the Riviera and Provence. This climate is characterized by hot summers and warm winters; rainfall is low and erratic throughout the year.

Mountain Zone: Mountain weather affects the Alps, Pyrenees and Massif Central, bringing with it cool summers with frequent rain and very cold winters with long periods of both sunny weather and rain or snow.

Oceanic Zone: Ocean weather affects the western seaboard of France from the Loire to the Basque region and the central regions: warm summers and mild winters with very heavy rainfall are common to these areas.

The notorious *mistral* is the normally seasonal wind which is caused by cold air being funelled down the Rhône Valley at high speed. It is a cold and dry and blows on and off during the winter and spring.

Overall, France has no very extreme weather, whether hot, dry, cold or wet and exceptions to this are very occasional. The following tables give the average temperatures of the main regions of France in degrees centigrade. The first column signifies the temperatures in winter and the second column those in summer.

Weather Chart

	Winter Average	Summer Average
Paris	7°	25°
Alps	3°	25°
Alsace	5°	26°
Aquitaine	9°	25°
Brittany	9°	24°
Corsica	12°	28°
Languedoc	11°	28°
Loire	8°	24°
Pyrenees	10°	27°
Normandy	8°	22°

Regions' Report

The French Connection

Before launching into a description of the various regions of France, it would be as well to pause and consider the historical links between the British, particularly the English, and the French. The Norman invasion of England in 1066 began a thousand years of antagonism and rivalry, conflict, and curmudgeonly cooperation that is the history of relations between the two nations. Britain has had connections with many countries from Norway to North America and from Palestine to India, but the French connection through geography and history, is the most enduring. In the 11th century, England, through the Norman invasion, became an extension of Normandy, to which was later added Gascony, acquired through dynastic marriage, and Picardy and Flanders. The French lands thus linked to the English crown in the 12th century, amounted to the western half of what is now modern France. The Normans brought with them to England, their culture, which included the French language, Romanesque and Gothic architecture and chivalry, mainly in the form of the knightly tournament. The exchange was however a two way street: English style went south to France, particularly south-western France which remained under the English crown for about the next three centuries. This long period of association saw the rise of the popularity of Gascony wines, shipped to England's ports in annual bulk consignments, and a glance at the history of some of the most illustrious Bordeaux châteaux (e.g Cantenac-Brown, Lynch-Bages) reveals their English origin; even Châteaux Margaux was originally the property of the English crown. In 1337 the English king, Edward III claimed the French crown and began the 'Hundred Years' War' of which Calais was one of the spoils which remained in British hands for over 200 years. Henry V, glorified by Shakespeare and Kenneth Branagh, pursued the British claim to France's lands, and Shakespeare's eponymous play ends on the high note of his era, the victory over the French at Agincourt in 1415. After that it was downhill for British claims to France. In 1429, with Henry VI on the English throne, a peasant called Jeanne, heard angelic voices, telling her to throw the English out of France and such was her rallying effect on her countrymen, that in less than four months the English were on the verge of defeat from the armies of Jeanne d'Arc. The English occupation of France was more or less ended when the British lost the battle of Formigny in 1450, and with it Normandy. This was followed by defeat at Bordeaux in 1453 and the countries were finally separated.

The next big era of conflict between England and France was the one for the colonies of the New World and the East. France bankrupted herself in the attempt to contend with wars both in Europe and overseas and the resulting overtaxation of the peasantry was one of the direct causes of the French Revolution in 1789. The French Revolution proved a mere hiatus in Franco-British rivalry as the rise of the formidable Napoléon Bonaparte and his plans for an Empire in Europe included designs on Britain. His ambitions were finally thwarted, as most schoolchildren learn on the plain of Waterloo in Belgium. Economically exhausted, France never realised her industrial potential in the nineteenth century, despite producing some of the world's best engineers like Monsieur Eiffel who built notable bridges (including one in Corsica) as well as the eponymous tower in Paris, and Ferdinand de Lesseps of Suez and Panama Canals fame. France in general and Paris in particular did however become synonymous with luxury goods, particularly fabrics for clothes and furnishings and household goods while Paris herself became a byword for fashion, luxury and elegance — a reputation it still lives on today.

The nineteenth century saw another flowering of cultural exchange between the two countries as the influence of the English romantics blew some of the cobwebs off dusty French classicism, while French settings became de rigeur for English and American novelists. The French language itself however, once the language of courts throughout Europe, never recovered its prestige as the international language of diplomacy enjoyed in pre-revolutionary times.

From the Grand Tour and the dawn of the age of travel as a form of pleasure (at least for the wealthy), came the habit of taking French holidays. Several Normandy seaside towns and Biarritz and Nice became very fashionable with 'Les Anglais'; while Paris attracted the highest society of all including British royalty. With this closer, sustained contact of the French and English, the French were able to reinforce their prejudices about the English and comment on their lack of sartorial style and physical disproportions, their gluttony and their inelegant manners. The English, it was said, went to France for pleasure, the French went to England for business (or as exiles from the various downturns of fortune inflicted on the royal and imperial dynasties). It became expedient, if not mutually comfortable, for the two nations to form the Entente Cordiale, a kind of alliance against the burgeoning power of a united Germany, and a Russia which was also looming on the horizon. During the wars fought as allies, both countries talked up their own contribution at the expense of the other. The First World War was probably won by the Americans turning up in vast numbers just in time; but to the French it was won at Verdun. The British meanwhile having lost a generation of manhood at Mons, the Somme and the other terrible battlefields, regard it as a victory won by their great sacrifice. In the Second World War, the French were contemptuous of the British tactical retreat at Dunkerque, while the British condemned the French for cooperating in part with the Germans, when France split between Free France and Occupied France. This, if anything, reinforced the British prejudice that the French were treacherous. Those of the Free French who had dealings with the British see it from another more friendly point of view, as an era which forged many bonds friendship and a French affection for many things British, including the British character.

In the post-war years, France overtook Britain economically and in world influence. A position she still retains today, despite the drawbacks of a lack of natural resources. There is little doubt in most Europeans' minds that the 'alliance' of Germany and France controls the destiny of the European Union; another source of contention between Britain and France.

The actual and symbolic linking of Britain and France by the Channel Tunnel has ended the separation of France and England once again and who knows, reduced the rivalry between them through mutual interests inextricably interlinked.

Regions and Départements

Many foreigners feel that they know very little about most of the French regions even if they have visited France many times over several years. This is understandable in that although a large and diverse country, popular tourism for many years was mainly confined to Paris and certain fashionable coastal regions, notably in the north and south of France. In recent years, however, the regions have gained a degree of autonomy, and under the current government's policy of decentralisation they have become much more self-promoting and accessible, and in addition, the majority have been transformed by economic development. Thus all the regions can be considered potential destinations for anyone wishing to settle and work in France: the choice will largely depend on the lifestyle desired, personal preference for a particular area, and/or regional employment opportunities.

The French sometimes refer to their country as *l'hexagone* and a quick glance at any map will show why. The country is very approximately six-sided with the Mediterranean, the Atlantic and the Channel on three 'sides' and the Alps, Pyrenees and the River Rhine on the other sides forming natural barriers between France and her neighbours. Internally, France is divided into 23 areas known as regions which are roughly equivalent to the Midlands or South Wales etc. in Britain. The French regions have a measure of autonomy, although this is a recent development and the system is nothing like as federally developed as it is for instance in Germany. In most cases the regional divisions correspond to the natural differences in geography between them.

Each region is sub-divided into départements which are comparable in size and function to British counties. Each of the 96 départements has an administrative centre which is either a major city or the counterpart of a county town. The départements used to be under the direct control of Paris. Now the regions have more influence the départements have rather subsided in importance although they are still crucial to the administration. The départments are sub-divided into communes which have their own authorities, very much like town or parish councils. Perhaps the most important point to register is that administrative matters are usually handled on a departmental basis, but when talking about culture, scenery or even cuisine the variations are usually defined on a regional basis.

Welcome and Information Facilities

As one would expect of a country with a huge tourist industry, France has no shortage of welcome and information centres, about 5,000 of them. The better known and larger towns and cities each have an *office de tourisme* while tourist bureaux *syndicats d'initiative* can be found in the main square or near the town centre of many smaller towns. The latter usually operate from more modest premises and for shorter hours than an Office Tourisme.

The main Office de Tourisme in Paris is open from 9am to 8pm daily. In addition, there are welcome offices *Accueil de France* at each of the main Parisian rail stations: Gare du Nord, Gare de l'Est, Gare de Lyon, Gare d'Austerlitz and Gare St Lazare and also at the main provincial railway stations like Marseille and Strasbourg and at the airport in Nice. All tourist offices provide multilingual assistance, maps and brochures and also lists of hotels, restaurants etc. The Accueil de France bureaux also provide a useful hotel booking service at the point of arrival.

Another useful organisation is the Formule 1 hotel chain of modern, budget hotels where a room costs Fr130 per night for up to three people. Optional breakfast is an additional F25. Entrance is by credit card after 7pm. A machine gives you a receipt with a code number which allows you to leave and enter both the hotel and the room. You therefore have to remember to take your receipt with you when you leave your room.

Further information about the regions, towns and cities of France can be obtained in the form of tourist and independent traveller's guides, which as a glance at any bookshop's French travel section will show, are readily available. Below are the addresses of some of the specialist travel and map shops which can provide a wider range of publications on France than general bookstores. In addition the French Government Tourist Office distributes many free booklets on France and will supply a list of maps and guides on request, or you can contact their web site (http://www.franceguide.com) which features a 2000-page France Guide which includes information available from the French Tourist Office, plus shopping, travel, motoring, regional information, theme guides and interactive multilingual correspondence pages..

Useful Addresses

The European Bookshop: 5 Warwick Street, London W1; tel: 0171-734 5259. French and other foreign language publications.

Hôtels Formule 1: (head office) 29 Promenade Michel Simon. 93166 Noisy le Grand Cedex, France. (tel: 1-43 04 01 00. Can supply a list of Formule 1, budget hotels (see above).

Federation Nationale des Offices de Tourisme et Syndicats d'Initiative: 280 Blvd. Saint-Germain, 75007 Paris; tel +33 1-44 11 10 30; fax +33 1 45 55 99 50; Minitel 3615 ITOUR; Internet: (http://www.tourisme.fr.).

Stanfords: 12-14 Long Acre, London WC2E 9LP; tel: 0171-836 1321. One of the largest map shops in Britain. Well-known French maps include the Michelin and Institut Géographique National (French Ordnance Survey) series.

The Travel Bookshop: 13 Blenheim Crescent, London W11 2EE; tel 0171-229 5260. Hundreds of titles for France including out-of-print and literary travel ones.

Office de Tourisme: 127 avenue des Champs Elysées, 75008 Paris (tel: 1-49 52 53 54).

France Accueil: 163 Avenue d'Italie, 75013 Paris. (tel 1-45 83 04 22).

The French Government Tourist Office: 178 Piccadilly, London W1V OAL ; open 9am-5pm Monday to Friday; tel 0891 244 123 (France Information Line; calls charged at 39/49 pence per minute; fax 0171 493-6594), publishes a useful free booklet *The Traveller in France Reference Guide* available on request or you can contact their web site (see above).

Regions' Guide

The following regional guide aims to introduce the different areas of France mentioning their salient points, general characteristics and advantages and disadvantages to be taken into consideration when choosing an area to live, work and or retire to.

Information on the industries and employment potential in each region is given in a separate report in *Setting up a Business*.

ALSACE

Main Cities: Strasbourg, Mulhouse.

Départements: Bas-Rhin, Haut-Rhin, Territoire de Belfort.

Office de Tourisme: 17 Pl. de la Cathédrale, 67000 Strasbourg; tel 03 88 52 28 28; fax 03 88 52 28 29.

Alsace is located in the far east of France and borders Germany to which, along with Lorraine it has belonged at various historical junctures. Consequently the region has a Germanic feel, evident in its people, dialects, architecture and cuisine. It is very scenic, largely unspoiled and generally an attractive area in which to live. The history of the Alsation wines predates even the Romans who are credited with having taken the vine to other parts of France. Beer is another local speciality as is the formidable *eau-de-vie*. The *truite bleu* (blue trout) is a local game fish which can be caught in the local rivers on acquisition of a permit from any Mairie (town hall) in the area.

Mulhouse is an important industrial area which enjoys a thriving economy. This has not always been the case however; Alsace was once very much a fringe region and somewhat underdeveloped. Its recent and rapid development is primarily due to its connections with Germany and its centrality within the EU which is certain to become even more important in future.

The area has excellent road connections to Paris (50 miles/80 km approximately) and also to Frankfurt in Germany and Basel and Zurich in Switzerland; as such, it is very much a euro-centre with promising employment potential for British expatriates. Property prices are currently higher than the French average.

Strasbourg The capital of Alsace, Strasbourg has been for centuries a staging point on the east-west trade route and its location on the Rhine made it an important centre for commercial river traffic. Nowadays it is the seat of the European Parliament. Strasbourg is a fairly small and compact city, but important economically and administratively. It has largely shaken off its quaint image of the past and is now set to become an important and dynamic Euro-city. It offers a high quality of life, with good housing and facilities. Currently the city is not overcrowded or congested but this may change in future. Taking into consideration Strasbourg's Euro-city status it may be particularly suited to executives and professionals.

AQUITAINE
Main city: Bordeaux.
Départements: Dordogne, Gironde, Landes, Lot-et-Garonne, Pyrénées-Atlantiques.
Office de Tourisme: 12 cours du 30 juillet, 33080 Bordeaux; tel 05 56 00 66 00; fax 05 56 00 66 01.

Aquitaine is a large region of south-west France and is probably one of the best known areas in France amongst holiday-makers and wine buffs. The Lot and Dordogne are dotted with foreign holiday homes and the area is very scenic, with rolling hills, forests and the attractive River Garonne valley: there is also an extensive Atlantic coastline. Despite being very far south Aquitaine does not have a hot and dry climate, and is generally considered to have some of the most pleasant and temperate weather in France,

Essentially the region is agricultural (containing some of France's most famous vineyards) and therefore largely quiet and unspoiled. The way of life is relaxed and property, apart from holiday homes, is modestly priced, though not cheap. Some areas can be very remote and inaccessible although the south of the region offers ready access to Spain and good TGV (Train à Grande Vitesse) connections provide easy access to Paris. This combination of rural quietude and accessibility has resulted in the area gaining popularity and attracting new residents. Biarritz on the coast near the Spanish border has been a popular and fashionable summer resort since the 19th century. It comes alive over the summer months and survives during the winter on the extortionate rates it has charged visitors in the tourist season. Bayonne is the other well known resort and is near Biarritz.

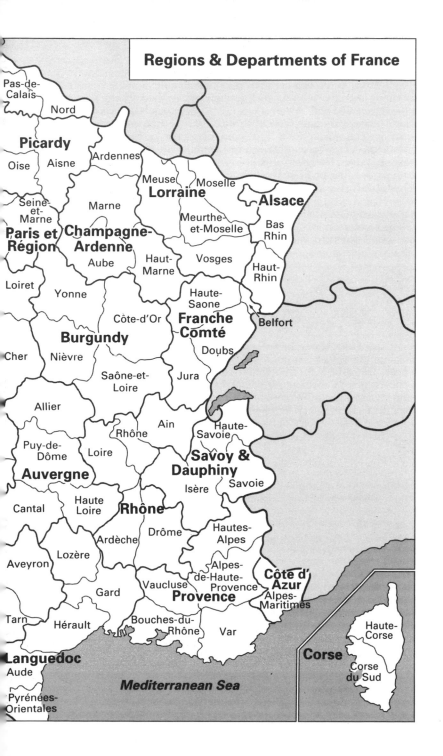

Regions & Departments of France

Pas-de-Calais

Nord

Picardy

Oise   Aisne   Ardennes

Meuse   Moselle

Lorraine

Seine-et-Marne   Marne

Meurthe-et-Moselle

Alsace

Bas Rhin

Paris et Région   **Champagne-Ardenne**

Aube   Haut-Marne   Vosges

Haut-Rhin

Loiret   Yonne

Côte-d'Or

Haute-Saone

Franche Comté

Belfort

Burgundy

Cher   Nièvre

Doubs

Saône-et-Loire   Jura

Allier

Ain   Rhône   Haute-Savoie

Puy-de-Dôme   Loire

Savoy & Dauphiny

Auvergne

Isère   Savoie

Cantal   Haute-Loire   **Rhône**

Ardèche   Drôme   Hautes-Alpes

Aveyron   Lozère

Alpes-de-Haute-Provence

Côte d' Azur

Gard   Vaucluse

Provence

Alpes-Maritimes

Tarn   Hérault

Bouches-du-Rhône   Var

Corse

Haute-Corse

Languedoc

Aude

Mediterranean Sea

Corse du Sud

Pyrénées-Orientales

Bordeaux: Bordeaux, situated on the River Garonne is a solid city built on the wealth of its mercantile classes and its former position as a great seaport. Following the loss of the French colonies and a decline in shipping requirements for various goods, the city fell into decline after the Second World War, relying mainly on the wine trade with which is is still strongly associated. Since the 1970s Bordeaux has become very much one of France's new techno-cities. Development has centred on electronics and a new container port on the nearby Médoc peninsula. The result is a very affluent and bustling city, despite its remoteness from the rest of France. However, it is not considered one of the most attractive or historically interesting of French cities. Bordeaux is a good place to live for those who hope to work within the various technical industries to be found in the city. These pay good wages and there is good (although not especially cheap) housing and facilities for employees in those industries. The city itself is not especially to be recommended for those who are retiring or who are looking for a relaxed pace of life. Apart from its business interests Bordeaux is also a very busy (and congested) convention and exhibition city.

AUVERGNE
Main City: Clermont-Ferrand.
Départements: Allier, Cantal, Haute-Loire, Puy de Dôme.
Office Tourisme: 69 Blvd. François Mitterand, 63000 Clermont-Ferrand; tel 04 73 93 30 20; fax 04 73 93 56 26.

Auvergne is one of the lesser known and more remote regions of France. It occupies much of the Massif Central — one of the three really mountainous areas in France apart from the Alps and the Pyrenees. In many ways Auvergne is a vestige of the France of former times and has a rich architectural heritage of châteaux and churches in thinly populated landscapes and hence offers a rather slow and gentle pace of life. The region contains some breathtaking scenery notably in National Park famous for its extinct volcanoes and is largely unchanged, apart from a small number of rather unattractive industrial towns, such as St Etienne.

The new A71 motorway extension connects the Auvergne area to Paris (300 km approximately) so the region is not as cut off as it once was, and retains its useful proximity to the Alpine resorts and the south of France. The Auvergne does not perhaps offer the best employment potential for prospective residents, but it does offer an unhurried pace of life with the added advantage of some of the lowest property prices in the whole country.
Clermont-Ferrand: Clermont-Ferrand is the lively political and economic centre for the whole Massif Central and the birthplace of the Michelin tyre company.

BRITTANY
Main Cities: Rennes, Brest, Nantes.
Départements: Côtes du Nord, Finistère, Ille-et-Vilaine, Morbihan.
Office Tourisme: Pont de Nemours, B.P. 2533 Rennes; tel 02 99 79 01 98; fax 02 99 79 31 38.

Brittany is another French region that has some echoes in British ears. Apart from the name and certain Celtic traditions however, Brittany is very much a foreign land. The ancient Breton language is one of a group of languages including Gaelic and Cornish, spoken by the pre-Roman tribes of Britain and Gaul. Breton like Welsh and Gaelic is still spoken, albeit by a dwindling number of Bretons, mainly the old. However the language has experienced a revival (in much the same way as Welsh has) over recent years. Other British associations also exist, such as old trading links with Cornwall, Wales and Ireland which can be traced back over hundreds of years. And there is an old district of Brittany still sometimes referred to as La Cornouaille, the French name for Cornwall. Brittany is very scenic, famous for its rugged cliffs which form an extensive coastline on the Atlantic and which gained renown as early as the 14th century in Chaucer's *The Franklin's Tale*.

Unfortunately the Atlantic-facing coastline also means that the weather, though fair in summer, can be very wild during the winter months and some areas are still remote with few facilities. However, the fact that most of Brittany is unspoiled and has a unique and inspiring culture with its own traditions and important literary figures including the novelist Henri Queffelec, more than makes up for these drawbacks. Towns like Quimper and Brest are busy but remain attractive. The area as a whole is popular with tourists and holiday-home owners with the result that property prices have been climbing steadily.

Rennes. The ancient capital of Brittany, Rennes, has only recently been designated its major city. Previously, economic dominance was held by Nantes (62 miles/100 km to the south) which is now capital of the Loire-West region. As a result of this, Rennes is only now starting to develop in its own right as a city of importance and it does not yet have the feel, nor the facilities, of a significant regional city. The advantage of this, however, is that the pace of life tends to be slower and more relaxed and property prices lower than might be expected. Employment opportunities in Rennes are increasing.

BURGUNDY
Main City: Dijon.
Départements: Côte d'Or, Nievre, Saône-et-Loire, Yonne.
Office Tourisme: 34 rue des Forges, B.P. 1298, 21022 Dijon Cedex; tel 03 80 44 11 44; fax 03 80 30 90 02.

Burgundy starts near the small medieval town of Auxerre and reaches down to just north of the metropolis of Lyon. It is another area of France whose name is famous thanks to the wine that takes its name from the region. In fact a map of the Burgundy area reads like a wine list from which Nuits St. Georges, Mersault, Chasagne-Montrachet, Mercurey, Pouilly-Fuissé are just some of the possible selections. For six hundred years Burgundy was an independent kingdom with its heyday in medieval times. Many of the great vineyards were run by religious orders whose expertise in cultivation and distillation was unrivalled in Europe.

Although prosperous, Burgundy's position in the hierarchy of the most economically important regions is not high; it is similar to the Auvergne in that respect. The area's countryside is not industrialized, and not especially attractive by French standards. Some parts are very isolated. That said, there is excellent access to both Paris and Lyon and beyond, by rail and A6 autoroute. These factors are sure to enhance future development of the region. Property prices are higher than average in Burgundy but there is only minimal interest from holiday and retirement homeowners. The region boasts no large cities and Dijon barely qualifies for city status as far as its size is concerned. Important towns within Burgundy include Villefranche, Macon, Bourg-en-Bresse and Chalon-sur-Saône and Beaune.

CHAMPAGNE-ARDENNE
Main City: Reims.
Départements: Ardennes, Aube, Haute-Marne, Marne.
Office Tourisme: 2, rue Guillaume de Machault, 51100 Reims; tel 03 26 77 45 25; fax 03 26 77 45 27.

Like Burgundy, Champagne-Ardenne is a region that gives its name to one of France's most famous products, and is yet another example of French, near-religious celebration of food and drink. Ever since a blind, 17th century monk accidentally discovered that stopping the bottles of fermenting wine in his abbey cellars with cork made them pop when drawn — whereupon he is said to have exclaimed 'Je bois les etoiles!' (I am drinking the stars) — the production of champagne has dominated most aspects of life in this area in one way or another. It has been the main source of regional employment and left its mark upon the culture and architecture of the region.

Despite the chalky rolling landscape that imparts special properties, to the wine, Champagne is not considered one of the most attractive areas of France and has not traditionally been popular with foreign residents although property is not expensive there. However, the region is convenient for Paris and the north (Ardennes) shares a border with Belgium (Brussels 62 miles/100 km approximately). Both these factors suggest good future development potential for the region. Apart from Reims there are no other major cities, important towns being Charleville-Mézières and Troyes.

CORSICA
Main Cities: Ajaccio and Bastia.
Départements: Haute-Corse, Corse du Sud.
Syndicat d'Initiative: numerous, including cours Napoléon, Ajaccio.

Despite being an island in the Mediterranean with Italian associations of longer duration than French ones, Corsica (La Corse), is nevertheless a bona fide region of France, albeit with a greater measure of autonomy than the mainland regions and a strong antipathy to being under anybody at all. Before 1768 it was a much disputed territory but in that year the French bought it outright from Genoa, then an independent maritime republic. Napoleon, who came from Ajaccio, is only Corsica's second most famous son (unless perhaps you are French), the first is Christopher Columbus, who was born in Calvi which was under Genoese domination at the time (which is why the Genoese claim Columbus as their son too). A descendant of Napoleon, Prince Charles Napoleon returned to live in Corsica in 1997.

The island is a mere 180 km long and a maximum of 80 km wide, and is sparsely populated, very mountainous with deep gulleys and tree covered slopes. The *laricio* pine which grows there is traditionally prized for ships' masts. The interior is covered with maquis (a mixture of wild flowers, herbs and dense scrub). A view of Corsica from the sea suggests a mountain rising from it. The beaches of the six-hundred-mile coastline, which bring the tourist hordes to the western side of the island in July and August, are magnificent. Apart from tourism and agriculture, Corsica is devoid of industry. In recent years more holiday home owners, particularly from Italy have been buying up property and prices, once rock bottom, are rising. There are few developments of the apartment/villa complex variety and no high rise blocks. Corsica has little potential as a place to live and work but retirement for those fit enough to enjoy the magnificent walks, or a holiday home are realistic options. The Corsicans' habit of occasionally dynamiting foreign owned villas and ignoring tourists, probably means that only those prepared to integrate as much as possible will be appreciated. The locals speak a blend of French and Italian. Slogans such as *I francesi fora!* (French get out), *Corsica Nazione* and others in support of the FLNC (Corsica's liberation movement) are daubed on any flat perpendicar surface, but it's hard to see liberation from France as very practical; especially as the country is known for its poverty and backwardness. One big advantage however, would be that Corsica would get to keep the profits of tourism, most of which are swiped by the mainland; but there again, France has poured money into Corsica for development and wants some return on the investment.

Largely free from any expatriate influences, Corsica offers a mainly good climate and the lazy pace of life you would expect from a backwater. It is possible to get a good impression of the island from the train but don't look for a TGV: the railway was inaugurated in 1888 and has 230 km of track, 12 bridges (including Gustav Eiffel's viaduct nearly 300 feet high) and 38 tunnels.

Bastia, is the commercial capital, while the small town of Corte, in the centre of the island, is the site of the island's university, only reopened a decade ago, after a very long vac of 220 years. A swathe of land through the centre is protected as the Park Natural Regional de la Corse and spectacular scenery can be found among the island's 20 or so peaks which surge up 2000m or more into the ether. Starting a business in Corsica would probably involve paying protection money, popularly known as 'revolutionary taxes' to the FLNC. According to fairly recent accounts, this varies from Ffr20,000-50,000 a year.

COTE D'AZUR
Main City: Nice.
Département: Alpes-Maritimes.
Office Tourisme: Acropolis Esplanade Kennedy, B.P. 4079, 06302 Nice Cedex 4; tel 04 93 92 82 82; fax 04 93 92 82 85.

The single département that makes up the Côte d'Azur must be one of the most exclusive of France. As such, a feeling exists among other French regions that it wishes to remain separate and considers itself superior to the rest of the country. The departement runs along the coast from the Italian border, encompassing Monaco, and reaching just beyond Cannes. It continues inland for about 50 km as far as the foothills of the Alps.

The tiny principality of Monaco, centred on Monte Carlo and backed by the Alpes Maritimes, is entirely independent from France.

That the Côte d'Azur is the most fashionable part of the south of France becomes evident from a run down of its resorts set amongst attractive and hilly scenery: Nice, Antibes, Cannes, Juan-les-Pins, St.-Jean-Cap-Ferrat and Menton. Indeed, it is an area almost totally dedicated to up-market tourism, culture and showbiz. This region has the ideal facilities and climate for holiday and retirement homes. However, the property and general living costs in the area are probably the highest in France and so it is really only feasible for those with considerable means who are not concerned with budgeting. Those seeking work would be ill-advised to set up here without first having a prearranged well-paid job and having looked carefully at the costs of accommodation. The high crime rate which plagues the area is a further disadvantage to take into consideration before making any final decision.

FRANCHE COMTÉ
Main City: Besançon.
Départements: Doubs, Haute-Saône, Jura.
Office Tourisme: avenue du Maréchal Foch, Besançon.

Franche Comté is an interesting but often overlooked region in the far east of the country. It shares a long border, and many other characteristics of culture, architecture and gastronomy with neighbouring Switzerland. The area is scenically outstanding mainly because of the long stretch of the Jura mountains which line the Franco-Swiss frontier and provide a landscape normally considered typically Swiss, rather than French. Franche Comté is popular with French tourists, but largely unknown to foreigners, whether as a place to holiday or to live. Much of the region is agricultural and unspoiled, Besançon being the only town of any size. Generally, the region is prosperous with good facilities; property prices tend to be higher than the French average.

One attraction of Franche Comté, which is could prove a magnet to Euro-residents, is the close proximity of Switzerland. Lausanne is only 85 km from Besançon along the N57, Geneva a little further. The possibility also exists of living in France (where living costs are much cheaper) but working in Switzerland (where wages are much higher). Switzerland issues a special work permit (the F permit) for this purpose.

LANGUEDOC-ROUSSILLON

Main Cities: Montpellier, Narbonne, Béziers.
Départements: Aude, Gard, Hérault, Lozère, Pyrénées-Orientales.
Office Tourisme: 78 ave de Piree, 34000 Montpellier; tel 04 67 58 67 58; fax 04 67 58 67 59.

Languedoc-Roussillon, usually just called Languedoc, is undoubtedly one of the regions of France which has undergone the greatest transformation in the last two decades. It has become economically important and dynamic thanks to the administrations of the French government's regional development agency, DATAR. It offers many of the things that are best about France all in one place, and is also an area that has attracted a large number of new residents, both French and some foreign. Languedoc is bordered by the Pyrenees, the Spanish frontier, the Mediterranean and the River Rhône and extends into the Massif Central. The region therefore has a varied range of of scenery and terrain from mountains to river deltas and coastal plains, to large cities and picturesque medieval villages. Much of the recent development and growth has been in the coastal strip. However, the traditional industry of the area is wine and the survival of this industry has resulted in the area remaining largely unspoiled. With all these different qualities Languedoc is potentially suitable for holiday homes, retirement or working. One drawback is that the prosperity of the area has fuelled a fierce demand for the available employment. A final factor to keep in mind is that the region is renowned for the independent outlook of its inhabitants as well as for its own language.
Montpellier. Montpellier was a sleepy but cultural city that has risen to the challenge of being the hub of one of the most progressive regions of the country. It has a liveliness and ebullience and together with Perpignan, Béziers and Nîmes, offers good employment potential and a relaxed attitude to life. The good weather of the Midi is another plus point. Housing, facilities and wages are good while property and living costs are very far behind those to be found in the more fashionable and more expensive Riviera and Provence.

LIMOUSIN

Main City: Limoges.
Départements: Corrèze, Creuse, Haute-Vienne.
Office Tourisme: boulevard de Fleurus, 87000 Limoges; tel 05 55 34 46 87; fax 05 55 34 19 12.

Limousin is France at its most rural and most remote. It is generally considered to be something of a gateway between the serious, industrious north and the relaxed, Mediterranean south of France. The region is very scenic and blends into the Auvergne region which lies to the east: it is possible to travel kilometre after kilometre without finding a city or even a town of much consequence. The capital, Limoges, is the only large town and as such it offers a very quiet way of life and few employment opportunities. Property and living costs, however, are among the cheapest in France. Those looking for a holiday or retirement home should find that excellent properties (especially those suitable for renovation) are available at what seem to be bargain prices compared to the prices being asked for holiday villas in the Dordogne, just to the west.

LOIRE VALLEY
Main City: Orléans.
Départements: Cher, Eure-et-Loir, Indre, Indre-et-Loire, Loir-et-Cher, Loiret.
Office Tourisme: place Albert 1er, 45000 Orléans; tel 02 38 24 05 05; fax 02 38 54 49 84.

Often called the Central Loire, this region is named from one of France's main rivers, the Loire which is to France what the Severn is to England. It winds its way from the Massif Central to the Atlantic Ocean beyond Nantes. The river gives its name to numerous départements and drains a vast area that is divided into two major regions also named from it. The Loire Valley is the inland Loire region and one of the most beautiful locations in all of France, mainly by virtue of its all round picturesque, rather than stunning, scenery. The Valley also enjoys some of the most temperate weather in France, even though it is quite far north.
A final recommendation for the area is that, reputedly, a very clear French is spoken here.
Apart from rural scenery the Loire Valley includes the famous *châteaux* of the Loire and consequently attracts convoys of tourists. The north-eastern part of the region (around the cathedral town of Chartres) is a popular roosting place for many Paris commuters, and the area as a whole attracts many native second home and retirement buyers, as well as foreigners. The region, while prosperous, has no great cities, although Paris is readily accessible on the A10, A11 and A71 autoroutes. Important towns in the area include Chartres, Orléans, Blois, Bourges and Tours. Generally the level of facilities available in the Loire Valley is excellent and inhabitants can enjoy a pleasant, unharried but modern way of life. Such quality of life is reflected in the prices which are considerably above average, and exorbitant for houses of charm. Real bargains are definitely the exception. The popularity which this region enjoys, however, is a just reflection of its capacity to suit most requirements.

WESTERN LOIRE
Main City: Nantes.
Départements: Loire-Atlantique, Maine-et-Loire, Mayenne, Sarthe, Vendée.
Office Tourisme: place du Commerce, B.P. 160, 44000 Nantes; tel 02 40 20 60 00; fax 02 40 89 11 99.

The Western Loire is the second region formed around the River Loire and covers the lower reaches of the river as it winds its way to the Atlantic. The Vendée and the Loire Atlantique share a romantically wild Atlantic coastline stretching nearly

200 miles. One of the main resorts is La Baule with a long sandy beach, typical of the region. Further inland is the renowned motor-racing venue of Le Mans in the Sarthe department, named from the river that runs through it.

Nantes: Nantes, on the coast of the Loire Atlantique is the commercial hub of the region. Until recently Nantes was part of Brittany but its role as the main Breton city has since been transferred to Rennes. Nantes has suffered from a decline in shipbuilding and associated industries with the result that people have been leaving, rather than moving to, this city; Property prices, living costs and facilities are currently very favourable. Although the city does not impress aesthetically, Nantes offers excellent access to the attractions of Brittany and the Atlantic coast; a combination to tempt holiday and retirement home buyers as well as those seeking work. The A11 provides a direct motorway link to Paris and a two- hour, inter-city TGV service is also available. The region is fairly convenient for Paris and quite easy to reach from the Channel port of St Mâlo or even from Le Havre, but is a long slog from Calais.

LORRAINE
Main City: Nancy.
Départements: Meurthe-et-Moselle, Meuse, Moselle, Vosges.
Office de Tourisme: 14, place Stanislas, B.P. 810 Nancy Cedex; tel 03 83 35 22 41; fax 03 83 37 63 07.

Lorraine, also known as Lorraine-Vosges, occupies the far north-eastern corner of France and shares a lengthy border with Germany and shorter ones with Belgium and Luxembourg. The region's proximity to Germany has resulted in the area falling alternately into the the clutches of France and Germany over the centuries and a strong Germanic influence, as in adjacent Alsace, remains.

Owing to its strategic importance, Lorraine is primarily known within France for its battlefields: Verdun, Metz etc. The scenery is generally drab and dotted with industrial towns and cities and to date the region has attracted few foreign residents, although its proximity to three other EU countries will no doubt prove advantageous for its future prospects. Access to the UK is good on the A26 and A4 autoroutes from Calais through Reims. Living costs are generally low, as are property prices.

Nancy. The capital of Lorraine-Vosges, Nancy is in many ways quite distinct from its own region: it is a reasonably attractive, uncongested and uncrowded city and not as industrialized as its hinterland. There is much commercial and academic activity in Nancy which is becoming something of an economic centre for Western Europe, not just France itself. The city enjoys a healthy prosperity, unlike some other parts of Lorraine and the facilities are excellent. In many ways the city of Metz, some 30 miles/50 km away along the A31/N57, carries equal status with Nancy. The nearby German city of Saarbrucken is also an important commercial city.

NORD-PAS-DE-CALAIS
Major City: Lille.
Départements: Nord de Calais, Pas de Calais.
Office Tourisme: place Rihour, B.P. 205 Lille; tel 03 20 21 94 21; fax 03 20 21 94 20.

The unfortunate plight of Nord, Pas-de-Calais is that it is one of France's smallest geographical regions with one of the most concentrated populations. It is comprised of several large towns and cities including Lille, Roubaix, Tourcoing, Arras and the major coastal ports of Calais and Dunkerque (Dunkirk). The urban sprawl also spreads across the border into Belgium. Lille is only 56 miles/90 km away from Brussels and a new autoroute, the Belgian A8, will soon link them.

This area, known as La Métropole du Nord, is France's only major conurbation outside Paris — France does not otherwise have large metropolitan sprawls, such as the West Midlands or West and South Yorkshire in the UK. The whole region is largely industrialized, including many declining industries, and is not the most scenically attractive of areas although some picturesque pockets still remain. On the other hand, local facilities are excellent, the region enjoys a closer proximity to the UK than does any other area in France (and endures a similar climate) and the Channel Tunnel entrance, to the west of Calais and linked to the A26 autoroute, provides potential for an economic boom in the area. The region also shares a border with Belgium, resulting in an inevitable Flemish influence. The influx of UK property buyers has forced prices up, but there are still many bargains to be found. Overall, despite the current high rate of unemployment within the area, prospects should improve, and Nord, Pas-de-Calais is most suitable for those intending to work in France; those looking for holiday and retirement property will find more attractive spots further west.

Lille. One of France's largest cities and not commonly thought of as attractive. However surprising it may be, Lille is stylish and not as built-up or spoiled as might be expected. Many people with employment in this area settle in Lille, rather than in one of the duller, industrial towns surrounding it. Lille is developing as a modern and well-organised, but uncrowded, city which offers excellent facilities and good housing: it is particularly noted for its efficient public transport service. Paris is less than two hours away by TGV and many of Europe's major cities can be reached quite easily by train and road.

NORMANDY

Major City: Rouen.
Départements: Calvados, Eure, Manche, Orne, Seine-Maritime.
Office Tourisme: Place de la Cathedrale, B.P. 666 76008 Rouen; tel 02 32 08 32 40; fax 02 32 08 32 44.

Of all the regions of France, arguably Normandy is the best known to the British for both historical and recreational reasons. William the Conqueror set off from there to invade England, the D-Day landings on the beaches there and evoke strong memories in those old enough to remember; while its other role as a social playground has attracted a British clientele to le Touquet, Deauville, Trouville etc. since the nineteenth century. Despite a continuing influx of *les Britanniques*, Normandy has a particularly strong local atmosphere. It is also one of the few places in France which does not produce wine — here the liquid products tend to be milk, cider and calvados (apple brandy). Normandy is unusual in that it is largely rural, but is also one of France's major and most important industrial areas; quiet, remote and scenic areas exist alongside heavily industrial and spoilt ones like the nuclear waste reprocessing unit at La Hague on the coast. Employment prospects for unskilled labour in Normandy are among the poorest in France, but foreigners with technical skills can find oppportunities in the high-tech industries which exist here. Normandy offers good access to the UK (via Dieppe, Le Havre and Cherbourg) which makes it popular with holiday and retirement-home buyers who find it reassuring to be so near Britain. Property prices tend to be low and bargains are readily available, with the exception of those areas which are popular with Paris commuters and weekenders. The culture, traditions and architecture of Normandy are very distinctive and the cuisine is some of the best in France, deriving much from the area's traditional occupations of fishing and agriculture. Overall, the province has major attractions likely to lure increasing numbers of foreign residents.

Rouen. An industrial city, Rouen lies on the banks of the River Seine: many of its industries are in decline, although some high technology ones continue to prosper. Like Le Havre, few consider Rouen an attractive place to live. More attractive residential towns are to be found nearby and on the coast, north east of Le Havre. The residential suburbs that do exist in Rouen are on the right bank of the Seine. Rouen does not quite succeed in communicating the air of importance to which, as a cultural centre for museums, art, sculpture and public monuments of all kinds, it is rightly entitled.

PARIS & ILE DE FRANCE
Main city: Paris.
Départements: Paris, Region Parisienne, Seine-et-Marne
Office Tourisme: numerous.

The Paris region, also known as Paris Ile de France, is one of the smallest regions by area, but the one with the greatest population. As in Greater London, the boundaries between the different départements and towns are not always clear and tend to merge into one another and to be known by various names. Until recently, Paris was the area in which most foreigners lived, mainly due to the fact that a largely centralized system of industry and commerce required that they work in the French capital. However, unless specifically tied to Paris by a job, few people, French or otherwise, would choose to live in the Paris region. Property and other costs of living are very high and the region tends to be extremely overcrowded. However, Paris is noted for its efficient and cheap system of public transport including the métro underground and the RER suburban train network which makes many of the outlying areas more accessible for city commuters.

The Paris region is not unattractive, its geographical position provides surprisingly mild weather compared to the surrounding regions, and the general facilities available are the best to be found throughout France. Additionally, the eastern portion of the region (Seine-et-Marne) is surprisingly rural. The rest of the Paris region is made up of many towns, some quite quaint, some modern, both groups well-planned and rather desolate. The surrounding towns, which inevitably fall under the influence of the capital, include Pontoise, St Denis, St Germain, Mantes, Versailles, Melun, Fontainebleau, Provins, Meaux, Bobigny, Nanterre, Creteil and Marne-la-Vallée.

PICARDY
Main City: Amiens.
Départements: Aisne, Oise, Somme.
Office Tourisme: 6 bis rue Dusevel, 80000 Amiens; tel 03 22 71 60 50; fax 03 22 71 60 51.

The Picardy region is one of the quieter and lesser-known French provinces. Historically it is probably chiefly known for its battlefields from both the Great War and the Second World War which are scattered throughout the region. Also the Forest of Compiègne, where the 1918 armistice was signed and the 1000-roomed royal palace of the same name which provided a retreat for royalty from the 14th century and was also lived in by Napoleon Bonaparte. Although some industry exists, Picardy is regarded as something of a backwater: lon,, straight roads and large, flat fields are the fairly monotonous hallmark of the area. Some parts of Picardy are remote and facilities poor although there are a few attractive areas and some marvellous medieval ecclesiastical architecture. No large cities exist, but important towns include Beauvais, Compiègne, Chantilly and St Quentin. Unfortunately, Picardy has not derived much benefit from its proximity to Paris, nor from its strategic position on the route both to Belgium and the Channel Tunnel; some suggest it may never do so. However, from the prospective resident's point of view, the main advantage is that property prices here are among the lowest to be found in France. This may prove to be a persuasive factor for those who either intend to farm in France or who are looking forward to a very quiet semi-retirement, whilst not being too far away from the UK.

POITOU & CHARENTES

Main City: Poitiers.
Départements: Charente, Charente-Maritime, Deux-Sèvres, Vienne.
Office Tourisme: 8 rue des Grandes Ecoles, 86000 Poitiers; tel 05 49 41 21 24; fax 05 49 88 65 84.

As the name suggests, Poitou Charentes comprises two small sub-regions which form one region. The area of Poitou Maritime is very scenic, featuring a long coast on the Atlantic, and subsequently is popular with holidaymakers. A tourist area it is characterized by thronged summers and deserted winters and its popularity with holiday and retirement-home owners has forced property prices up. Quite a distinction exists between coast and countryside. La Rochelle and Roquefort are resort towns, while Poitiers is something of a local commercial centre, offering a good, small-city, standard of living. Traditionally, Poitiers (formerly the duchy of Aquitaine's capital) forms the linguistic boundary between the *langue d'oie* and the *langue d'oc* (i.e. northern French where *oui* is yes and the southern dialects where *oc* is yes). Despite Poitiers's remoteness, La Rochelle is only 94 miles/150km away from Bordeaux.

PROVENCE

Major City: Marseille.
Départements: Alpes-de-Haute-Provence, Bouches-du-Rhône, Hautes-Alpes, Var, Vaucluse.
Office Tourisme: 4, La Canebière, 13001 Marseille; tel 04 91 13 89 00; fax 04 91 13 89 20.

Unfortunately for Provence, mass publicity in Britain has resulted in one of the best known regions of France becoming the one most in demand by potential British residents and in their wake, *les sightseers Britanniques*. However, despite this invasion, Provence has managed for the most part to retain its highly individual character. To the outsider it offers all that is typically 'south-of-France' by way of good weather, scenery, beaches, watersports, cuisine and fashion chic. However, Provence is more varied, both scenically and economically, than is usually assumed. The terrain is partly mountainous, partly hilly, and partly flat. Although famous for its tourist resorts and historic towns, Provence also has a great deal of industry, some of it heavy, in the Marseille-Toulon band of towns. The resorts of St Tropez and St Raphaël are in the east (note that the most fashionable part of the south of France, the Côte d'Azur, is not strictly part of Provence but a region in its own right) and major inland towns, generally considered pleasant, include Avignon, Orange, Digne-les-Bains and Aix-en-Provence.

Provence's vast number of holiday-home owners and retired people are not by any means solely British; many nationalities are attracted here by the good weather, the lifestyle and ambience. Over several years, such demand has inevitably put property prices beyond the means of many. Those who do manage to find something they can afford will also discover that the cost of living is generally very high and the main towns very crowded. Having said this, the sporting, social and cultural facilities are good and a Mediterranean atmosphere prevails, quite unlike anything to be found elsewhere. Considering the expense involved in living in Provence, those contemplating this area should either be comfortably off or have lucrative employment lined up. Seasonal work is also a possibility for those who wish to experience the idyll but are unable to afford to settle there.

Marseille Once thought of as France's second city, in recent years Marseille has been overshadowed, economically and in population, by Lyon. Marseille is a very compact and densely-populated city with an industrial hinterland which spreads out west and also east to Cassis, la Ciotat, Bandol, la Seyne and Toulon. Infamous as a tough and dirty city with a high crime rate, Marseille lives up to its reputation. Although the business and historic areas of the city ostensibly seem respectable enough, a profusion of social problems exists in these areas; however, the situation has improved in recent years.

Few people, French or otherwise, would actually cherish the idea of moving to Marseille without good reason. Yet, this city offers increasing numbers of high-paid jobs in the technological industries, all the facilities of a big city (and all the congestion), and relatively moderate housing and living costs. Marseille is also the French gateway to North Africa and Corsica and hence revels in a very cosmopolitan atmosphere. Tourists and holiday residents are not generally attracted to Marseille, which for those who do choose to live there is a positive advantage.

MIDI-PYRENEES
Major City: Toulouse.
Déepartements: Ariège, Aveyron, Gers, Haute-Garonne, Hautes-Pyrénées, Lot, Tarn, Tarn-et-Garonne.
Office Tourisme: Donjon du Capitole, 31000 Toulouse; tel 05 61 11 02 22; fax 05 61 22 03 63.

The Midi-Pyrénées region is one of the largest in France and is wedged between Aquitaine to the north-east and Languedoc-Roussillon to the south-east. As its name suggests it includes some départements which take in the magnificent Pyrenean mountains landscapes, while others are just as remarkable, for instance the Aveyron with its high plateaux, the Tarn with its stunning gorges, while yet others are in the Midi region. Scenically and atmospherically the region has a lot to offer and is and largely quiet and unspoiled with a favourable climate. Lot, and to a lesser extent Tarn-et-Garonne are some of the most popular target spots for holiday and retirement homes, but the entire area is fast expanding in popularity and attracting many new residents of all nationalities. Consequently, prices tend to be very much above average, although this is one area where it is still possible to find some real property bargains. Gers has been growing in popularity for some time. The British are often attracted to places with an English connection and Gers has plenty of those. Most of the 100 or so walled towns in the area were originally built by the English 600 years ago when the area of Gascony, of which Gers is a part, came under the English crown. The old town of Auch is the administrative centre of the Gers. The Spanish border is a two and half hour drive and the coast at Biarritz two hours. Contrary to expectation, the region is suitable for those seeking work: generally very prosperous, good opportunities are available in the capital city of Toulouse. Also surprisingly, the Pyrénées region is quite easily accessible including the ski resorts of St Lary Soulan and the Vallée de Luchon, with Bordeaux, Lyon, Spain and the south coast all within fairly easy reach; the A61 and A62 link the Atlantic and Mediterranean and Paris is only five hours away by TGV.

Toulouse. The focal point of the region for those seeking employment, Toulouse is a fast-growing and forward-looking city offering many employment opportunities. Central Toulouse is an attractive and historic city with a great deal of character, a fine old university and several art museums. The extensive suburbs, however, are modern and unattractive and include large shopping centres and housing estates. This cohesion of the traditional and the modern makes for an excellent quality of city life, with the added advantage of easy access to the local countryside. The prevailing high-tech industries mean that Toulouse tends to be a very executive and professional city. Wages are at the top of the French rates, but, correspondingly, property prices and costs of living are increasing.

THE RHONE VALLEY

Major City: Lyon.
Départements: Ain, Ardèche, Drôme, Loire, Rhône.
Office Tourisme: place Bellecour, B. P. 2254, 69214 Lyon Cedex; tel 04 72 77 69 69; fax 04 78 42 04 32.

Rhône is one of the regions of France which follows broadly geographic lines, taking in the long valley and plain of the River Rhône between the Alps and the Massif Central. The Rhône is another of France's major rivers and a focal point for industrial activity. It is this which has made Rhône one of the country's fastest expanding regions and a popular area for both the French and foreigners to move into in search of employment. Prices for property and costs of living tend to be quite high and although much of the region is agricultural it has become rather spoiled by development. However, the sheer employment potential and facilities available in the region do recommend it as a place to live. One other main attraction of the Rhône is its central location. Marseille, the south of France and Switzerland can be readily reached by autoroute and Paris is now only two hours from Lyon by TGV (quicker than by air shuttle). Thus, despite the industrial scenery within Rhône itself, it is now fairly easy to reach the surrounding, attractive countryside.

Lyon One of the first cities in France to push ahead with new technology, Lyon is now France's second commercial and industrial city and booming in economic terms. Major national and multinational firms have bases there in preference to Paris and a frenetic international atmosphere is the norm. Although not structurally very attractive, Lyon is set to become a key European city. Pleasant, reasonably-priced accommodation in Lyon itself is rare, and many people commmute to the city from surrounding suburbs. Facilities for entertainment and culture are superb, and the city is said to be the gastronomic capital of France, thus offering an enviable style of life for those with epicurean standards. Bourg-en-Bresse is another important centre within the region.

SAVOIE & DAUPHINY
Major City: Grenoble.
Départements: Isère, Haute-Savoie, Savoie.
Office de Tourisme: 14 rue de la République, B P 227, 38019 Grenoble; tel 04 76 42 41 41; fax 04 76 51 28 69.

Historically, Savoy and Dauphiny are separate regions but the French administration regards them as a single entity. The region lies in the French Alps and shares extensive borders with Switzerland and Italy and shares certain characteristics with both of those countries. Savoy and Dauphiny is one of the country's most scenic regions and harbours some of the most breathtaking and unspoiled spots within a developed country that one could possibly find. Despite its Alpine situation the region is not remote and offers a good, modern standard of living with a high standard of facilities but, needless to say, the weather can be severe. It is an area that has attracted large numbers of new residents as well as those wanting holiday homes, and property prices are rising accordingly. The Alps are the home of France's skiing industry and many resorts of all classes are to be found here. The area therefore has potential for those wishing to work in or run a business connected with skiing. The lakeside towns of Annecy and Evian have a milder microclimate, are only half an hour away from the main ski resorts and are expensive but popular places to retire to. In many ways, Savoy and Dauphiny are very untypical of France and do not offer the sort of lifestyle and character that are generally thought of as French. Important towns other than Grenoble include Mègeve, Annecy, Chambéry and Aix-les-Bains.

Grenoble. One of France's fastest developing cities, Grenoble is modern and prosperous, not remote or isolated as its location might suggest: many high technology industries exist nearby. Grenoble offers an attractive lifestyle in a clean, reasonably unhurried city with good facilities; considered a desirable place in which to live it is becoming more crowded with higher costs of living. Grenoble tends to appeal to executive and professional people and to ski enthusiasts; Courchevel and Val d'Isère are less than 62 miles/100km away. The city is well situated for connections to Turin in Italy, Geneva in Switzerland and Lyon. Paris is less than three hours away by TGV and provides a much easier access to Grenoble than by air.

Summary of the Regions' Attractions

Scenery: Brittany, Provence, Savoie & Dauphiny, Loire, Auvergne.

Sports and Outdoor Activities: Provence, Languedoc, Savoie.

Climate: Provence, Languedoc, Aquitaine, Côte d'Azur.

Culture and Strong Regional Traditions: Paris, Brittany, Alsace, Lorraine-Vosges, Languedoc, Provence.

Food and Social Life: almost anywhere and subject to personal opinion, but Normandy, Paris, Provence and Lyon are recommended.

Career Opportunities: Paris, Bordeaux, Toulouse, Lyon, Grenoble.

Low Costs: Nord-Pas-de-Calais, Normandy, Picardy, Limousin, Auvergne.

International Cities: Paris, Strasbourg (Alsace), Lyon (Rhône).

Remote Areas: Limousin, Auvergne, parts of the Pyrénées.

Getting to France

High Street travel agents can, of course, offer advice on travel to France by air, train or ferry. But there are also a number of travel agents in the UK that specialize in offering discount fares, particularly, but by no means exclusively, for young people.

Campus Travel (headquarters at 52 Grosvenor Gardens, London SW1W 0AG) is one of Britain's largest specialists in discount travel for students, young people and independent travellers. Of particular interest is their year-round flight programme to Paris. Campus has branches in Birmingham, Bristol, Brighton, Cambridge, Cardiff, Dundee, Edinburgh, Glasgow, Liverpool, London, Manchester, Newcastle, Oxford and Sheffield.

Another important organisation is Wasteels Travel (headquarters at 121 Wilton Road, London SW1V 1JZ; 0171-834 7066) — Europe's largest international rail specialist. In the UK they offer ROUTE 26 tickets for the under 26s. These tickets carry large discounts on standard rail fares to Europe. There is a wide choice of destinations and routes. All tickets are valid for two months, with the opportunity of stopping off anywhere along the chosen route. Other under 26 discount rail tickets can be obtained from Eurotrain (0171-730 3402) which is connected to Campus (see above) and Euro Youth (0171-834 2345) which is linked to British Rail International.

In addition to ROUTE 26, Wasteels also offers Inter-Rail Cards, rail tickets for the over 26s, Rail Cards and passes for France and other European countries, as well as cheap flights and travel insurance. Wasteels has around 200 shops spread throughout Europe, and assistance and advice is always available to any Wasteels customer at any of their offices.

Train: Via the Channel Tunnel, from the UK (London-Waterloo Station) Eurostar (a passenger only service) runs 13 trains daily to Paris. The train arrives at the Gare du Nord and passengers have to travel by the Metro to either the Gare du Lyon or Montparnasse to connect with TGV and other French rail services. For details of the TGV services in France see the *Transport* section of *Daily Life*. SNCF (French Railways) has a ticketing offices called Rail Shops in London (0990 30003) in Manchester and Glasgow; or telephone the free brochure hotline (0800 024000); if you are in London call in at French Railways House (179 Piccadilly, London W1V OBA). The service for passengers and their vehicles is Le Shuttle which leaves from the Cheriton Terminal in Folkestone (tel 0990 353535) and arrives at Coquelles at Calais. The short but boring journey takes 35 minutes and unlike the ferries and hovercraft the tunnel service is immune to bad weather conditions. Tickets can be bought through travel agents or at the station on departure. Other sources of information on train journeys to France are British Rail International (0171-828 0892), European Rail (0171-387 0444) and Special Trains International (0161-236 2960).

Motorists arriving with vehicles at Calais can put them on the Motorail service to popular holiday areas. Further details from Motorail (0171 203 7000).

Ferry & Hovercraft
Far from abandoning ship in the face of Le Shuttle, the ferry companies have increased their fleets, and in some cases revamped them to provide swish on board facilities. On the Dover Calais route there is P&O (0990-980980) and Stena Sealink (01233-647047) with departures every 45 minutes and a journey time of 75 minutes. Hoverspeed (01304-240241), on the same route has the same journey time as Le Shuttle.

Between Folkestone and Boulogne, the only service is the SeaCat (unfairly nicknamed the 'vomit comet'), a fast catamaran on 'skis' which lift the hull clear of the water and makes the crossing in 55 minutes; it is bookable through Hoverspeed.

From Ramsgate to Dunkirk the Sally Line (0800 636465) has a high speed service that takes 100 minutes, with five to eight sailings a day depending on the season, while North Sea Ferries (01482 795141) operate daily sailings from Hull to the Belgian port of Zeebrugge, which can make a useful alternative to the French ports during the busiest periods; it is only 19 miles further from Paris than Calais.

Depending on where you are coming from in the UK and where you are going to in France the other possiblities (which can include overnight sailings) are the Normandy ports: Portsmouth to Le Havre and Cherbourg (P & O), Portsmouth to Caen (Brittany Ferries 0990 360360). Brittany Ferries, as its name suggests, has a monopoly over the Breton ports: there are sailings from Portsmouth and Poole to St Mâlo, Poole to Cherbourg and from Plymouth to Roscoff.

Useful Addresses

Brittany Ferries: The Brittany Centre, Wharf Road, Portsmouth P02 8RW. Brittany ferries runs a property owners' club which entitles British residents who own French property, and who pay a one-off membership fee, to up to 33% discount on standard fares. For further details telephone 0990-360360.

Chez Nous: Bridge Mills, Huddersfield Road, Holmfirth HD7 2TW; tel 01484 684075; fax 01484 685852. Well-established agent that handles bookings for all the sea routes to France, plus air and Eurostar bookings.

Hoverspeed: Eastern Docks, Dover, CT17 9TG1.

North Sea Ferries: King George Dock, Hedon Road, Hull HU9 5QA.

P & O European Ferries: Channel House, Channel View Road, Dover CT17 9TJ.

Sally Line: Argyle Centre, York Street, Ramsgate, Kent CT11 9DS.

Stena Sealink: Charter House, Park Street, Ashford TN24 8EX.

Plane

Airports: Air services are now having to compete with Eurostar which takes 3hrs from London to Paris. There is plethora of flights and airlines to choose from including Air France (0181-742 6600), British Airways (0181-897 4000), British Midland (0345-554554) and Air UK (0345-666777) from Heathrow, Gatwick, Stanstead and London City to Paris-Charles de Gaulle (a.k.a. Roissy-Charles de Gaulle) and Paris-Orly. Most international flights go to Charles de Gaulle where you can walk from the arrivals hall into the TGV station (i.e. without leaving the airport). From Charles de Gaulle there are train connections to Lyon (two hours), Rennes (three hours) and Brussels (90 minutes), without going into central Paris. To get into Paris you take an RER (the urban train network) into the Gare du Nord. Orly Airport makes more sense if you are (a) going to south Paris or (b) if you are connecting with an Air Inter (France's domestic carrier) flight, as Orly is the hub for the domestic network.

Air Services: Over the last few years many new air services to France from the UK have sprung up, and such is the competion, that several have gone under, or been absorbed by British Airways. They fly from London's Heathrow and Gatwick airports to most large provincial French cities and from UK regional airports mainly to Paris but also to Nice, Lyon and other regional cities. The Air Travel Advisory Bureau (0171-636 5000 London; 0161-832 2000 Manchester) can give you the phone numbers of a few discount travel agents appropriate to your needs. The following airlines and agents can also provide further information:

Air France: Colet House, 100 Hammersmith, London W6 7JP.

Air UK: Norwich Airport, Norwich NR6 6ER. Flies from Stanstead to Paris-CDG.

Air Liberté: After going into receivership was taken control of by British Airways in 1997. Flies between London Gatwick and Bordeaux and London Gatwick and Toulouse; tel (UK) 0345 228899; Bordeaux: 56 34 53 53; Toulouse: 16 61 15 71 71. Also domestic flights in France.

British Airways: 156 Regent Street, London W1R 5TA; tel: 0181 897 4000.

British Midland Airways: East Midlands Airport, Castle Donington. Flies Heathrow/Nice; Heathrow/Paris CDG; Belfast/Paris (via Heathrow); East Midlands/Paris CDG and East Midlands/Nice.

Brymon Airways: based in Plymouth, Brymon is a subsidiary of British Airways and flies from Plymouth to Paris-CDG. For reservations tel 0345 222111.

Love Air: Building 44, First Ave, Stanstead Airport CM24 1QE; tel 01279 681435. Miniscule airline (3 Piper Navajo aircraft with 7/9 seats) operating between Lydd and Le Touquet.

Nouvelles Frontières: 2/3 Woodstock Street, London W1R 1HE; tel 0171-629 7772. Cost cutting flights from London to Paris and from Paris to many destinations in France and worldwide.

Euroglobe Travel: 0181-677 5124. Specialises in flights to France including charters and business travel.

Lupus Travel: 11 Vale Road, Tunbridge Wells, Kent TN1 1BS; tel 01892-533030. France specialists. Bargain flights to destinations nationwide in France and accommodation in Paris.

Dawson and Sanderson: 7A Victoria House, South Lambeth Road, London SW8 1QT; tel 0171-793 9364 (ext.33). Reduced fares on scheduled flights to the main French cities: Montpellier, Bordeaux etc as well as Paris.

Angel Travel: 34 High Street, Borough Green, Kent TN15 8BT; tel 01732 884109. Specialists in travel to France by ferry, air or rail.

Easyjet; (0990 292929) based at Luton Airport has £49 fares to Nice.

Coach Services

There are regular coach services from London to France. The biggest operator is Eurolines which is part of the National Express Group. In addition to the services listed below Eurolines run services in conjunction with the major ferry services through Calais, Caen, Cherbourg, Le Havre, Roscoff and St. Malo. For passengers from Scotland and the north of England there is a daily service via North Sea Ferries to Zeebrugge.

Eurolines (UK) Ltd: 52 Grosvenor Gardens, Victoria, London SW1W OAU; tel (0990 143219). London to Paris (incl. Euro Disney), Montpellier, Perpignan, Bordeaux, Nice, Chamonix, Grenoble, Strasbourg etc. plus the Channelink Services (see above).

Guides

Around and About Paris — The 13th-20th Arrondissements: by Thirza Vallois (Iliad, £15.95). There are also guides by the same author on arrondissements 1-7 and 8-12. The guides contain a wealth of historical detail and the type of hidden gems you would probably not find on your own. Also gastronomic recommendations.

A Little Tour in France: (Penguin £6.99) Henry James. A little out of date perhaps for the modern traveller, but gives an insight into sightseeing in a more elegant age.

Blue Guide France: Robertson/A & C Black (1988). £16.99 paperback. Detailed information on cultural aspects of France including art, architecture and history.

Guide des Maison d'Hommes Célèbres: Horay (£12). Who lived where, and when (in French).

The Loire Valley Everyman Guides, £16.99.

Living as a British Expatriate in France: (£9) from the French Chamber of Commerce in Great Britain, 197 Knightsbridge, London SW7 1RB; tel 0171-304 7021; fax 0171-304 7034.

Michelin Green Tourist Guide to France: A guide in English which covers all of France but is extracted from the series of Michelin Guides Verts on each region.

Ouvert au Public: Caisse Nationale des Monuments Historiques (1996) £16.50. The official French-language guide to 1,200 sites open to the public.

Paris-Anglophone Directory: (5th edition 1997). 2,500 Paris contacts organised in three sections, Travel & Tourism, Doing Business and Working and Living and Studying. Coverage includes, hotels, apartments, jobs, English-speaking doctors, lawyers and guides. Price 98 francs/US$14.95 from Anglophone S.A. (32 rue Edouard Vaillant, 93100 Montreuil; tel 1-48 59 66 58; fax 1-48 59 66 68; e-mail: (david@paris-anglo.com).

Three Rivers of France: (Pavilion £14.99). Freda White. Popular travel book covering the Lot, Tarn and Dordogne rivers of south-western France.

General Background & History

A Place of Greater Safety: (Penguin £7.99) The story of the French Revolution.

Citizens: (Penguin £16). Simon Schama's acclaimed history of the French Revolution.

Fatal Avenue: (Pimlico £10). Military history of the area from Lorraine to Normandy.

France 1848-1945: (Oxford University Press £17.99). Theodore Zeldin.

France Today: (1990, Penguin £8.99) John Ardagh.

French Provincial Cooking: (Penguin £15). Elizabeth David.

The Identity of France: (Harper Collins £25). Fernand Braudel.

The Last Great Frenchman: (Abacus £12.99) Charles Williams. A biography of General de Gaulle.

Jesuits: (Harvill £25) Jean Lacoutre. A study of the role of the Society of Jesus in French history.

The Price of Glory: (Penguin £7.99). Alistair Horne's account of one of history's grimest battles, Verdun in 1916.

Six Armies in Normandy: (Pimlico £10). John Keegan. An account of the Allied invasion of France.

French Literature and Literature Associated with France

La Bataille (the Battle) by Patrick Rambaud. Winner of the Prix Goncourt and the Grand Prix for fiction from the Académie Française 1997. An account of the notoriously bloody and fruitless Napoleonic battle of Essling which took place near Vienna in 1809.

Cross-Channel: (Cape £13.99). Julian Barnes's collection of short stories with an Anglo-French theme.

A Motor-Flight through France: (Picador £13). By the nineteenth/twentieth century American writer, Edith Wharton. An account of motoring through France with bygone stylishness.

A Moveable Feast: (Arrow £4.99). Hemingway in pre-war Paris.

Le Grand Meaulnes: (Penguin £5.99). English title *The Lost Domain*. The only novel of Alain Fournier, who died young in the Great War. A classic, fantasy tale of childhood (the lost domain of the title) passing into adolescence, set in the Sologne countryside.

The Horse of Pride: (Yale £12.95). Pierre Jakez-Hélias. Life in rural Brittany in the early twentieth century.

Paris, A Literary Companion: (Murray £11.99). Ian Littlewood.

Jean de Florette and sequel *Manon des Sources*: (Picador £6.99). Familiar to many through the films of the same names, these Marcel Pagnol classics arc almost obligatory reading, for anyone going to live in Provence.

Village in the Vaucluse (Harvard £9.95). Laurence Wylie. French rural life through the ages.

Madame Bovary: (Penguin £1.99). Gustave Flaubert's classic of love, lust and betrayal, set in Normandy.

Montaillou (Scolar Press £9.95). Emmanuel Le Roy Ladurie. The French historian's much lauded account of 14-century village life following the supression of the heretical Cathars.

Thérèse and *The Frontenac Mystery* (Penguin £5.99). Novels set in the Landes (south-west) region of France.

Tender is the Night: (Penguin £5.99). Scott Fitzgerald's Riviera-based novel about bright young things.

Travels with a Donkey: (Oxford University Press £4.99). Robert Louis Stevenson's classic account of walking in the Cevennes with an obstreperous donkey.

Residence and Entry Regulations

The Current Position

Now that the Europe has been a Union since 1993 when the Maastricht treaty was signed, this chapter may seem superfluous. Unfortunately, this is far from the case. Although the single market provides freedom of movement and residence throughout the EU for all its nationals there are still regulations which govern other EU nationals taking up residence in France.

These regulations have been greatly simplified in recent years but the fact remains that for the foreseeable future it will still be necessary to obtain formal approval to reside in France and be issued with a *carte de séjour*. This applies whether you are of independent means and intending to live in France but not to work there, or whether you are intending to work in France. If you are not a national of an EU country then the regulations are more involved.

In theory, the process of gaining the necessary permit is very simple. The fundamental premiss is that, providing certain stipulations are met, all nationals of European Union countries possess a basic entitlement to live in France.

EU Nationality

Nationals of most other EU countries, namely Belgium, The Netherlands, Denmark, Germany, the UK, Eire, Luxembourg, Italy, Spain, Portugal, Greece, Sweden, Finland and Austria, have a right to settle permanently in France. Despite Switzerland's non-EU status, Swiss nationals are afforded similar entitlements to those granted to EU Nationals.

It is not sufficient to be the holder of a passport of an EU country: one must also possess right of abode in that country. This will be indicated in the passport, in the case of a UK national, by the wording 'British Citizen'. Those who fulfil this criterion should follow the procedure for EU Nationals outlined below. Anyone in any doubt as to their status should check this with the passport authorities in their own country and with the French Consulate.

Passports

In order to take up residence in France a UK national must possess a current passport. Nationals of Belgium, Germany, Luxembourg, Italy and the Netherlands require only their national identity card.

Entry for EU Nationals

Alternatively, nationals of Belgium, Netherlands, Denmark, Germany, the UK, Ireland, Luxembourg, Spain, Portugal, Greece and Italy can travel to France first and then apply to take up permanent residence; they do not have to seek any permission or a visa before leaving for France or at the point of entering France. In other words, there is no difference at this stage whether one is entering France as a tourist or as a potential resident. Registration with the police or any other French authority on arrival is unnecessary.

Those who have a job to go to in France, or who intend to look for one on arrival, must apply for a *carte de séjour* within three months of entering the country. The criteria for acceptance varies according to whether one is retiring to France to live there permanently or semi-permanently, or whether one is going there to work. These issues will be dealt with later in this chapter.

Generally, the important point to note is that one can stay in France for up to three months without any further authorisation, but after this period one must have a residence permit and, usually, this will not be granted unless the applicant has either found a job, given evidence of adequate means of financial support, or started a business.

If unsuccessful in attempting to obtain a *carte de séjour* then, theoretically, you are unable to reside in France any longer. However, as EU passports are generally not stamped on arrival in France it is difficult to prove, or disprove, how long a visitor has actually been in the country.

However, it is as well to note that failure to apply for a residence permit can result in a fine of up to 10,000 francs.

The Carte de Séjour

To apply for a *carte de séjour*, you should contact the nearest appropriate authority once in France — they will supply the necessary forms. You should go either to the local *préfecture de police* (police station) or the town hall (*mairie*), any local person should be able to give directions to either. In Paris only, you must go to the police station of the arrondissement in which you are living.

The response to applications reportedly varies a great deal and some *préfecture* and town hall officials have been known to display the legendary hostility of the French towards the English, while their non-xenophobic colleagues elsewhere will be very helpful; will even brief you on the procedure in English, and will process the application quickly. The *carte de séjour* used to be issued free of charge but there is now a charge (stamp duty) of 150 francs for issuing and renewing it — the same amount that a French national pays for a *carte d'identité*. The time between application and receipt of a *carte de séjour* can vary from a few weeks to several months (up to seven months has been reported). In the meantime, if you wish to take up employment a receipt (*récépissé*) for a *carte de séjour* should be adequate.

The Procedure for Getting a Carte de Séjour

In general the ritual and the documents required vary greatly from office to office and from official to official. People who have been through this procedure report different versions of events, so one needs to be flexible.

It is as well to bear in mind that in France, one in four of the population works for the state and at least 10% of them have no discernible function. Therefore in order to forestall any hiccups on your way to official residency you should ensure that all the possible documents required are in your possession before you start your application, and remember that not one, but several copies of each are likely to be required and if possible obtained before you leave the UK:

All applications for a *carte de séjour* have to be accompanied by a valid passport, four passport photographs, a full birth certificate and marriage certificate (if applicable). You may also be asked for your birth certificate or marriage certificate officially translated. It is easier and much cheaper to get this done before leaving for France and the local French Consulate will supply a list of approved translators. Geoff Halstead who moved to France in 1993 described this procedure:

> *Birth, marriage certificates etc. have to be translated by a person on the French Consulate's approved list! Once the translations have been obtained (at a cost of about £15 each document) they have to be made into documents that are legal in France. This legalisation is performed by the French Consulate. The translations are counter-stamped and signed by a vice consul. The cost of this exercise is £10.80 per document. It should be noted that cheques are not accepted by the French consulate. They will however accept postal orders. Translation without consular legalisation could cause problems in France because they are not legal documents, and the originals although legal in the UK, may not be regarded as such in France.*

Employees will additionally need to present proof of having found both accommodation and employment within France. For the former, one needs to have either bought or rented a property. If the applicant has bought property, he or she should ask the notary (*notaire*) who handled the sale for a *certificat* for this purpose. In the case of rented accommodation, a receipt for the rent will usually suffice. If it is a friend's flat then they can provide an *attestation d'hébergement* (proof of lodging) and probably also their *carte d'identité*. The applicant will also have to produce a a contract of employment and should ask their employer to make out several copies of a *Certificat d'Emploi* on headed paper confirming the employee's passport number, the date from which they are employed and the gross salary; a pay slip (*bulletin de salaire*) will also suffice. The self-employed should provide some proof of being in business or of being self-employed if applicable. Those setting up in a self-employed capacity must provide evidence of their status, such as a membership of a professional or trade body, a VAT number, or registration on a trade register. Those who do not intend to work will require proof of income.

If you are seeking employment in France, some job centres and employers, sparked by France's recent clampdown on illegal workers, will ask for an additional document, a *fiche d'etat civil*, obtainable from the town hall and which requires the same documents as the *carte de séjour*.

Additionally, in some cases applicants have been asked for a medical certificate following a medical examination from a local doctor in France. Others have been asked for an affidavit, obtained from a Commissioner of Oaths in the UK, to the effect that they do not have a criminal record.

It is also advisable to know the full names, dates of birth and places of birth of both one's parents and also grandparents. Many legal and official processes in France require this information and all French nationals have documentation giving these particulars; probably because 40 per cent of French people have one foreign grandparent. Officials in France are often very surprised to find that foreigners do not know this information and it could hold up the procedure if you do not have it to hand.

It may take some time and several visits in order to satisfy the officials that they have the information they require. However, one should eventually be granted *carte de séjour* if all is in order. Initially this may be a temporary carte/receipt which is valid for three months and can be renewed until the residence permit is issued.

Check List of Possible Documents Required for the *Carte de Séjour:*
1. Passport (plus several photocopies of the main information-bearing pages).

Copies need to be stamped *copie certifiée conforme* at the local *préfecture* or town hall.

2. Passport photographs (you will need at least four of these for each member of your family).

3. Birth Certificate (this must be the full version and be accompanied by an official translation from the French Chamber of Commerce in the UK before you go, or from the local Consulate or lawyer in France. Don't forget to have several copies made up at the same time as the first otherwise you will have to get all the copies stamped at the town hall or *préfecture*.

4. Marriage certificate/divorce papers/custody order. If appropriate a marriage certificate (with official translation and copies) is essential, divorce papers may be needed to prove you are divorced, and if you are divorced and have children with you you will need a court order (and an official French translation and copies) confirming the children are allowed to leave Britain.

5. Proof of Residence: can be any of the above mentioned and or a receipted gas or electricity bill (*EDF/GDF facture*) or a phone bill (*facture France Telecom*).

6. Proof of date of entry into France. You may be asked this as you will recall, you have to apply for the *Carte de Séjour* within three months of arriving in France if you are intending to stay there. Travel tickets may suffice.

7. Proof of employment (see above).

8. Proof of financial resources (if not intending work) in the form of bank statements/letters. Letters from friends or relatives guaranteeing financial support must be officially stamped or notarised.

Students

Anyone studying in France will have to prove they are enrolled in an educational establishment, recognised by the Education Ministry, for the main purpose of following a vocational training course there and that they are covered by health insurance (as are members of their family accompanying them to France). Additionally, they will have to give an assurance in the form of a declaration or proof of adequate resources for support.

Residence Permit Renewals

The residence permit is considered long-term but will require periodic renewal. For a renewal you will go through the same procedure and formalities except that you will not have to produce proof of your antecedants'/descendants' relationships to you. It is necessary to apply for a renewal of the *carte de séjour*, before the existing one has expired. Renewals are normally granted on the following bases:

1. Students or persons who have been involuntarily inactive for more than twelve months in succession: a one year permit. If you are still employable but unemployed after the *carte de sejour* expires, the authorities may not renew it.

2. Economically inactive persons (generally, this applies to the retired) — the permit is renewed for five years at a time.

3. Others: when the permit is renewed for the first time, its validity is extended to ten years after which it will be renewed for a further five-year or ten-year period.

If you change your residence within France, you will have to inform the police station at your new place of residence within eight days of arrival. This is so that your new address can be entered on to the *carte de séjour*.

Summary

The official line is that the *carte de séjour* should be carried at all times; just as

French nationals are required to carry various identity documents for possible inspection. Until the *carte* has been received, officially one should instead carry a passport at all times.

EU nationals do not need any further authorisation, other than a *carte de séjour* in order to live and work in France: no visa or work permit is required. All potential residents require a *carte* but dependants (e.g. a spouse and children under 16) can be covered on the original application and for the same amount of time as the principal holder.

Note that those who wish to live in Monaco may require a visa before they are able to enter the principality and will have to then apply for permanent residence. Consult the French Consulate for guidance.

Staying on in France

If you want to stay on in France after working there as either as an employee or as a self-employed person, you are expected to fall into one of the following categories:

1. When you stop working you are of pensionable age under French law, have worked for at least the last twelve months and lived in France on a continuous basis for more than three years.

2. You have lived in France on a continuous basis for more than two years and have stopped working as a result of permanent disablement resulting from an occupational accident or illness that entitles you to a pension paid by the relevant French body and there is no other residence requirement needed.

3. After working and living in France for three years on a continuous basis, you have taken up work as a frontier worker (one who commutes to another EU country to work) but you are still resident in France.

4. You are retired having worked in another EU state, or have come from another EU state and are 'economically inactive'. Proof of adequate resources for support and insurance will be required. For further details see the chapter *Retirement.*

Entry for Non-EU Nationals

In order to be granted a visa, you need to have found work France and to have been granted a work permit, an *autorisation de travail* for the position. This is applied for by the prospective employer from the Office des Migrations Internationales (44 rue Bargue, 75732 Paris). Officially, non-EU nationals are not allowed to travel to France as tourists to look for work. Thus, it is usually necessary to fix up a job and to apply for a visa from outside France — with all the added difficulty which this entails.

Once the visa has been granted and is stamped in your passport, you can travel to France to take up residence. You should then apply for a *carte de séjour,*the application procedure for which is the same as that outlined in the section for EU Nationals.

Some special exemptions exist for non-EU nationals who wish to live in France temporarily as au pairs, students or trainees: for details contact a French Consulate.

Entering France to Start a Business

EU nationals who wish to enter France to start up a business are free to do so and no prior authorisation is required (further information is given on this in the chapter *Starting a Business*). The main difference in this case is that when applying for a *carte de séjour*, evidence of having registered with the the local Chamber of Commerce (*Le Chambre de Commerce*) will be needed instead of a contract of employment. This is usually a fairly simple matter and can be done once in France.

Non-EU nationals wishing to do the same thing require *une carte d'identité de commerçant étranger*, for which they should consult the French Consulate.

Entering France to Take Up a Trade

EU nationals are free to enter France to ply any trade whether it be plumbing, building or decorating etc. However, tradesmen should check to see if any qualifications which they hold are recognised in France. If this is the case, simply register with the Chambre des Métiers and produce documentation to this effect, instead of the contract of employment, when applying for the *carte de séjour*. Details of setting up in business in France can be found in the chapter *Starting a Business*.

Entering France with Retirement/Non-Working Status

EU nationals may retire to France or live there without having any means of gainful employment as long as they can prove they are able to support themselves financially. As already mentioned those who fall into this group require a *carte de séjour* (for further information see the chapter *Retirement*).

Having moved to France it is necessary to produce evidence of sufficient means of financial support, as well as the other documents mentioned above, to apply for a *carte de séjour*. If money has been deposited in a French bank then a statement will suffice, but if the bank is not French then a letter from your bank will be needed, translated into French by an approved translator, which specifies the balance of the account. There is no set amount which one must have in order to be considered self-supporting; it is very much dependent upon the discretion of officials. Ideally, however, one should be able to show a lump sum of 120,000 francs (approximately £13,000) capital, although this does not necessarily mean that this is an adequate annual income on which to live happily in France for one year.

The main difference to note is that a *carte de séjour* held by someone who is not working (and who does not intend to work rather than being just unemployed) will need to be renewed each year and further evidence shown of funds.

Consular Registration

Once you have taken up residence in France (i.e. you have been there for over three months), you should register with the Embassy or nearest Consulate. This can also be done on arrival if desired. In the case of the UK, there are British Consulates in all areas of France. This registration will enable the UK authorities to keep emigrants up to date with any information they need to be aware of as British citizens resident overseas, and enable them to trace individuals in the event of an emergency.

The Consulate can also help out with any information required regarding an emigrant's status overseas, or help with any diplomatic or passport problems. They may also be able to help in the case of emergency e.g. death of a relative overseas. However, they do not function as a source of general help and advice, nor act as an employment bureau.

Remember that passports will need to be renewed periodically: the nearest British Consulate can advise on this. It is also possible to maintain one's right to vote in UK elections once resident overseas, the Consulate can supply information on this also.

Nationality and Citizenship Once in France

As a passport holder of a foreign country permanently resident in France, an emigrant remains a national of his or her own country, not a French citizen. However, as an EU national one has most of the rights and obligations of a French national but no right to vote in national elections and no liability to military service.

It is possible for foreign nationals to apply for French citizenship after five years residence in France. However, in future there may be very little difference between the citizenship status of nationals of all the EU countries anyway. Citizenship is awarded at the discretion of the French authorities but the only basic requirements are that the applicant is of 'good character' and is fluent in French. Details can be obtained from the local préfecture.

In another area, France was aiming to crack down on *les clandestins/les sans papiers* (illegal immigrants) of whom there are an estimated three million living within her borders and who are estimated to be entering France at the rate of between 35,000 and 100,000 a year. The majority of such migrants come from north Africa, but there is a steady traffic also from Albania, Turkey (some fleeing the right wing backlash in Germany), Romania and even Pakistan, Angola, China and India. The main entry points are France's Mediterranean borders with Spain and Italy. The socialist goverment elected in 1997 is displaying its humanitarian bona fides by reversing the policy of its predecessor government by speeding up the naturalisation of about 40,000 illegal immigrants (instead of slowing it down). The claimants for naturalisation have to show they really want to settle in France and satisfy qualifying criteria which may include showing themselves already well-integrated into French life/having children born in France/students/political refugees in danger if they returned to their home country, and so on. Even with this change of heart, largely bought about by the high profile and celebrity protests against evicting them, the figure of 35,000-40,000 is somewhat down on the tally of 132,000 naturalised immigrants reached by a previous socialist government.

Summary

At this point, would-be French residents have all the information required to apply for and obtain authorisation to live in France permanently. Remember, however, that although the regulations are apparently very simple, the practice of applying can vary considerably. Local officials interpret the rules in many different ways and we are continually being told of different procedures that applicants are being asked to follow by local officials.

A general summary is that, as an EU national, as long as you have a job or business or can prove independent means, and have a home (whether bought or rented) you basically have a right to a *carte de séjour*. However, in practice it is again not so simple because the granting and withholding of residence permits entitles the authorities to a great deal of discretion as to whom they allow to live and work in their country. It is reported that those applying for categories of work which the authorities wish to keep for their own nationals may experience more difficulty than others.

Useful Addresses

French Embassy in London: 58 Knightsbridge, London SW1X 7JT (tel 0171-201 1000.

French Embassy: Cultural Department, 23 Cromwell Road, London SW7 2EN (tel 0171-838 2055).

All enquiries regarding visas, permits, procedures etc. should be sent to the French Consulate which has restricted hours for enquiries.

French Consulate: Service des Visas, 6A Cromwell Place, PO Box 57, London SW7 2EW; (0171-838 2000). Open 9am to 11.30am for visa applications, and from 4pm to 4.30pm for collection of visas.

Other enquiries:
The London Consulate deals with enquiries from England and Wales. Those living in Scotland should contact the French Consulate in Edinburgh. Those in Northern Ireland should apply to the Consulate in London:

French Consulate General: (including Customs dept.), 21 Cromwell Road, London SW7 2EN. Open 9am to midday Monday to Friday and Tuesday, Wednesday and Thursday also 1.30pm to 3.30pm.
French Consulate: 11 Randolph Crescent, Edinburgh EH3 7TT (tel 0131-225 7954). Open daily 9am to 11 am for visas.

British Embassy and Consulates in France:
British Embassy: 35 rue du Faubourg, St Honoré, 75008 Paris (tel 1-44 51 34 56; fax 1-44 51 34 01).
British Consulate General: 16 rue d'Anjou, 75008 Paris (tel 1-42 66 38 10).
British Consulate-General: 353 Blvd. du Président Wilson, 33073 Bordeaux Cedex; (tel: 5-57 22 21 10; fax 5-56 08 33 12).
British Consulate-General: 11 square Dutilleul, 59800 Lille (tel 3-20 12 82 72; fax 3-20 54 88 16).
British Consulate-General: 24 rue Childebert, 69002 Lyon (tel 4-72 77 81 70; fax 72 77 81 79).
British Consulate-General: 24 avenue du Prado, 13006 Marseille (tel 4-91 53 43 32; fax 4-91 37 47 06).

Setting Up Home

It is surprising to find that in a well-regulated country like France the French authorities are not certain how many British people are full or part-time residents there. One estimate puts the number of Britons with French private houses at about 100,000. There are about 62,000 registered British residents (i.e. holding a *carte de séjour*) in the whole of France; the rest being holiday or second home owners. Those wanting short break homes tend to head for Normandy and Brittany while Provence is the area for those who favour longer stays. Coastal property generally, is most in demand and usually commands a premium, while the Dordogne remains the most British-pervaded area of France. It is estimated that between 1987 and 1990 the number of British buyers rose from 2000 a year to over 20,000. In 1990 alone, it was reckoned that 14,000 houses were purchased in the Dordogne area which has attracted both permanent residents and holiday home owners. That this sharp rise of activity in the French property market coincided with the boom in UK property prices is no coincidence; the surplus cash thus generated by sales of homes in Britain financed many secondary residences abroad. At the end of the 1990's there is a much less spectacular demand for property in France than in the 'boom' years and while the estate agents optimistically talk of 'boomlets' in certain areas, there is no firm evidence that the market will reach a peak similar to the last boom. Having said that, the exchange rate at the time of press (almost ten francs to the pound) is generating another burst of interest in French property and there are more than a few estate agents specialising in France with smiles on their faces. This is in marked contrast to the lean last few years. Whatever happens to the currency conversion rate after France adopts the euro single currency in 1999, there is likely to be a continuing demand for French property for various reasons, not least from those who are going to work in France and those who wish to buy now and eventually retire there. The top end of the market will probably always be the Côte d'Azur where desirable properties command prices affordable only by lottery winners, the Russian mafia, pop stars and anyone else in King Midas's league.

The idea of acquiring a French home as an investment has become more widespread in recent years. Traditionally (except in Provence which has been fashionable for decades, and the Riviera which has been fashionable for over a century) the French have not regarded bricks-and-mortar as a copper-bottomed investment in the way that the British have. Nowadays however they have a firm awareness of the investment potential of choice properties in desirable locations, with the result that more people in France are home-owners than ever before; although ownership of the housing stock in France at 53%, is behind Spain (80%) and Italy (68%), but is greater than the Netherlands (45%), Germany (40%) and Switzerland (30%).

British buyers can find charming property for sale in most parts of France at much lower prices than in the UK. At the time of going to press, France is striving to meet the Maastricht criteria for joining the single currency and vendors frequently have to drop their prices. The majority of people moving from the UK will be able to use the proceeds of the sale of a UK home to buy a similar or larger

French property, and probably have money to spare afterwards. So far so good; but the costs of buying a property in France are some of the highest in Europe and can be as much as one seventh of the purchase price, while those characterful ruins so beloved of the British are the biggest pitfall of all, because of the renovation costs. Artisanal costs are much higher in France, and foreigners have an alarming tendency to get carried away by the choice of materials and possibilities on offer with the result that they spend more on the renovation and restoration than they paid for the property in the first place. Bankrupty or selling at a loss or, being unable to sell at all are commonplace. The estate agents files are full of tastefully converted an beautifully restored properties that have become a millstone to their owners.

Whether French property is a good investment and whether you stand to make a profit selling it on, is largely a matter of location. In recent years chalet homes in popular ski resorts have been touted as a sound investment, mainly because of the building restrictions in the Alps which means that demand outstrips supply. Another way of making money out of your property is to rent it out and, again, location is a crucial factor: piste-side apartments and Paris flats within easy reach of the Gare du Nord (where Eurostar terminates) will probably never be short of tenants, while isolated houses in remote parts of France probably will.

If you are hoping to sell to the French; think again. Not only do the French often prefer a new property, or better still an apartment, but they tend to see their larger, historic properties in a different light to the British. For them, a twenty-bedroomed château in its own parkland for £150,000 will seem overpriced and impractical on account of the heavy upkeep costs. Buying it in anticipation of future appreciation will therefore have little chance of success.

France has a unique system of property purchase and conveyancing. There are fundamental differences between the procedures under French and English law, and despite moves towards standardisation in many aspects of commercial life within the EU, property purchase procedures are unlikely to be standardised in the near future. The average UK property buyer is apt to see the French conveyancing system as cumbersome, expensive (which it is), and unnecessarily legalistic. However, in some ways the system makes sense particularly as it prevents gazumping and moreover, it is very thorough. Handing French real estate to chosen heirs is however problematic (see *French Wills* below). It is undoubtedly advisable to buy French property as a French person buys it, using French services rather than to try to buy property as you would in your own country though having your own legal or financial adviser may be useful (see below).

The aim of this chapter is to help the prospective resident to find the right home for them, and to offer a guide through the procedures necessary to buy, or alternatively, to rent property. This said, we can only present an overview, and it is strongly recommended that anyone considering buying property should take professional advice as well as consulting those who have already experienced the pitfalls and the procedures, in order to reach an informed decision about buying certain types of property. Due consideration should be given to the location, restoration and maintenance costs, the likelihood of being able to rent out to recoup some of the costs, the possibility of selling in the future, French income and capital gains tax and French inheritance laws.

Buying a Weekend Retreat

At the time of going to press, the combination of the Channel Tunnel's Le Shuttle (car service) and the 'ferry wars', plus the favourable rate of exchange mean that now is as good a time as it has ever been to buy a weekend place just across the

Channel with cheap fares and lower property prices as the incentive. If this is your aim, then it is important to be realistic about the journey time. Unless you have your own aeroplane, it is pointless travelling from anywhere north of central southern England as you will spend more time travelling than enjoying your property. Ideally you should live somewhere within easy reach of a short sea crossing or the Channel Tunnel. On the French side of the Channel, driving time should also be taken into consideration; if you can manage to find a property that meets your requirements and is close to a port (half an hour would be ideal), you will probably be more inclined to make frequent visits. However, many people are prepared to drive further afield. There are still plenty of properties in Normandy of the two/three bedroomed cottage and barn type, for around £10,000. They will need that much again spent on them to be habitable. Of course, Normandy is closer to the long crossing ports which can still mean spending more of the weekend travelling than enjoying your cottage. Convenient for the shorter crossings are the Pas de Calais, and the empty (some say bleak), gently undulating landscapes of Picardy.

Another point where you will have to be realistic, is about how often you are going to use the cottage. If you imagine it will be every weekend, or even every other weekend, you are probably being over-optimistic. Once you have realised that it is more likely to be used a lot in the summer, half-terms (if appropriate) and Easter (and maybe Christmas) holidays, you might consider the idea of buying with friends. This makes a lot of sense: financially, as it halves all the costs, and otherwise because it shares the responsability. If you are worried about circumstances changing or friendships failing, then you can form a property company (an SCI) which is dealt with later in this chapter. This enables any of the participating parties to sell their shares in the company if they want out. You can also will the shares on, which is not possible with privately owned property in France (see *French Wills and Inheritance Law* later in this chapter).

Rent or Buy?

Firstly, you must decide whether to buy or rent a home in France. This may depend on whether you intend to stay in France permanently or temporarily, and whether you intend to settle in one particular region or to move around in search of the perfect spot.

Certainly, it can make sense to rent, or if you are lucky, caretake (see below). Until you are really familiar with the area, you may not be able to decide whether or not to settle there.

However, in the present financial climate, when many experts consider French property cheap by European standards, there is a temptation to buy outright — especially in the already popular areas.

Traditionally, the French unlike the British, do not regard home-owning as a priority. They may well wait until their thirties before owning their first home; whereas in Britain most first-time buyers are in their early twenties. Many French people, especially urban dwellers, are content to rent an apartment or house and are not motivated to purchase: only about 51% of families own their own home. When they do buy a house, it is often a holiday house or second home.

Another serious consideration is that property ownership is accompanied by many commitments, such as maintenance, which are not always easy to tackle in a foreign country, especially if you are mostly absent. Additionally, if you wish to sell and move on it is not always easy to find a buyer in France — where generally speaking, people move around less than they do in Britain. However, even if your property fails to materialise investment value, it will probably have other less tangible advantages such as the privacy, sense of achievement and pride that home ownership confers and which rented property rarely does.

All types of property to rent are readily available in most areas of France and the prices, except in prime areas, are considered in line with costs of living in general. The legislation governing rentals, although subject to many changes over recent years, is fair and reasonable.

The concept of buying property freehold is much the same as in the UK or other countries. However, the system of renting property is very different. There is no direct equivalent of the British leasehold arrangement as all property in France is bought freehold, even in Paris. Owners of flats in apartment blocks are jointly financially responsible for maintenance of common areas. If you move in when spending on communal areas has been agreed, you will be liable for your share. Check that you know what these costs will be before signing the legally binding *Compromis de vente* . All these subjects are dealt with at greater length below.

Useful Addresses

Chez Nous: 85 Dobb Road, Holmbridge, Huddersfield, HD7 1QP (tel 01484 684075). Publish an annual brochure of British-owned French properties for rent. Prospective lessees buy the brochure and then deal with the owners direct.

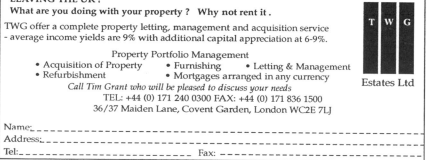

LEAVING THE UK !

What are you doing with your property ? Why not rent it .

TWG offer a complete property letting, management and acquisition service - average income yields are 9% with additional capital appreciation at 6-9%.

Property Portfolio Management

• Acquisition of Property   • Furnishing   • Letting & Management
• Refurbishment   • Mortgages arranged in any currency

Call Tim Grant who will be pleased to discuss your needs
TEL: +44 (0) 171 240 0300 FAX: +44 (0) 171 836 1500
36/37 Maiden Lane, Covent Garden, London WC2E 7LJ

T W G Estates Ltd

Name: _
Address: _
Tel: _ Fax: _ _ _ _ _ _ _ _ _ _ _ _ _ _ _ _ _ _ _

TWG Estates Ltd.: 36/37 Maiden Lane, Covent Garden, London WC2E 7LJ; tel 0171-240 0300; fax 0171-836 1500. Relocation agent who provide a comprehensive service for those wishing to sell or rent out their property when they relocate abroad. Deals with property in London and the Home Counties.

Leaseback

Leaseback schemes are a kind of halfway house between renting and buying and are for those reluctant to buy a home outright. You acquire the freehold at a discount (usually 30% or 35%) on the purchase price in return for allowing the property to be rented out by the agents for ten months out of twelve for the first nine or eleven years. At the end of the leaseback the property is yours or you can start another leaseback. This kind of arrangement usually applies to modern developments like Pont Royal, a vernacular style development in Provence. Although it can seem an attractive proposition, you have such limited use of the property that you might just as well spend the money on renting different properties in France.

Useful Contacts

Continental Metropolitan Estates Ltd.: Buchanan House, 3 St James's Square, London SW1Y 4JU; tel 0171-702 0033; fax 0171 702 2887. Agents for the Pierre et Vacances long term development project at Pont Royal in Provence. Leaseback scheme at 35% discount and owners can use their property for ten weeks annually for 11 years with no outgoings. The alternative is a 15% discount with 175 days owner use a year.

Pierre et Vacances: La Grande Arche, Paroi Nord, Cédex 61, 92054 Paris-la-Défense; tel 1-41 26 20 00; fax 1-41 26 25 72. Large French holiday company which pioneered leaseback. Properties available around France including ski resorts.

European Villa Sales; 01223-514241. Leaseback deals either side of £100,000 at Grand Ocean (with marina and golf course) near Biscarrosse in the south west.

Villas Abroad (Properties) Ltd.: 100 High Street, Hampton, Middlesex TW12 2SD; tel 0181-941 4499; fax 0181 941 0202.

Caretaking/Housesitting

For those who wish to reside in France but who want to move around the country there is an alternative to renting. Mr. Geoff Halstead and partner Mrs. Judith Lee left for France with the intention of taking up residence there for several years. However they needed to conserve funds as well as wanting to experience living in different parts of the country. Mr. Halstead offers his solution:

We did not want to buy a property in France because we wanted some degree of freedom to move. At first we considered buying a mobile home, but on a logistical basis it seemed daunting. We then thought the only real alternative would be to rent a series of properties in different regions, but this would have been expensive. Finances have however been eased because we have now arranged to be winter caretakers for a group of cottages in Brittany on a nil rent/ nil salary basis. In effect this means that we live rent free for seven months out of twelve.

To get this offer we placed an advert in *French Property News* offering our services as no cost 'guardians' (caretakers) to anyone with property anywhere in France. Judging by the response, there is potential for this kind of arrangement'.

There is definitely scope for caretaking British-owned properties that are only utilised in the summer months which an excellent way of getting to know a particular region (and to experience it in the harshest months) before committing yourself to a huge outlay. It is not however, a way to live in France for free, as Mr Halstead points out: *One must be able to afford general day-to-day living costs, fuel and electricity costs, and to have the means and wherewithal to survive the summer!*

Jayne Nash managed to get a housesitting job for her and her boyfriend by advertising in *The Lady* magazine. Of the three replies she chose one which involved looking after two houses, a dog, a swimming pool and 1000 hectares in the Dordogne. However she counsels against rushing into such an arrangement which may seem on the surface idyllic: 'We were there several weeks before we realised how difficult it was going to be to survive. Although we paid no rent, we still had to earn enough to live on and being in an isolated hamlet work was not easy to come by. I eventually managed to give some English lessons and my boyfriend did odd jobs'. She also advises drawing up a written agreement to be signed by both parties to avoid misunderstandings.

Home Swapping

An alternative to all the above which gives you a chance to explore a region before looking for a property is to swap your UK home with a French family. There are several agencies based in Britain that facilitate this and as France and Italy are much in demand you should allow about three months to set up a swap. They generally work on the basis that you pay a subcription to have your details entered in an exchange directory. Most of those participating are either professional people, with or without children, or those who are retired. The French agency for Worldwide Home Exchange Holidays is Interlink, details of which can be obtained from the following organisation:

Worldwide Home Exchange Holidays: GTI, Little Rylands Farm, Redmoor, Bodmin, Cornwall PL30 5AR; tel/fax 01208-873123. Email:100537,2242-@Compuserve.com
http://our world.compuserve.com/homepages/GTI — HOME — EXCHANGE
http://www.zbeng.com/ihea/green-theme

Two other agencies are:

Home Base Holidays Lois Sealey, 7 Park Avenue, London N13 5PG (0181-482 4258; fax 0181-482 4258; e-mail: 100522.2733@compuserve.com

Intervac International (Rhona Nayar); 3 Orchard Court, North Wraxhall, near Chippenham, Wilts. SN14 7AD (01225-892208; fax 01225-892011, e-mail: intervac.gb@msn.com).

How Do The French Live?

Typically, a home is not considered, by the French, as something to be intrinsically proud of. The architecture may be grand, but the French tend to pay less attention to the interior of their homes and to decoration than the British do.

The housing crisis of the post Second World War years lasted much longer in France, than in Britain or even Germany. Finally the country embarked on a massive building programme in the 1960's and 1970's of which the HLM (*habitation à loyer modéré*) is the most prolific result. This type of state housing brought about a substantial improvement in France's accommodation situation but did little to enhance the appearance of the peripheries of most of the big cities where they were built. Many of the new developments are characterless, and many of the new satellite towns created, especially around Paris, are bleak places, but at least they are built to a reasonably good standard and include all modern services. All new French homes built in the last 20 years are generally spacious, well equipped and built to very high structural standards which include sound-proofing.

Currently, most French people prefer new properties in convenient commuter-belt locations. This in part accounts for the large numbers of country properties, many suitable for renovation, which are available at seemingly laughable prices. This is one area, where the foreign buyer can cash in, as these properties, which UK buyers might consider charming and full of character, are frequently shunned by French buyers looking for modern and up-to-date property with easy commuter access.

Within France one can find all types of property; from large apartment towers to small, detached apartment blocks with just three or four flats, to terraces and detached houses. The semi-detached house is actually quite rare. Apartments are much more popular in France than in most other European countries and are not considered inferior to a house: currently 54% of the French population live in houses and 46% in flats.

Prices

Obviously it is difficult to give an accurate guide to all current property prices. However, any estate agent, whether in the UK or France, can provide information on current rates for different types of property in the various regions.

Prices are liable to vary considerably according to area (the Dordogne, Gascony and Provence are currently the most expensive regions), type of property and current demand. The severe slump of the early 1990's meant that bargain hunters were able to benefit from the insolvency of those unfortunate enough to find they could not meet their mortgage payments. Reposessed homes were put up for auction in large numbers and some incredible bargains were snapped up in this fashion. Auctions of reposessed properties remain one of the cheapest ways to by French property. Further details may be found later in this chapter.

Extreme bargains apart, French property prices generally are recognised as being lower overall than in the central and northern European countries. Compared with Britain for instance, prices of houses are still 50%-65% cheaper. For holiday areas, French prices are creeping up where specialised developments are being built, however, the French version is still cheaper than those on the Spanish Costas in all but the most sought after spots.

At the time of writing it is possible to buy a small cottage in a fairly isolated area of France for around £15,000. Such a property would certainly require some renovation, but would probably have basic services supplied and, if you are lucky, a roof in good condition. The average price for a three or four bedroomed detached house in good condition in a country area (not a holiday villa) is about £50,000-60,000.

One other point to take into consideration about prices is that when buying, a cash deposit will be required at the outset. This is normally 10% of the agreed price.

If you are buying a flat in a shared block check the price of the communal maintenance costs which should be given in the contract of sale.

The following table has been compiled to give some idea of the range of prices all of which have been converted to sterling at the rate at the time of writing

Property	Area	Price
One-bedroom studio	Val d'Isère	£35,500
two-bedroom flat	Paris 7th	£300,000
Modern four-bedroom house	Côte d'Azur	£205,000
Restored *mas* (farmhouse + half an acre)	Provence	£300,000
Village house in need of restoration	Gard nr. Nîmes	£35,000
7-bedroom house	Normandy	£52,000
new de luxe villa sleeping six	Cap d'Agde nudist colony	£38,600
Fully restored house with walled garden pigeonnier, tower and outbuildings	Tarn (south-west France)	£100,000

Other comparatively costly regions include any of the main commuter areas such as the Seine Valley and any areas popular with holiday-makers: Côte d'Azur, most of Provence and some regions in the west, including the Loire Valley, Poitou, and the Dordogne. Some parts of Brittany, although isolated, are popular for holiday homes and a little costlier than might be expected for rural areas.

In general the most isolated areas carry the lowest prices. Until recently some of the cheapest areas were those closest to the UK — for example, Nord-Pas-de-Calais and Normandy. Traditionally provincial areas, these regions are now benefiting from much closer links with the other EU countries including Britain via the Channel Tunnel, and prices have been forced up a little by buyers from the UK some of whom even commute to work in southern Britain from France. However there are still many bargains available. Price rises are also apparent in some border regions, including the Rhine départements, Savoy and the Lyon-Grenoble-Annecy triangle, which hope to benefit from the European connection.

Paris Only a minority of Britons would choose to buy a second home in Paris; someone living and working there would probably consider buying, but find that they can only afford to do so in one of the commuter areas near to Paris but easily accessible via the very efficient RER (urban train system). Needless to say, prices in Paris proper, do not echo the otherwise low level elsewhere in France but except in the most exclusive areas are still considerably cheaper than you would expect to pay for something comparable in London. In central Paris, domestic property is so expensive that most of it is rented. A one-room flat in central Paris would cost upwards of £80,000. As in other European cities, prices are worked out based on the square metres occupied and currently range from about Fr15,000 (£1,760) per sq.metre to Fr40,000 (£4,460) at the upper end.

Paris is divided into 20 areas (*arrondissements*) with their own distinctive character. Parisiens tend to refer to their address by arrondissement number as in 6th or 8th, with no further explanation which can be confusing to foreigners. The most fashionable and expensive areas are the 8th (the Right Bank, near the Champs Elysées) and 16th (Bois de Boulogne) where flats go on the market upwards of a million pounds. The 5th 6th and 7th (on the Left Bank near Notre Dame) are also fashionable while most of the 3rd and 4th (the Marais) district, formerly an aristocratic area, is experiencing a renaissance as is the trendy 11th (Bastille), a kind of Parisian Islington. Once you get as far north as the 18th (Montmartre and Pigalle), seediness sets in and prices drop. Other residential areas that are considered good (and therefore expensive) are in the western suburbs, within a 15 km radius of the centre; these include Meudon, Neuilly, St.-Cloud and Sevres.

However, despite the high prices and the add on costs (including local taxes these total 10-16%) Paris real estate prices have not increased for about six years and to those with enough money to spare for very desirable properties (at least £100,000-£150,000), Paris is beginning to look like an investment. £180,000 would buy you an apartment in a renovated 17th or 18th century mansion in the Marais. £300,000 would buy you a two-bedroom flat with kitchen and bathroom in a grand style town house (*hotel particulier*) in the Avenue Foch. A less exclusive market has recently developed from British people wanting apartments within walking distance of the Gare du Nord (where Eurostar terminates). If you are prepared to live in the unfashionable areas of the 9th, 10th and 17th arrondissements, you are likely to get much better value for your money. A studio apartment a stone's throw from the station could cost as little as £35,000 while a one-bedroomed flat would cost from £55,000. Such prices reflect the lack of modernity in the fixtures and fittings, but to compensate there are the gracious proportions of turn-of-the-century architecture complete with parquet flooring.

Most Parisians prefer to be up a floor, preferably with a garden or courtyard view, so prices for ground floor, or top of building (with no lift) flats will be lower. Other considerations are the size of the rooms (gracious high-ceilings mean higher fuel bills), and the proximity of a metro station. The biggest firm of estate agents in Paris is Bertrand, but many owners advertise their property themselves so it is worth studying the small ads of *Figaro* and the *Particulier* specialist magazines.

Hamptons (0171-824 8822), the British agent has a branch in Paris. Leonard Weil (+ 33 1-40 581 135), will handle buyers who wish to spend £160,000 plus. If you are in the happy position of having £300,000 or more to spare, contact the nob end agent Patricia Hawkes (+ 33 1-42 68 11 11). Rutherfords, the British agent (0171-386 7240) handles Paris property at the less elevated end of the market.

For Paris buyers there is also the convenience of having British origin mortgage lenders (Woolwich, Abbey National and Barclays International all have Paris branches) with bilingual staff and documentation in English.

Property Glossary

French	Abbreviation	English
Aménagé		converted
Bastide		Provençal country house
Bergerie		sheep farm
Cave		cellar
Chai		warehouse for wines and spirits
Chaumière	chaum.	thatched cottage
Colombage		half-timbering typical of Normandy
Dépendance	dépend.	outbuilding
En tontine		joint purchase
Une étable		cowshed
Fermette		farm cottage
Fosse septique		septic tank
fournil		bakehouse
Gentilhommière		gentleman's country seat
Grange		barn
Grenier	gren.	attic
Hôtel de ville		town house
Longère		Breton farm house typically long, stone-built
Un locataire		tenant
Lotissement	lotiss.	housing estate
Maison d'amis		weekend house
Maison bourgeoise		imposing mansion
Maison de maître		gentleman's residence
Maison paysanne		farm house
Mas		low, L-shaped Provençal farmhouse
Pailler		barn for straw
une pièce	pce.	one room, i.e. one-roomed flat
Pigeonnier		pigeon tower
Potager		kitchen garden
Portes-fenêtres à la française		French windows
Pressoir		press (cider) in Normandy, otherwise wine press
Société civile		property-owning company
Tout à l'égout	tt à l'égt	main drainage system
Verger	Verg.	orchard

Land Glossary

accidenté		hilly

une barrière	fence
le bétail	cattle
la culture	crop
le cadastre	land registry
droit de passage	right of way
un champ	field
un chemin	path
un étang	a pond
une fossé	ditch
hectare	approx 2½ acres
les inondations	flooding
kilometre carré	square kilometre
le marais	marshland
la moisson	harvest
Limite du terrain	boundary
le niveau de la mer	sea level
une pente	slope
un poteau télégraphique	telegraph pole
le proprietaire	landowner
un pylône	pylon
une source	a spring
stérile	barren
le système de fossés	drainage
une taillis	a copse
terrain à bâtir	land to build on

Useful UK Publications

There are now several magazines available in the UK on subscription which deal with the property market. Prospective buyers may find them useful as a general guide to prices as they carry pages of advertisements of properties for sale, rent and as holiday villas. Some are available from newsagents as well as direct from the publishers:

France: France Magazine Ltd., France House, Stow-on-the-Wold, Glos. GL54 1BN; tel 01451-831398; fax 01451 830869. A quarterly glossy for francophiles with a classified section including property sales and services. £16.50 per year from outside the UK.

French Property News: Wisefile Ltd., 2a, Lambton Road, London SW20 OLR; tel: 0181-944 5500. Monthly circulation about 18,000. No August issue. Available from the publishers or from the offices of some UK estate agents.

Focus on France: published by Amberstock Publishing, 532 Kingston Road, Raynes Park, London SW20 8DG; tel 0181-542 9088; fax 0181-542 2737. A magazine containing property classified adverts. Published quarterly.

French Property Publications

There are a number of specialised French publications aimed at private house hunters and others which can be of use to Britons looking for a French property. An *indicateur* is a directory.

Bulletin Officiel d'Annonces des Domaines: 15/17 rue du Scribe, 75436 Paris cedex 09; tel +33 1-44 94 78 00. Of interest to those wishing to attend government sales by auction of property, small businesses and goods that have been taken into official receivership. Published fortnightly.

La Centrale des Particuliers: 11 avenue Dubonnet, 92416 Courbevoie Cedex ;tel: +33 1 41 16 60 00; fax +33 1 41 16 60 09. Classified advertisements. Published weekly.

Constructions Neuves et Anciennes: 5 Ave de la République, 75541 Paris Cedex 11; tel 1-49 23 48 00. Published monthly.

De Particulier à Particulier: 40 rue du Docteur Roux, 75015 Paris; tel +33 1 40 56 35 35. Private adverts for accommodation. Published weekly. 14 francs.

Indicateur Bertrand: 43 Blvd. Barbès, 75018 Paris; tel 1-49 25 26 27.

Indicateur Lagrange: 64 rue du 8 mai 1945, 92025 Nanterre Cedex; tel 1-46 95 10 10. Also *Lagrange Anglais* a version adapted to the British market. Both monthly. 20 francs.

Choosing an Area

Although the section above provides a brief guide to the range of property prices in the different regions of France, it is also important to consider the city and regional information given in the *Introduction*, relating to the areas themselves. If you are intending to work in France, employment opportunities available in the different parts of France will then assume priority in the choice of area. There is a regional employment guide in the *Employment* chapter. As regards this aspect, remember that property is often cheaper in areas where there are few employment prospects. Although this will not concern those looking for holiday property or a retirement home, it is worth noting that some of the properties offered for sale via UK property magazines although cheap, are primarily intended for holiday use and hence are in areas with little employment potential.

Once a region has been selected then look at the départements which make up that region and narrow down the choice. Most of the 90 odd départements include one large town or a major city, three or four market towns and numerous villages. When choosing a property, accessibility to amenities and to good road and rail links are very important and can make all the difference to value. Many of the départements will have a large city or town but others only contain rural hinterlands, some of which can be quite isolated.

One feature of buying town property in France is that neighbourhoods tend to be more closely defined than elsewhere. In Paris, for example, each *arrondissement* (ward) is usually devoted to its own particular use, whether commercial, residential, or industrial. Make it quite clear to the estate agent what sort of neighbourhood you are looking for and ask for a selection of properties accordingly. As in most countries, each town or city will have its own broadly-defined upper, middle and working class districts. Once you are established as a long-term resident it may be possible, to make money on a property purchase by buying into an area which is upwardly mobile.

French Estate Agents and Property Register

It is perfectly practical to use a French estate agent (*agent immobilier*) to find a suitable property. An alternative is to consult central property registers. The Banque Woolwich (the French arm of the British Woolwich Building Society) offers potential clients access to the French property register. About half of all property transactions in France, are dealt with by estate agents, and the rest take place between private individuals, though in rural areas it is customary for the *notaire* to be the official intermediary. Many French estate agents, particularly in the north and other areas on which the British have homed in, have become quite used to dealing with English-speaking buyers; the most cosmopolitan of such agents will have bi-lingual or even native English-speaking staff.

The easiest way to locate agents is to look in the French property magazines such as *Living France, French Property News* and *France* where a wide selection of agents advertise their specialities and give French telephone numbers. One disadvantage of this method is that a large proportion of the property on offer is mainly for holiday use which may not be suitable, and may also be already restored and/or further up the price range than you may wish to go. You can also look for local agents under *Immobiliers* in the French yellow pages (available in main reference libraries in the UK). It is also possible to buy French telephone directories (in France telephone directories and yellow pages are combined) from BT International Directories (tel: 01772-793390 or fax your order on 01772 797797 and the cost of the directory will be added to your BT phone bill; express orders £10 extra; regular ones take ten days). Alternatively, one can contact the Fédération Nationales des Agents Immobiliers (see *Useful Addresses* below) and ask for a list of their members in the areas in which you are interested. The French Minitel network which has about 4 million domestic terminals in France has a property information service. It is however advisable to be in France to use it as access to the system is not widespread outside France. Another possibility is to contact one of British specialist property consultants who can put British buyers in direct contact French estate agents and notaires. One such agent is Sam Crabb's Consultancy in France (tel 01935-850274).

In France, the estate agent's profession is rigorously controlled by law. Agents must be professionally qualified and in possession of the relevant diplomas. Before estate agents can receive money on behalf of clients or buyers they must be in possession of a bond which secures that money for the vendor or the purchaser. What agents can and cannot do is very carefully controlled by the agreement they have with the vendor. It is worth noting that agents are not allowed to enter into any negotiations with you unless they hold authority from the vendor.

The estate agent must also be in possession of an annually issued permit for *transactions sur immeubles et fonds de commerce* (property and business transactions) issued by the préfecture de police. You may request to see any of the documents mentioned above. Estate agents must also hold professional indemnity insurance.

An estate agent's fees used to be controlled by law, now however they are unregulated. However, the fees charged by all estate agents must be displayed at their place of business. A commission percentage on a sliding scale from about 4% to 8% is usual and, as in the UK, the vendor is responsible for paying the agent his commission. However, check on this as in a few areas, principally in western France, the purchaser is expected to pay some or all of the commission.

The function of the estate agent in France is to help the vendor and the purchaser to reach an agreement. In order for the sale to take place the offer of purchase has to be accepted. This is followed by the signing of a *compromis de vente* which sets out the details of the agreement between the vendor and the purchaser. The signing of this document may take place in the estate agent's office (or the notaire's). However, estate agents are not empowered to authorise the next stage of the sale the *acte authentique* which should be done before a notaire (see below).

UK Estate Agents

During the French property sales boom of the late 1980's dozens of UK firms entered the French property market. Some of these companies were connected with established High Street estate agents, or they dealt exclusively with French property. These days there are fewer British agents dealing with sales of French property. Some may act both as estate agents and letting agents for British owned properties. The easiest way to locate these companies is by checking in the French property magazines mentioned above. An alternative method is to contact them though through the Federation of Overseas Property Developers, Agents and Consultants (FOPDAC), P.O.Box 3534, London NW5 1DQ; tel: 0181-941 5588. This body represents a handful of estate agents who are members of the organisation and meet FOPDAC's strict criteria. A list of them can be provided on request.

The main advantage to using UK-based agents is that they will know the areas and the sorts of property that generally appeal to UK buyers, whereas a French agent may find it difficult to understand their exact tastes and requirements. These agents, as well as arranging mortgages, viewings and help with legal details, can also provide lots of inside information on the ins-and-outs of living in France as well as on buying property. Some UK agents will have associates overseas for whom they act as a sub-agent; check at the outset if they charge fees. Costs of purchasing a French property are often inflated because of agents' commissions which come on top of hefty legal fees (see below).

Some of the UK agents have formed themselves into groups whose members can locate property in any part of France: Property in France is one such as is Groupe France comprising Alpine Apartments, Barbers, La Collection Française, Northern France Properties, and Sifex.

Whether one chooses to use a French or UK estate agent is very much a matter of personal choice. Many people feel more secure dealing with a company in their own country, but there is no reason why dealing with a good French agent should present any difficulties.

Some UK agents have set up offices in France:

Agence Christol: B.P.50, 25 Blvd Gambetta 34800, Clermont-L'Herault; tel +33 4 67 96 00 60; fax +33 4 67 96 29 09

Anjou Properties: Agence Transimmo, 30 rue Victor Hugo, 49150 Baugé; tel +33 2 41 89 16 94; fax +33 2 41 89 24 49.

Edwin & Carole Cottey: 93 les Dauphins, Cavaliere, 83980 Le Lavandou; tel/fax +33 4-94 05 86 76. Search, purchase and sale of properties in Provence, Var and Côte d'Azur.

Entreprise Tredinnick: Chalembel, 63980 Fournols; tel +33 4 73 72 16 44; fax +33 4 73 72 16 86. Internet: >> http://www.french-property.com/ent-tred/index.htm. <<

Espace Immobilier: 15 blvd. de la Liberté, B.P. 51, 34701 Lodeve Cedex; tel +33 4-67 44 45 85; fax +33 4-67 44 13 72; Internet: >> http://www.french-property-news. com/french-property-news/espace.htm. Specialise in the Herault region of the Languedoc.

Penny Proudlock: Team Overseas tel/fax +33 553 36 33 48. South West France including Lot-et-Garonne, Tarn-et-Garonne, Lot, Dordogne and Gers.

Prince Estates (France) S.A.R.L.: tel 01451 820726; fax 01451 810790. Deals only with Normandy. Office in Caen.

Provence Property Sales & Services Network: +33 490 65 18 73; fax/tel +33 490 65 16 59.

Rural Retreats Ltd: tel +33 4 68 91 57 93; fax +33 4 68 91 67 93. E-mail: 101771.2453@compuserve.com

Rousillon Properties Int. Ltd. 4 Route de Laroque, 66690 Sorede, France; (tel +33 4 68 89 2911; fax +33 4 68 95 46 87.

Useful Addresses

Fédération Nationale de L'Immobiliers (FNAIM): 129 rue du Faubourg, St Honoré, 75008 Paris; tel: (1) 44 20 77 00; fax (1) 42 25 80 84.

Syndicat Nationale des Professionnels Immobiliers (SNPI): 91 rue de Prony, 75017 Paris; tel (1) 42 27 82 05).

French Government Tourist Office: 178 Piccadilly, London SW7 6EW; Publishes an information leaflet listing addresses of UK estate agents who deal specifically with French property and with various areas of France.

The following is a list of some UK estate agents which deal in French property:

Alpine Apartments Agency: Hinton Manor, Eardisland, Leominster, Herefordshire HR6 9BG; tel 01544 388234; fax 01544 388900; e-mail zigi@aaa.kc3ltd.co.uk.

Authentic France: Margon, Burton Street, Marnhull, Dorset DT10 1JJ; tel 01258 821372.

Barbers: 110 Westbourne Park Road, London SW2 5PL; tel 0171-221 0555; fax 0171-221 0444.

Beaches International Property Ltd: Hagley Hall, Hagley, Stourbridge, W Midlands DY6 9LQ; tel 01562-885181; fax 01562-886724.

Corsican Properties: Rutherfords Business Park, Marley Lane, Battle, East Sussex TN33 ORD; tel: 01424-774368. One of the very UK agents that deals with Corsican property.

Domus Abroad: 4 Gardnor Road, Hampstead, London NW3 1HA; tel 0171-431 4692 (24hrs); fax 0171-794 4822.

Dordogne & Lot Properties: 348A Woodstock Road, Oxford OX2 8BZ; tel 01865 558659 (24hrs) or 513143.

Eclipse Overseas: 29 Stuart Road, Highcliffe on Sea, Christchurch, Dorset, BH23 5JS; tel 01425 275984; fax 01425 277137. Residential and commerical property in Normandy, Charente, Loire, Vendée and Brittany.

European Property Market: Waterloo Chambers, Fir Vale Road, Bournemouth, Dorset BH1 2JL).

European Property Search: 9-11 St Cross Road, Winchester, Hants S032 9JB; tel 01962-853568; fax 01962-870008. Has associates in many French Regions.

European Villas Sales: 195 Chesterton Road, Cambridge CB4 1AH; tel 01223-514241; fax 01223-562713.

French Property Shop: Wadhurst Road, Mark Cross, East Sussex; (tel 01892-852449). South-west France: Charente, Charente Maritime, Dordogne, Gironde, Lot, Lot et Garonne.

France Med: BCM House, London WC1N 3XX (tel 0181-645 0773; fax 0181-645 0822). Deals only with upmarket property on the Côte d'Azur.

Francophiles Ltd: Barker Chambers, Barker Road, Maidstone, Kent ME16 8SF; tel 01622-688165; fax 01622 671840. Property searches in Normandy, Brittany, Pas de Calais and the south west.

Futura S.A.R.L. Properties in the Dordogne, Lot-et-Garonne and Gironde. UK office: 01787-224770; fax 01787 223084; French office: 00 33 5 57 46 27 06; fax 00 33 5 57 46 38 10.

G.A.K. Williamson: P.O.B. 100, Alresford S024 02B; tel 01962-771937 & 01962-734999.

Gascony Property: 12 Royal Terrace, Southend-on-Sea, Essex SS1 1DY; tel 01702 390382; fax 01702 390415; Internet: http://www.french-property.com/gascony.htm/

Gowers: 15 South Street, Bridport, Dorset DT6 3NR; 01308 420077; fax 01308 458231. Various French regions.*Holland & Holland:* 30 West Street, Bognor Regis, West Sussex PO21 1XE (tel 01243-822764; fax 01243-841257). Deals mainly with the north of France and some other regions.

A House in France Ltd.: 11 Mountview, Mill Hill, London NW7 3HT; tel 0181-959 5182; 0181-906 8749.

Hexagone France Ltd: Webster House, 24 Jesmond Street, Folkestone, Kent CT19 5QW; tel 01303 221077; fax 01303 244409. Northern France specialists.

International Property Shop: 58 South Street, Exeter, Devon EX1 1EE (tel 01392-211022; fax 01392-413666).

Homes in Real France: 3 Delgany Villas, Plymouth PL6 8AG; tel 01752 77177. Western and southern France, old and new properties.

J.L.M.: 109 Kenilworth Road, Fleet, Hampshire (tel 01252-621143).

La Collection Française: 66 High Street, Manton, Marlborough, Wilts. /SN8 4HW; tel 01672-516266; fax 01672-514402; or tel + 33 251 51 31 25; fax + 33 251 51 51 31 25. Specialises in sales of properties in western France — from the Deux-Sevres to the Dordogne.

Latitudes, 14 Pipers Green Lane, Edgware, Middx HA8 8DG; tel 0181-958 5485; fax 0181-958 6381.

Maison France: Green Lane, Pilham, Gainsborough, Lincs.DN21 3NU; tel 01427-628537; fax 01427-628855. Various areas.

The Nyrae Group: Nyrae Properties (Overseas), Old Bank House, Arundel, West Sussex, BN18 9AD; tel/fax (24hrs) 01903 732554; tel 01903 884663; fax 01903 884629.

Paul Clifford & Partners: Almeley Manor, Herefordshire HR3 6LB; 01544 328455.

Specialists in the Lot/Tarn and Garonne border area only. Offices in the UK and France.

Philip Lockwood UK & Overseas: 71 Coventry Street, Kidderminster, Worcs. DY10 2BS; tel/fax 01562-745082.

Pierre & Vacances: 3 Shepherd Market, London W1. Actually one of the largest French agencies, but has a London office. Specialises in apartments in fashionable places like St. Raphaël and in the alpine resorts.

A Place in France Ltd:, 34 Middle Street, Portsmouth P05 4BP; tel 01705-832949.

Properties in France: 34 Imperial Square, Cheltenham, Glos GL50 1QZ; tel 01242 253848; e-mail: 101720.1306@compuserve.com

Propriétés Roussillon: Roussillon House, 29 Aversley Road, Kings Norton, Birmingham B38 8PD; tel 0121-459 9058; fax 0121-458 1325.

Provence Property: The Old Ale House, Stedham, Midhurst, Sussex GU29 ONQ; tel: 01730-816044; fax 01730-816913.

Sifex: Phoenix House, 86 Fulham High Street, London SW6; tel: 0171-384 1200; fax 0171-384 2001.

Spratley & Co: 60 St. Martin's Lane, London WC2N 4JS, tel. 0171-240 2445.

Villas Abroad Ltd: 100a High Street, Hampton, Middx TW12 2ST; tel 0181-941 4499; fax 0181 941 0202.

Waterside Properties: tel 01892 750011; fax 01892 750033. Specialises in all types of French property and land with a waterside location.

Western France Properties: 25 Vanston Place, London SW1 1AZ; tel 0171-386 0026. For the Vendée, Charente, Charente Maritime, Deux Sevres, Dordogne, Lot et Garonne and Lot.

Finding Property

There is generally no shortage of property to buy in France, of all types and sizes and in any state from totally derelict, dilapidated but habitable, partly or completely restored, modern apartments, vacant building plots etc. and it should be quite easy to locate a selection of properties for consideration. There are several ways of doing this, most of which have already been mentioned above including: consulting the French Property Register (can be contacted in the UK on 0181-995 8335) or using Minitel (the French Internet), subscribing to a French property publication or using the services of a UK estate agent with associates in France. If you choose one with a wide network you will be able to cover a wide choice of areas from one source.

It is currently possible to find and buy property both from within and from outside another country. In fact, you could buy French property without ever actually having visited France. Although buying a property unseen is not recommended, you can certainly track down possible properties and make a shortlist before making a visit and the final decision to buy.

There are various ways to find a property other than by visiting an estate agent. In France, just as elsewhere, some people decide to sell their property privately, rather than by using an agent, perhaps by placing a notice on the property that it is for sale (*à vendre*) or by press advertisement.

Some people take a few weeks holiday in France and combine it with a search for a suitable property. Apart from travelling around the chosen area, the best source of reference is the *Property For Sale* sections of newspapers. Both the national and regional French newspapers carry these sections. It is possible to obtain these in most European countries either at city news-stands or by special order with a newsagent. Some of the most useful are:

National newspapers: *Le Figaro, France Soir, Le Monde, Le Parisien*

Main Regional newspapers:
La Dépêche du Midi
Le Dauphine Libéré — *(Rhône/Dauphigny region)*
Nice Matin — (Côte d'Azur)
Ouest France — (Brittany — published in Rennes)
La Voix du Nord — (Nord/Pas-de-Calais)
L'Est Républicain — (north-eastern France)
Le Progrès — (Lyon)
Le Républicain Lorrain — (north-east)
Sud-Ouest — (Bordeaux region)

Newspaper property advertisements are placed by both agencies and private individuals. Unless your French is very good the agencies will be easier to deal with, especially if they are English-speaking. However, subject to your language proficiency, there is no reason why you should not deal privately with a French vendor, as long as appropriate professional advice is taken. Contacting French vendors direct can be a way of locating less glamorous properties which are not aimed at the holiday-home market and may therefore be cheaper and in many ways, more authentically 'French'.

Use all the available sources when looking for a house and then draw up a list of the properties which are of interest and which you would like to view. Illustrated particulars are usually available from most agents.

Useful Addresses
Internet French Property: < http://www.french-property.com >. Web site that advertises French properties. Also reachable by phone (01702 390382/fax 01702 390415; e-mail: 100711.1647@compuserve.com and 12 Royal Terrace, Southend-on-Sea, Essex SS1 1DY.
Minitel Research Services: 61 Warwick Square, Westminster, London SW1V 2AL; tel 0171-828 8133 (help desk open 9am-10.30pm Monday to Friday). Service providing searches of databases offering properties for sale by price.

Finance

Once a property has been found and a purchase price agreed, the next step is to sign a preliminary, legally-binding contract *le compromis de vente* (or a *promesse de vente*), and to open a French bank account ready to pay the deposit (likely to be 10% of the purchase price). One of the quickest ways to transfer money is through the Inter Bank On Line System (IBOS) operated between the Royal Bank of Scotland and Crédit Commercial de France (CCF), whereby you can transfer funds instantly between the UK and France (for details of other methods of transferring money to France and opening French bank accounts, see *Banks and Finance* in the *Daily Life* chapter). If for some unforeseen reason you are unable to proceed with the purchase you will lose the deposit unless you can persuade the vendor to allow you to include a get-out clause (*clause suspensive de prêt*) in the preliminary contract. If you are not a cash buyer and intend to obtain a mortgage which you later find you are not able to get, you will then be able to reclaim your deposit. The preliminary contract should also state the amount, term and interest rate which you expect for the proposed loan. Provided that all these details and the get-out clause are inserted in the compromis de vente then you should not lose your 10% deposit (see *Property Offers and Preliminary Contracts* below).

If you have not already made preparations to obtain a mortgage you will now have time to do so as there is usually a delay of two to three months between the signing of the *compromis de vente* and the second part of the process, the signing of the *acte authentique de vente* (a.k.a. *l'acte final*), the document that finalises the sale. Choosing the right system of finance for property purchase is a complex matter in any country. However, non-residents of France can freely import funds into France for property purchase. Certain taxes have to be paid if the property is sold, before the net proceeds can be exported from France and these are dealt with below. There are many companies active in the provision of finance for buying property in France and many companies both British and French have now become adept at handling this type of transaction. There is thus no reason why borrowing to buy should be any more difficult than doing the same thing in your own country. However, the appropriate procedures and conditions concerning a mortgage will differ substantially according to whether you choose to raise a mortgage with a UK or French bank, with French francs or sterling.

Note that when France joins the on 1 January 1999, the value of the French franc will be fixed on the Euro until it is phased out entirely from 1 January 2001.

The following sections indicate the various advantages and disadvantages involved in each procedure.

French Mortgages

Generally speaking, the French institutions take the view that the purchase price is the value of the property and they will lend any portion of this (although the more you can afford to pay on deposit, the more favourable the terms). Conditions of the loan include that payment should not exceed a third of your net income including all existing commitments. Any spare 'income' could be used for further repayment of the mortgage. The amount which one can borrow is then decided by working out how much one can 'afford'. An important point to note is that joint incomes are combined, as are outgoings.

A French bank or specialised property finance institution would take first charge over the property as security and would normally lend over a term of 15 to 20 years either at a variable or fixed rate of interest. All mortgages in France are repaid by the capital and interest method: endowment or pension linking are not used at all.

When taking out a mortgage in French francs/Euros, special consideration must be given to the prevailing exchange rates which will affect the cost of the loan relative to your UK income. The usual mortgage interest rate is fixed for the whole term of the mortgage; this type of loan is almost unknown in the UK, but is the norm in Europe and also in the USA.

As well as the 'fixed' rate of interest for French mortgages, there is also a 'variable' rate, which can fluctuate, but not by the large amounts seen in the UK over the past year. Indeed these rates are often fixed for a period and then 'capped and collared' and can only move by a small percent (usually not more than 3%) each year.

There are various fees associated with borrowing in France. This includes an arrangement fee to the bank (which usually includes valuation costs) and extra costs to the *notaire* (property-conveyancing lawyer) for the registration of the mortgage at the Bureau des Hypothèques.

The maximum amount which can be borrowed in France on a property over five years old is normally 80% of the purchase price, not including notaire's or estate agent's fees. New properties are treated differently, in that if they are under five years old, the purchase price should include VAT (TVA) of 20.6%. It is possible to borrow up to 95% of the purchase price ex-VAT. In practice 100% mortgages are available but special terms would have to be negotiated.

The largest banks which offer mortgage facilities in France are Banque Nationale de Paris, Credit Lyonnais and Société Géenérale. Credit Agricole functioned as a specialized mutual credit organisation until 1982 but now trades, more or less, as a mainstream bank. Note that as in the UK, mortgages on a property cannot be transferred from owner to owner as is possible in the USA. Additionally, a further arrangement, known in France as an *épargne logement* is available. Under this scheme one must save a minimum amount with a bank each month for a period of five years. After this time has expired one is guaranteed a mortgage to purchase the chosen property.

Useful Addresses
Abbey National: 163-165 avenue Charles de Gaulle, 92200 Neuilly sur Seine; tel +33 1 46 37 30 30; fax +33 1 46 37 51 38.
Abbey National plc, Foreign Services, 21 Prescot St. London E1 8AD; tel 0171 612 5018.
Abbey National: Les Arcades de Flandre, 70 rue Saint-Sauveur, 59046 Lille, Cedex.
Abbey National: B.P. 219, 59404 Cambrai, Cedex; tel: 3-27 73 33 40.
Banque National de Paris (BNP).: Key to France — U.K. tel: 0171-823 8994.
Banque Woolwich: 9 rue Boudreau, 75427 Paris Cedex 09; tel +33 1 42 68 42 68; fax +33 1 47 42 72 72.
Banque Woolwich: 87 Avenue Francois Arago, BP 801, 92008 Nanterre Cedex.
Banque Woolwich: 9 rue Boudreau, 75009 Paris; call Mary Fort on tel +33 1 42 68 42 20; or in the UK: Freephone 0800 400 900 and ask for the brochure *Helpful Hints on Housebuying in France.*

Conti Financial Services: 204 Church Road, Hove, E Sussex BN3 2DJ; freephone 0800 018 2811; tel 01273-772811; fax 01273-321269. Conti have many years of experience arranging finance for clients (both UK and non-UK nationals) purchasing properties overseas and is an independent mortgage broker.
Credit Agricole: Mortgage à la Francaise, Client Liaison, 135 Fleet Street London EC4A 2ED; 0171-427 0007; fax 0171 427 0010 — will send out an information pack on mortgages in France on request.
Credit Agricole du Calvados: 14050 Caen, Cedex; tel: 231 55 62 00; fax 231 55 65 07; contact: Vincent Gray. For banking requirements *within* the Calvados region.

Cred'Immo: Crédit Mutuel de Bretagne, 29808 Brest Cedex 9, France; Monsieur Rouzic tel: 2 98 00 23 72; fax 2 98 30 52 10.

Finance from the UK

A number of people planning to buy property in France arrange loans in the UK, taking a second mortgage on their UK property and buying with cash in France. Alternatively, it is now also possible to approach French banks, based in London, for a sterling loan secured on the French house. If you are considering borrowing in the UK, then the method of calculating the amount that may be borrowed is worked out at two and a half times your primary income plus any secondary income, less any capital amount already borrowed on mortgage. Sometimes two and a half times joint income, less outstanding capital is possible.

Naturally this would be subject to a valuation on any UK property and you could expect to borrow more than 80% of its value in total. A second charge or a new first charge would be taken by the lender. Some lending institutions charge a higher rate for a loan to cover a second property.

You should also be aware that you may be liable to lose some UK tax relief if a UK property is re-mortgaged. If you currently have relief on loans for home improvement or double tax relief on loans for home improvements then this tax relief could be lost.

Costs incurred will be arrangement fees for the bank/building society, legal costs, including mortgage registration costs. You will also have to pay for a revaluation of your UK property. In contrast, there will be no extra fees to pay on a French mortgage. Make sure, however, that if a loan is arranged in the UK all the details of this are included in the *clause suspensive de prêt* in the *compromis de vente*.

While the vogue among the British for owning French property may have peaked, it has not abated, and French and British financial institutions in the UK and France offer finance specifically for the purchase of property in France. The following can all provide assistance:

Useful Addresses

Abbey National: (Head Office) tel 0171-612 4000 ask for a free copy of *Buying Property in France*. Abbey National has a branch in Paris.

Banque Transatlantique Representative Office: 36 St. James's Street, London SW1A 1JD. Handles mortgages on upmarket properties in selected Paris and provincial areas and helps with tax limitation strategies. Information pack avaialble on request; tel 0171-493 6717, fax 0171 495 1018.

Crédit Agricole: London Branch, Mortgage à la Française, 23 Sheen Road, Richmond, Surrey TW9 1BN; tel 0181-332 0130.

Crédit du Nord: London Branch, French Property Finance Department, 66 Mark Lane, London EC3R 7HS; tel: 0171-488 0872; fax 0171-488 0874.

French Mortgage Consultancy. Peter Davies, 5 Landsdowne Close, Worthing, Sussex BN11 5HF; tel/fax 01903-249777. Advice on the most advantageous way to purchase an overseas property.

French Mortgages and Property Insurance: The Mortgage Shop: Jersey; tel 01534-89830; fax 01534-21302.

Templeton Associates: tel 01225-422282; tel/fax 01225 422287. Consultants for mortgages, remortgages and comprehensive financial advice for buying in France.

The Mortgage Procedure Once You Have Moved to France

Someone who has moved to France and started work may find .obtaining a mortgage to be surprisingly difficult. The French bank or other lender will want to see not only three months pay slips but also a French tax return and the *carte de séjour*. As you will be unable to produce all of these documents for about six to nine months after arriving in France, it is as well to consider renting property for an initial period of a few months.

If you are going to buy your first property in France, work there and continue to do so, you may qualify for a low interest mortgage from one of the credit immobiliers designed to help first time buyers.

Exchange Risks

Mortgage providers and the National Association of Estate Agents vary in advising would-be French property purchasers to borrow in French francs (the Euro from 1999) or sterling. If, as seems the case at the time of press, Britain does not join the single currency in 1999, but France does there will always be some fluctuation in exchange rates between the Euro and sterling, at least a mortgage in Franch francs/Euros on a French property provides better security against such movements.

If, up to 1999, the franc increases in value against sterling then a UK purchaser will have to make higher repayments on a monthly or, preferably, quarterly basis. However, the value of the property in sterling will also have increased. Similarly, if the value drops, then payments are reduced, as is the value of the property and the loan. The general advice is that if the mortgage does not represent a significant part of your income, and is less than half the value of the property then the mortgage should be in francs/Euros. If your French mortgage represents a large part of your income then sterling might be better. Obviously, if your income is in French francs/Euros for the foreseeable future then it would make sense to borrow in that currency as taking the mortgage out in French francs or Euros means not worrying about exchange risks.

Exchange Control

Since France has effectively abolished any exchange control on the movement of currency it is possible to import or export French francs to or from France without limit. However, funds should always be transferred via a bank rather than in a suitcase. Additionally, with a bank transfer, a record of the origin of the funds is kept, so that if in the future controls are reintroduced it should not be such a problem exporting the sale proceeds; the latter may, however, be subject to Capital Gains Tax (*impôt sur les plus valeurs*).

Mortgage Comparison Table

	French Mortgage	UK Mortgage
Types available:	Mostly repayment only	Repayment or endowment or pension mortgages,etc.
Maximum % of value:	80% of valuation	95%, possibly more advanced
Maximum compared to income	Payments not to exceed one third of disposable income	Typically $2\frac{1}{2}$ x main salary plus second salary
Repayment period:	20 years maximum	25 years, sometimes more
Repayments made:	Monthly or quarterly	Monthly only
Interest rate:	Usually fixed,but variable becoming more common	Usually variable, rarely fixed

Finally, note that professional advice is essential for anyone proposing to raise a mortgage either in the UK or France.

Useful Addresses

Sam Crabb Wickham Farm, Marston Magna, Yeovil, Somerset BA22 8DT; tel 01935 850274). Formerly part of the French property and mortgage consultants, Crabb and Templeton Associates, Sam Crabb set up as an independent consultant in late 1993.

Conti Financial Services: see page 72.

French Mortgage Consultancy: Peter Davies; tel/fax 01903 249777.

Copropriété

Copropriété, is an important concept in the purchase of French property. In France it is very common because a large number of homes are apartments or sometimes houses which share communal facilities or, for example, are on a private estate.

At this point it is useful to point out the situation as regards freehold and leasehold purchase of a property. As you will know, in the UK and some other countries you can either buy a property outright for an indefinite period — freehold, or alternatively, simply lease it, in effect, buying the right to use it for a fixed period, for example, 99 years.

In France, most property is freehold, however, if you buy a flat the situation is somewhat different. In the deeds one will have a number of shares expressed in fractions (*tantièmes*) of the common areas (*parties communes*) while owning one's own flat (*parties privatives*). The possession of tantièmes gives the flat-owner voting rights in the syndic, or management committee (see below). The two elements of ownership: communal areas and private dwelling are both saleable but not separately.

The operation of any apartment building or development where dwellings are grouped together on land common to all residents is regulated by French law:

Le Règlement de Copropriété: The Règlement is the deed of co-ownership. It is a complex document but basically similar for every copropriété. Amongst other things, the Règlement shows the exact boundaries between the apartment and the common areas, sets down the general rules which apply to the building, including a requirement to appoint a syndic, to hold periodic meetings and to designate responsibility for service and maintenance charges etc., and it fixes the service charges and the method of payment.

If the property to be purchased is bound by the laws of copropriété (this should be stated in any sale particulars and it is normally obvious if the property is part of any sort of shared development). You should ask your legal adviser to explain the règlement to you in detail. If you do not specifically ask it may be automatically assumed that you are aware, as most French purchasers would be, of the main implications involved.

Syndicat de Copropriétaires: This brings together the co-owners and their conduct is clearly set down in the Règlement. The requirements are that the syndicat de copropriétaires meet at least once a year. At this meeting the co-owners will negotiate the budget proposed for the forthcoming year, discuss any imminent maintenance work and sometimes, appoint a new syndic.

These meetings are potentially a very good way of getting to know neighbours and minimizing the sort of disputes which occur between neighbours. Some co-owners take the meetings very seriously, others may see them as a tedious chore to be dealt with as quickly as possible.

Syndic de Copropriété: Each copropriété is run by the syndic. He or she is appointed by the owners to manage the arrangement on a professional basis, not as a caretaker (although many apartments also employ the latter). The syndic's main duties are to arrange maintenance, repairs, insurance, and payment of bills for communal services. He or she will then collect the service charges to cover this, plus management fees, from the individual co-owners.

In many cases the syndic is a professional within a firm which is in the business of managing copropriété. Occasionally the syndic may be one of the residents, perhaps a retired professional, who does it as a sideline. In either case, the syndic is accountable by law to the owners for his or her expenditure and conduct.

The co-owners have the right to appoint or dismiss a syndic. Obviously, there are good and bad sydics and it is preferable to have the former variety, since the quality of the syndic can make a great difference to the running of the block and to the costs involved. Despite this, many co-owners often resign themselves to making do with whatever syndic they find themselves stuck with.

Service Charges

Even if the process of reading the règlement is left to an adviser then one should at least know how the service charges are compiled. The copropriété system means that these are likely to be much higher than service charges in the UK, where some of the expenses which constitute the service charges and are shared by the copropriété would be the responsibility of individual tenants or leaseholders.

The actual budget for the copropriété is voted on at the meetings and set according to the majority vote. Some owners favour a lavish budget, others try to cut costs to the bone. It is always advisable to obtain past service charges accounts to make sure that one is happy with the level of spending.

Service charges will typically include all maintenance of the communal areas and gardens and will often include insurance. Whether they include water and heating varies from case to case. Service charges may vary from apartment to apartment depending on the number of communal services each receives. For example, an apartment with three bedrooms will use more heating than one with two, but their contribution to the upkeep of the garden may be the same.

All in all, the system of copropriété is far more common in France than in Britain, although it is in fact a very sensible and logical idea. Although the whole thing can and does go sour in some cases, it usually ticks along reasonably effectively and there is a great deal one can do to improve things by taking an active interest in the arrangement.

Legal Considerations

UK Legal Advisors

Although it is perfectly practicable to carry out property purchase consulting only French legal professionals there is a cautious school of thought which recommends that before signing any French legal documents, you should know exactly what they contain. For this reason, many prospective purchasers like the reassurance of having documents checked by a British-based firm of solicitors with expertise in this field. Despite the single market and free movement of goods, people and services, British trained lawyers cannot practice in France without being members of the French bar. Also, notaires who have the vital role in property purchase, have the monopoly on conveyancing in France and access to their profession is very restricted. In order to become a notaire you have to buy a licence (*Charge de Notaire*) from someone who is giving up the profession. It is not therefore possible to have all the French legal processes dealt with by British-based legal exponents. However, many British firms have formed partnerships with their counterparts on the other side of the Channel with whom they can liaise.

Fees charged by British-based legal firms for checking an agreement vary, but firms may charge a fixed rate, normally not less than £100. Subsequent consultations are paid for on an hourly basis. Others may charge a flat rate for an entire package ranging from £500 upwards, depending on the price of the property and the amount of legal work involved.

There are a couple of main get-out clauses (*conditions suspensives*) which can be included in the *compromis de vente*: the *clause suspensive de prêt*) has already been mentioned but there is a second condition suspensive: the *certificat d'urbanisme*. This is to cover the purchaser, if the property is affected by any planning requirement of which he or she was unaware. This can include highway extensions and alterations. If there are any other conditions suspensives which the the purchaser wishes to include, for instance an unfavourable survey result, then this will have to be done with legal consultation as such clauses are uncommon in France. If building or extension operations are envisaged it is also possible to subordinate completion to the approval of the proposed construction.

The notaire (see below) is not traditionally an advisor working exclusively for one or other party. He or she is a mixture of state appointed conveyancer and professional practitioner with a responsability toward the transaction rather than to one or other party.

For partisan legal advice you will have to appoint your own advisor.

British solicitors who understand French property law are listed under *Useful Addresses* below. Others can be gleaned from the various publications already mentioned *Focus on France, French Property News* and others. You could also try John Venn and Sons, Solicitors & Notaries (95 Aldwych, London WC2B 4JF; tel 0171-395 4300; fax 0171-395 4310) who are international lawyers and advisors to the Federation of Overseas Property Developers, Agents and Consultants.

An additional legal consideration is that the French Napoleonic Code, upon which the French system of law is based, is very different from UK laws which govern inheritance and property succession. Very briefly, it is impossible to disinherit natural children and it is therefore problematic to leave all property and assets to a surviving spouse. It is therefore important to get good legal advice to find a way round this if you consider that you may have a legal problem. See *French Wills and Inheritance Laws* below.

Useful Addresses
The following are British-based or British lawyers in France, with expertise in French-conveyancing:

Bennett & Co Solicitors: 39 London Road, Alderley Edge, Cheshire SK9 7JT; tel 01625-586937; fax 01625 585362.
Henry C.F. Fowkes: Toulouse; tel +33 5 61 34 01 85.
Jane Hood-Williams: 52 Rectory Road, West Bridgeford, Nottingham NG2 5BU. tel: 0115-9455433.

John Howell & Co Solicitors: 17 Maiden Lane, Covent Garden, London WC2E 7NA; freephone 0800-652 2000; tel 0171 420 0400; fax 0171-836 3626. Experts in French conveyancing and French inheritance law with their own qualified French lawyer.

John Howell & Co
Solicitors & International Lawyers
The specialists in Spain, France & Portugal

- We deal **only** with legal problems involving Spain, France & Portugal.
- We have our own qualified overseas lawyers working with us in London.
- We have 23 Associate Offices in Spain, France & Portugal.
- We also act as estate agents for Spanish, French & Portuguese property.

17 Maiden Lane, Covent Garden, London WC2E 7NA ● FREEPHONE: 0800 652 2000
FAX: 0171 836 3626 ● Email: info@europelaw.com ● Internet: http://www.europelaw.com

Howard Kennedy: 0171-636 1616.

Liliane Levasseur-Hills: 69 Pullman Lane, Godalming, Surrey GU7 1YB. Fully qualified French notaire offering comprehensive services including : buying and selling French property, French inheritance law and French taxes.

Nationwide Independent Solicitors Group: tel: contact Mr Kirk on 01284-763333 for a list of member firms in the UK.

Sean O'Connor & Co: Bilingual solicitors, 4 River Walk, Tonbridge, Kent TN9 1DT; 01732-365378; fax 01732-360144.

Pannone & Partners: 123 Deansgate, Manchester M3 2BU; tel: 0161-832 3000; fax 0161-834 2067.

Penningtons Solicitors: Dashwood House, 69 Old Broad Street, London EC2M 1PE, tel 0171-457 3000; fax 0171-457 3240. Paris office: 23 rue d'Anjou, 75008 Paris; tel + 33 1 44 51 59 70; + 33 1 44 51 59 72.

Prettys Solicitors: Elm House, 25 Elm Street, Ipswich, Suffolk IP1 2AD. tel: 01473-232121; fax 01473-230002.

Graham Platt: Qualified both in Britain as a solicitor and admitted to practise as an advocat in France. Deals with property, company, litigation and probate; Leeds (tel 01132 467161; fax 01132 467518) and in York (tel 01904 610820; fax 01904-646972).

Russell, Cook, Potter and Chapman: 2 Putney Hill, Pitney, London SW15 6AD; tel: 0171-789 9111. Contact: Sally Osborne.

Thrings & Long Solicitors: Bath, Avon; tel 01225-448494; 01373-465431; fax 01225 319735; contact: Anthony Wilkin.

French Wills and Inheritance Law
It is important that anyone contemplating buying property in France should be aware of French Succession Law. If British property owners do not take due precautions they will find the distribution of their French real property subject to French inheritance law which is quite different from English law in that the deceased may not dispose of their entire estate to whomsoever they wish. French law firstly favours children of the deceased who are *héritiers réservataires* and are automatically entitled to a specified share of the estate (*La Réserve Héréditaire*). This applies also to children from a previous marriage. If there are no children, then grandchildren, parents of the deceased, grandparents and cousins, in that

order of precedence, will be the beneficiaries of part of the estate. Where there are surviving children, property and assets are shared in equal part amongst them. This explains why there are so many small parcels of land and farms in France and why it sometimes takes a long time while the several owners of the property you wish to buy are all contacted. The remainder of the estate (*quotité disponible*) is left to be disposed of according to the wishes of the deceased. With one child, half the estate must go to the child and the remainder can be disposed of according to the will of the deceased. With two children two thirds of the estate must go to them and with three or more children three-quarters of the estate must be divided among them. The law discriminates in favour of children before spouses. Under French law of succession, a surviving spouse is not strictly an heir but is entitled to a reserved portion of one-quarter, but only in life interest. The status of a surviving spouse often needs improvement by using the disposable portion and a lawyer can be very useful in helping to achieve the best possible position.

There are certain legal expedients which can be brought to bear on the situation, especially if you want your spouse to inherit. The position of a surviving spouse can be improved by a *usufruit* (usufruct in Roman/Scots law) whereby the entire property can be left to the survivor during his or her lifetime), subject to not exceeding the disposable portion. This and various other possibilities should be discussed with a legal advisor. The alternatives include *la clause tontine*: In Britain couples often buy their property as joint tenants. In France if a husband and wife purchase property jointly they are *proprietaires indivis*. Unless another arrangement has been made they will then each be deemed to own a half share. However on the death of one spouse, half the property will then be subject to the normal French inheritance laws as described above. However, it is possible to opt for a joint tenancy by inserting *la clause tontine*. This can only be done at the time of purchase i.e. it cannot be added retrospectively. The effect of the clause is to vest the property entirely in the surviving spouse who has the freedom to dispose of the property as he/she wishes. The disadvantages are however that inheritance tax may be charged on the same property twice and may not therefore be tax efficient when used with some properties. It may be open to attack if there is a significant disparity in ages between the spouses and/or there is no evidence that both spouses made a real contribution to the purchase price.

Another possibility is to buy the property through a French property owning company, a *société civile immobilière* (SCI). It is quite usual for groups of property buyers to form their own. This has the advantage of avoiding French inheritance laws (but not French inheritance tax) and thus makes it easier to (gradually) transfer property to heirs. Acquiring a property through an SCI adds £1000-£3000, or even more depending on any additional fees that might be charged for legal expenses. Subsequent transfer (i.e. after the property purchase has been completed) might not avoid the heirship problem, and would cost up to £5,000; about 3% of the value of the property.

The above are just guidelines to some of the main ways of avoiding French inheritance laws. It is strongly recommended that you take expert legal advice from one of the UK-based law firms with expertise in this field (see *Useful Addresses* above) as the legal principles associated with avoidance techniques are extremely intricate and if used ineptly can well lead to other legal or tax problems.

Useful Publications

Buying and Selling Residential Property in France: (£8) published by the French Chamber of Commerce in Britain (197 Knightsbridge, London SW7 1RB; tel 0171-304 7021; fax 0171-304 7034).

Buying and Selling a Residence in France: Keith F C Baker and Georges Daublon available from Tolley Publishing Company (Tolley House, 2 Addiscombe Road, Croydon, Surrey CR9 5WZ) for £24.95 or telephone the order hotline (0181-686 0115).

Solicitors and Notaries

Once a French property has been decided on the whole procedure is completely different to that which you would follow in the UK; professional advisors are also used in a very different way.

In the UK, you would probably instruct a solicitor to act as a conveyancer, or you could try to do it yourself. However, buying a property in France does not involve a legal advisor as a matter of course, but must involve a notaire. If you wish to engage a solicitor in the UK to oversee the whole purchase there are a number of firms which specialize in this. However, it is quite possible to complete the purchase successfully and satisfactorily without professional advice of this nature. Note however that a French notaire, unlike a UK solicitor, cannot possibly advise on the legal implications of a purchase as it affects your own situation in the UK.

The reason that a solicitor is not necessarily needed in France is due to the involvement of the *notaire* in property purchase. The notaire has no direct equivalent in the UK: he or she is a legal official appointed by the state to see that contracts, and this includes contracts for property purchase, are properly and legally prepared and formalised under the law. In this particular role the notaire is a highly qualified and responsible conveyancing solicitor in his or her own right. He or she is an entirely impartial adviser for both parties. There are approximately 7,500 notaires in France divided up into 5,000 practices. Once regarded as a rather dry and dusty profession, the average age of the notaire has fallen and many dynamic women and men are attracted to the profession. Notaires can be consulted on a wide range of specialities. They can deal with tax and fiscal matters and advise on the management of private estates. It is an interesting point to note that where the notary is acting for the state, for instance, in property transactions, only a part of the notarial fee goes to the notary, the rest goes to the state.

In most cases, the notaire will simply prepare the contract of sale according to law and see that it, and all the necessary supporting documentation, is properly handled. However, a notaire can also help in negotiating the sale of property and some can even offer mortgages.

Hence, a purchase once properly handled by the notaire, is secure from a legal point of view. The notaire also has a full indemnity insurance and a compensation fund. The conduct of notaires is strictly regulated by the Ministry of Justice and the Chamber of Notaries and they are bound by their profession to give sound legal counsel.

Finding a Notaire

The buyer is entitled to appoint the notaire who will then mostly act for both parties on an impartial basis: for this reason it is not necessary to have two solicitors or notaires.

However, in many cases the vendor will want to use his or her own notaire and this may save work if the notaire is already familiar with the vendor and the property in question. However, one should, perhaps, remain slightly suspicious of such an arrangement as although notaires are overwhelmingly highly professional and ethical, a notaire chosen by the vendor may, in some cases, feel entitled not to make it his or her positive duty to point out any drawbacks or problems that he or she is not legally obliged to point out, whereas a notaire you had selected might be more proactive. It often comes down to asking the right questions which is where having your own legal advisor can be most helpful.

If buyer and vendor cannot agree on the choice of a notaire then they can employ two, and the fees will then be shared. If a buyer retains a notaire to act as an adviser or consultant in a property purchase or sale, rather than just as an independent conveyancer the role of the notaire comes closer to that of a solicitor in the UK in that he or she is acting in the client's interests which contrasts with the notaire's normal role of conveyancer in which they are assumed to be an impartial supervisor. The use of an additional notaire as an advisor is optional.

Notaires can be contacted through the Chambre Départementale des Notaires in each département. The Centre d'Information des Notaires (1 boulevard de Sébastopol, 75001 Paris) will also provide further information. Some British estate agents can put those wishing to buy French property directly in touch with notaires and bi-lingual assistance. There are some English-speaking notaires, but by no means all are familiar with property purchase by foreigners.

Notarial Fees

It is usual for the buyer to pay the notaire: the fees broadly divide into two different categories.

A notaire who has acted as an advisor for a sale or purchase is entitled to charge scparatc fccs for this service. Notarial fees are fixed by state tariff. It should always be checked what these separate fees will be beforehand: shop around if necessary. Similarly, a notaire who has negotiated a sale is entitled to a commission in the same way that an estate agent is. The vendor is usually liable for the cost of the commission, which is usually a little less than that required by estate agents, but again one should always check on this.

The main charges to consider, however, are those levied for the actual conveyancing, which will reimburse the notaire for professional services, the costs of any documents or information obtained, land registry fees, and any taxes or stamp duties paid. Charges vary a little from region to region but, generally, notaires have similar fees and charges, the total bill typically being between about 10% of the purchase price for resale property and 4% for new property or fairly new properties (under five years old) and more for properties which include a large garden or parcel of land.

It should also be noted that TVA (VAT) is charged on the sale of new or fairly new property at 20.6% in France (and the first resale, if within five years of original construction); this should however already be incorporated in the asking price. The reduced stamp duty compensates in part for this.

These charges seem excessive to the UK buyer, but are the norm in France and so it is understandable why the French themselves often prefer to live in rental accommodation. However, the lower cost of property generally in France should still make purchase worthwhile, provided that you do not spend an excessive amount on renovation and are not dependant on making a profit when selling.

Surveying

It is not usual practice in France to have a survey carried out on property you are intending to buy. It is often not considered necessary as the original builders and vendors are obliged to give certain guarantees and warranties as to the condition of the building. However, it is worth asking the notaire to verify whether the property is guaranteed or not.

If you decide to have a survey done the cost may be considerable. Probably the best way to find a local expert in surveying (*expert-géomètre* or *arpenteur* is to enquire locally. Most estate agents or notaries are able to arrange this for you, although any estate agent can give a simple evaluation of a property on which you wish to make an offer. Obviously, in the case of old property being sold at a low price it is strongly advised that a survey be done. If you get a full structural survey done by a French expert then the report will have to be translated into English unless your French is good enough to understand the array of technical terms. The alternative is to get a British surveyor or builder, a number of which have set up in France, to do the survey. Addresses of such surveyors can usually be found in the advertisements sections of the magazines already mentioned (e.g. *French Property News, Focus on France* etc). There are also Chartered Surveyors based in the UK who have representative offices in France such as Hadleigh Consultants based in Birmingham and Tarn-et-Garonne. There are also British based surveyors who are willing to inspect properties in any part of France but sending a surveyor to the south will obviously add considerably to the charges.

Useful Addresses
Benson & Rogers-Coltman: Market House, Craven Arms, Shropshire SY7 9NN; tel 01588-673314; fax 01558-673359. Contact: Mr P A Wright.
Curchod Continental: 54 Church Street, Weybridge, Surrey; 01932-855270.
Hadleigh Chartered Surveyors: 16 Highfield Road, Edgbaston, Birmingham B15 3DU. Tel: 0121-6259977; fax: 0121-6257766.
Agence et Union (French office of Hadleigh), Place de la Halle, 82140 St Antonin Noble Val; tel + 33 563 30 60 24; fax + 33 563 68 24 67.

Survey Glossary

bill	*une facture*
concrete	*le béton*
double glazing	*double vitrage*
downstairs	*en bas*
estimate	*un devis*
floorboards	*les planches*
invoice	*une facture*
plaster	*le plâtre*
rot	*la carie*
roof support	*une armature à toit*
roof tiles	*les tuiles*
rooms	*les pièces*
rotten	*pourri*
slate	*l'ardoise*
stonework	*la maçonnerie*
surveyor	*un géometre* (also *un arpenteur*)
upstairs	*en haut*
wiring	*installation electrique*
woodwork	*la boiserie*
woodworm	*vers de bois*

The Purchase and Conveyancing Procedure

Property Offers and Preliminary Contracts

Once various properties have been selected, viewed, and your new home has been chosen, the next step is to make an offer. It is quite in order to make an offer of between 5% and 10% less than the asking price, depending on any professional valuation given. Only in a few very popular areas will such an offer not stand a chance of being accepted. Make the offer direct to the estate agent, or direct to the vendor if it is a private sale.

The procedure of making an offer must be handled very carefully in France. Once an offer has been made and accepted, a preliminary contract, is drawn up and the deposit paid. There are two main types of preliminary contract: the *promesse de vente*, which is binding on the vendor alone, or the more usual *compromis de vente* which binds both the vendor and the purchaser, except in certain specified cases (see below). Reneging on the *compromis de vente* incurs a financial penalty of at least the deposit. This process avoids both the possibility of 'gazumping' and also the possiblility of the buyer reducing the offer at the last minute.

La Promesse de Vente (Promise of Sale)

The less usual type of contract is the *Promesse de Vente* which binds the vendor to selling to the purchaser but allows the latter an option to buy within a defined period (usually three months). The vendor promises not to sell to another buyer during the agreed period while the purchaser deposits 10% of the purchase price (known as *une indemnité d'immobilisation*) with the notary. If the purchaser changes his or her mind and withdraws from the agreement within the time specified, they will forfeit the deposit. Get out clauses (*conditions suspensives*) such as being turned down for a mortgage, are the same as for the *compromis de vente*.

Compromis de Vente (Sale Agreement)

The more usual and generally recommended form of preliminary contract is *le compromis de vente*. This is binding on both the seller and the purchaser so that the seller is committed to selling to the purchaser and the purchaser is committed to buying from the seller. If the purchase is dependent on the buyer being granted a mortgage or bank loan, the compromis de vente should include a *clause suspensive* to that effect. This means that if the mortgage application fails the compromis de vente will be rendered null and void and the purchaser may regain his or her deposit.

The *clause suspensive* may not be used as a convenient excuse to get out of the sale agreement, as the seller is entitled to try to find a suitable mortgage if this clause is invoked. Other circumstances in which it is possible to back out and have the deposit refunded include when the ownership of the property cannot be established, or if it is the subject of a mortgage which cannot be repaid.

The main thing to note about the compromis de vente contract is that although it binds the buyer to the purchase it can incorporate a limited number of 'escape' clauses to be used in strictly specified circumstances.

The other clauses of the *compromis de vente* include such specifications as the agreed price, description of the property, the vendor's right to sell and sets a date for completion of the sale (usually no more than three months later). Its basic function is to establish that the sale proceeds on terms which are acceptable to both parties. In itself, the *compromis de vente* may well be a very simple contract prepared by the estate agent and not a complex document prepared by the notaire. Thus it is important to make sure that you do not sign a *compromis de vente* mistaking it for an unbinding 'Agreement to Purchase' as an estate agent might use in the UK. Take professional advice if in doubt.

In summary, therefore, it is important not to make an offer on a property or to make a preliminary contract without being sure that this is the house you want and having first taken any professional advice you feel is required.

The Deposit

A deposit of usually 10% of the purchase price must be paid when the *compromis de vente* or the *promesse de vente* are signed. The sum is held independently by a notaire or estate agent and these professionals are bonded in order to protect such deposits. If the buyer then withdraws he or she will forfeit the deposit to the vendor, and if the vendor backs out he or she may be liable to pay a larger amount (sometimes double the deposit) in compensation.

There are certain get-out clauses (*clause suspensives*) which the buyer may include in the *compromis de vente* so that if, for example, the buyer's mortgage application fails he or she will not forfeit the deposit.

There is considerable importance attached to the term used to describe the deposit: if it is referred to as a *dedit* (forfeit), then the buyer can withdraw from the agreement but will forfeit the deposit. If it is the vendor who wishes to withdraw, he or she may do so but must pay the buyer a sum which can be double the deposit.

If the deposit is termed *acompte*, neither the seller or the buyer may withdraw from the agreement, and so legally, the sale is enforceable.

Enquiries

Once the *compromis de vente* is signed the next stage is for the notaire to make various enquiries to ascertain that there are no legal obstacles to the proposed sale. The notaire's work here is very exhaustive and he or she is professionally insured and bonded in order to certify the accuracy of the work. The notaire's remit does not include a structural survey of the building which will have to be arranged separately (see above). The notaire's function is to check for possible defects in the documentation pertaining to the property. The main enquiries which may be made are:

1. Verifying the identities of both vendor and buyer as well as of previous owners, including an examination of the deeds.
2. Checking whether any third parties hold rights or obligations which would affect the sale or the buyer's use of the property.
3. A land registry check is carried out at the Conservation des Hypothèques to ensure that there are no planning objections to the property. The notaire may also appoint a land surveyor (*géomètre*) to check on the description of the extent and boundaries of the property.

These checks will ascertain if any current mortgage exists on the property. If one does, the notaire will need to know that it can be redeemed before the purchase can be completed, perhaps from the proceeds of sale. This procedure can be completed, at its quickest, in two weeks but can take up to two months.

Acte Authentique de Vente (Deed of Sale)

Once a notaire has carried out all the required searches into title etc. he or she will prepare a draft of the final deed of sale (*acte de vente*), which forms the basis of the conveyancing. Both parties are entitled to a copy of this draft document, known as *le projet de l'acte*, prior to signing and you may wish to have it examined by your own professional adviser. Needless to say the draft contract will be in French, even if you have previously been able to obtain English explanations of the results of the notaire's enquiries.

The *acte de vente* is similar to the draft contract that would be prepared by the vendor's solicitor in the UK. It reconfirms all the information about identity of the property, previous ownership, rights, etc. as have been investigated at the enquiries stage. The contract and supporting documentation also sets down a date for the signing of the contract, a date for taking possession of the property, and a statement of the agreed price and associated conveyancing charges.

Before the *acte de vente* is signed the buyer will have paid the 10% deposit, probably from a French bank account opened for the purpose, to the notaire who as stakeholder will pay it into a special stakeholder account (*compte séquestre*). On the day the acte de vente is completed, the notarial fees, stamp duty and land registry fees should be paid to the notaire who will also confirm that the mortgage funds have arrived (if you are not paying in cash).

Signing the Contract (L'Acte Final)

If there are no further queries then the buyer and the vendor, and their professional advisers (if appropriate), are required to meet at the notaire's office on an appointed day to sign the contract.

If you do not wish to, or cannot, visit the notaire's office in person, you can give a power of attorney (*une procuration/un pouvoir*) authorizing another person to represent you at *l'acte finale*. This can be someone in the notaire's office. This can also be done for any signatures that are required at any stage of the purchase. The power of attorney can be prepared for you by any other notary in France but ideally, if you can plan ahead it should be arranged at the same time as the compromis de vente. Some, but not all French consular officials are empowered to carry out notarial duties and can sign a power of attorney. Failing this it can be arranged through a solicitor in the UK but if it is not a procedure with which they are familiar be sure to check with the French Consulate on the exact format required, as the slightest mistake could result in it being rejected by the notaire.

The signing of a contract can be a lengthy procedure. If there are any further enquiries or queries it is quite usual for them to be sorted out at this point so that the purchase can go through as planned, rather than putting back the date for completion. Finally, note that it may be necessary to produce various documents, such as birth and marriage certificates, when the signing of the contract takes place; check this beforehand.

Tying up the Ends

Once the *acte authentique de vente* is signed and the property price paid, the deal is completed. The notaire lodges a copy of the deeds at the land registry (*cadastre*), and if you have taken out a loan or mortgage, a copy with the *bureau des hypothèques*. It is also the notary's job to deduct any taxes or outstanding mortgages the vendor may owe, as well as his own charges, from the money received from the buyer before passing it on to the vendor. Of course, the buyer owns the property as from the date agreed and the money is safe as the notaire is bonded to hold such payments. For this reason, it is essential to make sure all payments go through the notaire and not direct to the purchaser.

Although the notaire's fees may seem high, remember that in most situations there will not be any other bills to pay. Of course, if the notaire has also been used as a consultant, or if a UK solicitor has been employed, their fees will be extra.

It is clear that there is an advantage in employing your own notary, when any further professional assistance with property matters is required. The notaire will already know something of you and the property in question, and in the case of death, for example, it is usual for the notaire to deal with the property that may be involved in the estate.

Paying for New Property

Payment of the balance will be due at the signing of the contract, so it will be necessary to liaise with a bank and, perhaps a mortgage company, to ensure that everything goes smoothly.

Those who intend to import money from the UK should obtain details of the procedure from their bank. Currently there are no limits on the amount of money which one may transfer to France, it may, however, need to be declared to customs so that it can be exported without restriction in future.

All payments have to be made in French francs, no matter what currency you might have borrowed in. This is always specified in the contract and is the basis on which fees and taxes are calculated.

Note that France joins the single European currency in 1999 and that the French franc will be fixed on the Euro from 1 January 1999, until it is phased out. At the beginning of 2002 euro notes and coins replace the national currencies of nations participating in the European Monetary Union (EMU).

If purchasing a French home depends on the selling of a present one, remember that it is very rare to arrange things so that you receive the money from one home in the morning and use it to purchase the new one the same day. The same tends to apply even if one moves within France at a later date.

Beware of vendors who might request part of the purchase price in cash. The way in which property is paid for and taxed in France, and the fact that a notaire earns a percentage commission means that this is a not uncommon tax dodge. Needless to say, it is illegal and may increase any tax due on a future sale.

Insurance

It is compulsory in French law for property-owners to insure their homes for third party liability (*Responsabilité Civile Propriétaire*). This should be done as soon as the purchaser has completed the acte de vente; it is obviously essential when renovation work starts. Although it is not compulsory by law to insure against other risks like fire, theft, water and other damage, it is probably advisable that property owners do so. In some cases the new owner can carry on the previous owner's insurance. This in any case is liable to happen by default as in France policies tend to be renewed automatically unless they are formally cancelled. You will however need to register the policy in your own name.

There are various types of property insurance in France and your estate agent can advise and arrange a policy for you. Note that tax on insurance premiums in France is much higher at 9% than Britain's 4%. Alternatively you can look to British brokers who provide policies for property owned overseas. Holiday Homes Insurance, established over a number of years as an insurer for Britons' second homes abroad, now offers a buildings and contents insurance that has been drawn up to comply with EU regulations. The usual French system of insurance is to calculate the premium on the square meterage of buildings, Holiday Homes can arrange a type of deal more usual in the UK, based on the value of the building and contents. Their policy is issued in English with premiums and claims payable in sterling. There is a French translation and schedules are issued in English **and** French, which saves the expense of having a translation made.

If you are keeping your UK residence, some brokers will extend the British Household insurance to cover home and contents abroad.

HOLIDAY HOME INSURANCE

Special facility for all Europe

HOLIDAY HOMES INSURANCE SERVICES

Scottish Mutual House
27-29 North Street
Hornchurch, Essex RM11 1RS

Telephone: 01708 458222
24 hour answerphone: 01708 458222
Facsimile: 01708 453555

Main Points about Household Insurance in France

Household insurance in France automatically covers both buildings and contents unlike in the UK where both covers can be taken out separately. The terms below include both basic and optional cover. Check with your insurer which are optional.

House Insurance Glossary

English	French
Liability to third parties	*responsabilité civile du chef de famille*
Legal Costs	*défense-recours*
Fire	*incendie*
Snow	*neige*
Water damage	*action des Eaux*
Storm	*tempête*
Hail	*grêle*

Window breakage	*bris de glaces*
Theft — vandalism	*vol et vandalisme*
Legal protection	*protection juridique*

Useful Addresses:

British Insurance and Investment Brokers Association: 0171-480 5083.

Institute of Insurance Brokers: 01933 410003.

Europ'AGF: AGF insures more than ten million people in 38 countries. Their UK correspondent is Dan Silvey, AGF Insurance, The LUC, Suite 2, 2nd Floor, 3 Minster Court, Mincing Lane, London EC3R 7DD; tel 0171-617 4500; fax 0171 617 4517). AGF offers a comprehensive service to those relocating abroad and/ or buying a second home overseas. They have links with seventeen European countries, so if you relocate again in Europe, you can take your insurance with you.

Holiday Homes Insurance: Scottish Mutual House, 27-29 North Street, Hornchurch, Essex RM11 1RS; tel 01708-458222; fax 01708-453555. Specialists in providing cover for Holiday Homes in Europe with Policy wording to meet the local requirements, including the payment of Insurance Taxes. Premiums and claims in sterling. Policy wording in Englsih with French translation available.

John Holman: 01277-633345. Has overseas house-insurance designed for owners of property in Europe (expatriates and holiday homers).

Barlow Redford & Co: 71a High Street, Harpenden, Herts. AL5 2SL; tel 01582-761129; fax 01582-462380.

O'Halloran and Co: 01522-537491. Will arrange cover for holiday homes in Europe.

Copeland Insurance: The Andrew Copeland Group, 230 Portland Road, London SE25 4SL; tel 0181-656 8435; fax 0181-655 1271. Buildings and contents insurance for France and a special scheme for classic cars in France.

Property Insurance: The Mortgage Shop, Jersey; tel 01534-89830; fax 01534-21302.

Property Insurance Abroad: P O Box 150, Rugby CV22 5BR; tel 01788-550294; fax 01788 562579. Will provide a free quote.

Jon Watson: 01734-568800.

Woodham Group Ltd.: 1 Goldsworth Road, Woking, Surrey GU21 1JX; tel: 01483-770787. Insurance Consultants linked to Holmans (above).

Useful Publications

A Home in France: Jane Hawking.

At Home in France: a guide to buying and renovating (Alegretto Publications £6.99).

(The Daily Telegraph) Buying a Property in France: £8.99.

Buying and Selling a Residence in France: £24.95 (0181-686-0115). Keith Baker and Georges Daublon. Keith Baker is a Notary of the City of London and a solicitor, while Georges Daublon was a Notaire and is now a senior partner in a large French law firm.

Buying and Selling Residential Property in France: (£8) from the French Chamber of Commerce in Great Britain, 197 Knightsbridge, London SW7 1RB; tel 0171-304 7021; fax 0171-304 7034.

Buying and Renovating Property in France: (£7.95). Available only direct from the author, J Kater Pollock, Flowerpoll Ltd., The Granary, Mill Lane, Linton, Cambridge CB1 6JY.

French Housing, Laws & Taxes: (£6.95) by Frank Rutherford who has been buying and selling property in France for 27 years. Available by mail order from

Amberstock Ltd., Rapid House, Wandle Bank, Wimbledon, London SW19
1DW; tel 0181-542 3562.
A Complete Guide to Buying a Home in France: (Simon & Shuster £6.99) by V.
Menkes-Ivry.
*Home and Dry in France (or A Year in Purgatory), How and How Not to Find, Buy
and Restore a French Property* by George East (available through *Focus on
France*).
*The Overseas Homeowners Handbook (David & Charles) Geoffrey Pilgrem; tel
01273-474167.*

Purchasing Uncompleted Property

At this stage it is appropriate to discuss the procedure required for buying
property that is not yet constructed or not fully constructed (*acheter sur plan/en
l'état futur d'achèvement*). Although the vast majority of purchasers buy a house or
apartment that has already been lived in, or at least completed, others may be
interested in buying what is currently a plot of land with the building on it in
whatever state of construction. This is most likely to be the case if you are looking
for a holiday property on a resort development in which case you will be buying
through a property developer (*promoteur*).

Obviously, prospective buyers will need to satisfy themselves that the design and
fittings of the property will suit their requirements. When a purchaser buys such a
property, the developer transfers all ownership in the land and the building work
so far and the purchaser then pays the vendor in instalments as the building work
progresses. The intervals when payment will be made are defined in the contract
and are regulated by law. It is advisable to have specific guarantees in favour of the
purchaser inserted into the contract and it is advisable to employ professional legal
advice for this kind of contract. This can be done either in France by employing a
notaire as a consultant, or in the UK, by obtaining the services of a solicitor with
experience of such matters. It is especially important to check the method of
ownership which is being proposed. If you are buying through an estate agent
check also whether or not you are required to pay some or all of the estate agent's
commission on the sale, as this is customary in some areas. One final point to
remember is that you are entitled to appoint the notaire if you so wish. As a
developer may well try to insist that their notaire handles the transaction, you need
to decide whether this is in your best interests. One advantage of this is that the
involvement of several notaires may make it easier to find out about any possible
drawbacks, rather than a single notaire handling everything from buying the
original site to the conveyancing of the finished properties. Again, check on the
usual rate of fees demanded for these services.

Time-share: As already mentioned, most French property sales are similar to what
would be freehold in English law, probably within a copropriété arrangement if it
is an apartment or on an estate. However, especially on a holiday development,
there may be some sort of timeshare (*(Multi-Jouissance/Multi-Propriété*) arrangement, or some management agreement (*Nouvelle Propriété*) usually known as
leaseback (see details at the beginning of this chapter). Such arrangements are, in
some ways, totally at odds with the usual basis for buying property and so
obtaining unbiased professional advice is strongly recommended.

Buying a Plot for Construction of Property

If you find a suitable plot of building land for your purposes you have to obtain a
certificat d'urbanisme (town planning certificat) from the local authority. You will
then have to sign either a *Compromis de Vente* or a *Promesse de Vente* (for details

see above). Once you have acquired ownership of the land and have draft building plans you must apply for planning permission (*permis de construire*) at the local *mairie*. You have two years from the granting of the *permis de construire* in which to begin building.

Two types of contract are open to those building their own property:

Le Contrat d'Entreprise (The Company Contract): With the Company Contract you engage the services of one or more companies and give them a copy of the plans. The contract specifies the timetable and payment schedule. The fees can be fixed or liable to review. This type of contract puts the onus of supervision and coordination on the person commissioning company services and who therefore has to coordinate the whole project.

Le Contrat de Construction (The Contract of Construction): For obvious reasons, this is the more usual contract for new building. You deal with one professional who oversees and is responsible for all the construction work. The payment schedule is governed by law and you are entitled to certain specific guarantees for the building work etc.

Location Vente

This system of purchase by instalments has been operating in France for about 50 years. It also occurs in the UK and is a way of buying property that you cannot otherwise afford. The vendor, usually a company, rents out the apartment or the house concerned and incorporates into the contract a unilateral promise to sell (*promesse unilatérale de vente*). The contract is activated when the buyer deposits an agreed sum (usually three to 5%) and thereby gains immediate occupation and the possibility to buy at the end of a fixed period, using the monies paid during the renting period to finance the purchase. There are disadvantages to this method of purchase in that rents are generally higher than than average and sometimes the price is indexed to cover increased maintenance costs over which the potential purchaser has little control. The rental period generally lasts two to three years.

Auction Sales *(Ventes aux Enchères)*

Some of the best property bargains obtainable in France are those bought through auctions held by the courts or notaires. There are several reasons why property is sometimes sold at auction: it may be an asset of a bankrupt which has been seized by the courts to pay off creditors; the other auction holders are notaires who sell properties repossessed by the banks or other finance providers in settlement of debts, or when a deceased person's estate has to be disposed of. The main point about such sales is that the aim of the sale is not to get the market value of the property it is simply to raise enough from the sale to settle outstanding debts and to pay their fees. Information about such sales can be obtained from the French courts, notaires and in some cases newspaper advertisements a few days before the sale. The trick is to find out what the reserve price is and pitch your bid slightly above. Prospective buyers must be able to show they have the resources to meet the price required in either cash or approval of a lending organisation. If the sale is through the courts, you may find the process of *vente à la chandelle* (auction by candle) still used in some parts of France, which can add a slightly fantastical air to the proceedings. Also fantastical are the lawyer's fees of about £800 for 15 minutes work. The prospective buyer must be accompanied by a lawyer who places the bid on the buyer's behalf. For a candle auction, if no counter bid has been received after three, twenty-second tapers have been lit and expired the bidding is closed and the property belongs to the highest bidder. French law does however, allow ten days for a higher offer to be made to the seller in writing, through the courts, provided that it is 10% higher. In practice this is not a frequent occurence but if it happens, another and final candle auction will be conducted approximately two months later.

If a notaire is handling the sale, he or she will issue a deadline for the submission of bids. Bids are delivered in sealed envelopes. At the hour appointed for the sale, the envelopes are opened by the notaire and the property goes to the highest bidder.

The main problem from the point of view of the British buyer is that the timescale for public auctions is very tight and it is difficult to find out about the properties to be sold at auction from the UK. They do not even receive much publicity locally — notaires will circularise a few local real estate agents and possibly place a newspaper advert.

The best way to find out about notaire property auctions is to contact notaires in the region which interests you. Estate agents may be able to help you with such contacts.

Renovating Property

For several reasons, home improving work in France is a notoriously problematic undertaking but this does not stop foreigners falling in love with dilapidated properties in rural areas and entering into the imbroglio that renovation can entail. The canny French prefer new properties which do not need time-consuming maintenance. One reason why home renovations cause problems is that building, plumbing and electrical services are generally more expensive than in the UK. For a foreigner, there is the added problem of trying to translate or interpret specialised terminology; difficult even when it is in your own language, but virtually impossible in a foreign language. A pocket-sized publication *English/French Dictionary of Building, Property and Gardening* has been compiled by J. Kater Pollock, (price £6.95 from Flowerpoll Ltd. The Granary, Mill Lane, Linton, Cambridge CB1 6JY) and is a good starting point in this respect, it includes such indispensables as butt hinge (*paumelle*) and rim lock (*serrure apparente*).

If you are having improvements or renovation carried out on your French property in your absence, then it is generally easier to use a UK builder or architect who has experience of working in France as it is extremely difficult to supervise a renovation job from 500 miles away.

If already living in France, however, and planning to renovate your home, whether for domestic or commercial aims, then it makes sense to employ local traders. In this case it is essential to check both the availability of local specialists and the prices they charge, as well as the work to be undertaken, before buying a property. There are tempting properties in France for the equivalent of £10,000, but this could, for example entail a re-roofing job in a very remote area with little chance of a local builder doing the job for anything less than 80,000-100,000 francs (approximately £8,000-11,000). Thus it is essential to have the property carefully checked by a conveyancer who will produce a full report on the work needed, before you enter into any kind of commitment. The truth is that many British buyers get carried away with renovation and end up spending as much again, and frequently more, in restoring a property as they paid for it. Frequently, having got into this state, they are then obliged to sell it at a loss — so be warned.

It is possible to reduce some of these problems by using an estate agent who is also a builder and so can advise you on the plumbing, electrical and other matters involved in renovating property. Espace Immobilier (see *useful addresses* below) offers such a comprehensive service, in the Languedoc region of southern France.

In the case of major renovation it is advisable to use the services of an architect, if not to design anything, then to supervise the work: professional supervision is a statutory requirement for building works over a certain size. If considering any major changes or extensions then you have to apply to the local mairie for the necessary consents and permissions. (see below). Separate approval is required for new drainage systems or alterations.

The French do not really understand the appeal of 'Do it Yourself' so it is not always easy to obtain the materials needed for DIY maintenance and renovation work.

Finding a Builder/Tradesman

In France as everywhere else, there are reliable builders and there are charlatans. The problem of distinguishing between the two is especially difficult for the foreigner as normal powers of perception tend to be neutralized by a susceptibility to Gallic charm. Whatever precautions you employ, one unavoidable eventuality, however sterling the building work, seems to be that the cost will greatly exceed your expectations. This may be due to the dishonestly low estimate you were given, or more likely, that you get carried away by the enthusiasm of your specialist carpenter, mason etc. and give him *carte blanche*. Also bear in mind that renovated property is often more difficult to sell than unrenovated because many people prefer to buy property to do up in their own style rather than to make do with someone else's taste. You may therefore never recoup the money you spend on renovation. Indeed, if you can sell the property at all, it will probably be at a price below the one you anticipated. However, a properly carried out renovation will give you a great deal of satisfaction and with any luck you will not want to sell it until the property market has picked up. Alternatively, if everything turns out to confirm your worst nightmares about renovation, solace yourself with the thought that there could still be mileage in writing a picaresque book about the eccentricities and waywardness of French artisans.

Probably the best way to find a builder is through local recommendation. However glowing the testimonial it is still probably advisable to consult the local *Chambre des Métiers* for a list of registered builders and to find out how long the firm tendering for your custom has been in business. French builders are prone to bankruptcy because competition is cut throat and there are always more firms than jobs available to support all of them.

For smaller renovations you will probably need one or more specialists: typically a bricklayer/mason, plumber, carpenter, electrician and perhaps a thatcher. You should always request an estimate for any work requested and for large building projects do not pay a larger deposit than 10 to 25% depending on the size of the job. For individual tradespeople, you will probably have to pay more up front. Some clients keep at least 20% of the fees back until several weeks after the work is completed to allow time for defects to show up; especially for major building work. However if you feel secure about the quality of workmanship, this may not be necessary. Those who have taken the trouble to plan their renovations, do the necessary research and learn the precise building terms (in English and French) so that they can communicate with their builder and are on site daily to monitor progress, generally encounter fewer problems than those who are absent, and do not take trouble to plan the operation carefully.

An alternative to using a French builder or artisan is to employ one of the dozens of British builders who have set up business in France. Many of them have renovated their own properties so you can inspect their handiwork before employing them. There is usually a selection of their advertisements in the English-language property magazines e.g. *Property in France, Focus on France* and *French Property News.*

Building/Renovation Glossary

English	French
attic conversion	*l'aménagement du grenier*
builder	*le maçon*
builder's merchant	*le marchand de matériaux*
carpenter	*le menuisier*
central heating	*le chauffage central*
electrical socket	*la prise*
drainage	*l'evacuation des eaux usées*
estimate	*le devis*
mains sewerage	*le tout-à-l'égout*
partition wall	*la cloison*
plumbing	*la plomberie*
roof check & repairs	*l'entretien et les réparations du toit*
septic tank	*la fosse septique*
water supply	*l'alimentation en eau*
wiring system	*l'électricité*

Useful Addresses

Adrian Barrett: Chartered Surveyor, Chartered Builder. Structural surveys, architectural and interior design, permis de construire, invitation of tenders, overseeing building work, bi-lingual service, new houses, alterations, conversions, extensions; tel 01722-333583.

Espace Immobilier: 15 Blvd. de la Liberté, B.P. 51 34701 Lodeve Cedex; tel +33 4 67 44 45 85; fax +33 4 67 44 13 72; Internet http://www.french-property-news.com/french-property-news/espace.htm; UK address: 34A, Kings Avenue, Eastbourne, Sussex BN21 2PF; tel 01323 737147. Comprehensive purchase and renovation service from an estate agent/building contractor dealing with Languedoc in southern France. Also land purchase and building from scratch.

Fédération Nationale des Promoteurs-Constructeurs: 106 rue de l'Université, 75007 Paris (tel +33 1-47 05 44 36; fax +33 1 47 53 92 73). National guild of builders and developers.

James Matthews: bilingual architect working in France and the UK. UK tel 0181-347 5970.

*Conseil Régional de l'Ordre des Architectes d'Ile de France:*140 avenue Victor Hugo, 75016 Paris (tel (1) 44 05 86 00).

Conseil National de l'Ordre des Architectes: 25, rue du Petit Musc, 75004 Paris; tel (1) 53 01 95 55; fax (1) 53 01 95 69).

Planning Permission

Once you have seen its potential and invested in a property you many want to make alterations, extensions, convert outbuildings into gîtes or carry out other alterations which require planning permission. The rules regarding protection of conservation areas and historic buildings in France are stringent but do not relate to every detail of the interior and exterior as in the UK. French planning regulations are more concerned with the external appearance of buildings while the interior details are left more-or-less to the house-owner. Therefore if the projected alterations are to the interior and will not severely alter the external appearance a *note de renseignements d'urbanisme*, obtained by the notaire during his or her enquiries during the conveyancing process will be adequate.

Certificat d'Urbanisme (Town Planning Report). Permission is required if a change of use of a building is intended, For instance if stables are going to be converted into a dwelling. The application for a CU can be made by anyone though it is often done by the notaire or a *géomètre* (surveyor). If a *certificat d'urbanisme positif* is granted then a *permis de construire* (building permit) can be applied for at the *mairie* (town hall). If you are buying a property with the intention of converting it then you should apply for planning permission *before* signing the acte de vente (deed of sale) and have the granting of planning permission included as a *clause suspensive* (get-out clause) in the *compromis de vente* (preliminary agreement).

The application will come under the scrutiny of the mayor and the town council and will be handled by the Direction Départemental de l'Equipment (DDE), subject to whose approval the mayor will issue the necessary certificate. The mayor is a far more important and influential figure in France than in the UK. Especially in small communities, he or she can be influential in persuading the DDE to grant approval. It is therefore advisable and courteous to arrange a meeting with the mayor to put forward your proposals. If your property is in the vicinity of a historic monument, the application will also have to be submitted to the office of historic monuments headed by Monsieur l'Architecte des Bâtiments de France. This august-sounding personage has an absolute power of veto which is not infrequently exercised.

The above procedure applies if the net surface area to be constructed does not exceed 170 square metres. Only living areas should be included, parking space, and non residential parts of the building, e.g. cellar, unconverted attic, do not count. There are more generous specifications for buildings to be used for agricultural purposes. For additions to existing buildings the limit is 20 square metres. Otherwise, should the area of 170 square metres be exceeded then you will have to use an architect to officiate over the application for building permission.

Permis de Construire: This is the application for building permission which has to be lodged at the town hall. It must be submitted, together with plans of the work intended: these could take the form of a photograph or drawing showing the existing buildings and surrounding land, and a drawing showing the proposed alterations including the precise dimensions. The notations on the drawing should be in French and it may be advisable, to seek the services of a professional architect. The property owner can either deliver the application in person and obtain a dated receipt, or send it by recorded delivery. The town hall must display within its premises a notice of the application lodged within 15 days of the receipt of the application. Also within the same period a letter should be sent to the applicant notifying him or her of the date (usually two months hence) by which a decision will be made. If no notification is received by the stated date the application can be deemed to be tacitly approved. However, just to be certain you can request an attestation from the town hall to the effect that no negative decision has been taken. A *permis de construire* automatically expires if no construction takes place within two years, but can be extended for a year if an application is relodged not less than two months before it is due to expire.

Swimming Pools/Minor Extensions

Open-air swimming pools and certain minor extensions or alterations do not usually require a full *permis de construire*. However, a less convoluted permission is still required in the form of a *déclaration de travaux exemptés de Permis de Construire*. Approval is applied for in the same way as a *permis de construire*, but is more often than not automatically granted. Grounds for refusal include proximity to a listed building.

Renting Out Property

Once the French property has been acquired it is possible that the owner may wish to let all, or part, of it, either as a business, or just until he or she assumes permanent occupation. There is good potential for summer holiday lettings in France, especially on the Côte d'Azur, Brittany and in many towns along the west coast. Well placed property in ski resorts also has good renting potential, especially if you can let it to a tour operator for the season. However, doing this involves important tax implications, particularly for non-residents. For a start, the law requires that non-resident ownership is registered with the Centre des Impôts des Non-Résidents (Secteur d'Assiette No 6, 9 rue d'Uzes, 75094 Paris Cedex 02; tel 1 44 76 18 73; fax 1 42 36 16 84). Revenue from letting is known as *revenus fonciers*. Non-residents in receipt of any income obtained from sources based in France should obtain forms 2042 and 2044 from the French Embassy or Consulate in their own country, or from the above address. Returns have to be submitted annually to the Centre des Impôts des Non-résidents in Paris, before 30 April. It is usually possible for the property owner to appoint a representative in France to deal with taxation affairs and the notaire may well be able to arrange this. Note that a financial penalty may be incurred by registering late.

The main point to remember about letting out a property in France is that if you rent out your property for all or part of the year, you will be subject to French income tax of at least 25% on your French income. This is payable in three annual tranches, normally due 15 February, 15 May and in September. This applies even if one remains a non-resident. However, there is a double tax agreement between the UK and France which enables one to offset some, or all of, the French tax liability against UK taxes. It is also possible to get tax reductions against costs incurred for repairs and maintenance, mortgage interest, management and security expenses, and a 10% allowance to cover depreciation and insurance. It is strongly advised that individual advice is taken from an accountant or financial adviser in the UK. If resident in France and letting property as a business then you will be liable for French income tax as part of your regular income; in this case do not register as above.

The notaire and any estate agent will be able to draw up a letting contract for you (see *Renting Property* below). An estate agent who is appointed to supervise the lettings for you the owner, must be licensed to do this.

Alternatively, some of the UK estate agents who deal in French property also operate a summer letting service (see *UK Estate Agents*).

Chez Nous: a very useful organisation to know about is Chez Nous (Bridge Mills, Huddersfield Road, Holmfirth HD7 2TW; tel 01484 689199/fax 685852; e-mail: John Smith@cnts.demon.co.uk.). Chez Nous publish an annual catalogue of over 1,500 private homes available for renting in France. They also have a website (http://www.cheznous.com.) Owners pay for an advertisement in the catalogue and prospective holiday-makers contact the owners direct. Properties in the Chez Nous catalogue cost from £90 per week for a cottage to £900 per week for a château and many prices in between.

If you have the time to deal with prospective lessees yourself, you are more likely to get the rental monies more quickly (an important consideration if you are paying off a mortgage). Some letting agents on the other hand, have an amazing range of excuses for not handing over the money they have been paid by the tenants, until months afterwards.

Gîtes: Many rural properties in France come with outbuildings suitable for conversion to *gîtes ruraux*, holiday accommodation which can be registered and let under the auspices of the national *Gîtes de France* organisation. Some départements give grants for gîte conversions as they encourage regional tourism. Grant application forms are obtained from the mairie and grants, usually in the region of 30%, are subject to conditions including that the accommodation should be available to let for a minimum of three months per year for ten years. There are regulations regarding the standard of accommodation which must be kept up for the gîte to be accepted on the national scheme. These include detailed specifications about the fittings, even down to the type of mattresses to be used, and the regularity of refurbishment is also stipulated. The gîte is liable to regular inspection to verify its condition. If you wish to be included in the Chamber of Agriculture booking system there is a weekly fee of 12% of the rent. Participation in the Gîtes de France booking system is subject to a higher fee of about 15%. Bearing in mind the expense of maintaining a gîte and the fact that they are one of the cheaper ways to holiday in France there is not a great deal to be made from the average gîte. Those in popular resort areas will fare best.

Selling Your Property

Recently, this has a sore point with many Britons trying to sell their renovated properties as the market has been sluggish except for the higher priced properties in the most desirable areas. Many would-be sellers, especially in the north dropped their original asking prices by anything from 12 to 20% in order to achieve a quick sale. Others have been falling behind with their mortgage payments. To date, many have suffered being respossessed and often as not have ended up having their dreams knocked down in a *vente à chandelle* (see *Auctions* above) which achieves nothing like the market value of the property. Notwithstanding any individual disappointments in selling a property, and the forced drop in price of many properties (despite extensive improvements), anyone who is a   non-resident foreigner, selling a property in France, should take into account the French tax implications.

In normal circumstances it is unlikely that someone would want to sell a property immediately after completing purchase of it. However, it is possible that someone might want to move to another part of France, or perhaps to sell up and return to the UK at some stage.

The sale would be initiated in much the same way as in any other country; the property can either be sold privately, or an estate agent (sometimes a notaire) can be approached to handle the sale. As already stated, estate agents are heavily regulated by law in France, and you are entitled to request a breakdown of their charges and commission. Additionally, if the estate agent is to negotiate with purchasers on your behalf if, for example, you have left France, he or she must be given clear authority to do so. It is also worth noting that in certain parts of France, one can require that the purchaser pays the agent's commission.

The actual purchase and conveyancing procedure will proceed in the same way as for a purchase, but of course this time you are the vendor. A preliminary contract will be made and if the vendor decides later to break this, it could lead to a liability to pay the purchaser 20% of the property value. The *acte authentique de vente* will then be prepared by the notaire and signed in the usual way. If, by this time the vendor has lived in France for several years he or she will probably not require a legal advisor. When selling a property in France one does not receive the proceeds of the sale from the notaire on the day of the sale. It can take at least 14 days, possibly longer, before the notaire hands over the net amount to the vendor. During this period the vendor does not receive any interest on the money from the sale.

One of the notaire's tasks before handing over the money from the sale is to deduct any outstanding mortgages on a property from the proceeds and forward them to the lender. The notaire is also obliged to deduct any taxes, for example Capital Gains Tax and to forward them to thc tax authority. Normally, non-residents are liable to pay capital gains at 33.3% or if they are non-residents categorised as *Marchands de Biens* (dealer in real estate) by the French tax authorities the rate is 50%. There are various reductions allowed against capital gains liability: for each year of ownership after the second year there is an allowance of 3.33% and after 22 years an entire exemption from capital gains is allowed. Capital gains tax is also waived if the property is one's main and only residence. The tax is calculated on the capital gain made, but does allow for, expenses (i.e. of purchase or sale), and index-linked gains which can be deducted.

Renting a Property

Renting a home is not considered inferior to buying one in France, and renting is much more popular than in the UK. People are content to rent a house with no ambitions to buy it; although the situation is changing gradually. Rented homes of all types are available from small apartments and studios to town houses and farm houses. Large manor houses and châteaux are also available for those whose aspirations reach that high. The choice will obviously be regulated by your financial situation and to a lesser extent by the area in which you choose to live.

In large French cities most of the rental accommodation is in apartments and there is often a good selection of studios (bedsitters), which can be quite large and well-appointed. The reason for this is not because of a shortage of space or because apartments are particularly cheap, but basically because the French generally prefer the convenience of flats.

Apartments sometimes come in large blocks of several hundred, and although slums exist in France, French high rise flats tend to have a better reputation and be of a higher standard than their equivalents in the UK. At the other end of the scale, some blocks may comprise a detached building of just three or four small flats.

Some apartment developments are owned and rented out by large property companies. It is quite common, however, to find small blocks of privately-owned flats with the owner living in one of the apartments, or somewhere nearby. Living in such an apartment block can be both a good way of getting to know French people and of integrating into the community.

Rents

It is difficult to give a guide to typical rents. Generally, however, they are reasonable when compared to other costs of living and, property for property, are almost certainly lower than in the UK. Obviously variations do occur geographically. As you would anticipate, Paris rents are the highest and those in the Côte d'Azur and parts of Provence not much lower. Any area which is popular with holiday-makers will have highly inflated rents on desirable properties if not all year round, at least in the peak holiday season when farmhouses with swimming pools and all mod cons can cost £800 + per week. As with purchase prices, rental costs in isolated and rural areas may seem very cheap if compared to those of other northern European countries.

The following survey, compiled at the time of writing shows the following typical levels of rents, quoted in pounds sterling:

Property	Area	Rent per month £'s (unfurnished)
3 bed flat	Paris suburbs	£1,080-1,620
1 bed flat	Paris suburbs	£840-1,200
2 bed town house	Normandy	£300-480
3 bed detached	Montpellier, Herault	£420-780

In addition to the rent there may well be compulsory insurance cover and service charges, especially in the case of an apartment block, to budget for. In the case of such apartments it may be that the building is a copropriété, jointly owned and run by its co-owners. Some of the residents in the copropriété may be owner-occupiers, whereas other apartments are rented out to tenants by their owners.

Finding Accommodation

A great deal of accommodation is found by word of mouth and personal contacts. This makes the situation a little difficult for those looking for property from outside France or who do not know a local area very well.

The main ways of finding rented accommodation are by newspaper advertisements in regional and local newspapers. A selection of these are given in the section on property purchase. Some of them circulate or are available by order in the main European countries. Note that descriptions of French properties specify the total number of rooms in the living area, rather than the number of bed-rooms as in the UK, so *quatre-pièces* will be a three-bedroomed apartment with a sitting room plus kitchen and bathroom.

Holiday Lets

A possibility for short-term accommodation is to look in the UK national newspapers, for example, *The Daily Mail* and *The Times*. UK owners of French property sometimes advertise holiday lets here which might be worth considering. Alternatively, try the French property owners magazines like *French Property News*, where French property agents, estate agents and individual property owners advertise: both can be located in the French Yellow Pages which is available in major reference libraries in the UK.

As there are comparatively few foreigners wanting to rent property for the long term in France, as opposed to outright purchase or holiday lets, you will not find many landlords with whom you can deal in English. Agents who sell French property to UK buyers will be able to do so, but not all of these deal in rental property.

Documentation for Renting

Once you have located a suitable property it is necessary to act quickly to secure it. The following documents will be required by the agent/landlord and if you have them ready in advance, you will improve your chances:

Bail au Nom Propre (Lease in your own name)

1. Photocopy of your passport (pages with name, date, and place of birth, dates of issue and expiry).

2. Employer's attestation of employment, stating salary. Note that the agent/landlord will expect your salary to be four times the amount of the rental. If this is not the case, a letter of guarantee is normally required from an employer etc. saying that in the case of non-payment of rent, they will pay the monthly rental for the period of the lease.

Rent Agreements

Rental accommodation in France is surrounded with a barrage of rules and regulations. Indeed, it may well be more complicated than the procedure involved to buy the property outright and, it is not usual to call upon a lawyer to help with property leases, there is not generally anyone to guide you through the process. You may have to rely on the goodwill of the estate agent who will be familiar with rental agreements.

The main reason for the very complex situation as regards renting is due to the major legal changes which have taken place in recent years. The reforms were initiated by the socialist government which in 1981 introduced various laws giving greater security to tenants, these laws, as is the French custom, are known after the minister who introduced them, La Loi Quillot. In 1986 however, La Loi Quillot was altered by the right wing government and these new regulations are known as La Loi Mehaignerie.

La Loi Mehaignerie

Leases taken after 23 December 1986 come within the province of La Loi Mehaignerie. Despite this there is still a great deal of confusion in France, among landlords and tenants alike, as to the precise differences between the two laws. An important point to note is that neither laws apply to holiday lettings or to the sub-letting of accommodation and therefore give little security of tenure and no protection against rent rises to such tenants.

The provisions of La Loi Mehaignerie afford reasonable basic protection to the *locataire* (tenant): The tenant is entitled to a written agreement (though it need not be a formal contract), which must detail all the terms and conditions of the rental, some of which are regulated by law and cannot be changed by a lease.

The Rental Agreement

The following items form the basic rental agreement:

1. If a rent review clause is included in the lease it can only be exercised once a year, and even then the rent may only be increased by a statutory amount linked to the Cost of Construction index.

2. A landlord/lady can ask for a bond and deposit, but the latter may not exceed the equivalent sum of two months rent and this must be returned to the tenant within two months of the end of the lease, less any outstanding rent.

3. The tenant is obliged to pay certain service charges and to insure with a suitable company (see *Insurance* below) of his or her choice. Typically, electricity is metered and paid for by the tenant, although water charges may be part of the

service charges. (for further details see *Utilities* below). The tenant is also responsible for ensuring the property is used sensibly and for certain items of maintenance.

4. It is advisable to have an inventory (*état des lieux*) of the contents of the property and their condition prepared at the start of the lease in order to avoid any later dispute; a *huissier* will prepare this for a fee. The huissier is an official peculiar to France, who, apart from being a bailiff, is also authorized to prepare legal statements on traffic accidents. In any legal proceedings it is the huissier's statement of facts which will be taken as correct, and which will prevent a landlord/lady denying responsibility for repairs, etc.

Another provision of La Loi Mehaignerie is that a rental must be granted for a fixed period of at least three years and the tenant must give three months notice of leaving, unless he or she has lost or changed jobs, in which case the notice required is only one month. A tenant cannot be made to leave before the end of the agreed period unless he or she breaks the terms of the lease. At the end of the set period the tenant has certain rights to renew, although these are not absolute, and the landlord/lady is entitled to vary the terms of the new agreement.

It is advisable to obtain professional advice according to your individual situation: an independent estate agent can be retained as an adviser.

Useful Addresses

A Flat in Paris: 31 Avenue de la Motte Picquet, 75007 Paris; tel + 33 1-40 61 99 11; fax + 33 1-45 66 42 79.

Paris Appartements Services: 69 rue d'Argout, 75002 Paris, France; tel + 33 1-40 28 01 28; fax + 33 1 40 28 92 01; e-mail www.paris-appartements-service.fr. Rental

of furnished flats in the heart of Paris and weekly cleaning service for a minimum of a week from 500 francs per day (plus utilities). including tax and weekly change of linen.

Paris Relocations: 15 rue Vignon, 75008 Paris; +33 1 53 30 41 00. Run by Eva Demichellis. Paris and the Paris suburbs only.

Cosmopolitan Services: 113 bld Péreire, 17th Arrondissement; tel 1-55 65 11 65.

Executive Relocation France: 30 rue de Lubeck, 75016 Paris; tel +33 1 47 55 60 29; fax +33 1 47 55 60 86.

Relocation Service: 57 rue Pierre Charron, 8th Arrondissement; tel 1-42 89 09 15.

Payments Required Before Moving In

Once you have agreed the terms of the lease, you will be required to pay a deposit (*dépot de guarantie*) equivalent to two months' rent. This deposit is refundable when you leave provided that you can show the condition of the property is the same as when you arrived. In addition, you will need to pay one month's rent in advance, plus other costs such as the registration tax and building charges.

If you have used an agency there will be a commission which is usually split between the lessor and the lessee. However, if the accommodation is furnished the lessee is normally liable to pay all of the commission. As stated, agents' fees are high in France and are likely to be 10% of the annual rental. It is therefore considerably to your advantage to locate rental accommodation by word of mouth or through newspaper adverts placed by individuals.

Renting and Copropriété

Finally, a prospective tenant should be especially aware of situations where the property to be rented is part of a copropriété, as many apartment blocks are. In such a case the landlord/lady is obliged to provide the tenant with certain details of the règlement de copropriété.

Aspects of renting which one would typically consider to be the responsibility of the landlord, such as outside maintenance, will in fact be the responsibility of the copropriété. In this situation, however, the tenant does not become one of the co-owners of the copropriété and any defects with the property should be taken up with the landlord and not with the copropriété or syndic. This said, the tenant will probably have to make payment towards the service charges to the copropriété.

To summarise, the terms and conditions of leasing a property work fairly smoothly for both parties once the initial complexity of the lease has been sorted out. Although the legislation in force provides quite a good level of protection against bad landlords, it tends to be quite difficult to solve tenant-landlord disputes by the processes of law, making it particularly important to choose a property and a landlord with care.

Insurance for Tenants

A tenant (*locataire*) should always arrange appropriate insurance for the property. Apart from being sensible and prudent, it is a legal requirement that one has third party insurance for property. One would probably wish also to extend this basic insurance to cover all risks, including theft and damage by fire: these comprehensive policies are known as *Assurance Multirisques*. Obtaining this cover may be compulsory in the case of a rented property, but the tenant has the right to open a policy with whichever insurance company he or she chooses; the landlord/lady cannot dictate this.

If your rented home is part of a copropriété then, in most cases, this will provide, and charge you part of the cost of the *multirisques* insurance to cover the building as a whole. However, the specifics of this arrangement should be carefully checked in each case, as the *copropriété* insurance may not cover damage and/or theft which is limited exclusively to your private areas of the building.

If the tenant wishes to arrange his or her own insurance then it should first be ensured that the previous tenant's insurance is cancelled, rather than it just being assumed that this has lapsed.

Insurance rates are on a scale of charges according to the square meterage and the location. There are some areas, including Paris, Marseille and parts of the Côte d'Azur where the high levels of petty crime make it difficult to obtain more than a very limited theft insurance at anything like a reasonable price.

A wide range of insurance companies is available to deal with home, motor or life insurance in France; a useful address for general information is Centre de Documentation et d'Information de l'Assurance (2 rue de la Chausée d'Antin, 75009 Paris; tel +33 1 42 47 94 40; fax +33 1 42 47 94 40). In the case of property insurance, the firms compete with each other for business, so it is worth looking around before choosing. One can go to a broker, agent or direct to some of the companies; use the French yellow pages (pages jaunes) for guidance.

Since the introduction of the single market in the EU it has been possible for an insurance company in one EU country to insure property in another. Some British companies have taken advantage of this (see *Insurance for Homeowners* earlier in this chapter). Thus a UK company can provide insurance for property or other goods in France. Remember that in any aspect of French insurance it is essential that written evidence is obtained which proves that a policy exists before taking responsibility for the property concerned.

Moving In

Inevitably, setting up and running a home in France is initially likely to be both a traumatic and chaotic process. However, a few general pointers should be of great assistance when, for example, out shopping for furniture, or having essential services (e.g. telephone, electricity) connected.

Furniture and other Furnishings

The market for household furniture in France splits into two very distinctive sections. On the one hand there is cheap, budget and rather basic furniture available from chain depots; while on the other hand, you can choose from high quality, well made and expensive goods from smart or artisanal shops. Indeed, this is a description which applies to many aspects of French life as the French do not believe that quality can come cheap. Many areas of France have a reputation for high quality, handmade furniture, and this is often evident from the numbers of small, backstreet, craft workshops to be found in most French towns. Despite this, the French tend to have a preference for contemporary furniture and designs. Collecting antiques or reproductions is not generally such a passion in France as it tends to be in the UK. For those with the time and inclination, and who do get a buzz from finding the genuine article, it is possible to pick up some bargains in the provincial bric-a-brac and second hand markets (*les brocantes*) and sale rooms (*dépôt ventes*) found all over France. The *dépôt vente* is also a useful place to know should you wish to sell household items that have been superseded. You deposit the item with the owner of the *dépôt vente* and agree an asking price. The price of the objects is reduced by 20% every month they remain unsold, and when they finally find a buyer, the owner of the *dépôt* takes a commission. Unfortunately Batsford Publishers' useful little book *Antique Fairs and Auctions of France* by Peter Manston is now out of print. It gives the dates and times of the markets throughout France as well as useful hints about buying from them, so it may be worth trying to track down a second hand copy. For more information about buying antiques in France, see *Shopping* in the *Daily Life* chapter.

Those who want to furnish a home or holiday home cheaply but who are not at leisure to scour the flea markets and antique fairs, will find there are various chain stores like Monsieur Meuble which operate along the lines of MFI. These are usually to be found in the large out-of-town commercial centres along with the hypermarkets. When furnishing a house remember that France is a very large country which has several very different climatic and weather zones. In the north, the weather is very much like the UK; the eastern regions can be bitterly cold in winter and in the southern regions the climate is Mediterranean — mild in winter and very hot in summer. It is worth bearing this in mind and furnishing your property accordingly. One option to consider is bringing some furniture from home with which to furnish the new property: the transportation and customs procedures involved are discussed in a *Removals* below. However, first consider if your UK furniture is appropriate for your new location as regards climate and space available.

If you a furnishing a home in northern France, it might be worth checking out the excellent and regularly revised *Factory Shop Guide for Northern France* published at £9.95 by Gillian Cutress and Rolf Stricker (0181-678 0593). As well as the many fashion outlets, the guide has details of household goods outlets selling everything from cutlery, crockery and glassware to cookware, towels and tapestries all on sale at well below retail prices.

Local Taxes

There are two types of property tax in France, *taxe foncière* and *taxe d'habitation* both of which are calculated on the basis of an assumed rental value (*valeur locative*). These taxes are payable annually on 1 January and it is the person owning or occupying the property on that date who has to pay the full amount. It is the tenant's duty to notify the local authorities when he or she assumes residence in that area, although the notaire will sometimes do this.

Taxe Foncière: This is a land tax which is levied on the owner of any plot of land, except where the buildings are used exclusively for agricultural or religious purposes. The payment of the *taxe foncière* is waived for two years on land where building or restoration work has recently been carried out. In certain cases the period during which the taxe foncière is not payable may be extended, for instance, on areas of land where buildings have been newly constructed. This tax, as mentioned above, is calculated on the basis of assumed rental value as decided by the relevant department of the *cadastre* (land registry). The annual rate is adjusted in line with inflation.

Taxe d'Habitation: This is an occupancy tax is levied on all property residents in France, regardless of whether they are the tenant or the owner of the property in which they live. If the property is unoccupiable, ie is being completely renovated, it should be possible to get a temporary exemption. This should be negotiated with the *Direction des Impôts, Trésor Public.* It will be necessary to describe the state of the property (i.e. uninhabitable, backed up by photographs of the interior and exterior). Unoccupied, but habitable holiday homes are however liable for *taxe d'habitation.* There are however, various reductions which one can claim from this tax if the applicant is either retired or has an elderly, dependent relative living with them: further details can be obtained from the local mairie. The *taxe d'habitation* is also calculated on the basis of an assumed rental value by the local council and is adjusted annually to take account of inflation. There have been suggestions that part of the basis for the tax should be income related but at the time of writing no decision had been finalised about this. The amount levied by this tax varies according to région, département and town. The returns on this tax are allocated to the various public authorities which serve the area, to cover the cost of refuse disposal, local schools, street lighting, etc. Overall, the *taxe d'habitation* combined with the *taxe foncière* is likely to be less than the UK's council tax on a similar property and in a corresponding area.

Utilities

Electricity
The domestic electricity supply in France is 220v AC, 50Hz. The supply is reliable and provided by a state-controlled company, Electricité de France (EDF) which, apart from supplying the power, also employs electricians whom you can call on for repairs, etc. As in the UK there are different tariffs suitable for the heavy domestic user. For instance a day time rate (*heures pleines*) and an off peak period (*heures creuses*) at night. The off peak rate is about half the cost of the full rate.

Notify EDF when you are moving in so that the supply can be connected. Electrical installations in new properties, or extensions to systems, must be inspected before they can be connected and it should be a condition of purchase of any new property that the wiring passes the EDF examination. When a new house owner or tenant first becomes a customer the company may require a security deposit against bills, this especially applies in the case of non-residents; in both cases this sum will later be refunded.

Old French houses may still have dangerous wiring, and rewiring is almost certainly essential in any property that needs renovation. In newer properties, the supply is usually properly installed with adequate sockets. Most new installations have built-in fuses which disconnect the supply in case of the slightest short circuit or power leak.

Sockets are of the round pin type, with some having two pins and others three (including an earth). Not every socket is earthed as in the UK and an appliance which requires earthing must not be used in a two pin socket. Wiring colours are the same as the UK (live-brown, neutral-blue, earth-yellow/green). Appliances imported from countries using 220v will work in France with no difficulties. Those from countries where 110v is used, like the USA, cannot be used. Most appliances from the UK where 240v is used will work satisfactorily but, unless they have a voltage selector (see back of the appliance) appliances with a motor (e.g. washing machines) may run a little slower and it may be a better idea not to take them. TV sets from any other country, including the UK, will usually not work due to differences in the TV systems.

Electricity is metered with a standing charge and the bill is usually rendered every two months; although other periods including six-monthly are possible. There is also a small local tax added to the bill and VAT with separate rates for the standing charge and on the consumption. One tip when paying any bill to an official body is to pay it well in advance to avoid risk of disconnection as cheques and bills can take a long time to go through the system and if you do not pay promptly there is minimal hesitation before you are cut off. Unlike the UK where you get a reminder and a notice of disconnection, there is no such leeway in France.

If you are likely to be absent more than present then it is advisable to have an outside meter otherwise, if your meter is not read, you will get an estimated bill of enormous proportions.

You would expect French electricity, which is largely generated from nuclear power, to be some of the cheapest in any modern country. However, with VAT (TVA) and a local tax added to bills they can be surprisingly large.

If you are considering purchasing a property that is not connected to the electricity supply then you should carefully consider the the cost factor involved. EDF charges for linking you to the nearest main cable depending on the distance required for the connection. It will almost certainly cost hundreds if not thousands of pounds. Those who are very remotely situated could consider having a generator installed and rely on bottled gas for heating and cooking. This would certainly be a viable option for a holiday home that is only occupied for a few weeks of the year.

Gas

The use of mains gas is not as common in France as the UK, and since the supply system is not extensive, it can work out more expensive than electricity. However, many householders hedge their bets against supply problems by having cookers with both electric and gas rings combined.

Piped gas is found only in towns and cities and is supplied by Gaz de France (GDF). Gas in bottles (obtainable from the local supermarket or supplier) or large built-in tanks (filled by tanker) is more usual, especially in country areas. Suppliers and delivery services for bottled gas are widespread. As with electricity, gas bills (for piped gas) are rendered every two months and TVA (VAT) is added.

Water

The water supply is of a good standard and as safe to drink from the tap as in the UK. Despite this, most French people have bottled mineral water to drink with meals and at other times.

There has been a severe water shortage in many parts of central and southern France in recent summers. In a few localised areas this has produced a parched, dusty scenery more suggestive of southern Spain or Greece. In such areas it may be as well to check the reliability of the water supply when one is looking for properties.

Piped water is supplied by one of France's largest private companies Générale des Eaux, through its countrywide subsidiaries. Billing details vary but all supplies are metered. The water meter will be sited outside the property. As the water is metered it is especially important to report leaks quickly and not to leave any taps dripping in a holiday home between visits there.

Owing to the need to conserve water, especially in the drier, southern areas, most houses have showers, rather than baths. Some property owners have their own spring or well on their property, but before tapping into it an analysis is essential. If the property is not connected to the mains and you want it to be, it is essential to get a quote. Like electricity, the cost will vary depending on how near you are to the mains. The pipe connecting your property to the mains and the metre will probably have to be laid underground and the digging and filling in of any trench costs extra i.e. it may not be included in the quote.

Telephone

The telephone system in France has been modernised from one of the most derided to one of the most efficient and up-to-date in the world in less than two decades. France now has 32.4 million telephone lines and innovation in services offered is constant and ongoing. There are discount plans for domestic and business users such as the *Primaliste* plan for residential subscribers and *Avantages Partenaires* for small businesses. Many of these plans are similiar to those offered by British Telecom. For instance, for a flat monthly fee, residential subsribers can save between eight and 20 per cent on international calls with *Primaliste Internationale* and benefit from the *France Telecom Assistance Internationale* support service.

France Telecom used an ingenious marketing ploy to introduce new technology when they encouraged over five million domestic customers to accept a Minitel teletext terminal free of charge. Minitel terminals (a kind of simplified computer) can be easily connected to the telephone. In most areas they are still provided free of charge. There are now 6.5 Minitel terminals, providing subscribers with thousands of information services from 25,000 information providers ranging from holiday reservations to dating services as well as providing a nationwide telephone directory. Prospective students can even use them to find university places. Such was the success of the project, that these terminals are an indispensable part of many people's telephone system. Unfortunately for Minitel, although it was ahead of its time, it has been left standing by the global Internet which offers all the same services at increasingly competitive prices. You have to pay up front for Minitel, it's all in French, and some subscribers claim you need a degree in logic to work out the tariff structure. Sadly, after all the effort and inspiration that went into Minitel, it is almost certain to be superseded by the global internet.

Telephones can be installed readily and quickly in most locations. In very remote locations the cost of connection is another matter — perhaps another reason for the seemingly bargain price of the house? If the property is for holiday use, however, the lack of a telephone may not be a problem. As with most utility services, bills are rendered every two months and TVA is added.

At the time of press France Telecom was being partially privatised although the French government will remain the majority shareholder with 51% of the stock. Shares are being sold both on the Paris and New York markets. In preparation and to establish itself as a Global operator, France Telecom linked with Deutsche Telekom AG and Sprint Corporation of the the the USA in 1996.

Removals

If it were feasible, you would probably not transport your belongings to France, and so save money on removals; but the fact is, almost everyone possesses some things to which they feel inextricably attached and most of us cannot deny ourselves the comforting presence of items that remind us of home. Additionally, you should take into consideration that some goods are much cheaper in the UK than in France and it may therefore be worthwhile transporting them over (or under) the Channel.

FRENCH CONNEXION

Regular removals to and from France and throughout UK; Lloyds insurance. Full packing service. Container storage. Single items to whole house. Small family firm offering personal, efficient, reliable service. Free estimates. Discounts on return loads.

UK 01935 872222   Fax: 01935 873094

Start with a list of 'essential' items. Then try to cut it down to a minimum. Electrical household appliances (*électro-ménager*) are almost always much more expensive in France and it may be worth taking them (as long as they are compatible — see 'Utilities' above). However, there may be difficulties with electrical repairs and ordering new parts as a great many home appliances in France are of French design and manufacture.

Anything of substantial weight will be very expensive to move and some furnishings may not be suitable if moving to a warmer part of France. For instance heavy curtains are not practical, and delicate antiques, particularly those made of wood are especially vulnerable to humidity and high temperatures.

If you intend to take only a small quantity of items, it is possible to transport them yourself, perhaps using a hired van. It will however be necessary to obtain clearance from the the van hire company. Depending on how impatient you are to have your French property fully furnished, you can do it gradually; taking a trailer-load with you from the UK each time you go.

The alternative is to use a removals company which in most cases can take care of everything, including packing, collection, storage and delivery. If you are going for a less comprehensive service, choose a company experienced in overseas removals, and which can readily provide a quote for any destination. The British Association of Removers (BAR, 3 Churchill Court, 58 Station Road, North Harrow, Middx. tel 0181-861 3331) will provide a list of firms and general information on moving possessions overseas. BAR also has an International Movers Mutual Assurance fund set up by the overseas group of the BAR. This means that clients' interests are protected if a member company goes bust. This means that money will be refunded or another member company will carry out the removal.

Useful Addresses

The following companies all have experience of overseas removals:

*Allied Pickfords:*Heritage House, 345 Southbury Road, Enfield, Middlesex, EN1 1UP; freephone 0800 289 229.

H Appleyard & Sons: Denby Way, Hellaby Industrial Estate, Rotherham, Yorkshire; tel 01709 549718.

Burke Bros. Moving Group: Head Office, Fox's Lane, Wolverhampton WV1 1PA; tel 01902-729030; fax 019028-27837. Weekly service to all parts of France.

David Dale International Removers: Dale House, Forest Moor Road, Harrogate; tel: 01423-867788; fax 01423-863255.

Cotswold Carriers: Unit 9, Worcester Road Industrial Estate, Chipping Norton, Oxon; tel/fax 01608-642856. Full and part loads to and from France.

Eardley's Removals & Storage: Stoke-on-Trent; tel: 01782-616421; fax 01782-715381.

French Connexion: The Old Vicarage, Leigh, Nr. Sherbourne, Dorset DT9 6HL. Regular removals to and from France and throughout the UK; single items or whole households; tel 01935-872222; fax 01935-873094.

Jay Bee Removers: freephone 0800 289 121; tel: 0181-574 3929; fax 0181-574 2713. From the UK and Ireland to France.

Peter Adams (Watford) Ltd: 208 Station Road, Edgware, Middlesex, HA8 7AR; tel: 0181-958 3155; fax: 0181-958 6399. Ordinary removals or complete package including measuring up French residence and supplying furniture.

Simpsons of Sussex Ltd.: Whitehill Road, Crowborough, East Sussex TN6 1JU; tel 01892-654544; 653834. Fax: 01892 667479.

Tooth Removals: Unit 13/14, Ascot Road, Clockhouse Lane, Feltham, Middx. TW14 8QF; tel 01784 25152; fax 01784 248183.

Whites the Movers: from the UK to anywhere in France; tel: Andover 01264-362024; fax 01264 362024; tel Newbury 01635-49144.

Customs Regulations

Since January 1993 it has been possible to move your household goods and appurtenances to your French residence with the minimum of documents (see below), or customs formalities except random checks to which all traffic entering France is liable.

Special regulations apply to the import of motor vehicles (see below) which must have been tax-paid and registered in your home country prior to import. Certain goods are restricted including firearms and medicinal drugs. As there is a chance that you will stopped by customs in a random check, you should have in your possession a notarised certificate of ownership of a French property. A carte de sèjour is an additional useful proof of residence if applicable.

Whether you are hiring a firm of professional removers or loading up a van with your possessions, there is the same minimum of formalities. Reports vary considerably as to the attitude of French customs officials. Some who have been through the procedure found French customs ignored them, while others have undergone a very thorough check. As long as a sincere attempt is made to cooperate with French customs they can be quite helpful. The French Consulate will provide comprehensive details on the customs procedure and a leaflet *Importation d'un Véhicule* (Importing a Car) and the regulations on restricted goods. Above all ensure you have official proof of French residence as mentioned above.

General Conditions of Import

1. Nationals of other EU countries may take any household goods and effects into France, tax and duty free, whether they are new or not.
2. It is advisable to carry a certificate of ownership of French property in case you are stopped in a random customs check.
3. There are special regulations regarding the import of a car (see below).

Taking Your Car

Some expatriates will probably take the view that it is not worth importing a UK model car with right hand drive to France: it will be inconvenient to drive and worth very little when you come to sell it.

If you do decide to import a car to France then the regulations are as follows:

1. You can import into France one vehicle which has been acquired in another EU country, duty free (*en franchise*). Until recently, you had to have owned it for a minimum of six months and have not less than 6000 km (3,728 miles) on the clock; a precaution designed to prevent anyone reselling cars in France for profit. However, according to the French fiscal authorities, the period of ownership and the mileage requirements are waived completely, provided that the owner has paid VAT in the UK and can produce the original bill of purchase as well as the vehicle registration document issued in the UK. Also that they can convince the French authorities that they are taking up residence in France.

Commercial vehicles do not qualify for duty free entry, but motor cycles, caravans and mobile homes do — and on the same terms as cars.

2. Be sure to take the registration document (V5), tax disc, MOT (if applicable) and insurance papers. Under EU regulations, insurance taken out in the UK is now valid in France. You should check with your insurance company about this.

3. Make sure customs officials are told that the car is for permanent import. There will be additional form filling at the border, and forms will be provided which are required to register the car in France. Note that cars which are to be based permanently at a secondary or holiday home will normally be admitted free of tax.

4. It is necessary to register the car in France within one year of taking up residence and obtain a *carte grise* (French registration document).

Obtaining the Carte Grise

Procedures may vary slightly from region to region, but normally the first step is to contact either the préfecture, or the Direction Régional de L'Industrie de la Recherche et de l'Environment (DRIRE) who will send a leaflet requesting the following documents:

Demande de Carte Grise: more formally known as *Demande de Certificat d'Immatriculation d'un Véhicule.*
You will also have to purchase a Timbre Fiscal (tax stamp) from a tabac (tobacconist) for about £20.

Justification de l'origine du véhicule (certificat de vente): The original bill of sale for the car. Although the French consulate specifies that one should have this document, in practice not everyone can supply one, for instance if they have bought the car privately, secondhand. Apparently, if all other documents are in order, this will not cause problems.

Titre de circulation étranger: Vehicle registration document from your own country.

Quitus from the French Inland Revenue: Even though there is no duty to pay on a vehicle being permanently imported this document is still required in order to prove that the vehicle is exempt from VAT. It should be obtained from the *Centre des Impôts* nearest to where you are going to be based in France.

Rapport de Contrôle Technique: This is the French equivalent of an MoT

Certificate. The fee varies from issuer to issuer and also depends on the size etc of the vehicle. Costs should probably be in the region of £40 + .

Failure to pass any of the sections means that repairs/modifications have to be carried out. Almost always, modifications to the exhaust will be needed and also the headlamps will need to be changed for driving on the right (temporary black tape stickers and yellow varnish will not do). You will also need a letter from the head office of the vehicle manufacturer confirming that the model and type of car has been approved for France. This involves writing to the head office in France. Brace yourself for a shock at the fee some companies charge for this — in some cases as much as £80.

Once all the documents have been mustered you can take the vehicle to the nearest *centre de contrôle de véhicules* where the car will be thoroughly checked and tested and any remaining problems listed for rectification before all the paperwork can be finalised and taken to the préfecture. The préfecture issues the Certificat d'Immatriculation more commonly known as the *carte grise*. Before the carte grise is handed over, proof of identity and residence must be shown.

The final step is to buy the *vignette* (annual tax badge) from the relevant department of the préfecture and to collect the licence plates. The cost of the *vignette* varies depending on the department and the type of car. An average cost would be in the region of 1000 francs (about £110). British expatriates should then write to the DVLA in Swansea advising them that the vehicle has been re-licensed in France.

At the time of writing the entire process of importing a car from the UK into France is likely to cost several hundred pounds.

Useful Addresses
French Consulate General: (Customs Department), Kingsgate House, 115 High Holborn, London WC1V 6JJ; tel 0171-831 0142; fax 0171-831 2143. Can answer your questions on importing a car.
French Fiscal Attaché: Kingsgate House, 115 High Holborn, London WC1V 6JJ; tel 0171-831 9048. Deals with VAT and income tax queries.

Pets

Many people moving to France in the long-term will want to take their dogs and cats with them. A maximum of three animals is allowed and all dogs and cats must be at least three months old. To import cats and dogs into France, a health certificate and a vaccination certificate are required. At the time of press, it is thought that pet dogs and cats (*chiens et chats de compagnie*) may also require an electronic identification tag (microchip), or a tatoo to enable the animal to be identified; although the Ministry of Agriculture, Animal Export section in Surrey, did not seem to think either the tag or tatoo were compulsory. It may therefore be advisable to check the latest requirements with the French Ministry of Agriculture in Paris (see address below).A rabies vaccination is compulsory only for Corsica or for animals being introduced onto camping grounds, holiday parks or participating in shows in areas affected by rabies.

For other information about Pets, see the relevant section in *Daily Life*.

Useful Addresses
D.J. Williams: Animal Transport, Littleacre Quarantine Centre, 50 Dunscombes Road, Turves, Nr Whittlesey Cambs PE7 2DS; tel 01733-840291; fax 01733 840348. Pet collection and overland delivery service. Will collect from your home, arrange all the necessary documentation. Also return home service from Europe provided.

Ministry of Agriculture, Animal Export: Hook Rise South, Tolworth, Surbiton, Surrey KT6 7NF; tel 0181-330 8184. Details and an application form for a Ministry of Agriculture export certificate can be obtained from the above address.

Ministére de l'Agriculture et de la Pêche, Direction Générale de l'Alimentation, Sous-Direction de la Santé et de la Protection Animales, 175 rue du Chevaleret, 75646 Paris, Cedex 13; tel +33 1 495 581 77; fax +33 1 495 55111. Contact: Dr B Vallet. Can confirm the latest requirements for importing domestic pets into France.

Daily Life

Anyone who goes to live in a foreign country, will initially find that the multitude of daily rituals, previously taken for granted, now pose seemingly insurmountable challenges. The intention of this chapter is to provide, as much as possible of the practical information required to cope successfully with various aspects of French life. If you have not already decided whether living and working in France is for you, the following information could help you make up your mind, or, assuming that you have already made the decision to go, it could act as a day-to-day survival guide. Note, however, that there are bound to be regional and local variations in most of the aspects covered — so it is always advisable to check details with those who are already living in the region to which you are going, or with other appropriate sources. In France there are particularly striking differences between town and country which may affect the procedure required in doing even the most mundane things. The key to unravelling daily life in France is often the ability to speak the language reasonably well. Thus, the first section of this chapter covers this aspect, with subsequent sections dealing with other aspects of daily life, which, if handled successfully, can make living in another country an enriching, rather than a daunting, experience.

The French Language

There is probably little need to elaborate here on the philological background of the French language. Traditionally, most Britons learn some French at school but only a very small proportion go on to develop a skill at using it. A romance language derived from Latin, many French words are comfortingly familiar thanks to the common root with some English ones. Like English, French is also a great literary language, indeed according to the French, it is the cultural language of Europe and being able to converse in it, is in itself is indicative of a cultured person. It is ironic therefore, that despite the most intense chauvinistic efforts of the Academie Française to find French alternatives to the accumulation of English and American words (usually known as franglais), which have pervaded the language since the 1960s, many of these have now been awarded wide acceptance and recorded in the 1992 edition of the French dictionary of the Academie Française, (previous edition 1935). Words such as *le weekend, le fast food, le blazer, le bluejean, le bestseller, un camping* and the slightly misleading *le babyfoot* (table football) are now officially part of the French language.

Is it Essential to Learn French?

If you intend to find anything more than a very basic job then it will be necessary to speak, or to be prepared to learn to speak French accurately and fluently.

However, this does not just apply to job-seekers. It may be considered acceptable for tourists not to speak the language of the country they are visiting, but anyone intending to live there for all or part of the year should, as a matter of courtesy as well as practicality make an effort to learn French. Family members of a foreign resident working in France may also need a grasp of French for school, or shopping and social purposes.

Many Europeans, for example the Danes, Greeks, Belgians and Spaniards, are very adept at speaking foreign languages, and will often willingly speak English, or put up with English-speakers' laborious attempts to master their tongue. However, despite the common misconception that English is widely spoken in France, the French are not generally any more competent linguists than the British. This situation is excacerbated by the fact that the French are excessively proud of their language and even if they can speak a foreign language frequently choose not to.

Learning French

As already mentioned, many British people already have some familiarity with French from their schooldays. However, it may still be necessary to begin from scratch unless you have had a chance to practise in between, and retained a mastery of basic grammar. There are various ways to go about learning the language which are dealt with below.

Self-Study Courses

The advantage of self-study courses is that they enable students to absorb material at their own convenience and learning pace. The possible disadvantages are that a large degree of self-motivation is required and it is not possible to practise spontaneous conversation. Thus while they are a good way of drumming in the basics, ideally they should be complemented by a language course/evening class, or conversation exchange with a mother-tongue speaker. Most self-study courses consist of course books and audio-tapes. There are also courses aimed at those who require French for commercial purposes for instance the BBC's *Get by in Business French* and *French Means Business*. The BBC has a large share of the self-study market and they have a range of courses for general French at different levels which enable one to learn at one's own pace. Further details can be obtained from the BBC Mail Order/Shop in Newcastle (tel: 0191-222 0381). Some courses on the market are aimed at holiday-makers so check the contents of the course carefully to find the most appropriate. Linguaphone (Carlton Plaza, 111 Upper Richmond Street, London SW15 2TJ (0181-333 4898; fax 0181-333 4897) have courses which range from beginner to very advanced level with prices from £49.99 for a video course to £399.90 for a minilab executive course. Audio-Forum (2-6 Foscote Mews, London W9 2HH; tel 0171-266 2202; fax 0171-266 2314) have a range of courses for everyday French and business situations that incorporate the latest colloquialisms and specialist courses in French phonology and French for lawyers.

CD-Rom multimedia language learning is the latest addition to the self-study market. Eurotalk (315-317 Kings Road, Fulham, London SW6 4RF; tel 0171-371 7711; fax 0171-371 7781; e-mail: 100442.1701@compuserve.com), has a range of quizzes, games and stories in French as well as a learning programme *Ecoutez-Bien*, mainly aimed at children and anyone who can only learn languages if it is made fun.

Adult learners of French might like to consider subscribing to the quarterly journal *Bien-Dire* (9 rue J. Soulary, 69004 Lyon; fax +33 4-78 30 87 03; website: http://biendire@compuserve.com) which comes with audio cassettes of selected articles and contains news, practical information and as well as articles on France and an English translation).

Language Courses in the UK

Alliance Française de Londres: French Courses, 1 Dorset Square, London NW1 6PU; tel 0171-723 6439. The Alliance has about a thousand centres worldwide and is sponsored by the French government. It offers part-time day or evening French courses and intensive courses. UK Alliance teaching centres are in: Belfast, Bristol, Cambridge, Esher, Exeter, Glasgow, Milton Keynes, Oxford and Manchester. There are in addition about 30 Alliance social circles in the UK.

The Berlitz School of Languages: 9-13 Grosvenor Street, London W1A 3BZ; tel 0171-915 0909. This is an international organisation which offers language tuition specifically tailored to the individual's requirements. The cost of the courses available can vary enormously depending on the standard of the student and the intensiveness of the course. One major advantage of the Berlitz schools is that courses begun in the UK can be completed in France: branches in the UK are also located in Birmingham, Manchester, Leeds and Edinburgh.

inlingua School of Languages: 28 Rotton Park Road, Edgbaston, Birmingham B16 9JL; tel 0121-4540204; fax 0121-4563264. Inlingua is another organisation with a worldwide network of privately-owned language schools: there are approximately 280 schools in all of which 240 are in Europe. The schools only employ native French speakers as teachers. At the Birmingham centre all teaching is residential on a one-to-one basis. The cost of a forty-five minute session starts at £26. The most intensive course (50 lessons) costs £1,670 for a week including board, lodging and activities. French courses can also be arranged at centres abroad. There are also inlingua branches in Cheltenham and Torquay.

Institut Français: 14 Cromwell Place, London SW7 2JR; tel 0171-581 2701; fax 0171-581 2910. All types of courses including business French.

Classes The advantage of evening classes is their low cost compared with commercial intensive courses run by private schools. The disadvantage is that most classes only have one two to three hour session per week so it is advisable to supplement the classes with a conversation exchange (see below) or an Anglo-French social/cultural group so you can consolidate through practice, what you have learned in class.

Most local colleges of further education run language courses from beginners to 'A' level standard, and the courses run for the academic year, usually from September. A year's non exam course is likely to cost in the region of £100, while GCSE and 'A' level courses are even cheaper. Those interested should contact the modern languages department of their nearest college of further education.

Private Tutors/Conversation Exchange It is always worth checking the Personal Columns in the UK national and regional press for the possibility of finding a private tutor; alternatively post a 'French Tutor Wanted' advertisement on suitable notice boards e.g. in libraries and schools. The aim should be to find a native French-speaker who can provide individual tuition in the specific areas in which you require help. Alternatively, if you are already following a course, either self-study or evening classes and you just want to practice speaking then you can try to fix up a private conversation exchange with a native speaker in the UK who will speak French with you in return for similar practice in English.

Language Courses in France. Various French language courses are available in

France for foreigners. These courses are aimed at a range of abilities and needs, and are sometimes arranged as learning holidays, possibly including accommodation with French families. Many French universities offer such courses and can be approached for details. A booklet listing all of the universities in France which offer these courses can be obtained, free of charge, from the Ministry of Foreign Affairs in France. Some companies in France which also organize courses include: Linguistic Services (Pujols sur Ciron, 33210 Langon; tel 556 76 66 44; fax 556 76 65 42) and APRE (PO Box 5032, 34032 Montpellier).

EF International Language Schools (Kensington Cloisters, 5 Kensington Church Street, London W8 4LD; tel: 0171 795 6675/0171 878 3550; fax; 0171 795 6625); is part of EF Education, the world's largest private educational organisation. EF provides highly intensive personalised language training for the business world as well as courses for adults of 16 years and over in small groups. EF students learn on location in France, studying in an international environment while living among native speakers to maximise exposure to the language and culture. The experience and expertise of EF's instructors, the flexibility of weekly course start dates as well as the pleasant and professional course centres in France all translate into convenient and effective language learning for students of all levels and abilities.

The Eurolingua Institute (Havre Saint Pierre, 265 allee du Nouveau Monde, 34000 Montpellier, France (tel +33 467 15 04 73; fax +33 467 15 04 73; e-mail

eurolingua_institute@msn.com; internet http://www.eurolingua.com: UK office tel 0161-972 0225; fax 0161-972 0225) is the largest pan-European organisation of its kind, currently teaching six languages in nine countries, and providing unique and affordable opportunities, for people of all ages (16-75 years) and from all walks of life, to learn languages in the countries where they are spoken. In France, one-to-one and group homestay programmes take place at Eurolingua's French language institute, *Eurolingua Espace Langues* in Montpellier, south of France, and a wide range of regional centres.

The British organisation Cultural and Educational Services Abroad (CESA, western House, Malpas Truro, Cornwall TR1 1SQ; tel 01872-225300; fax; 01872 225 400; email:language2cesa.demon.co.uk) has been an agency organising language courses abroad for over seventeen years. The minimum course is two weeks but private tuition programmes can be arranged in France for a week ina choice of locations. CESA provides comprehensive advice to clients of all ages (from 14-60 +) and caters for a wide range of linguistic abilities from non-existent to degree level.

Useful Addresses
Association pour la Diffusion de la Pensée Française, 28 rue de Bourgogne, 75007 Paris, France; tel + 33 1 40 62 80 62; fax + 33 1 40 62 80 63; produces a booklet *Répertoire des centres formations* (cours de francàis langue étrangère) giving details of French language courses all over France. It can be obtained free of charge, from French diplomatic services in your own country. In the UK this is from the French Embassy, Service Culturel (0171-838 2055).
The Franco-British Society: 162-168 Regent Street, London W1R 5TB; tel/fax 0171-734 0815). Club promoting Anglo-French relations.

It is also a good idea to find out if any Anglo-French clubs or societies exist in your area, as these may organize social events or discussion groups. Check with your local further education institute or local library. It is also worth contacting the Franco-British Society which arranges various discussion groups and social events concerned with Anglo-French culture and relations.

Shops and Shopping

Shopping in France, is a revelation if you are used to the mass production in the sale of food in the UK and even more in consumerist United States of America. This may have made the whole process very efficient but also very uninteresting. One shopping mall or superstore is much the same as another, although most try to convince us otherwise. Of course France has its share of hypermarkets around which family shopping increasing revolves, but for the moment at least, alongside them traditional specialist and family shops still survive. It is therefore possible to enjoy efficient individual service and to appreciate the quality and variety of the goods themselves.

Food Shopping

The quality of foodstuffs and the cost of eating out in France are viewed by many people as reason enough for going to live there, and few countries can rival the range and appeal of the regional specialities for sale in French shops. Some indication of the emphasis on gastronomic merchandise in France is that as much as a quarter of the average French family budget is spent on food and drink although there are some signs that more of this is being spent more on convenience foods than hitherto.

While traditional, independent food shops, which offer individual service and top quality goods, are still prolific in France there is also the other end of consumerism in the form of the massive hypermarkets (*hypermarchés*) like Auchan, Mammouth and Leclerc, which sell every product imaginable at competitive prices while still paying keen attention to quality. Supermarkets (*supermarchés*) in France tend to be smaller and more expensive than in the UK, and are more like self-service grocery stores. The Monoprix chain is one of the less expensive.

For expatriates living in Paris, Nantes, Strasbourg, Toulouse, Reims, Marseilles, Rouen, Lyon or Villiers en Bière (near Fontainebleau), there is the reassuring presence of a Marks and Spencer foodhall where you can buy marmalade, Dundee cake, muffins, sandwiches (British style), farmhouse cheddar, oatcakes and all the other 'typically British' food that expatriates are liable to miss and which are otherwise hardly available in France. Central Paris now has two branches, a new one in the rue de Rivoli (opposite the Richcliu wing of the Louvre) opened in 1997, barely ten minutes walk from the flagship branch next to l'Opéra. This tries frantically to keep Parisiens in sandwiches which disappear from the shelves at the rate of thousands per day.

Most shops keep long and convenient continental hours, typically from 8am to 7pm (allowing for much regional variation). Small shops take an afternoon break which lasts longer the further south one travels. In some areas it is usual for shops to be open on Saturday, and part of Sunday, but to close on Monday. In cities, especially Paris, some shops may close for a long summer holiday in July and August.

Apart from the hypermarchés where you can buy everything, shops in France tend to segregate trades. For example, the *boulangerie* sells bread and sometimes biscuits while the *pâtisserie* sells cakes and pastries and may also be a café. Similarly, the general butcher is the *boucherie*, but for pork one must visit a *charcuterie*. Sometimes the charcuterie will also sell a range of cooked meats, not just pork. A *boucherie chevaline* is a butcher which sells horse meat, while a *traiteur* sells ready made up meat dishes, often for the catering trade. Fresh fruit and vegetables are best bought in open markets held several times a week, but most towns have a greengrocer, usually as part of a shop selling *alimentation* (general provisions). *Primeurs* are early fruit and vegetables but can also mean greengrocers.

Wines of all types and qualities are amazingly cheap in France, and one of the pleasures of being an expatriate in France is being able to enjoy the local wines and to buy direct from the local producers. This applies to other consumables, particularly cheeses. Stronger alcoholic drinks produced in France are about the same price as the UK, or slightly more expensive, but you are likely to find better quality and more choice than you do in the UK.

Non-Food Shopping

The commendation of shopping in France does not extend so enthusiastically beyond food shopping. As far as non-food shopping is concerned, French consumers tend to have less choice and more expense than in the UK or the USA. Opening hours are shorter for non-food stores, although hypermarchées are open late most evenings and sell virtually every general-use line imaginable, from clothes to car body panels and tyres.

When small-store shopping, it is important to know where to go for different items; in a *pharmacie* one will only find drugs and medicines, probably not toiletries, and perfumes are only sold in *parfumeries*. A *quincaillerie* is a hardware shop. Newspapers and magazines are most commonly sold at a tobacconists *un tabac* or news-stands, and not in anything that compares to W H Smith.

When it comes to buying domestic appliances, such as cookers, fridges, microwaves, TV's and video recorders, the French pay a lot more for such goods than you may be used to. Once, the main reason for this is that in the past cheap Japanese and Far-Eastern imports were restricted or highly taxed, and consequently many of the goods available in the shops were of French manufacture only. As domestic appliances are more expensive to produce on a small scale than the Japanese and Far-eastern made goods which we buy in the UK, the cost of this is reflected in the French shop prices. In many cases it is possible to save money by importing appliances from the UK, although this is likely to involve problems with compatibility, spares and servicing. Now that France has abolished controls on foreign investment non-French goods are increasingly available, Daewoo microwaves and televisions are now being made in France and many other companies including Sharp and Philips produce electrical goods there.

Clothes are also very expensive in France, partly due to the reputation which the country holds for quality and style in this area, and also because of the lack of cheap imports available. Thus, you can save a great deal of money by importing your clothes from the UK. Generally, French people tend to have a very small wardrobe of high quality, expensive clothes. Since many French clothes are well-made and stylish, it is often worth looking in second-hand (*d'occasion*) clothes shops and for period clothes, the *marchés aux puces* (flea markets) can yield some real gems.

The Parisian flea markets are good for clothes and other things and can be a fascinating way to consume hours. Three of the best known are situated on the *Périphérique*: the Puce de St-Ouen at Clignancourt, is in fact many markets from smart to downright shanty, all in the same neighbourhood. For example you can buy posh antiques at Marchés Vernaison and adjacent Dauphine while Marché Serpette has a more eclectic range of goods and junk and so on until you descend into the ropey areas where there seem to be more shifty looks to the square metre than nifty bargains. You have to go to the other side of Paris to get to Porte de Vanves market which is the place to look for second hand clothes and domestic bits and pieces, and where you can find quality items amongst the junk. In the east of Paris the Marché Porte de Montreuil is the most junky of all the markets which is thronged with those from France's ethnic minorities haggling over a veritable scrapyard of discarded items.   It is possible to hunt out bargains, particularly in factory shops (*les magasins d'usine*), and there is a handy guide to help you do this: *The Factory Shop Guide for Northern France* (£10.95 including postage) is available from the authors, Gillian Cutress and Rolf Stricker (1 Roseberry Mews, Rosebery Road, London SW2 4DQ; tel 0181-678 0593; fax 0181-674 1594). It is regularly updated, and will help to track down designer clothes from among others Daniel Hechter and Descamps, designer children's clothes including Petit Bateau and Osh Kosh. In the household department there are Le Creuset seconds (about a third of UK prices) and coordinated household linens from Calais to Boulogne and eastwards into Belgium and southwards as far as Troyes. There are 234 shops listed including the factory outlets, with maps and detailed instructions on how to reach the outlets.

TVA

Taxe sur la Valeur Ajoutée is levied on almost everything in France, including food, books and utilities. Since the 1st January 1993, the various rates of VAT which existed on different goods and services in France have been reduced to two: a standard rate of 20.6% and a reduced rate of 5.5%. The reduced rate applies to food, medicines, travel, most hotels, books, and utilities; standard TVA at 20.6% is levied on most other goods and services. These disparate rates account for the fact that while some things in France seem comparatively cheap, others seem expensive.

Duty-Free Shopping/Customs Allowances in the EU

Although there is now free movement of goods and services within the EU duty-free shopping (i.e. at ports/airports/on ferries etc) for items for personal use, will not be abolished until 30 June 1999. Until this date, duty free sales are subject to the same customs allowances which apply to travellers entering the EU from a non-member state. The limits in force are one batch from each of the following categories: 200 cigarettes/100 cigarillos/50 cigars/250gm tobacco; also one of : 2 litres still wine/1 litre of spirits or liqueurs over 22% volume/2 litres of fortified/sparkling wine/; also 60cc/ml perfume/250cc/ml toilet water; also other goods including gifts and souvenirs up to £36 worth.

There are also guidelines, (but no precise limits except on credibility) for duty paid items for personal use, bought in one EU state (e.g. in supermarkets and shops) and taken to another. Above all the citizen will have to satisfy the customs that the items are for personal use and not for resale in another country. The guidelines are in the region of 10 litres of spirits, 20 litres of fortified wine and 90 litres of wine of which not more than 60 litres is sparkling. The guidelines for tobacco products are roughly quadruple the the duty-free allowances.

Cars and Motoring

Driving Licence

On July 1 1996, a standard model of EU driving licence was adopted in order to make licences understandable and acceptable thoughout the EU. However, many drivers in the EU will still have valid licences that predate the standard version and all of these, if valid their country of origin, are still valid in France. Visitors to France can drive on a licence issued by any EU country, without any further formalities. An international driving permit is neither required nor recommended, however, provisional driving licences are not acceptable and car drivers must be at least 18.

Once a residence permit has been issued and you intend staying in France for longer than a year, then you will have to exchange the British licence for a French one. At the time of going to press, there is confusion about whether this includes even the pink UK licence which follows the EU standard type. This should not be necessary. It is permissable to continue driving on any other UK licence for up to 12 months, provided that it is accompanied by an official French translation.

You should therefore exchange your UK licence for French one (a) if it is of the old, pre-EU standard type, or (b) if you wish to add a new category of vehicle. To exchange your licence for a French one, you should apply to the nearest préfecture (*Service des Permis de Conduire*), taking the UK licence and an official translation of this. A medical certificate and/or eyesight test is sometimes required. Provided that you obtain a French driving licence within 12 months it is not necessary to take a French driving test; if you leave it any longer than this, however, a test will be required. French driving licences do not remain valid until the driver reaches the age 70 as in the UK, and the renewal period varies according to age and the type of licence.

Importing A Car

The basic procedure for importing a car to France has already been explained in *Setting up Home*. As long as the car has been bought and registered in the UK, and appropriate UK taxes and VAT have been paid, there should be no problem importing the vehicle duty free; assuming one is taking up permanent residence in France.

Once resident in France it is necessary to re-register the car and to have French number plates (*plaques d'immatriculation*) fitted. This procedure begins at the nearest préfecture. The documents required to do this may vary, and different offices may request different documents. However, at the very least your passport, *carte de séjour*, and car registration document (V5) will be required.

It is also necessary to have vehicles inspected for roadworthiness; this is done at the Service des Mines. It is as well to obtain details of the test requirements, which are not especially rigorous, beforehand. (For further details see *Setting up Home*, page 109).

After this procedure has been completed one receives French registration documents and road tax stickers. Once permanent residence has been taken, car insurance should also be amended: you will probably have to change to a French insurance company (see below).

If importing a car to France, whether on a permanent or temporary basis, note that minimum tyre tread requirements are higher in France than in the UK. Additionally, it is compulsory for foreign registered cars to have a nationality badge, and right hand drive cars must be fitted with headlight beam converters.

France is the only major European country to insist on yellow headlamps. It is no longer compulsory to convert headlamps to yellow on a foreign registered car but it is advisable if only to avoid the natives flashing at you. Kits to do this are available at car accessory shops.

Buying a Car

If you decide to sell your current car in order to buy a left hand drive one on moving to France, you will find that French makes, basically Renault, Peugeot and Citröen, dominate the market. An advantage of French-made cars is that it is much easier and cheaper to obtain spares and to service them and although UK and other European cars are available, service facilities and the general level of garage know-how about them can be patchy. Fords and up-market German makes are perhaps less common than in the UK and Japanese cars are comparatively rare.

French car prices are currently, overall, a little higher than in the UK. It is difficult to make a direct price comparison, however, as cars sold in France tend to include much less standard equipment than in otherwise identical models.

Those who wish to buy a new car should go to the appropriate franchised dealer. New cars are almost always sold at list prices, so, although it is still worth shopping around and asking for a discount, large discounts on the list price are not customary as in the UK. Most dealers have their own financing deals which generally involve a deposit of 20 to 30 per cent of the purchase price and and the remainder in monthly installments over three to five years; but the interest rates are high. You might do better getting a bank loan as the interest charged is generally lower. If you take out a bank loan to buy the car, make sure that both it and the bank loan are insured. The supplying car dealer will, of course, arrange all the relevant paperwork including a temporary statement of ownership (*carte grise*). Used cars are also available from franchised dealers. These mostly only sell used cars up to one or two years old, and are usually a reputable source and offer appropriate warranties.

If you choose to buy a used car from outside the franchised dealer networks then a great deal of care and caution is required: this applies whether buying privately, perhaps from a newspaper advertisement, or from a dealer. Used car dealers in France have a very poor reputation, even worse than in the UK, and, despite recent legislation intended to prevent just this, dangerously defective cars are by no means rare. Few dealers sell models more than five years old. The préfecture in the département in which the car is registered should issue the seller with a *lettre de nongage* which means there are no outstanding debts (e.g. hire purchase) on the car. If the car is over five years old, the seller must provide evidence that the car has been checked and issued with a *contrôle technique* which lists the faults that need to be put right before the sale. The purchase of a used car must be registered at the prefecture. You will need to take with you a certificate of sale which is an official document supplied by *préfectures* to sellers; the cancelled *carte grise* (log book), and the *Autobilan* (test certificate), as well as all your own identity documents are all required for this.

If you buy the car outside the area you are living in then you will need to get the car re-registered locally when you are back home.

A useful publication is *L'Argus*, the French car guide. It provides details on how much you should pay for particular models and the purchasing process.

If you live in Paris, there is an incentive scheme to encourage the purchase of electric cars which are tax exempt and entitled to free parking. The number of electric charge-up stations is planned to reach over 100 in the near future, though with Paris traffic jams being what they are, your batteries may run down before you get to one.

Running a Car

Running a car in France, as in any other country, can be expensive and also requires a great deal of official documentation. Garage services, for both maintenance and repair work, tend to be very expensive. It is because of this, and also because of the costs and limitations of insurance, that many motorists do not have their cars properly serviced or repaired, even after quite major accident damage. However, when considering the generally dilapidated state of the average French person's car, it is as well to remember that the French do not cherish their cars in the same obsessive way British motorists tend to do.

Petrol in France is currently a little more expensive than in the UK and both leaded and unleaded is available; diesel fuel, as elsewhere, is cheapest.

The main documents required by car owners are:

Registration Document (*carte grise*). This is supplied when you register or buy a new or used car, and should be handed on to the buyer when you sell it. If you move to another département then you must re-register your car at a préfecture there within three months: this involves obtaining a different registration number and new number plates.

Insurance Certificate. You will also receive an insurance sticker which must be displayed on the vehicle's windscreen.

Tax Disc (*vignette*). This should be affixed to the windscreen and will need to be renewed each November. Make sure that you are given the receipt for the tax disc and ensure that you keep this when buying a used car: the fee involved varies according to the car but is quite modest except for luxury cars. Tax discs can be purchased from the tabac.

Note that cars do not necessarily need an annual safety test unless you are intending to sell them (see below).

Car Insurance

Car insurance is comparatively expensive in France partly because all premiums include taxes at an average rate of 36%. Even higher *cotisations* (premiums) are charged for cities and areas which have a notoriously high crime rate. Another factor affecting insurance charges is the high collision rate (one every 85 seconds according to one estimate). It is particularly important to shop around and to find the best deal possible. The basic legal requirement for French car insurance is third party liability, and many owners of what seem quite new cars risk taking out no greater cover than this, though most will also have cover for accidental damage to the vehicle. Comprehensive insurance is available which will cover most risks, including damage to your own car. It is particularly important to examine each policy and to see what is and what is not included, as various policies do not necessarily cover the same risks, and the insurance inclusions and exclusions will certainly vary from a UK comprehensive policy.

Green cards are no longer required by motorists travelling to France. If you are taking up permanent residence you will require a new policy that complies with French requirements: ask various companies and/or brokers for quotes as they all compete against each other for business. One of the main French insurance companies, AGF, has a motor/household insurance division in the UK at Milton Keynes (tel: 01908-690888; 0990-660066) and a commercial insurance division in London (0171-617 4500). If you are in France, it should be a simple matter to locate local brokers. AGF also has subsidiaries all over Europe so the service offered to British nationals going to France can be continued if they move elsewhere in Europe.

There are various peculiarities of French motor insurance. Firstly, the *bonus/malus* system: although one gains a useful no-claims bonus and discount for not claiming each year, one also gains a claims supplement and loading if a claim is made, which can make insurance very expensive. Basically, to get the maximum discount (50%), you need to provide the French insurance company with proof of no fault claims for thirteen years.

Another difference to be aware of is that many comprehensive policies will reduce cover to third party only, if any accident or damage occurs because the driver was breaking road traffic law. If you want a policy that is tailored to the usage of the car, it is possible to arrange insurance based on the car's mileage (*kilométrage*). It is necessary to carry proof of insurance with you when travelling by car. Should you be unfortunate enought to be involved in an accident it will be necessary to complete a *constat à amiable* (agreed accident statement).

As with house insurance, it is usually necessary to give a long period of notice (sometimes three months) before cancelling a policy and one is liable for premiums until that notice expires. Overall, the French motorist has good reason to be envious of the comparatively reasonable cost and generous terms of motor insurance in the UK. At the time of press the European Commisssion had proposed new legislation aimed at making cross-border car insurance feasible by requiring insurance companies to appoint agents and representatives in all member-states in order to deal with claims arising from an incident in a member country other than the one in which the insurance was taken out. But this legislation is, as they say, still on the drawing board.

Main Points of Motor Insurance in France

Compulsory cover for third party liability

No restriction on drivers (vehicle can be driven by any driver with the insured's permission).

The no claim bonus cannot be protected.

The maximum no claim discount is 50% (13 years with no liable claim).
When taking out insurance with a French provider, the proposer must provide sufficient proof of his/her insurance cover 13 years back in order to claim the maximum no claim discount.

Insurance Glossary

English	French
No claim bonus/discount	*bonus*
Third party liability	*responsabilité civile*
Comprehensive insurance	*assurances touts risques*
Fire and theft	*vol et incendie*
Windscreen damage	*bris de glaces*
Accidental damage	*dommages a votre vehicule*
Personal accident/bodily injury to the driver	*garantie conducteur*
Policy excess	*franchise*

Selling a Car

Remember that you cannot sell or otherwise dispose of a car imported duty free within 12 months without paying the TVA on the import. As far as documentation is concerned, selling or part exchanging a car in France is more complicated than in the UK. You have to obtain the appropriate certificate of sale form from the mairie or préfecture and, to complete this in duplicate and then to send one copy back to the registration office. The other copy and the *carte grise* registration document go to the purchaser, as does the vignette.

The main difference between selling a car in France and England is that in France, if the car is five or more years old it must be submitted to a mechanical inspection (*Contrôle Technique*), after which, if successful, it will be issued with a test certificate (*Autobilan*). Thus, no matter how recently another, similar test has been done on the vehicle, you must arrange and pay for this beforehand. Legality apart, no sensible buyer would want to pay very much for a vehicle over five years old which does not have an inspection certificate.

The Vignette

The *vignette* is the French car tax badge. However, it operates somewhat differently to the UK version. It is generally slightly cheaper than UK road fund tax and also varies in cost depending on the engine size and and car age and also the region of registration. Older and smaller-engined cars registered in the Drôme will cost less less than brand new Ferraris registered in Paris. It is important to note that the vignette is not registered to a particular car as is the UK road tax, which is why they are liable to be stolen, particularly around the time of annual renewal in November. The vignette must be displayed inside your windscreen by law, together with the insurance *vignette, vignette d'assurance* which will be provided by the insurance company.

It is advisable to keep the receipt for the tax *vignette*, as if it is stolen, you can replace it without paying again, if you still have the proof of purchase.

Roads

Twenty-five years ago, French roads, except for main roads, were of very poor quality and full of *nids de poules* (potholes): however, these days French roads are among the best in Europe and the motorway system, over 5,000 miles of it, largely constructed since 1969, is also excellent, if expensive. France and Italy are the two

EU countries which charge motorists for using the motorways. French roads are classified as follows:

A — Autoroute (Motorway or M grade road in UK). With few exceptions these are toll roads (*Autoroutes à Péage*). Tolls vary but are usually in the region of 30 francs per 100 km. You pick up a computer card when you join the motorway and you pay on exit. It is inadvisable to exit via a lane signed *telpéage* without the special card required, as you will cause a hold up and a state of over excitment (*rage de la rue*) in other drivers. Another hazard of autoroutes is that computerised tills introduced in late 1997 will deliver a printout that not only tells you how much to pay but also how fast you have been driving. If you have exceeded the speed limit a flashing red light on the till will alert the operator to summon *les flics* (police) who will promptly fine you up to a maximum of 2,500 francs.

N — Route Nationale (A grade road in UK). These are usually quite good and single or dual carriageway, but they usually pass through towns which can slow a journey down.

D — Route Departementale (B grade road in UK).

Overall, the road network is very comprehensive and there are now autoroutes extending from Paris to every corner of France. For example, the A6 and A7 to Marseille and A1 Autoroute du Nord to the Belgian border. The latest stretches at the time of print were the A75 (routed across the Massif Central) from Clermont-Ferrand to the Mediterranean, and in the north, the A16 from Dunkirk to Abbeville on route to Normandy. However, roads may not be as well signposted as they are in the UK so make sure you have good maps like the Michelin 1:200,000 yellow series.

The French tend not to be great long distance travellers so traffic is very often quite light, with the definite exceptions, however, of Paris and some major city centres and during the main holiday months. Since nearly all French workers take a month's holiday in either July or August the worst days, such as 31 July and 1 August when departing holiday makers meet returning ones, the journey between the Mediterranean and Paris can easily take 17 hours. On Bastille Day (14 July) it is nothing to have a tailback of more than 50 km on the autoroutes going south from Paris. For nearly twenty years the the French government has used a cartoon character called Bison Futé (Crafty Bison) to warn motorists, through the mass media, of impending bad traffic days and to advise, by means of maps, available at service stations, alternative secondary routes which are designed to circumvent the traffic jams.

Driving

In common with most nationalities, the French are renowned for their own particular style of driving, and it is advisable to adapt accordingly (with as little risk to personal safety as possible!). Although the basic rules of the road are very similar in France to the rest of Europe, as are most road signs, there are some differences. It may seem needless to point out that in contrast to what has become a British peculiarity, the French drive on the right. It is a sad fact however, that the majority of accidents caused by Brits occur after they pull out from a picnic spot, hypermarket, or petrol station and forget this vital fact, thus finding themselves on the wrong side of the highway.

Those particularly concerned about driving in France, together with those who cannot yet drive, should take lessons with a local driving school (*l'auto-école*). Before you can start with a driving school, you will need to produce some ID (e.g. *carte de séjour*) and proof of your address (you can use a receipt for rent, or an electricity or telephone bill), and excise stamp and four photographs. Drivers who have had held a licence for less than one year are restricted to 90km/h (55mph).

It is advisable to obtain a copy of the French Highway Code before leaving the UK. Some of the fundamental rules follow:

Speed Limits. The speed limit on all autoroutes is 130kph (80mph); however, this reduces to 110km/h (65 mph) in wet weather, and is 110km/h on non-toll autoroutes. The speed limit on dual carriageways is 110km/h and 90km/h (55mph) on single carriageways — both reduced by 10km/h in wet weather. A new speed limit of 50 km/h has been introduced for foggy conditions where visibility is reduced to 50 metres. *Rappel* means the restriction is continued.

The limit in towns varies between 45km/h (30 mph) and 60km/h (38mph). Often a town name sign acts as the start of a speed limit and that same sign crossed through with a bar signifies the end of the limit.

The Priorité Rule. One of the most important rules to remember when driving in France is the *priorité à droite* which means you must give way to traffic joining from the right from another road (but not driveway) however minor. Thus, you must stop, as emerging drivers will not and, similarly, they will not be pleased if you stop when it is your right of way. This rule generally applies in towns and on minor roads. It used to apply also on major roads but this is generally no longer the case. If a major road does have priority this will be indicated by a sign in the form of a red diamond with a white border and sometimes by a red triangular sign reading *passage protégé*: this right of way ends when the same sign appears crossed through with a black bar.

One must also be careful at all junctions to see who has priority. *Cédez le passage* means give way, but *Stop* means just that! Give way when entering a roundabout (at one time traffic on the roundabout had to give way) and also watch out for a typically French rather 'casual' observance of traffic lights.

Other Rules

Minimum driving age: in France this is 18, not 17 as in the UK.

Seatbelts: seat belts must be worn by anyone travelling in the front or back of a car, and children under ten are not allowed, by law, to be carried in the front of a car unless they are in an approved, rear-facing seat.

Parking: parking is controlled by a *zone bleu* in many towns. This involves buying a parking disc (available from news-stands and small shops) which displays the time of arrival and depature: parking is restricted to a maximum of 90 minutes. Yellow lines do not prohibit parking in France, instead this is usually indicated by a sign rarely seen in the UK, a blue circle with red border and red diagonal slash.

Road Signs: Apart from the signs mentioned above, some of the most common are: *déviation* (diversion); *chaussée deformé* (uneven road edges or temporary road surface) and *gravillons* (loose chippings).

Police and Fines

Disregard for the various rules of the road is widespread in France, despite the reputation of French traffic police for being very strict, and the fact that more restrictive laws concerning driving are continually being introduced. Patrols and radar traps are commonplace in France and the breathalyser is also used widely: the penalties for exceeding the legal alcohol limit rise relative to the amount of excess alcohol. The legal blood/alcohol limit is 50mg per 100 millilitres of blood; slightly lower than the UK's 80mg.

Fines for any offence, including illegal parking, tend to be very high, and are usually rendered on the spot: up to £330 for minor offences and £4000 for drink-driving. Disqualification from driving, for anything from a week to several years (for drunk driving), is also imposed more frequently than in the UK and in some cases it is possible to have your licence taken away at the roadside. If the charges are the most serious ones: not stopping after an accident or manslaughter, there is an automatic court appearance and the maximum penalty is two years in jail and up to £23,250 in fines. While these are serious offences from anyone's point of view, the more controversial one is dangerous driving, a charge imposed at the magistrate's discretion if the motorist is deemed 'to have deliberately put the lives of others in danger'. There does not need to have been an accident, it is enough to have witnesses. This carries a maximum penalty of a year in prison and a fine of £1,165 and is additional to whatever other charges and fines the magistrate may have deemed appropriate.

It is advisable to carry all driving documents with you when motoring, this includes licence, registration document, insurance papers, and also your passport or *carte de séjour*, whichever is appropriate.

Breakdowns, Thefts and Accidents

There is no exact French equivalent of the AA or RAC which operates on a national basis. However, there are motoring organisations one can join which will arrange for a local garage, rather than their own service vehicle, to attend the breakdown. You can extend your AA or RAC assistance cover to France, or you can join an international assistance organisation like Europ Assistance.

Emergency Telephones: *bornes d'appel d'urgence* or emergency terminals (tall, orange pillars marked 'SOS') can be found on autoroutes and on some other major roads. On autoroutes (motorways) they are spaced at approximately 2km intervals and about 4km on other major routes; there are even some at strategic points on *départmentales* (D roads). On motorways and major roads they are positioned opposite each other on both sides of the road so that people do not try to cross a fast road to reach one.

They can be activated by pressing and releasing the button marked '*pour demander au secours* (to summon help) and then speaking into the large oval metal panel. Your call will be answered by the local emergency services or police station. Each telephone is numbered and you should give this number to whoever answers and tell them the location of your vehicle. If the call is to report an accident, give as many useful details as possible: the number of the telephone, the number of vehicles involved and the state of any injured. Accident calls are relayed to the SAMU (*Service d'Aide Médicale d'Urgence*) and the *sapeurs pompiers* (fire brigade). If there is a language problem, try to get a French person to make the call. You should display the red warning triangle from your car.

If you have broken down, the emergency services will send out a *garagiste* although it is unlikely he will perform AA or RAC type roadside diagnosis and repairs. It is more likely that you will be towed to his establishment for a hefty fee; the fact that the cost of this is state-regulated is no consolation when you get the bill.

Vehicle thefts and break-ins are very common in French cities and foreign registered cars tend to be particularly vulnerable, so take the usual precautions. In country areas, however, such crime is virtually unknown.

It is compulsory for all cars to carry a red hazard warning triangle which must be used in the case of a breakdown or accident and also carry a spare bulb kit. One must stop if involved in any accident, however slight. French drivers tend not to call the police if possible and this is only usually required if someone is seriously injured.

A few years ago, the number of fatal motor accidents in France (which has a similar sized population to the UK) was more than double that of Britain at nearly 9000 annually. The French Transport Ministry bought in a barrage of new regulations to improve matters including licence penalty points. It emerged in an analysis of the accident statistics in France that men are twice as likely as women to be killed on the road and around half of all accidents involve only one vehicle. The worst time for accidents is Sunday afternoon after the traditional Sunday lunch.

If you are involved in an accident then you have to fill in a report form, which should be supplied by your insurers and kept in the car at all times so that it can be filled in on the spot. This document is known as a *constat à l'amiable* and is a standardized form being used increasingly in various parts of Europe. In some cases, where there is disagreement as to who is to blame for the accident, it is usual to call a *huissier*, a legal official who will prepare an official and impartial statement of facts for insurance or legal purposes.

As was highlighted by the car accident that killed Princess Diana in Paris, it is a criminal offence in France not to try to assist persons in danger, or if that is not possible to summon assistance. The maximum penalty is five years imprisonment and a fine of half a million francs.

Transport

Air

Air transport, both to and within France, is efficient and reasonably priced. Owing to the size of the country it is also a service which is more regularly used than in most other European countries, although the expansion of the high speed train network (see below) is proving tough competition on some routes.

The main airline is the state company, Air France, which operates most international services and the major domestic ones. The state-owned domestic airline formerly known as Air Inter, was absorbed by Air France and is now Air France Europe. The domestic services carries nearly 18 million passengers a year and operates hundreds of internal flights a day. Air France Europe also provides a shuttle air service (La Navette) between Paris Orly and Nice, Marseille and Toulouse. TAT (bought up by British Airways) and much smaller airlines also offer domestic flights, as do provincial airlines such as Air Vendée. The train-fly service, which is linked with Eurostar, has proved popular as a way to get to provincial French cities via the capital. There are also cheap internal apex one-way tickets (book 14 days ahead) e.g. Paris to Nice for £37.

You can of course fly from almost every capital city in the world to Paris. In the case of the UK, it is possible to fly from nearly every regional British airport to Paris and to some major provincial cities such as Lyon, Marseille, Nice, Bordeaux and Strasbourg. Surprisingly, air tickets for travel within France can work out cheaper than driving (because of autoroute tolls and petrol prices) and on some routes the prices are competitive with rail travel. There are always special offers for limited periods and special fares for 'affinity groups' (under-26s, families, over 60s and students up to 27 years). Full details can be obtained direct from Air France in France; the UK office deals only with international flights.

Useful Addresses
Air Canada: 7 Conduit Street, London W1R 6AT; tel 0990-247226. Toronto to Paris (Charles de Gaulle).

Air France: Colet Court, 100 Hammersmith Road, London W6 7JP; tel 0181-742 6600; +33 1 44 08 22 22.

Air France Europe: Head Office: 45 rue de Paris, 95747 Roissy-Charles de Gaulle Airport, France (1 41 56 78 00; fax 1 41 56 34 98).

Nouvelles Frontières: 2/3 Woodstock Street, London W1R 1HE (0171-629 7772; brochure line 0171 493 2435). Major French travel agent operates between UK and France (Paris, Provincial France and Corsica). Also does charters from Paris to the Caribbean (Martinique, Guadeloupe, St Martin); the Indian Ocean (Réunion, Mauritius and the Seychelles; the Pacific Islands (Tahiti, Noumea, Easter Islands).

TAT: (0345-222111) TAT is linked with British Airways. Routes include: Gatwick-Poitiers-Tours-Brive; Gatwick-Paris-Lyons; Gatwick-Marseilles.

Bucket Shops

France has only had bucket shops since 1991, since when they have become commonplace for selling charter tickets at bargain prices. Last minute tickets (*vente de dernière minute* or VDM) are widely available on Minitel or by telephone. Some airlines have even opened their own bargain basements as they have realised that selling off seats cheaper than usual is better than not selling them at all. Travel agents also sell bargain tickets, but generally add their own costs and so are slightly more expensive.

Useful Contacts

Dégrif'Tour, Réductour: Minitel 36-15DT or 36-15RT.

Routard: Minitel 36-15.

Nouveau Monde: tel 1 43 29 40 40.

Access Voyages: tel 1 44 76 84 50.

Nouvelles Frontières: (see also above). Minitel 36-15.

Charter et Co: tel 1 43 55 30 00.

Cash and Go: Minitel 36-15 Cashgo; tel 1 53 93 63 63.

Jumbo Charter: fax 1 46 34 12 55.

Go Voyages: tel 1 49 23 27 00.

King Tour: Minitel 36-15; tel 1 42 85 01 83.

Etapes Nouvelles: fax 1 48 74 26 46.

Rail

France has an extensive rail system, of 35,000 km of line serving 3000 destinations and it is one of the most modern in the world. Half of all long distance rail traffic in France is high speed and 75% of all passengers are on the high speed services. This model of a modern rail system is run by the Société Nationale des Chemins de Fer Français (SNCF), a nationalised company in which a great deal of public money has been invested. State subsidy helps keep down customer charges but not running costs, and the level of deficit tends to be billions of francs annually. Trains are generally punctual, which no doubt has something to do with a system of bonus reductions for drivers whose trains are late without cause.

All French towns and cities of any size are linked to each other by rail, although it is frequently necessary to travel between them through Paris. All the main cities have commuter lines and various types of trains are available.

The TGV: the apogee of the rail system is the impressive 187 miles/300 km per hour TGV (*Train à Grande Vitesse*) whose growing network currently links Paris to all south-east France as well as Bordeaux, Toulouse, Lille, Brittany and Switzerland. From Lille it links up with the Channel Tunnel. Some of the latest services at the time of print, mean that using Eurostar from London, passengers can travel to Bordeaux, Nantes and Quimper without going to Paris, thanks to the 102 km rail ring which by-passes the capital through stations at Massy, Chessy and Charles de Gaulle Airport. The Lille connection also serves Lyon and the south. The Paris Lyon route sports the newer Duplex (double-decker) TGV which is the nearest you'll get to a flying sensation on land.

Other Services: the non-TGV express trains, include those which travel to other European cities, and local trains. Prices vary with the speed of the service and time of travel and a wide range of reduced fare passes exist in cluding the EuroDomino runabout which gives unlimited travel for three, five or ten days in any month and includes the TGV (though you still have to pay for the obligatory advance booking). Other discount deals of up to 50% are the *Carte Vermeil* for senior citizens over 60; the *Carte Kiwi* for families; *Carte Carissimo* for under 26s and the *Carte Couple* for couples. Season tickets are also available.

Train tickets: can be bought at stations and some travel agents. The SNCF computerised booking system was subject to some teething problems during 1993; for instance its determination to declare trains fully-booked when this was far from the case, and by declining arbitrarily to register some cities. It is possible also to book tickets via the telephone Minitel system. TGV seats must always be booked in advance and there is a supplement. All rail tickets must be validated (*composté*) in the orange, automatic, date-stamping machines located at platform entrances-— there are usually no ticket collectors on platforms, only on the trains.

The Motorail service, by which it is possible to transport both car and passengers overnight by train, is particularly useful for those travelling from the north or from Paris to the southern regions of France. It is pricey, at about £600 return for a family of four, but this has to be offset against the cost of going by car with autoroute tolls and higher petrol costs, and the boredom factor if small children are on board.

For sheer scenic indulgence the narrow gauge Chemin de Fer Provence runs between Nice and Digne in Provence.

The Paris rail terminals and the areas they serve are as follows:

Gare D'Austerlitz	Southwest, Bordeaux, Spain
Gare de l'Est	Strasbourg area and Germany
Gare de Lyon:	Southeast, Lyon, Switzerland, Italy
Gare Montparnasse:	West, Brittany
Gare du Nord:	North, Channel Ports, Channel Tunnel (see below), Holland, Belgium.
Gare St Lazare:	Normandy

Channel Tunnel & Eurostar:
Eurostar in France: tel 08 36 35 35 39.
Le Shuttle: tel 0800 127127
British Rail: Paris tel 01 44 51 06 02.

Paris Métro

The Métro is the urban underground system that carries five million passengers a day plus another five million on the RER regional network that links into the suburbs. Buying a book of ten tickets, a *carnet* is cheaper than buying single tickets which cost about 90p for a single journey anywhere within the city of Paris and about 50p with a carnet ticket. If you are staying in Paris for several weeks it is worth investing in a monthly ticket at 243 francs (about £26). During the summer of 1997 when pollution was at its worst in Paris, ticket prices were slashed by half to get motorists to use public transport.

Coach and Bus Transport

France has a reasonable system of long distance coach services, some of which are operated by SNCF. The only effective way to obtain current details is to apply directly to tourist offices in France.

In the major French cities the bus system is integrated and coordinated with the underground (Metro) and the commuter rail lines. For these, although one can pay in cash on the bus it is much easier, quicker and cheaper to buy an appropriate concessionary pass or to book tickets in advance.

Sea and River Transport

For details of the sea crossings between southern and northern Britain and northern France and Belgium see the *Getting There* section at the end of the *General Introduction*.

From France itself Société Nationale, Maritime Corse-Méditerranée operate ferries between Marseilles and Toulon and a choice of vessels to Corsica: The NGV *Asco* and *Aliso* are fast ferries which run from the end of March and can speed you from Nice to Corsica in two and three-quarter hours. Fares cost about £29 one-way per person and about the same for a car. The plusher vessel *Napoleon Bonaparte* (what else?) operates an overnight service between Marseille and Corsica. Prices from about £36 one-way for a passenger and £50 one-way for a car. You can book in France (+ 33 4 91 56 32 71) or London (0171-491 4968).

Useful Addresses
French Railways: 179 Piccadilly, London W1V 0BA (tel 0171-409 3518).
SNCM: 179 Piccadilly, London W1V 9DB; tel: 0171-491 4698.

France's network of navigable waterways is a vast 5,600 miles (9000 km). If you haven't taken your own cruising craft with you, then it is possible to hire boats of almost any size from cabin cruiser, up to converted commercial barges (*péniches*) which can sleep up to two dozen people plus several crew. The main canals are in the north where canals and rivers are linked and have to be shared with commercial traffic heading for the ports. Popular regions for pleasure cruising include Burgundy; the great river Rhône; the Midi (the Canal du Midi connects the Atlantic with the Mediterranean); and Brittany and the Loire on the rivers: Vilaine, Sarthe, Mayenne and Loire.

Useful Publications
Carte Guide Navigation Fluviale: very detailed series of maps by Navicarte, published by Editions Grafocarte (ISBN 2 90498 510 7). Available from the UK supplier (IMRAY 01480-462114), or from the French publishers (Navicarte, Port Autonome de Paris, Service de la Plaisance, 2 Quai de Grenelle, 75015 Paris, France).
Guide to the Inland Waterways of France: (1992) David Edwards May (ISBN 0 852880820) at £24. Also available from IMRAY (see above).

Tax and the Expatriate

In the future it is conceivable that tax systems throughout Europe may become completely integrated, but at present this is far from the case. As a result of the different tax regimes which exist in different countries there are major complications involved in a move overseas. This does not just apply to tax affairs in the host country; a move will conjure up many tax implications in one's home country also. The situation is rather more simple, however, if you are leaving the UK, and thus the UK tax system, for good. Tax regulations are more complex if you are buying a second home (*une résidence secondaire*) in France because then you are obliged to become involved in two very different tax systems.

It is advisable to take individual and independent financial advice before committing yourself to a move to France. This will ensure that no unnecessary tax is paid, and should also minimise eventual tax bills. If you do not already have an accountant who is experienced in expatriate taxation then the addresses of Franco-British tax consultants can be obtained from the French Chamber of Commerce in Great Britain (197 Knightsbridge, London SW7 1RB; tel 0171-304 7021; fax 0171-304 7034) .

Useful Addresses

Blackstone Franks: (Barbican House, 26-34 Old Street, London EC1V 9HL; tel 0171-250 3300; fax 0171-250 1793; e-mail 100073.3506@compuserve.com). Also offices in France. Specialists in the expatriate financial sector who publish an invaluable book *Living in France* (£6.99) which gives full details of the tax implications of moving to France.

Brewin Dolphin Bell Lawrie Ltd. Stockbrokers: 5 Giltspur Street, London EC1A 9BD; tel 0171-246 1028; fax 0171-246 1093. Services include international portfolio management with offshore facility for those domiciled or resident outside the UK. Contact Robin Lindsay-Stewart.

HANSARD EUROPE LIMITED

When in France....

Hansard Europe Limited, a Dublin-based offshore company, offers products designed exclusively for the French market.

Hansard French products have been designed to be tax-efficient with regard to French tax and life assurance regulations.

For more information about Hansard Europe Limited or the Hansard Group, please contact Product Support on +353 1 278 1488.

"Dedicated to the orderly creation of wealth."

Hansard Europe Limited, P.O. Box 43, Enterprise House, Frascati Road, Blackrock, Co. Dublin, Republic of Ireland.
Telephone: +353 1 278 1488 Fax: +353 1 278 1499
Internet: http://www.hansard.com
Ligne directe pour les francophones : + 353 1 283 6740
Registration No. 219727 Dublin, Republic of Ireland.

Hansard Europe Ltd: P.O. Box 43, Enterprise House, Frascati Road, Blackrock, Co. Dublin, Republic of Ireland; tel +353 1 278 1488; fax +353 1 278 1499. Hansard have products aimed at the French market and designed to be tax efficient with regard to French tax and life assurance regulations.

Siddalls International Parc Innolin, 3 rue de Golf, 33700 Bordeaux-Mérignac; tel +33 05 56 34 75 51; fax +33 05 56 34 75 52 (UK tel 01329-288641). Can help you build a pension fund geared to your needs and provides full investment, tax and inheritance planning.

Wiggin & Co Solicitors: The Quadrangle, Imperial Square, Cheltenham, Glos. GL50 1YX; tel 01242-224114; fax 01242-224223. European Lawyers and tax advisors.

The Question of Residence

Any person who spends more than six months (183 days) per year in France has to pay French tax on his or her worldwide income. Taxable income includes income from work, letting and leasing, trade enterprises, returns on investment, annuities and speculative capital gains (except, in certain circumstances, on the sale of a principal residence). Before moving to France it is therefore important to consider where your main residence will be for tax purposes. The important point to note is that you do not necessarily escape one country's income tax and become subject to another's just by moving there. It all depends on where the tax authorities consider you are resident for tax purposes, and also where you are domiciled — the two not necessarily being the same thing.

Procedure for Residents. The situation is reasonably straightforward if you are moving permanently to France. You should inform the UK Inspector of Taxes at the office usually dealt with of this fact and you will be sent a P85 form to complete. The UK tax office will usually require certain proof that you are leaving the UK, and thus their jurisdiction, for good. Evidence of having a sold a house in the UK and having bought one in France is usually sufficient. If you are leaving a UK company to take up employment with a French one then the P45 form given by your UK employer and evidence of employment in France should be sufficient. You may be eligible for a tax refund in respect of the period up to your departure in which case it will be necessary to complete an income tax return for income and gains from the previous 5 April to your departure date. It may be advisable to seek professional advice when completing the P85 which needs to be completed carefully. Once the Inland Revenue has been satisfied that an individual is no longer resident or domiciled in the UK, they will close the appropriate file and not expect any more UK income tax to be paid.

Procedure for Non-Residents. If you are buying a second home in France, whether for long holidays or retirement, etc. then the situation as regards taxation is more complicated in that you remain liable to UK tax but may also acquire liability for French tax. This may also be the case if you are maintaining any sort of financial connection with the UK, e.g. if one still owns and rents out a home in the UK, thus generating an income. If this is the case then an accountant in the UK must be consulted for individual advice, otherwise you may find that both the UK and French tax authorities will consider you liable for income tax on your income, no matter where it is earned. Some people who have moved to France but spend long holidays or business trips back in the UK have found that the UK Inland Revenue still consider them domiciled in the UK for tax purposes.

Personal Income Tax

Known in France as *IRPP (Impôt sur le Revenu des Personnes Physiques)* this tax ranges from the minimum of 12% on annual taxable income between 22,210 francs and 48,570 francs (approximately £2,414 to £5,280) to the maximum of 56.8% on taxable income above 277,730 francs (approximately £30,200). However this gives a somewhat misleading picture as there is a vast range of income tax allowances in France: These include allowances on alimony payments, dependent children up to the age of 18, adult children up to the age of 25 in higher education, disabled dependants etc. This means that there is a very great variation in the actual percentage of tax for which individual taxpayers are liable. The highest wage earners will find that they pay more tax in France than in the UK, while the average French employee takes home a little more net income than his or her UK counterpart. Deductions for national insurance contributions work out much higher than in the UK at about 18% for executive and managerial staff, but are deductible from the gross salary.

Anyone earning any sort of income in France will find the French tax authorities will have an interest in it, regardless of whether they have officially taken up residence or not and whether or not they have a *carte de séjour.*

Income and Allowances

Income tax is calculated upon two sources of income, earned (*impôt sur le revenu*) and unearned (*impôt des revenus de capitaux*). If a resident has only an average income and interest on bank deposits, the latter tax will not apply as tax is deducted from bank interest before the account holder receives it. As explained in the section on banking, it is also possible to hold a deposit account where interest is payable free of tax.

Tax allowances in France are fairly generous and it is for this reason that many French tax payers contribute less than those in other European countries even though the tax rates do not appear substantially lower. If you have anything more than a very simple financial situation, professional advice is necessary in order to take best advantage of the allowances available. The latter relate to certain property and home expenses, interest on certain loans, and allowances for dependants. Married couples, for example, are allowed a 50% allowance on their taxable income and this increases with each child they have.

The minimum income, below which one is not liable to pay any income tax, is set along similar lines to that in the UK: at the time of writing this is 33,450 francs (approximately £3,635); in the UK the level is £4,045. Above this amount, however, tax rates are levied on a sliding scale rising in degrees of about 10%, with each additional segment of income being subject to a higher rate. At present the lowest possible rate is 12% of taxable income and the highest is 56.8%, with the average taxpayer probably paying less than 30%.

Finally, a special wealth tax (*impôt de solidarité sur la fortune*) came into effect in France as of 1 January, 1989. However, as this does not apply to those with incomes of less than approximately four and a half million francs (about half a million sterling) with tax starting at 0.5%, this will probably not be a great source of anxiety for many readers.

Registering for Income Tax

The procedure for those who have moved to France to take up a job or start a business must register with the *inspecteur des impôts* shortly after arrival. As income tax is not deducted by PAYE, as in the UK, you will be sent an income tax return to complete in due course: in this case, as we have said, you should no longer be liable to UK tax. Note that foreign nationals working in France for the first time should normally expect to pay their tax in September of the year following their arrival. Therefore if a UK citizen arrives in France in September, he or she will not pay any income tax until two years following their arrival. Thereafter, the system reverts to normal see *Income Tax Returns* below).

Income Tax Returns

Once registered with the French tax authorities they will send you a tax return (*déclaration fiscal*) every year. A husband's tax return usually applies to his whole family's income as head of the household. It is not usual for a wife to be assessed for income tax separately. The French tax year runs from February to February. A tax return must be filed by the last day of February of the year following the year when the income is received or the capital gains realised. For income earned in 1997 therefore, a return must be filed by the end of February 1998. Once you have registered with the tax authorities a form will automatically be sent to you, but if not, is essential to request one as otherwise a penalty of 10% is automatically levied, even if the return is a day late.

An income tax return should take into into account any deductable allowances, and is adjusted eventually to take account of changes in salary or circumstances. Should a tax payer become unemployed, he or she must obtain a signed declaration and inform the collector of taxes (*percepteur*) before leaving employment.

There are two methods of payment allowed in France, the more usual of which is to pay one's tax bill in three instalments (*tiers provisionnels*) The first two payments are provisional and are payable annually on 15 February and 15 May: these instalments are calculated at a third of the previous year's total tax bill. The third instalment, the balance, is due on 15 September by which time the tax collector will have details of the previous year's income and will have made any necessary adjustments. The second method of payment is by monthly instalments (*Mensualisation*) by direct debit from the tax payer's bank account: on the eighth of each month from January to October a tenth of the previous year's tax bill is deducted. Additional deductions will automatically be authorized by the taxman in November and December if one is earning more than in the previous year. Monthly payments are a useful budgeting aid as they spread the burden of payment over the whole year and serve to allay any worries about having to pay three large instalments. However, those with a keener economic sense would probably prefer to have their money earning interest for them and will therefore opt for the three-instalment method, only whipping their money out of an investment account just in time to meet each tax deadline.

The latest date at which claims against over assessment or overpayment can be made is 31 December of the second year following the year in which the tax notice was issued. Claims must be made in writing and only the tax payer can sign the claim form. If possible it is advisable to file a claim before any payment is made in order to claim a deferment of payment. Before leaving France foreign employees must pay any taxes due for the previous year and the year of departure. A return for this income must be submitted to the tax office in the ten days preceding departure and the tax paid before departure. Following payment of outstanding taxes a tax clearance (*quitus fiscal*) certificate from the French revenue saying you have paid all your tax bills will be issued. Where departure is before 31 December, the previous year's taxes are applied and if this results in an overpayment then a claim for excess tax should be made.

The French Tax System

Currently about 40% of the total tax revenue in France comes from VAT (TVA as it is known there). Income tax is also a major source of revenue, representing 20% of the total tax revenue. Interestingly enough, the French consider themselves grossly overtaxed even though they pay less than most northern European countries.

At present the tax system is overburdened with administration and as a result not only is it difficult to obtain guidance and assistance from the tax authorities, but errors, mistakes and both over and under-assessments do occur. Another problem is that tax evasion, as well as tax avoidance, tends to be something of a national pastime in France, with most people not seeing the former as being particularly unethical. The unfortunate result of this is that if the tax authorities do start to investigate then they often take a very hard line: they have powers to assess tax at whatever level they see fit unless the tax payer (or, perhaps more appropriately non-tax payer) in question can give sufficient reason for them not to exercise this authority.

A Note for Non-Residents

It may be a good idea for those intending to live in France on a temporary basis not to register with the French authorities, nor to advise the UK authorities of their new situation until professional advice has been taken: to do so may result in paying tax unnecessarily. The best way of proceeding will depend largely on how much time is spent in each country. Generally, UK tax cannot be avoided if more than six months each year is spent in the UK. An accountant will advise whether it would be better to be resident in either the UK or France for tax purposes and what to inform the authorities in each country.

Taxation for Non-Residents and Double Taxation

It is important to realise that it is not only those who work in France who are liable to French income tax: it is also possible for non-resident French property owners to become liable to French income tax based on an estimated letting value. Current French law requires foreign non-resident property owners to register with the Centre des Impôts des Non-Résidents (for futher details see *Setting up Home*). However, people who fall within this category will not necessarily have to pay any tax, as the amount taxable may be reduced by property expenses and offset against UK income tax.

Occasionally the question of double taxation arises. This will mainly concern those who have moved to France on a temporary basis and is a situation where both the French and UK income tax authorities consider the resident liable to pay income tax to them from one income. For example, some holiday property owners have found that both authorities have claimed income tax on rental income from their property. Fortunately, a double taxation agreement exists between both countries so that while in the short term, one may have to pay both bills, subsequently a refund will be made from one or the other.

Other Taxes

There are a range of taxes in France which are similar, or sometimes even identical, to taxes which operate in other European countries. Although such taxes often operate differently in practice, the principles on which they are based remain the same.

Capital Gains Tax

Capital Gains Tax (*l'impôt sur les plus values*) will not affect most tax payers but anyone hoping to make money from dealing in French property on a regular basis should bear the following in mind. If a home is a principal residence then any capital gains made on a subsequent sale will not be taxable. This enables people to move house within France, or to change their country of residence, without being penalized financially.

If a home is a secondary residence or a holiday home Capital Gains Tax will still not be charged in France provided that this is paid in the UK. Such an exemption is only permitted once and is hedged with restrictions, notably that the vendor must have had free use of the property (i.e. it has not been leased out). If this is not the case and the vendor sells the property within two years of purchase then CGT is levied at 33.3%. A small consolation is that legal expenses and agents' commissions can be deducted for the amount payable. CGT is reduced by 5% each year after the first two years.

Death Duties

Within six months of the death of a person resident in France, his or her successors in title must send to the tax collection office that handles his affairs, a succession return giving details of the deceased's assets and any tax that is due. Inheritance taxes (*droits de succession*) are due on the total assets (both in France and abroad) of anyone domiciled in France. Those not domiciled in France pay death duties only on assets within France. Joint tax agreements mean than inheritance taxes paid in France may be reclaimed from the UK tax office.

The level of death duties payable by heirs is on an ascending scale based on the nearness of kinship to the deceased, the furthest relatives paying the most at 60%, whilst children and spouses pay the least, from 5% to 40%, depending on the value of the legacy. Immediate kin are also permitted an automatically tax-free inheritance of up to 300,000 francs (roughly £30,000). There is also a 25% reduction on certain *inter vivos* (between living persons) gifts to legal heirs.

Useful Addresses

Franco-British Chamber of Commerce: 197 Knightsbridge, London SW7 1RB2; tel 0171-304 7021. Will provide a list of Franco-British tax consultants.

French Fiscal Attaché: Kingsgate House, 115 High Holborn, London WC1V 6JJ; tel 0171-831 9048. Enquiries for tax information in writing only.

Direction des Services Généraux et de l'Informatique: 92 bvd Ney, 75878 Paris, Cedex 18; tel +33 1 49 25 12 45. Further tax information.

Association de Comptables: 151 rue Montmartre, 75002 Paris. Professional association of French accountants.

Hereward Philips: Prospect House, 2 Athenaeum Road, Whetstone, London N20 9YU; tel 0181-446 4371; fax 0181-446 7606. A UK chartered accountant, experienced in dealing with most tax matters relating to expatriates and non-UK residents.

Banks and Finance

Banking Requirements

At an early stage in planning a move to France it may be advisable to open a French bank account. Even before you move to France, you will need funds to pay the costs related to buying or renting a property, legal fees and deposits etc.; so this does not just apply to those who are moving to France permanently. Even once you have your holiday home in France it can be useful to have a French bank account as regular bills, such as those for local taxes and utilities can be paid by direct debit from your account when you are not in residence.

Having said this, in the short term it is possible to manage without a French account. Credit cards and travellers cheques issued by UK banks are accepted in France. However, the fees which are charged for these services can make a long-term stay in France, without a French bank account, very expensive.

Eurocheques: Eurocheques have come in for a steadily mounting rejection in France where banks are trying to reduce the number of paper transactions. Unfortunately, during 1995 and 1996 there seemed to be only a limited number of banks (mainly Crédit Agricole) which would accept them. Some holiday home owners had also become used to relying on the Post Office to cash Eurocheques, but in 1996 they joined the French banks in boycotting them. By the time of press, the advice is, that since only a few banks and bureaux de change (which charge a high commission) are accepting Eurocheques, you should carry a variety of alternatives such as a credit card, travellers cheques or a debit card. Visa Delta debit cards are widely acceptable for withdrawals or payment for goods, while cards with the Cirrus logo can be used to withdraw money from from cashpoints displaying the same logo.

Credit Cards: There is a difference between French and UK issued credit cards: French cards have a microchip and users enter a PIN into the card machine, or give their PIN at the check out when making a purchase. UK cards have a magnetic strip (regarded as old fashioned in France) and customers are not used to providing their PIN when buying goods. French retailers have taken to refusing to accept the British version although, provided that you can give your PIN, there is no valid reason for their doing this. You should check with your card issuer for advice, before going to France.

Another credit card caveat, this time from the providers of Card Protection Plan insurance is that France is the worst country for recorded credit card theft, and Paris and Nice are the worst areas.

Keeping a UK Account: many expatriates decide that, even after moving permanently to France and opening a French account, to keep a bank account in the UK. This account may then be drawn on if you return to the UK for a holiday at some point, or if you need to order any home comforts from the UK by mail order.

Money Transfers

It is a simple matter to transfer money from a UK bank account to a French one, or vice versa: simply provide your UK bank with the name, address and account number of your French bank account. The procedure is known as a bank transfer in the UK and, in France, as *un virement*. The Royal Bank of Scotland and Credit Commercial de France (CCF) have recently joined the IBOS instant money transfer system. CCF has 180 branches in France and you can transfer money to any one of them from the Royal Bank of Scotland branches in the UK on the same day. There is another fast way of transferring funds through an international computer system called 'Society of Worldwide Interbank Financial Telecommunications' (SWIFT). You should enquire at your bank for further details. Transfers usually take 24 (sometimes 48) hours.

Another possibility is Girobank Eurogiro. This takes three working days to transfer funds between post offices and there is a fixed charge, no matter what the amount, and it is considerably cheaper than the SWIFT inter-bank system. Even cheaper is the ten-day service. New customers simply open an account at the post office solely for international transfers. This system is adequate for holiday home owners and those who want their pensions sent to them at minimal cost.

The fastest way (and the most expensive) way of sending money is the Telegraphic Transfer (TT). Western Union and American Express are the two best known companies. The transfer simply involves a person paying the money at the sending office and within 15 minutes it can be collected at the receiving office; literally while you wait. Western Union can be reached in Paris on 1 43 54 46 12.

Exchange Control

UK Exchange control regulations were abolished 1979 and as far as the authorities are concerned you may transfer money from, or to, the UK without restriction. Exchange controls in France were abolished more recently, in January 1990. The main implications of the removal of exchange control regulations are that as a French resident you can open an account in any country and take an unlimited amount of money out of France. However, it is obligatory to inform the French inland revenue of any new account on your annual tax return. In addition, international transfers in excess of 50,000 francs or a foreign currency equivalent other than bank transfers, must be declared to the authorities (BNP Central Records) who will provide a certificate confirming customs approval. Likewise anyone, resident or non-resident, entering or leaving France with more than the equivalent of 50,000 francs in cash must declare it to French customs.

Choosing a Bank

If you already have an account with Barclays, National Westminster, Lloyds, Abbey National, Woolwich or the Midland banks, all of which have one or more branches in France, it may be useful to stay with them, as they will be especially aware of any problems you are likely to experience at the outset. You may therefore wish to ask your current UK bank if they have branches or associated companies in France which could attend to all the details of opening accounts. Barclays has the largest number of branches in France and the National Westminster Bank has branches in all large cities including Paris, Bordeaux, Lyon, Marseille, Nantes, Nice, Strasbourg and Toulouse. Lloyds and the Midland have one branch apiece in Paris. Since January 1993 banks from any EU country have been able to open branches in any other EU country without any regulation except from their country of origin. It is therefore likely that there will be an increasing number of foreign banks, including UK ones, setting up branches in France.

State owned, part state owned and private banks exist in France. As part of the conservative government's privatisation policy, government holdings in all kinds of companies, including banks are in the process of being sold off through the international markets. The major clearing banks are Banque National de Paris (BNP), Crédit Lyonnais and Société Générale. The Société Générale, the BNP and Crédit Lyonnais have all been subject to privatisation. These are the equivalents of UK clearing banks can be found in the boulevards and market places of cities and towns, large and small throughout France.

Minitel Banking

French banks are the subject of many complaints from the French themselves. They have archaic opening hours: some close for lunch and, owing to regulations dating back to 1937, all have to be closed for two days a week. At the time of press a change of legislation to allow commercial banks to open six days a week and the introduction of more flexible working hours seemed likely in a long overdue overhaul of the 60-year-old legislation. Some banks close on Mondays and are open on Saturday. There are usually long queues and service can be mind-numbingly slow. For those willing to use the Minitel for banking, life can be a lot easier. With Minitel you can transfer money between your accounts, buy and sell shares, read your statements and get instant readings of the Paris stock exchange. Thus you need only go to the bank in person to make deposits and collect your cheque book. The latter can also be posted to you.

Co-operative Banks/Mutual Credit Organisations. There are many such institutions in France which began as regional community assistance organisations working for the mutual benefit of client and organisation. Although these operate exactly like mainstream banks and offer most banking services, each office is an independent organisation, rather than a branch of a clearing bank. Credit Agricole is the largest organisation of this type and with almost 10,000 offices worldwide is found in almost every town of any size. The mutual credit organisations are cooperatives and it is possible to become a member and invest in their shares, along the lines of a UK building society. You are usually required to become a member if a loan or mortgage is needed but this is optional if one merely wishes to deposit money or to have a cheque account with them.

If you have taken a mortgage with a French bank this branch may also be the logical choice for your bank account, and this, anyway, may be insisted upon by the bank in question.

There are many corporate banks and finance companies in France, such as Banque Paribas, which provide business banking facilities but not personal accounts. Savings banks (*caisses d'épargne*), are also to be found although these can only offer a limited range of services such as savings accounts and loans for property, similar to UK building societies.

The Post Office. When looking at banking in France it is worth considering the post office (PTT) which offers cheque accounts and savings and investment schemes and has more branches in France than any bank. The French equivalent of Girobank is, CCP (Compte Cheques Postaux).

Opening an Account

A piece of basic advice for those intending to open an account with a French bank is to choose one of the larger branches; it may not be the most accessible but it is far more likely not to close for lunch or all day on Mondays as rural branches tend to do.

One option for those who know where they will be based in France is to open an account through a French bank's UK branch. However, although several large French banks have UK offices not all of them provide such a service. Credit Lyonnais (Broadwalk House, 5 Appold Street, London EC2A 2JP; tel 0171-374 4014) will send an information pack on opening an account before you go. Credit Agricole (Client Liaison, 135 Fleet Street, London EC4A 2ED; tel 0171-427 0007) will also help you open an account with your nearest branch in France. Opening an account before leaving for France is likely to save a lot of bother, particularly if you have difficulty speaking French. However, once you are in France all your dealings will be with the branch where you have your account. As they are unlikely to have staff who speak English, it is advisable to brush up your French or find some other method of making financial transactions in France that does not involve French banks.

Alternatively, you can open an account in France in person. French banks have recently been trying to improve their image and consequently bank managers and manageresses (*gérant(e)* or *responsable de l'agence*) tend to be more accessible than they used to be, and to make an effort to meet new clients personally. When opening a French bank account be prepared, if requested, to show all your identification documents, including passport, *carte de séjour*, property deeds or rent documents, birth certificate etc. and in addition, proof of income such as pay slips or a tax return is also required. The banks must satisfy themselves that you are not banned from operating a bank account, as frequently happens to those who misuse them in France (see below). You will also require a reference from your UK bank, preferably in French. However, all this bureaucracy can be avoided by opening an account from a UK branch of a French bank like Crédit Lyonnais or Crédit Agricole. As in the UK, cheque books and monthly statements will be posted to your home address.

Banking hours are typically 9am to 4pm, possibly with a lunch hour, although late opening until 7pm is being introduced at some of the larger banks. Banks close early on the day before a bank holiday.

Bank Accounts

Various types of account are available in France which broadly compare to those in the UK in that there are current accounts, deposit accounts and also various types of savings plans.

A current account is known as a *compte de chèque*. It is illegal in France for banks to pay interest on credit balances. There are no maintenance charges but there are many more transaction charges e.g. on direct debits, on most current accounts whereas most personal banking customers in the UK expect free banking if their account remains in credit.

There are many different types of deposit accounts (*comptes sur livret*) in France: the interest rates and minimum deposit periods vary from bank to bank. In France individuals are allowed a deposit savings account on which the interest paid is free of tax and which is very similar to the TESSA/ISA accounts available in the UK. The limit to these accounts is about £8,000, although the interest rates paid are modest. Most banks offer these schemes under varying brand names.

Cheques

French cheques are written in very much the same way as British ones, but with the information positioned differently: the banks will supply a specimen if asked. In France cheques are not negotiable to a third person. When paying cheques in to your bank account it is necessary to sign them on the back; failure to do this may mean that the banks will return them to you, thus delaying the clearing process. Cheque guarantee cards as such are not used, and so when using a cheque you may be asked for some other form of identification. However, when opening an account one should request a debit card, the Carte Bleu, which is similar to a 'connect' or 'switch' card in the UK. As well as being preferred by traders to personal identification for large amounts of money, the Carte Bleu also enables you to draw out money, and to obtain a current statement of account, from cash machines throughout the country.

Clearing Cheques. The French banking system is well-organised, although not as efficient or as quick as that in the UK, due generally, to the fact that the French do not place a great deal of urgency on banking matters. Whereas a cheque takes three days to be cleared in the UK, in France cheques usually take longer to clear from, or be credited to, an account, especially if they are from, or destined for, a bank account in a different branch in another part of France, or if they have come from abroad. In most cases, deposits of foreign cheques made out in French francs will be credited only upon actual receipt of the funds from the payer (known as *crédit après encaissement* or CAE). The other kind of cheque clearing is *sauf bon fin (SBF)*, when you are credited for the cheque within six days, but the credit can be withdrawn if the cheque is returned unpaid.

In some cases it can take as long as twelve days to clear a cheque. Thus, it can sometimes be hard to keep track of one's finances. There is no such thing as a post-dated cheque in France; it will be considered valid from when the bank receives it, regardless of the date on it. However, if the date is more than a year old, it will not be cleared.

Bouncing Cheques. One of the main differences between the French and British banking systems is that in France it is a serious offence to write a cheque with insufficient funds to meet it. A period of 30 days is allowed for the account to be put in order. Should this prove impossible the bank automatically blocks the account for a period of one year, during which time the offender is banned from writing any further cheques. This is known as an *interdiction*. The offender's details are kept on a central list by the Banque de France for a period of three years, in case he or she tries to open another account. If this should happen then the police are informed.

Stopping Cheques. Along with getting automatic overdrafts, British people are used to being able to stop cheques for a variety of reasons, including buying faulty goods. In France it is not possible to do this without legal repercussions that will keep the lawyers happy for months at your expense. In other words it is not the simple solution that it is in the UK.

Bankers Cheques: (*chèques de banque*) cannot be treated as cash in the same way as they are in the UK. Bankers drafts have to be paid into your account and cleared in the normal way.

Charge Cards and other Banking Services

Credit cards do not exist as such in France. Instead, charge cards are issued. Each month, the total accrued to the charge card is automatically debited from your account. A good many banks provide charge cards, for which an annual fee is payable. Probably the best-known is the Carte Bleue which is very widely accepted in France. There is also an international version, the Carte Bleu/Visa, but this still has to paid off at the end of each month. Needless to say, one can also use UK cards, with Visa being preferred, in France.

Charge cards are quite widely accepted in France, although not to the same extent as in the UK or USA. These cards can also be used to withdraw cash from cash dispensers and most large shops, hypermarkets, restaurants, hotels and even autoroute tolls accept charge cards. There are also card-operated petrol stations and the new minimum service, 24-hour 'pit-stop' hotels where access is by credit card. However, do not take this for granted in remote rural establishments. Most petrol stations now take cards.

Direct Debits. (*les prélèvements automatiques*). As in the UK, direct debits are a convenient way of paying regular bills for utilities, especially if you are only based in France for a few months of the year or are making only periodic visits there. As already mentioned, services like electricity and telephones will be cut off far more readily in France than in the UK, if payment is late and by getting your bank to pay such bills automatically you should prevent this. A similar service can be arranged through the Post Office.

Domestic (i.e. internal) money transfers are known as *virements*, while international ones are *transferts*. The Girobank equivalent in France is CCP (Compte Cheques Postaux).

Main Commercial Clearing Banks
Banque Paribas: 3 rue Antin, 75002 Paris; tel +33 1 42 98 12 34; fax +33 1 42 98 11 42.
Barclays Bank SA: 21 rue Lafitte, 75009 Paris; tel +33 1 44 79 79 79; fax +33 1 44 79 72 52.
CCF: 103 avenue des Champs Elysées, 75008 Paris; tel +33 1 40 70 70 40; fax +33 1 47 23 71 04.
Crédit Agricole: 26 quai de la Rapée, 75596 Paris Cedex 12; tel +331 44 73 21 41.
Crédit Lyonnais: Secretariat Général (head office), Service Clientèle, 19 Bvd. des Italiens, 75002 Paris; tel +33 1 42 95 15 89; fax +33-42 95 65 48.
Lloyds Bank International: 15 avenue d'Iéna, 75783 Paris Cedex 16; tel +33 1 44 4342 32; fax +33 1 44 43 42 05.
Midland Bank: 20 Avenue Rapp, 75332 Paris Cedex 07; tel +33 1 44 42 70 00; fax +33 1 44 42 71 36.
Société Générale: 29 Blvd. Haussmann, 75009 Paris; tel +33 1 40 98 20 00.

Useful Address
Girobank plc: Midlands Region, Lyndon House, 62 Hagley Road, Birmingham, West Midlands, B16 8PE; tel 0121-454 9876.

Banking Glossary

English	French
annual Percentage Rate (APR)	*TEG*
annuity	*l'annuité*
automated banking lobby	*libre service bancaire*
automated teller machine (ATM)	*guichet automatique*
balance	*le solde*
bank code	*code banque*
bankers draft	*un chèque de banque*
bank identity record	*relevé d'identité bancaire (RIB)*
bank statement	*un relevé de compte/extrait*
beneficiary	*bénéficiaire*
bounced cheque	*un chèque sans provision*
branch	*agence/guichet*
branch code	*code guichet*
in cash	*en espèces*
bridging loan/finance	*crédit relais*
cash	*argent liquide*
cash dispenser	*Distributeur automatique des billets (Dab)*
cash withdrawal	*un retrait d'espèces*
cheque book	*un chèquier/carnet de chèques*
cheque	*un chèque*
cheque deposit	*remise de chèque*
coins/change	*la monnaie*
commission charged on receipt of an international currency transfer	*un commission de repatriement*
cash withdrawal	*retrait d'espèces*

credit your account	*approvisionner*
counter (bank counter)	*guichet*
current account	*compte de dépôts*
debit	*un débit*
deposit	*un dépôt*
to deposit money in an account	*déposer de l'argent*
deposit account (for savings with a passbook)	*compte sur livret*
direct debit	*un avis de prélèvement*
endorse (i.e. sign the back of a cheque)	*endosser*
exchange rate	*le taux de change*
expiry date	*date d'expiration*
foreign currency	*la devise*
fees	*les frais*
investment	*un placement*
insurance cover for accidental death (for a savings account)	*parrainage/compte parrainé*
joint current account	*compte de dépôt joint*
a mortgage	*crédit hypothécaire*
mutual fund	*société d'Investissement á capital variable (SICAV)/ fonds commun de placement (FCP)*
overdraft	*un découvert*
overdrawn account	*un compte débiteur*
overdraft charge	*agio*
personal loan	*un prêt personnel*
PIN number	*la code confidentiel*
power of attorney	*un procuration*
previous balance	*ancien solde*
profitability	*la rentabilité*
repayment schedule	*le tableau d'amortissement*
remittance	*remise*
secured loan	*un prêt garanti*
seizure of funds	*saisie attribution*
share	*l'action*
share in a cooperative	*un part sociale*
standing order	*ordre permanent/virement automatique*
to stop a cheque	*faire opposition*
transfer	*un virement*
valid	*valable*
value date when a transaction is actually credited/debited to/from an account	*jour de valeur*
tax	*l'impôt*
to withdraw money (from an account)	*retirer (de l'argent)*

Money

On January 1 1999 France will join EMU (European Monetary Union) and the euro (single European currency) will be introduced. The franc will exist alongside the euro but its value will be fixed to the euro. Overnight in 2002 the franc and other national currencies of countries participating in EMU will be replaced by euro notes and coins.

The franc is divided into 100 centimes. On credit/charge card slips and elsewhere when prices are printed or written, it is customary for a comma to be used to divide francs and centimes, not a decimal point as in the UK. Confusion is sometimes caused by the continuing reference, among certain groups, to the old franc. In the early 1960's the franc was devalued by a factor of 100 — thus 100 old francs became one new franc. However, it is occasionally referred to by the very old, and by those who consider it fashionable, to quote a price or value in old francs. This should be borne in mind and checked if a price seems much higher than expected!

Franc notes (*billets*) come in values of: 20, 50, 100, 200 and 500.

Coins (*monnaie*) come in values of: 1, 2, 5, 10 francs and 10, 20, 50 centimes. Some coins (e.g. the 10 francs) are also issued in different designs. Small change is sometimes referred to as *petite monnaie*.

Insurance and Hospitals

The Health Care System

In general the French hospital and health care system is very good, and standards equal those found in Germany and Switzerland. The system is a combination of private and public health care services: a national health care service is available but it functions in a totally different way to that in the UK. One cannot obtain free treatment in every hospital, and it is sometimes necessary to pay for treatment and to then claim back the cost from the authorities.

One point to bear in mind is that once Britons leave the UK they are no longer entitled to use the British NHS free of charge, unless they return to the UK permanently. Of course, treatment is available in the case of any accident suffered while on a visit here, but routine treatment cannot be claimed free of charge.

When visiting France, whilst still resident in the UK, most treatment can be obtained under the E111 and a reciprocal agreement. However, as with any journey abroad, it is a good idea to take out travel insurance which includes health benefits.

There are not a great many English-speaking doctors in France and although your local British Consulate will be able to direct you to a suitable doctor or hospital, obviously the majority of medical staff will speak French only.

Health Insurance Contributions

All French workers are required to contribute to the social security system (*séecurite sociale*). This applies both to the employed and self-employed. The contributions are calculated as a percentage (usually about 18%-20% of a managerial salary) of taxable income: employers must also pay a contribution towards their employees costs. A foreign individual must begin contributing once in possession of the *carte de séjour* , and register at the local sécurité sociale or health insurance office, *(caisse primaire d'assurance maladie)*. The address can be obtained from the local *mairie*. These contributions provide for a range of health and social security benefits for the contributor and his or her dependants.

Note that, foreigners who are non-residents, even though they are from elsewhere in the EU will only receive doctor/hospital treatment if they pay first and then apply for reimbursement. British expatriates working in France while continuing to pay UK national insurance contributions will be covered if they have applied for form E101 or E106 (depending on their length of stay). Maximum cover is for five years.

Those on business trips or short stays or visits who are not covered by an E111 will have to choose between returning to the UK for free treatment or paying up front to go to a French hospital. Charges would be in the region of £750 per day for an in-patient (non-serious) including treatment and drugs, accommodation and food and up to £2000 for more intensive treatment (e.g. serious heart operation requiring intensive care). Note that anyone requiring unexpected emergency treatment will still be treated without paying first.

Social security contributions are generally much lower in the UK than in France. In some cases by as much as 50%. During visits to the UK Britons can also continue to use the British National Health Service while living and working in France, provided that they are still registered with the DSS in Britain. However, this dispensation is only while they remain UK resident. Once they have become a French resident they will have to start paying French social security contributions in order to be able to use the French health service. Alternatively, they can take out private medical insurance.

Those who have retired to France and are entitled to a UK state pension should obtain form E121 from the DSS in Newcastle upon Tyne (see address below) before they leave the UK.

If you retire early without a state benefit you will not be covered by French social security. However, there is a concessionary period of up to two and a half years during which you can still receive UK National Health treatment, provided that your British National Insurance contributions are up to date and that you have obtained form E106 from the DSS in Newcastle upon Tyne before you leave the UK.

If a foreigner is living in France, temporarily or permanently, without working (but is not retired) then it may be possible to join sécurité sociale voluntarily. However, most people in this position prefer to take out private health insurance or at least travel insurance, as this is typically cheaper for short-term visitors and also provides better benefits.

The French National Health System
What Social Security Entitles You To

Payment into sécurité sociale entitles both you and your dependants to medical treatment, and other expenses, free of charge up to a statutory limit for each type of treatment. Often, sécurité sociale pays for only a percentage (usually 75%-90%) of the treatment and (40%-70% for medicines) and the patient must pay the remainder. Sécurité sociale will only pay the full cost of treatment for more serious illnesses and in specific hospital practices. Hospitals and general practices are basically allowed to charge what they like for their services. However, in each locality a group of doctors from certain hospitals and general practices agree to charge fees within the limits set by sécurité sociale. Therefore, if one uses the facilities which these hospitals and practices (known as *conventionné*) offer, treatment undertaken should not cost any more than is stipulated by the authorities. If you want to cheque the rates for *conventioné* treatments, you can do so on Minitel (3614 Infoprat). The alternatives to this are either to opt for totally private treatment, or to make up the difference between conventionné rates and whatever the hospital or practice which you have chosen charges. Private health treatment is extremely expensive and the vast majority of people choosing this option take private health insurance (see below) to pay for it. The facilities in conventionné hospitals tend to be basic but are generally considered good.

French Private Health Insurance

Thus, an element of personal contribution is involved between the cost of treatment, even in conventionné facilities, and the percentage (say 75%) that sécurité sociale pays. In certain cases this difference could amount to quite a lot of money and consequently most people take out an insurance policy specifically to cover this shortfall. The premiums involved are quite low and most industries, occupations and professions have special plans (*mutuelles*) which employees can join to cover this. Joining such plans can sometimes be a condition of employment, in other cases contributions are paid as part of the employment package.

The E111

In the initial moving period, or on holiday visits, or while on a speculative visit to France to look for work, one will probably not be covered by sécurité sociale, and in such cases, you can take out private travel insurance. However, it is also possible to obtain free, or mainly free, treatment under a reciprocal agreement which exists between some EU countries. To qualify for such treatment one must obtain form E111, (known as the E-one-eleven), available from the DSS Overseas Branch (Newcastle upon Tyne NE98 1YX; tel 0191-213 5000) or Department of Health and Social Services, Overseas Branch, Lindsay House, 8-14 Callender Street, Belfast BT1 5DP (for those living in Northern Ireland). Once in France, anyone who requires treatment should go to a conventionné doctor, dentist or hospital. Although they will probably have to pay for treatment, up to 75% of this can then be refunded, as long as the procedure detailed in the E111 is followed. However, you should note that as a percentage of the treatment costs are still not covered by the E111 is is still necessary to have travellers health insurance cover for the balance.

An E111 Normally expires after a three-month period and is not valid once one has left the UK permanently or is employed in France. It can sometimes be renewed and it is also possible to get an 'open ended' E111 if one is making frequent trips abroad for a longer period than three months. However, once a permit de séjour has been applied for (i.e. after three months in France) permanent arrangements should have been made. Explanatory leaflet SA29 gives details of social security, health care and pension rights within the EU and is obtainable from main post offices, doctors' surgeries, hospitals and also from the DSS Overseas Branches in Newcastle and Belfast. It may be of use to those intending to move to and work in France. Leaflet T4 gives general health advice to travellers, contains the application form for an E111 and gives a country by country breakdown of what treatment the E111 entitles you to.

Private Medical Insurance

Those who are going to France seeking work, or who spend a few weeks or months a year there, will require private medical insurance to cover the balance of the cost not covered by the E111 (see above). If you already hold private health insurance for the UK, you will find that most companies will switch this for European cover once you are in France. With the increase of British and foreign insurance companies offering this kind of cover, it is worth shopping around as cover and costs vary. One of the best known UK companies is BUPA International (Russell Mews, Brighton BN1 2NR; tel 01273-208181; fax 01273-866583; Website www.bupa.com/int). BUPA offers a range of schemes from insurance aimed at holders of the E111, to full-scale private patient plans (International Lifeline).

Another major UK insurer is Expacare Insurance Services (Dukes Court, Duke Street, Woking, Surrey GU21 5XB; tel 01483-717801). Expoacare's International Health Plan - Area 1, premium rates (Europe only) provides cost-effective health insurance for expatriates of all nationalities who are based in France; for details contact D. L. Pryor on 01483-717801.

Western Provident (01823-623565) also provide medical insurance for expatriates. The standard of healthcare in France is uniformly high, those who take out private patient's plans that allow for treatment in France should have no qualms and it may cut the waiting time which may otherwise be necessary for some treatments.

Using Doctors and Dentists

It is as well to line up a doctor/GP (*médecin généraliste*), dentist or optician who can be consulted if necessary, soon after arrival. You do not have to be registered with a particular doctor or practice and can visit any doctor in any part of the country as need dictates. Most people will obviously choose a doctor near where they live or work for convenience. Before making an appointment you should check the charges in advance of any medical or dental practitioner as if they are not *conventionné* (part of the French national health system), a very large contribution will have to be made. Most of these services will provide immediate treatment in the case of an emergency. Night and Sunday duty doctors can usually be contacted through the local police station (commissariat de police).

It is normal to pay the full costs of any consultation with a doctor or dentist immediately. A receipt, known as a *feuille de soins*, will be given for this. If any prescriptions (*ordonnances*) are purchased they will have a price stamp (*vignette*) attached which must be retained. Once the treatment is over sign and date the feuille, attach any vignettes, and send it to the Caisse Primaire d'Assurance Maladie, of which there are several in each département. In due course a refund of the appropriate percentage of the charges will be received — a minimum of 75% of the cost of treatment and 40%-70% of the cost of medicines. A refund cannot be obtained for medicines which are bought without a doctor's order.

Chemists: (Pharmacies). French doctors have a wonderful selection of remedies at their disposal and there is a tendency to prescribe elaborate pharmaceutical compositions, when an over-the-counter remedy would be just as beneficial. All medicines in France are expensive so you should ensure you are covered by a combination of the E111 and travel insurance, or by national or private health schemes, if you need prescriptions. When your local chemist is closed at a weekend, holiday etc. there will be a sign on the door, as in the UK, of the nearest duty chemist (*pharmacie de garde*). These are also usually given in the regional newspaper.

Using Hospitals

In an emergency, aid can be obtained from any hospital with casualty facilities. The emergency ambulance will select the closest. If less urgent treatment is needed then your doctor or specialist will refer you to an appropriate hospital: this might be a conventionné hospital, or a private one if such a preference has been indicated. Out-patient treatment is charged for and the cost must be recovered as for doctors and dentists.

In the case of in-patient treatment the system varies. Some hospitals are publicly-run and some are private clinics. They may charge the full cost and provide a certificate which can be used to reclaim a part of the charges as described above. Other hospitals may claim the sécurité sociale contribution direct from the Caisse Primaire, and just expect you to pay the balance (e.g. 25% for medical treatment). Note that treatment for serious illnesses is refunded at 100%. Some hospitals make a fixed daily hospital charge (*forfait journalier*) accommodation charge which sécurité sociale does not cover and this could be up to the equivalent of £90 to £120 per day.

Sometimes it is possible to agree in advance with social security that they will pay your expenses for an operation or treatment in a private clinic under a *prise en charge* if the amount is in excess of 600 francs. This amount is subject to constant revision more or less in line with inflation.

Ambulances: In France, unlike the UK there is no national ambulance service but each area has its own *Service d'Aide Médicale Urgence* (SAMU); national telephone number 15. Once you or the person assisting you dials this number the operator takes down the name, address and symptoms of the patient and connects the caller with the doctor on call (*docteur de permanence*). According to the demands of the situation, a doctor or ambulance team will be sent to administer first aid or transport to hospital. Charges are levied correspondingly.

Reclaiming Medical Fees

At the end of a course of treatment any expenses which have been paid out and which are recoverable under sécurité sociale need to be reclaimed. All the necessary documentation, receipts and vignettes required to do this will be provided by the hospital. Follow the procedure carefully and ensure you claim for everything that is covered in one application. Note that the time taken by the health insurance office to refund the money can vary from a few days to several weeks or months.

It is advisable to be privately insured for the portion of medical expenses that are not covered by sécurité sociale. These can then be reclaimed separately from the insurance company. Again, the doctor or hospital etc., will provide the necessary documentation. Under this arrangement, if extra insurance has been taken out, the medical treatment will cost nothing except perhaps a very small policy excess. The general rule to remember in France is that everyone is entitled to fairly good, cheap medical treatment under a reasonably effective national health service system. However, most people take additional steps to improve the level of care to which they are entitled and to gain further protection against costs involved.

Useful Addresses

Anglo-American Pharmacy: 6 rue de Castiglione, 1st Arrondissement, Paris; tel 01 42 60 72 96.

British and American Pharmacy: 1 rue Aubert, 75009 Paris. (fax 01-42 65 29 42; tel 01-47 42 49 40).

Pharmacie des Champs: 24-hour opening; 84, av des Champs-Elysées, 8th Arrondissement; tel 01 45 62 02 41.

Caisse Nationale d'Assurance Maladie des Professions Indepéndants (CANAM), Centre Paris Pleyel, 93521 Saint Denis Cedex; tel: 01 49 33 38 00. Advice on National Health insurance. Has 174 local *organismes conventionnés* and 31 regional offices (*caisses maladie régionales*).

Caisse Primaire d'Assurance-Maladie de Paris: Division des Relations Internationales, 173-175 rue de Bercy, 75586 Paris Cedex 12. (tel 01-40 19 55 23). Information and refunds.

DSS Overseas Branch: Tyneview Park, Benton, Newcastle Upon Tyne NE98 1YX (tel 0191-225 5251/225 5298).

American Hospital: 63, bld. Victor Hugo, Neuilly-sur-Seine, Paris; tel 01 46 41 25 25.

English Medical Centre: 8 bis rue Quinhault, 78100 St Germain-en-Laye: tel 01 30 61 25 61.

Hertford British Hospital: 3 rue Barbès, 92300 Levallois-Perret, Paris. (tel 01 46 39 22 22).

Hôpital Hôtel Dieu: 1 pl. Parvis, Notre Dame.

Health Insurance

BUPA, BUPA International, Russell Mews, Brighton BN1 2NR (tel 01273-208181; fax 01273-866583; Website www.bupa.com/int).

Expacare Insurance Services: Dukes Court, Duke Street, Woking, Surrey GU21 5XB; tel 01483-717801; fax 01483-776 620.

PPP Healthcare: Phillips House, Crescent Road, Tunbridge Wells, Kent TN1 2PL; tel 01892-508959.

Worldwide Health Insurance ASA Inc., USA; tel 1-602 968-0440.

Social Life

France is renowned for offering a rich and colourful ambiance. The general atmosphere of the country and temperament of the people, to say nothing of the favourable climate, will offer many opportunities for an interesting and rewarded social life.

Unfortunately, or fortunately, depending on one's view point, France is not a country which tends towards a highly-organized social life and although clubs and societies do exist they are not so widespread as in the UK. Much of the social life in France is based on, or starts with, a meal with friends, consequently one needs to make a definite effort to socialize and make friends within the local community. As there are rumoured to be more British people in the Dordogne than any other region of France, it is likely that you might be less inclined to make the effort to integrate with the French in that area with so many compatriots on hand to socialise with.

However, there seems to be little point in moving to France if you are going to be totally insular and socialise only with other British people.

The French

Although it is fair to say that it is not the custom of the French to offer an exuberant welcome to foreigners as is typical of say Americans, neither are they unfriendly and xenophobic as some commentators seem to want us to believe. Having said this, it is a commonplace observation that Paris has the reputation of being the coldest and most unwelcoming city in Europe for any foreigner. However, this is not true of the country as a whole and, certainly in rural areas, people are often very welcoming and helpful.

That the French are a nationalistic and proud race, however, is a generalisation difficult to refute and from time to time concern amongst the French that their patrimony is being sold off piecemeal to Britons and other foreigners manifests itself, chiefly through the strident declarations of the right wing nationalist (Le Pen's) party. Such campaigns fuel an attitude among nationals that all things French are best — true in some cases certainly, and should remain unsullied by foreign influence. This attitude can engender a lack of curiosity about other countries and cultures. It can also be turned to advantage, as those who show an interest in France will endear themselves to their French neighbours and colleagues and thus this is an effective way of getting to know people when new to the country. The reputed hostility between the French and British (specifically the English) is more often than not an amiable rivalry, although the French are said to be particularly jealous of the dominance of English over the elegance and romance of the French language.

The best course of action is to show an interest in and respect for France as a whole and the single most effective way of doing this is to learn the French language. However, always stand up for the principles of your own country because the French, probably more than any other nation, particularly respect patriotism.

Meeting People

The best and easiest way to meet people anywhere is through work. However, this may be more difficult in France than elsewhere because of the sharp dividing line which exists between work and home, business and pleasure: colleagues in France who have worked together for many years may never become anything more than acquaintances without a great deal of effort. If this is the case, then try to make the first approach, perhaps by inviting colleages home to meet the family or for a drink or meal: this is unlikely to offend and at worst would be considered some curious foreign practice. Senior business people almost always invite colleagues or contacts for a meal in a restaurant, rather than in their home, and the choice of the right place is crucial. A last piece of advice — when invited anywhere in France remember that, unlike in the UK, the words of Louix XIV, *l'exactitude est la politesse des rois* (punctuality is the politeness of kings) still hold true.

Other than through work, it can be difficult to make friends in the local community as the French do not tend to drop into a neighbour's home uninvited, or to invite them in to their own homes until a certain amount of intimacy has been established. Apart from in the smartest circles, French people can also feel that their homes are only open to family and well established friends (*les vrais amis*) which, to the British anyway, is an unfamiliar discrimination. However, locals are usually glad to introduce new arrivals to the local club or society and thus it may be helpful to develop a previously unrealised enthusiasm for archaeology, bridge, boules or architecture; as appropriate. Needless to say, amongst younger people there is much less formality generally.

Unlike schools and corner shops in the UK, the French equivalents seem to offer few opportunities for social contact and in towns and cities there is the usual impression that everybody is too busy to say more than 'hello'. One of the best ways of forming social contacts is to not be afraid to ask for help, or to offer it, to neighbours and people in the local area or at work: such attempts at integration will stand a much better chance of success if carried out in good French. Those who live in an apartment block should try to form an acquaintance with the caretaker (often a female or a couple). The copropriété regime which operates in many apartment blocks can also be a good means through which to meet people.

Churches may provide a way of meeting both locals and other expatriates. Although France is predominantly Catholic, a number of Protestant churches exist, including those in Paris, Lyon, Marseille, Nice, Strasbourg, Bordeaux, Biarritz, Toulouse, Cannes, Caen and Grenoble.

Finally, do not forget that you are not alone as an expatriate in France and it will inevitably be easier, at least initially, to make friends with expatriates of any nationality who are in a similar position to yourself. There are already many British people living and working in Paris and notable (although still rather small) British expatriate communities in the Côte d'Azur, Provence, Languedoc, Nord-Pas-de-Calais and Normandy.

Social Attitudes

Considering that France is a predominantly modern and forward-looking country, social attitudes can often be quite backward and in some ways old fashioned. After a lapse in the 1960's, the family unit is currently enjoying an increased popularity in France and family members are likely to keep in quite close touch although extended families are now largely a thing of the past. Despite this resurgence of family values, however, one fifth of French children are born to single-parent households.

France harbours all the social problems which exist in any developed country and, as elsewhere a tendency persists to ignore these problems until they flare up in a major incident. Perhaps the largest on-going social problem in France is immigration, arising from the large number of Arab and African immigrants from the former French colonies in North Africa. However new regulations have been introduced to make obtaining residency status more streamlined than in the past (see *Residence and Entry* chapter). The other major social problem is youth unemployment which the government elected in 1997 is trying to combat with new measures (see *Employment*).

The aristocracy, bourgeoisie and working classes still exist in France, although distinctions between the three are less tenable than ever before. In particular, traditional bourgeois values are now less repected and less prevalent than at any time in the past — with the exception only of the French Revolution.

About 32% of French women work and as a result a tendency exists for young women to want to keep their own identity and careers after marriage. The number of civil-law marriages taking place in France is declining whereas common-law marriage (*union librée*) is widespread. Living together before marriage is generally considered perfectly respectable with long-term relationships carrying equal social status with marriage.

When dealing with people socially it is usual, initially anyway, to adopt a formal manner, unless they indicate otherwise. First names are used sparingly, and anyone who begins an acquaintance on a first-name basis will probably be considered over-familiar and even rude, rather than friendly. French children are taught from a young age to shake hands with people on arrival and departure (as is customary for people of all age groups throughout Europe). Children will also commonly refer to adults as 'Monsieur', 'Madame' or 'Mademoiselle'. Neighbours may well always address you as one of the above, without it ever being considered unfriendly and you should do likewise. Similarly shopkeepers, restaurateurs, postmen/ women and anyone of your daily aquaintances should be addressed in a similar manner.

Entertainment and Culture

Perhaps the most popular entertainment, and one which is also considered as part of the country's culture, is eating — preferably at restaurants or bistros. Eating out, whether this constitutes little more than a snack and a drink or a considerable meal, is the basis of much French entertainment and social life. Every city, town and village has bars, cafés and restaurants in abundance, and standards are usually high and prices low in all but luxury establishments. Restaurants almost always reflect regional character and it is very important to learn (preferably through first-hand experience) which are the best ones in the area. Sunday is the main day for eating out and restaurant meals are very much a family affair.

The availablity of other night-time entertainment is as various as the regions of France. Of course, Paris is an acknowledged European centre for theatre, opera and ballet and is also where many world-famous art galleries and museums, are situated. However, there is often a considerable choice of all the above in other large cities and, unlike in the UK, even small towns and rural areas have their own theatres and music and arts festivals. French nightclubs and discos are fashionable but tend to cater for a more upmarket clientele than in the UK. Cinemas are widespread throughout Paris, which boasts approximately 200 of them, with foreign films being shown in their original language on the Champs Elysées and in the Left Bank area. French tastes in music are as diverse and as well catered for as in any other European country. Particularly popular in recent years have been bands and singers from Mali, slightly tempered by western influence.

Most regions of France have an extraordinarily rich patrimony a large part of which is completely unknown to most foreigners. Museums, ancient sites, historic houses, magnificent architecture and art galleries are to be found in profusion and are a good means of familiarizing oneself with the culture, language and people of France. In most areas great importance is placed on local traditions, such as festivals and carnivals. The most infamous national festival is 14 July, Bastille Day, when in Paris there is a three-day celebration involving firework displays, open-air balls and dancing through the city streets.

Sports and Pastimes

The French used not to be renowned for being a great sporting nation , either as participants or spectators. However, the importance attributed to sport internationally and its general popularity, have more than quadrupled the number of regular practitioners of all kinds of sports in the last 25 years. This trend is reflected in the increase in the number of sports clubs and facilities to be found throughout France.

Watersports and skiing remain the most popular participant sports and this is hardly surprising when one considers the ideal climate and natural facilities offered in large parts of the country for just these activities. Swimming and waterskiing retain their popularity, while sailing and windsurfing are the current manias: fresh water and deep-sea fishing are also favoured. Ski resorts, scattered throughout the Alps and the Pyrenees, are frequented by millions of French people each year. For the French, skiing is not an elitist sport and although some alpine resorts like Courchevel, Les Arcs and Megève have a reputation for being chic and expensive. There is also cross-country skiing in the Vosges and the Massif Central, particularly the latter. Skiing in France is obviously cheaper for the French as no international travel is required and it is now common for all types of people to take a skiing holiday each winter and many Parisians drive regularly to the Alps for skiing weekends.

Other popular sports include football, rugby (especially in south-west France) tennis and of course cycling whose main event the Tour de France is internationally famous. Golf still continues to be popular but exclusive in France, and is largely practised in private clubs. Cricket is also played at 38 clubs among 800 players, 200 of them French (and rumoured to be better bowlers than batters). Traditional blood sports, such as hunting (with deer and wild boar, not foxes, as quarry), shooting and fishing retain their popularity in France, as do other traditional, but less aggressive pastimes, such as French bowls (*pétanque*), chess and bridge.

The sports facilities which do exist in France are generally excellent and even the most modest town now has a public swimming pool (*piscine*).

Apart from approved sports facilities in towns, successive recent governments promoted *colonies de vacances* where children from less well-off families who cannot afford to go on a family holiday can at least send the children away for a subsidised holiday run by qualified *moniteurs*. It is estimated that such colonies provide holidays for a million children a year.

There is also a considerable French following for rambling and hiking, which has rocketed in less than ten years from being one of France's least popular sporting activities to one of the most popular. The Poitiers region alone has about 30 official clubs for the sport. The governing organisation is the Fédération Française de la Randonnée Pédestre based in Paris. France's main hiking paths are called Grandes Randonnées (GRs) and these include GR20 which winds through the Corsican mountains and Gr58 in the Queyras (in the south-east) and the the GR65 pilgrim route to Santiago di Compostela, and the GR10 in the eastern Pyrenees. There are also day-circuit routes (GR de Pays) which are marked with red and yellow painted slashes. Around towns and villages are the shorter promenades (PRs) with yellow signposts. One of the results of this explosion of ramblers in France is an adverse reaction amongst landowners who have taken to blocking off some routes to keep the hordes out. Overall French official paths seem to be a lot less crowded than the most popular British ones.

Information on all sports is available either from tourist offices, or the Ministry of Youth and Sports (Ministérere de la Jeunesse et des Sports, Direction des Sports, 78 rue Olivier de Serres, 75739 Paris Cedex 15; tel 1-40 45 90 00.) Information on all aspects of sports for young people can also be obtained from the Bureau de la Communication du Ministére on 1-40 45 92 07.

Holidays

The French way of life is not to work 9am to 5pm, Monday to Friday and then to relax in the evenings and at weekends. Instead, the idea of taking 'le weekend' is fairly new to France. The French usually work from 8am to 6pm, with a long, two-hour lunch break, all year round with one long break in the summer. All employees are entitled to five weeks annual holiday and it is usual to take three or four weeks in July or August and then one week at Christmas and/or Easter. As a result, many firms and small businesses close completely for a month in summer. Paris and its suburbs are almost deserted by the Parisians in August. The vacuum in the capital is filled by foreign tourists, while French holiday resorts and the roads to them solidify with the French *en vacances.*

Although this arrangement seems bizarre and lemming-like to the British worker used to two weeks away in the summer and lots of long weekends, to the French it is a very civilised habit which recognises the importance of the quality of life. Most older holiday makers stay within France, usually in the south (although the Atlantic coast and Brittany are also popular) while the more intrepid investigate neighbouring countries on motoring holidays, and an even smaller number fly off to their holiday homes in Corsica, northern Italy, and the Spanish islands. Obviously there are other, more adventurous travellers, but these tend to be younger. Usually armed with the relevant Guide du Routard (a kind of French equivalent of the Rough Guides), they are generally worse linguists than their British counterparts and even if they know another language, are unenthusiastic about demonstrating it. This may explain why some of their favoured destinations are those where French may be understood: the Mahgrebian countries of north Africa, former French West Africa and increasingly, Vietnam.

A staggering one in six French households owns or has access to a second home (*une résidence secondaire*) in France — a greater proportion than any other country in the world. These flats or houses are mostly situated in seaside resorts, mountain regions or in rural countryside; they are used as holiday homes, for long weekends and frequently intended as retirement homes for the largely urban population of France whose romance with the rural idyll is at least as strong as that of the British. Owning a secondary residence has come to constitute what amounts to a French national characteristic, and is not restricted only to the affluent. Camping vans and caravans account for 9% of secondary residences in France which is an indication of the strength of the urge to get back to nature which in France manifests itself through numerous caravan parks and campsites.

Schools and Education

Education in France

The French education system is still regarded as one of the most thorough in the world but there have been some complaints about its rigour in recent years, though from pupils, rather than from parents or employers. However, the system continues to produce highly literate and numerate pupils and good academic results. Despite the country's rich culture, French schools place particular emphasis on the sciences, which accounts for the country's leading position in many scientific and technical industries.

French education is highly centralised with a national curriculum that ensures national uniformity. At one time school timetables were identical in every school in every part of the country. Now, however, the regions have a limited amount of autonomy in this respect. The system is almost entirely based on state schools (*l'écoles publiques*), not to be confused with British-style public schools. Less common are the private schools (*l'écoles privée*) which are often religiously based: although fee-paying, most of these are also, in part, state or church subsidised.

State financial assistance can be direct, in the form of allowances given at the beginning of the school year for six to sixteen-year-olds on the basis of family income. Transport support is also provided. Sometimes, municipalities award scholarships to support pupils in their studies.

Education in France is compulsory, by law, from six to sixteen, and is free, except for universities which charge fees. Parents may be expected to pay for books and materials which can amount to £200 + per pupil per year, although generally, such costs are borne by the municipality (for primary schools) and by the *conseils généraux* (county councils) for *colléges*. Although some schools work from Monday to Friday, the traditional French system of having Wednesday afternoon free is still prevalent.

Much emphasis is placed on a pupil's own determination and commitment, with little encouragement, as such, from teaching staff, many of whom lecture rather than teach. The recent education act (see below) makes allowance for sports as part of the secondary education curriculum and has also abolished the separation of children into academic and vocational streams at the end of the fifth grade. Instead children either move up to the fourth grade, or repeat the fifth. Another innovation of the Act is to encourage all children to study at least two modern languages in the fourth and third grades.

The main difference between the English and French approaches to education is acknowledged to be that while English education focuses on bringing out the individual, the French system concentrates on training the mind. Another difference is the time spent in French schools on written French compared with English in English schools. In France, grammar and sentence construction are closely scrutinised. Thus it is that in France that, generally speaking, all manner of people can argue clearly and articulately. There is no doubt about it, the approach in France is more intellectual.

Under EU regulations, any EU citizen must be treated in the same way as national citizens in having access to French education if they so wish.

The school year normally starts at the beginning of September and lasts for 36 weeks.

1989 Education Act

The changes brought about by the education act were not major but they represented a shift of emphasis by redefining education into *cycles pédagogiques* and setting target attainment levels for each cycle, rather than for the end of each year of schooling. Thus nursery school is included in the *cycle d'apprentissages* (introduction to basics) for 5-8 year-olds which also includes the first two years of primary school. The next cycle is the *cycle de consolidation* (8-11 years) then *cycle d'observation* (11-13 years), *cycle d'orientation* (13-15 years) and finally *cycle de determination*.

Under the 1989 Education Act French school term dates are fixed three years ahead based on the new theories for the optimum periods for work and rest that were deemed to be most pedagogically effective. It was decided that the 36 weeks of the school year should be divided into five terms of seven weeks for the first four and eight or nine for the last one.

The Structure of Education

Although not compulsory, nursery schooling (*l'école maternelle*) for two to six year olds is free and widely used. Under the 1989 Education Act a place at nursery school must be available for any three-year-old whose family wishes it, in a school as near as possible to their home. There is also pre-nursery school (*jardins d'enfants*) for two and three-year-olds.

Compulsory primary education (*l'école primaire/école élémentaire*) begins at six. Under the French class-grading system pupils begin in the eleventh grade and work upwards to the first. Grades eleven to seven comprise the primary stages. These are followed by the next stage, secondary education (*collège*) which begins at the age of eleven and lasts until age 15. There are different stages of secondary school: the collège d'enseignement secondaire (CES), and then *lycée* or technical school (*le lycée technique*) from the age of fifteen. A lycée corresponds roughly to a grammar school while a CES is more like a comprehensive. A leaflet, *Primary and Secondary Education in France* available from the French Embassy (Information Service) in London (0171-235 8080) explains the education system in detail.

In the third grade, depending on their aptitudes and the advice of teachers in consultation with their parents, students will either embark on studies leading to the baccalauréat (see below), or take technical or vocational options leading to various qualifications: *Brevet de Technicien (BT), Brevet d'Etudes Professionelles (BEP)* or *Certificat d'Aptitude Professionnelle (CAP)*. A leaflet called *After The Third Class* is obtainable through the Office National d'Information sur les Enseignements et les Professions (ONISEP).

The first grade is the last year of compulsory education. Around 75% of pupils stay on after the first grade in *la classe terminale*. Most of the terminale prepare for the baccalaureat examination taken at the ages of eighteen or nineteen. The *bac* is a highly competitive exam and only around 50% currently pass, but as it is essential for entry into many professions and university it is extremely sought after. Students can choose the emphasis of the bac from several options including literature, mathematics and sciences but within each of these categories all the subjects are compulsory. The different types of baccalaureate are rated in importance: baccalaureate 'A' which is arts-based is ranked lowest, while the science-based baccalaureate 'C' is considered the most prestigious. Those who have passed the baccalaureat are known as *bacheliers*.

Further Education

As in the UK the number of young French people entering further education is rising, though for years the percentage starting university courses was around 30%, much higher than in the UK where the percentage was about 19% at a similar period. The result of such a high rate of entrants is that the university system is overstretched. In the UK, students try to go to the best centre for their chosen discipline, or failing that, to wherever they can get in with their 'A' level results, regardless of location or preferences, whereas in France it remains usual to go to the nearest university. This is not by any means obligatory, and indeed it is perfectly possible for someone from Montpellier to study in Paris, but it is not encouraged — for instance cheap university accommodation is not so readily provided as in the UK. In order to cope with an increasing number of students the French government has been expanding the number of places available, in some cases even renting space to do this. There are around one hundred existing institutes of higher education and among them over seventy traditional universities. Largely due to the rapid expansion of higher education, Many French universities do not enjoy quite the same reputation as the rest of the education system: for example they are not as well respected as those in the UK. Of the top ten French Universities, five are in Paris, and the number one is the *Université Paris-Dauphine* (a.k.a. Paris 1X), which has close links with industry and commerce and specialises in economics and business studies. No such patchy reputation exists for the grandes écoles which are regarded as the source of industrial and commercial grey matter by France's employers. The écoles have their own entrance examinations on top of the bac; one, the ENA, takes only graduates. The grandes écoles generally offer three-year courses in a variety of subjects and their emphasis on applied or vocational aspects. Almost all France's engineering and business education and much of the scientific education and education for the elite in public service has traditionally been the preserve of the écoles. The universities on the other hand offer much more academic courses and some major vocational education particularly in law, computer science and all medical studies.

Unlike the UK, France has no central clearing system for allocating university places and applicants must apply to individual universities in person. In Paris, infamous queues, reminiscent of the first day of Harrods' sale, usually form outside the universities as soon as the bac results are known. In order to alleviate this unseemly scramble for further education (to which every bachelier is automatically entitled) application for places at Paris universities through the Minitel system was tried out in 1990.

The Structure of Higher Education Courses

The systems of the grandes écoles and the universities are very different. The écoles award *diplômes* which takes three years (five, if you include the two years intensive preparation for the entrance exam).

University studies are divided into cycles. The third cycle is for postgraduate studies. Various diplomas and degrees are awarded by universities and these are known familiarly by their acronyms: DEUG, DEUT, DESS etc. The more recognizable ones are: *la licence, la maitresse* and *le doctorat* which correspond to the BA, MA, and PhD. A distinguished additional qualification, the *Habilation à Diriger des Recherches*, authorizes the holder to direct the studies of research students and is awarded at professorial level.

After two years a university student is awarded either a DEUG (*Diplôme d'Etudes Universitaires Générales*) or a DEUST (*Diplôme d'Etudes Universitaires Scientifiques et Techniques*. The DEUST is more vocationally oriented and includes a compulsory *stage* (practical experience training).

The DEUG or DEUST gives entry to the second cycle of study which also lasts two years. At the end of the first year a *Licence* is gained and the fourth and final year leads to the *Maîtrise*. For some technical subjects only a *Maîtrise de Sciences et Techniques* (MST) is awarded. Other specialised *mai[cii]trises* are: *maîtrises de sciences de gestion* (MSG), or a *maîtrises de méthodes informatiques appliquées à la gestion* (MIAGE). There is also a second cycle university qualification, *magistère*, for a period of study in a vocational subject. It includes a *stage* in industry and is at a slightly higher level than a *maîtrise*, although there is considerable drop out at earlier stages.

Qualification levels are often expressed as *Bac* + x (i.e. the number of years of study). The majority of graduates will be *Bac* + 4 which is roughly the same as a *diplôme* from a *grande école*.

In addition to the *diplôme* or various university qualifications, many graduates are now taking additional qualifications at technician level in an effort to combat graduate unemployment. These qualifications can be obtained at *Instituts Universitaires de Technologie* (IUTs) and also be taken on a part-time study basis at other institutions. The qualifications include: *Brevet de Technicien Supérieur* (BTS) and *Diplôme Universitaire de Technologie* (DUT). At *Instituts Universitaires Professionnalisés* (IUPs) the technical qualifications are a *diplôme d'études universitaires professionnalisées* and a *mâtrise* awarded at the end of the first and second years of study respectively. Both IUTs and IUPs are technically part of the university system, but they offer very specialised qualifications.

Postgraduate Study

There are various levels of postgraduate studies at the universities. One year of study leads to either a *Diplôme d'Etudes Approfondies* (DEA) or the *Diplôme d'Etudes Supérieures Spécialisées* (DESS). Generally speaking the DEA is regarded as preparation for a doctorate for which thesis preparation is normally one or two years. The DESS is thought of more as a vocational qualification complete in itself. The doctoral system in France has been overhauled and there is now only a single *doctorat* which has replaced the *doctorat du troisieme cycle* and the *Doctorat d'Etat* which were for advanced academic research. In theory, a doctoral student can drag out their higher education for *Bac* + 9, because for a doctorate he or she needs a DEA and then an additional two to four years of study. At doctoral level, much of the research done in French universities is supported by the *Centre National de la Recherche Scientifique* (CNRS). The CNRS publishes a series of *Annuaires* with details of its activities and a *Répertoire des Unités de Recherche du CNRS* which lists the main centres of research.

Continuing/Adult Education

France has no equivalent of the Open University of the UK. However, any Briton can study with the Open University while being based in France. Nonetheless, France is very keen on continuing education (*education permanente*) and there are various schemes for encouraging those in employment and others to keep learning for further study and qualifications. There are also studies aimed at retired people. Universities are very active in this area, and so enquiries at your local university in France are a good place to start.

MBA Courses

There are a number of MBA courses and business schools in France that attract French and foreign students. Perhaps the best known is INSEAD, a pure business school, based at Fontainebleau. In addition, five of the Grands Ecoles offer two year MBA courses:
L'Ecole des Hautes Etudes Commerciales (HEC)
L'Ecole Supérieure des Sciences Economiques et Commerciales (ESSEC)
L'Ecole Supérieure de Commerce de Paris (ESCP)
L'Ecole Supérieure de Commerce de Lyon (ESCL)
Le Centre d'Enseignement et de Recherche Appliqués en Management de Nice (CERAM)
In addition the *Ecole des Affaires de Paris* (EAP), also called the European School of Management, has a European Masters in Management programme which includes one year in France and a year each in two of its overseas branches in Germany, the UK and Spain. Also, the Institut Supérieur des Affaires (ISA), HEC School of Management, 1 rue de la Liberation, 78351 Jouy-en-Josas, Paris; tel +33 1 39 67 73 82 and Groupe ESC Lyon, 23 ave Guy de Collongue , 69132 Ecully Cedex which has close links with the Cranfield School of Management in Bedfordshire.

The Grandes Ecoles

Many French students planning their future careers dream of entry into the grandes écoles which which occupy much the same place in the higher education system of France as the ancient universities of Oxford and Cambridge do in Britain or the 'Ivy League' universities in the United States, i.e. they represent the highest academic achievement. Most of the dozen or so top establishments which merit the term, grandes écoles, were founded in the 19th century to train academic elites in the new technical and scientific subjects and to provide top calibre staff for the military, civil service, business, education and research cadres of France. The majority of grandes écoles are controlled by the ministry to which their speciality is linked, which means, in effect, that they are outside the university system.

Some of the best known grandes écoles are in Paris: the Ecole Polytechnique is one of the oldest having been founded in 1794 to teach engineering; it later changed to military engineering under Napoleon. To this day it remains closely linked with the military: its director is a general and students wear military uniform on important occasions. Although graduates are awarded a *Diplome d'Ingénieur* and the rank of second lieutenant, many resign their commissions on graduation and head for the fleshpots of industry and commerce. Ex-Polytechnicians are known as *Anciens X.*

Founded about the same time as the Ecole Polytechnique and equally famous is the Ecole Normale Supérieure, originally founded to train lycée teachers for the whole of France. Its students are divided into *scientifiques* and *littéraires.* Nowadays it also produces top researchers as well as its fair share of notables: public figures including President Pompidou and Sartre have been amongst its graduates.

Probably just as famous as the above is the Ecole Nationale d'Administration (ENA), founded in 1945 by de Gaulle as a training establishment for top civil servants (*hauts fonctionnaires*). Unlike other grandes écoles only graduates are accepted. From the ENA they pass into the highest echelons of state administration, the Grands Corps d'Etat, including the French equivalent of the Treasury, Inspection Générale des Finances. Posts are also allocated in the diplomatic and other administrative careers including the prefectoral system. Past alumni (known as *énarques*) include five of the last seven prime ministers, former Presidents Giscard d'Estaing and Jacques Chirac, , Elizabeth Guigou, Minister for European affairs under Mitterand, Michel Rocard, Laurent Fabius, and over 200 German civil servants.

Other grandes écoles include *écoles vétérinaires, écoles de commerce,* five *écoles des mines* (formerly for mining, nowadays for general engineering). There also exist grandes écoles for the sciences and humanities.

Entrance to the Grandes Écoles

Apart from the ENA, prospective entrants for the grandes écoles should have the baccalaureat, preferable with distinction (*mention*), after which they are required to complete a rigorous preparatory course (*classe préparatoire aux grandes écoles or CPGE*) lasting two to three years at the end of which they sit a fiercely competitive examination (*concours*). About 50% of candidates drop out at the preparatory stage and an even greater percentage are weeded out by the entrance examinations. With such high standards it is hardly surprising that the reputation for excellence in the grandes écoles persists. There are rumblings of criticism against such elitism which, it is said, confers life membership of an exclusive club on the already privileged (i.e. those from professional and higher cadres backgrounds). In 1976 it was estimated that 1% of entrants to the grandes écoles were from a blue-collar background (compared with 12% at French universities generally).

Primary & Secondary Education

The *Mairie* in each municipality is responsible for registering pupils in primary and nursery schools. It can also provide parents with the addresses of the regional and district education offices which carry all the necessary information on entry to secondary education (first and second cycle). For information on pre-university education, parents should make the town hall of their municipality their first stop.

Foreigners in French Higher Education

About 100,000 foreigners (approximately 13% of the total intake) enrol for higher education (*l'enseignement supèrieure*) in France annually. Applicants from the UK must have 'A' Levels which are officially recognized as the equivalent of the baccalaureate. Anyone with resident status applying from within France will follow the same system as the French. Applications for the UK can be made by obtaining an admission request (*une demande d'admission*) from the cultural section of the French Embassy in London. The same department will also supply detailed information on further education in France, including French government scholarships to study in France.

Applicants will also require a thorough knowledge of the French language. Special preparatory courses are available both in the UK and in France and a language test is obligatory before the start of the academic year. Further details are obtainable from the French Embassy (see above).

French student identity cards are obtainable from the Centre Regional des Oeuvres Universitaires et Scolaires (CROUS) of which there is one in every university town. The CROUS at 8, rue Jean Clavin has a special bureau, the Service de l'Action Sociale, to deal with students' problems.

Student Programmes of the European Union

The SOCRATES-ERASMUS Scheme: The EU inspired ERASMUS (European Action Scheme for the Mobility of University Students) was started in 1987 and enables students from one EU country to study at a university in another EU country for up to one year on a bursary awarded by the EU. The scheme is administered from Brussels at the Erasmus Bureau (70 rue de Montoyer, 1040 Brussels, Belgium; tel 02 233 01 11; fax 02 233 01 50). The deadline for applications is 31st October in the year preceeding the proposed academic year of study. Applicants from the UK can contact the UK Socrates-Erasmus Council (c/o Students Grants Council, The University, Canterbury CT3 7PD; tel 01227-762712; fax 01227-762711).

Leonardo da Vinci: (Leonardo Technical Assistance Office, 9 ave de l'Astronomie, 1030 Brussels, Belgium; tel +32 2 2227 0100; fax +32 2 227 0101). Provides for university students and recent graduates to undertake periods of industrial training with companies in other states. The maximum duration is 12 months. The scheme does not supply bursaries, so it is up to individual employers to decide. However the scheme will subsidise language tuition and day-to-day subsistence (food and travel allowance).

Lingua Action C: like ERASMUS, this is part of the Socrates programme and involves the appointment of prospective teachers as language assistants in other member states. Further information from the Central Bureau for Educational Visits and Exchanges in London (tel 0171-389 4004; fax 0171-389 4426).

Useful Publications for Students

Higher Education in the European Community — A Student Handbook: (£14.95 European Commission). Obtainable from bookshops or libraries. Contains information on courses on offer and entry qualifications, scholarships, insurance, costs and advice for disabled students.

The European Choice — a Guide to Opportunities in Europe: published by the Department for Education (Sanctuary Buildings, Great Smith Street, London SW1P 3BT; tel 0171-925 5000). Gives details of all the various EU schemes to promote student mobility and also information about financial support.

Useful Addresses

If coming from outside France, with qualifications from another country these can be checked with a branch of NARIC; and the following organisations can also assist.

NARIC Bureau: Bureau de l'Evaluation, de l'Information et des Comparaisons Internationales (DAGIC 7), 110 rue de Grenelle, 75007 Paris.

Mastères Spécialisés (available in French only) from the Conférence des Grandes Ecoles, 60 Blvd Saint-Michel, 75272 Paris.

NARIC (Network of National Academic Recognition Information Centres):Minis-tère de l'Enseignement Supérieur et de la Recherche, Direction Générale des Enseignements Supérieurs, Service des Formations, Bureau de l'Orientation et de l'Insertion professionnelle des étudiants: 61-65 rue Dutot 75732 Paris Cedex; tel +33 1 40 65 66 19. Publishes the brochure *Organisation générale de l'Enseignement Supérieur en France* (available in English).

Bureau de l'Information sur les systèmes éducatifs et de la reconnaisance des diplômes — DRIC A2: (enseignement du secteur scolaire) 110 rue de Grenelle, 75007 Paris; tel +33 1 40 65 65 90.

French Embassy Cultural Dept: 23 Cromwell Road, London SW7 2EL; tel 0171 838 2055; fax 0171-838 2088.

French Institute: 17 Queensberry Place, London, SW7 2DT; tel 0171 838 2148; tel 0171 838 2145.

European Business School: 27 Blvd Ney, 75018 Paris.

The European School of Management (EAP): 6 Ave de la Porte de Champerret, 75838 Paris, Cedex 17.

INSEAD: Blvd de Constance, 77305 Fontainebleau.

Central Admissions Office for the five MBA schools is at: HEC, 1 rue de la Libération, 78351 Jouy-en-Josas.

French Schools

Foreign residents' children living in France will have three main schooling options: to attend boarding school in their native country, to take up the exciting opportunity to go to a French state or private school, or to go to an international school in France.

It is perfectly possible for British expatriates to send their offspring to French state schools although their decision to do so may depend on the stage of education reached and whether or not a complete change of system and coping with lessons in a foreign language, would constitute more of a disruption than a benefit. Whilst all parties concerned would need to discuss carefully the ramifications of, for instance, learning about *nos ancêtres les Gaules* (our ancestors the Gauls) rather than about, our ancestors the Anglo-Saxons etc, it is probably true to say that younger children will be the most easy to integrate into the French system as they have the least difficulty in becoming bilingual. Older children already embarked on a UK examination course may well be unsure of how they would manage in a French school. One possible way of finding out would be by spending an academic year at one such school, and providing the children are at least fifteen this can be arranged through an international education programme such as that run by Intercultural Education Programmes (IEP). The other possible problem that school students may have to consider is that if their parents return to the UK they may have to switch back into the UK system. Since there is as yet no system of equivalents in the EU, except at final year level this contingency would need careful consideration. One possibility is to find a school in the UK that teaches the international baccalaureat that can be followed in other countries including France, where it is taught. Please note that it is not the same as the French bac.

Those who decide to send their children to state school in France will be obliged to send them to the one designated for their area. The local *services des écoles* (schools information service) in the town hall (*mairie*) can supply a list of local schools at all levels. Information and advice about the French schooling system can be obtained in the UK from the Parents' Association (APEL) of the Lycée Française in London. However, as an initial source of information the French Embassy in London produce free explanatory leaflets on the French education system.

Alternatively those who are interested in private schools will find both day and boarding schools exist. If you are able to afford private schooling, one of the advantages is likely to be smaller classes which would probably prove a less intimidating environment than large state school classes, especially for pupils who are hesitant in French. Supplementary lessons in the French language could be arranged until fluency has been established.

Another way of gaining a standard of fluency necessary to attend a French school is for children to attend a language course, preferably in the long summer holidays before term begins. British language course consultancies, such as Cultural and Education Services Abroad (CESA) offer advice on such matters free of charge, and will make all the arrangements once a suitable course has been located.

Counselling and information on French private schools is obtainable from the Centre National de l'Enseignement Privé, the Service d'Information des Familles and the Centre National de Documentation sur l'Enseignement Privé.

International schools which cater specifically for the international community are based mainly in or near Paris (also Cannes, Lille, Lyon and Nice — see below) which means that you would have to live within easy reach to make this option practicable. The American schools follow the US curriculum but with some emphasis on French language and culture. Such schools include: the American School of Paris, the International School of Paris and the Marymount International School, all of which are English-speaking.

Alternatively, there are a number of bilingual schools, including the Lycée International de St. Germain en Laye, and the International School of Paris. The former follows the National French curriculum but also provides courses in the history and culture of other countries in the language of that country, which can be incorporated into the international baccalaureate; the US curriculum is also offered. The latter has particular expertise in the international baccalaureate.

The only school in France to offer the UK curriculum is the British School of Paris which takes pupils from four to eighteen years and caters fir English-speaking children of over 30 nationalities. It is a non-profit association of France and is managed by a board of governors under His Excellency the British Ambassador. The British School is located on two different sites in the western suburbs of Paris. The Junior School at Bougival, uses a mixture of new and traditional methods based on the National Curriculum with emphasis on instruction in the French language. Both music and drama, together with varied sports and extra-curricular activities are available. Computer instruction is also given to the Upper Juniors. All staff are involved in providing pastoral care and arranging extra-curricular activities.

International schools can also be found elsewhere in France: the Bordeaux International School started in 1988 and provides a British-style international education for ages four to nineteen and intensive language courses for teenagers and adults. There is also the International School of Sophia Antipolis near Nice which specialises in International and French baccalaureate education and also the English-speaking European School at Mougins (Cannes).

Places in bi-lingual and international schools tend to be much in demand and entrance requirements stiff, so plans need to be made well in advance.

Which course of action you take will very much depend on circumstances. Take advice from the schools and advisory bodies involved. Most children embarked on UK GCSE and 'A' Level examination courses may be best left undisturbed. Younger children may be able to pick up sufficient French depending on their ability. It is generally accepted that toddlers who have not yet mastered English can probably learn enough French, if they are immersed in it, to start in the French system at nursery school so that by the age of six they can compete perfectly well with French children at primary school. Those foreign residents whose children have been through the French education system are more than satisfied with the pedagogical standards. It is alas still true that French schoolchildren have a wider range of knowledge because they study more subjects at a higher level than their English and Welsh counterparts who are forced to specialise so early. This probably accounts for the general French perception that the English are badly-educated and ignorant.

International Schools in Paris

American School of Paris: 41 rue Pasteur, 92210 St Cloud; tel (01) 41 12 82 82; fax 01 46 02 23 90. US curriculum and international bac. English.

British School of Paris: 38 quai de l'Ecluse, 78290 Croissy-sur-Seine (tel 01 34 80 45 90; fax 01 39 76 12 69 senior school; tel 01 39 69 78 21 junior school). UK curriculum. English.

College International de Fontainbleau: (Anglophone section), 48 rue Guerin, 77300 Fontainbleau; tel 1 64 22 11 77; fax 1 64 23 43 17.

Ecole Active Bilingue: 52, Avenue Victor Hugo, 75008 Paris; tel 1 45 00 11 57. British/American/French curricula. French and English.

Ecole Active Bilingue Jeannine Manuel: 70 rue du Théâtre, 75015 Paris; tel 1 45 75 62 98; fax 1 45 79 06 66. French national curriculum and international bac.

Eurécole: 5 rue de Lübeck, 75116 Paris; tel 1 40 70 12 81; 1 40 70 91 07. National and International curricula. French, English, German, Spanish.

The International School of Paris: 6 rue Beethoven, 75016 Paris; tel 1 42 24 09 54; 1 45 27 15 93. UK & US curricula and international bac. English.

Lycée International de St Germain en Laye: Boite Postale 230, 78100 St Germain en Laye; tel 1 34 51 74 85; fax 1 30 87 00 49. US and French National curriculum and optional international bac.

Lycée Marcel Roby, American Section: 6 rue Giraud Teulon, 78100 St. Germain en Laye, Paris; tel 1 34 51 00 96; fax 1 34 51 95 70. US and French curricula. French bac (international optional). French and English.

Marymount International: 72 boulevard de la Saussaye, Neuilly-sur- Seine 92200; tel 1 46 24 10 51; fax 1 46 37 07 50. US curriculum. English.

United Nations Nursery School: 40 rue Pierre Guérin, 75016 Paris; tel (1) 45 27 20 24. US and national curriculum. English.

Outside Paris:
American International School on the Côte d'Azur: 15 rue Claude Debussy, 06200 Nice; tel 493 21 04 00; fax 493 21 69 11. US and UK curricula and international Baccalaureate. Instruction in English.

Bordeaux International School: 53 rue de Laseppe, 33000 Bordeaux; tel 556 44 27 95; fax 556 79 00 47; US and UK curricula. English and French.

Cité Scolaire Internationale de Lyon: (Section Anglophone) 22 ave Tony Garnier, 69361 Lyon, Cedex 07; tel 478 69 60 06; fax 478 69 60 37. UK and UK curricula. English and French.

CIV International School of Sophia Antipolis (Nice): B.P. 097, 06902 Sophia Antipolis Cedex; tel 492 96 52 24; fax 493 65 22 15. International bac, French national curriculum. English and French.

College Lycée Cevenol International: Chambon-sur-Lignon, 43400 St. Etienne; tel 471 59 72 52; fax 471 65 87 38. French national curriculum, international bac and national curriculum with international option. French and English.

College et Lycée de Sèvres: International Sections, rue Lecocq, Sèvres 92310; tel 1 45 34 30 06; fax 1 45 34 76 63. English, French and German.

L'Ecole des Roches: 27130 Verneuil sur Avre; tel 232 23 40 00; fax 233 32 23 40 48.

Mougins School: (Cannes) 615 Av Dr Maurice Donat, Font de l'Orme, B.P. 101, 06250 Mougins Cedex. tel 493 90 15 47; fax 493 75 31 40. UK and US curricula. English.

Strasbourg International School: Chateau de Portalës, 161 rue Mèlanie, 67000 Strasbourg; tel 388 31 50 77.

Information about Education
APEL, Lycée Française: 35 Cromwell Road, London SW7 (tel 0171-584 6322).

Centre d'Information et de Documentation Jeunesse (CIDJ): 101 Quai Branly, 75740 Paris Cedex 15; tel 1 45 66 40 20.

Centre National de Documentation sur l'Enseignement Privé: 20 rue Fabest, 75007 Paris (tel 1-47 05 32 68).

Centre Regional des Oeuvres Universitaires et Scolaires (CROUS): 8 rue Jean Calvin, 75005 Paris (tel 1-47 07 61 70).

European Council of International Schools: (ECIS), 21b Lavant Street, Petersfield, Hampshire GU32 3EL; Tel: 01730-268244. Can provide a list of schools abroad offering the British Curriculum.

French Embassy: Service de Presse et d'Information, 58 Knightsbridge, London SW1X 7JT; tel 0171-201 1000; fax 0171-201 1053.

Ministère de l'Education Nationale et De La Culture: 110 rue de Grenelle, 75357 Paris Cedex 07; tel 1-49 50 10 10; fax 1-45 51 99 47.

Office National d'Information sur les Enseignements et les Professions (ONISEP): Service de vente par correspondence; 46-50 rue Albert, 75635 Paris Cedex 13; (tel 1-40 77 60 00); fax 1-45 86 60 85.

Academic year pupil exchanges with French schools
Cultural and Educational Services Abroad (CESA): Western House, Malpas Truro, Cornwall TR1 1SQ; tel 01872-225300; 01872-225400.

Intercultural Education Programmes (IEP): Ground Floor Suite, Arden House, Main Street, Bingley, West Yorkshire BD16 2NB (tel 01274-560677).

Study Associates International: Gold Peak House, Wilmerhatch Lane, Espsom, Surrey KT18 7EH. Director: Mrs. Legge. Tel: 01372-272853.

The Media

Television

Overall, French television programming tends to be mediocre; many educated and middle-class French do not watch it at all. The last survey showed that 66 per cent of French people said television insulted their intelligence. However, news broadcasting is good and as listening to the television is one of the best ways of learning French it is a good idea to have one. There is a shortage of high quality, nationally made programmes, mainly because the funding for these is lacking. American and British productions are dubbed into French and soap operas, are very popular though liable to be frowned upon by the guardians of French culture. The main French television channel TF1, was charged with not showing enough French programmes in 1992. This is some indication of the fact that French television is much more regulated than its British counterpart. Another regulation does not allow films to be shown before 11pm on Saturdays, so as to encourage people to go to the cinema.

With the advent of cable (*câble*) and satellite (*la chaîne cryptée*) TV, the average French viewer has a choice of scores of stations from a growing number of countries. In addition there are several pay-as-you-view channels. France's Europe-wide TV cable and film group, Canal Plus, is half owned by a grouping comprising cable giant Générale des Eaux, publishing and media conglomerate Havas and the Societé Générale bank. So far some 19% of French homes have a subscription to Canal Plus based around movies and sport and a certain anti-conformist element depicted in its satirical and humorous output. Satellite is growing faster than cable. It is estimate that half the viewers of satellite TV are the immigrant families (who can receive broadcasts from their own countries). There are basically six regular channels in France some of which are national, others vary regionally. TF1 (Télévision Française 1) is the main channel watched by a third of viewers. It has been privatised since 1987. State-owned FR2 (previously Antenne 2) is often rated better than TF1 although news coverage is poorer, despite its popularity. FR3 is also state-owned and tailors its programmes to each region of France. Canal Plus (Channel 4) is a privately-owned (see above) international subscription channel launched in 1984 — a special decoder is required. Arte replaced La Cinq, which folded in 1992. It is jointly funded by France and Germany and broadcasts on channel 5 from 7pm to just after midnight. As its name suggests its output is largely cultural programmes (some of them bewilderingly obscure). Channel 6 (M6) has been on the air since 1987 and is a light entertainment channel. In addition it broadcasts American series and soft porn movies.

The French are able to receive at least sixty satellite channels, from seven countries, relayed by seventeen satellites. Paris-dwelling BBC lovers who tuned to BBC World Service Television on Fridays found their lifeline gone when it was replaced in 1994, for a variety of reasons, (rumoured to be sinisterly connected with promotion of the French language), with La Chaine Info, a relentless 24-hour news channel. It is now necessary to have an extra decoder and pay a higher tariff for the privilege of being a BBC WST viewer. If desperate, you can get your friends and relations back home to send you videos. Other BBC channels are not available in France. You have to live in Brussels to get BBC 1.

Cable television arrived in France in 1986 and there are now at least 100 cabled French towns offering a range of programmes from French, Italian, CNN (American) and Spanish networks. Cable subcribers pay a monthly fee.

There is little point taking a television and video recorder to France from the UK (although black and white portables may work) as different broadcasting systems are used.

Television Licences
An annual television licence is required, the cost of which is currently 449 francs (about £50) per year for a colour TV set. There are certain exemptions including those over 64 years of age and those on low incomes below the taxable threshold; in 1997 this was 66,140 francs (about £7,189) for a couple and slightly less for a single person. The licence fee and tax thresholds are liable to yearly revision (upwards).

Radio
Radio in France is divided into the public-sector, whose channels are presided over by Radio France, the national company, and RLPs (Radio Locales Privées, a.k.a *radios libres*), private stations which have sprung up since deregulation in 1982.

The selection of national radio stations available in France is not extensive but it is one which caters for all tastes and like the BBC is also public service broadcasting. National stations include the oldest, *France Inter* (general interest, news and topical debate). *France Culture and France Musique* which are similar to BBC Radios 3 and 4. A special service, *Radio Bleue* is aimed at the elderly.

Other channels which come under the aegis of Radio France include a network of nearly 50 local radio stations; *France Info*, a continuous news channel covering all France; *Radio France Internationale* (RF1), France's world service for the international community which is on the air 24 hours and broadcasts in 14 languages to five continents.

Other National Radio Stations: There are a number of private radio stations very popular in France, but which orginate from outside the country. These include *Europe I* which belongs to the Hachette multi-media group and *RMC (Radio Monte Carlo)*.

Private Local Radio Stations:
Since deregulation the FM band has been crammed with private local radio stations — one estimate put the number at 1500. The surviving stations are mostly music channels with national networks: *NRJ, Nostalgie* and *Skyrock* are some of these. Minority interest stations also exist.

Receiving the BBC in France: It is possible to receive various English speaking stations throughout France, including the BBC World Service which has its own monthly magazine *London Calling* which keeps you up to date with any changes in the broadcasting frequencies. Contact the Subscription Department (World Service, Dept. G, Bush House, London WC2 4PH). In northern parts of France the BBC national radio stations can sometimes be received, depending on the local terrain, weather conditions and time of day.

Newspapers
One French person in two reads a newspaper at least two or three times a week and 40 per cent read a newspaper every day. The newspaper industry in France has

had its price wars similar to those in the UK. Despite such attempts to boost readership, the younger generation are not as inclined as their parents to develop a taste for newsprint, and reader numbers, especially of the important dailies, are declining. Other factors working against newspapers are the rapid rise in production costs and the power of the print unions — still a force to be reckoned with in France, and the high cost of the end product (almost £1 a copy) also limits readership.

Considering the size and diversity of France, the total of 85 regional and national (i.e. published in Paris) newpapers is not surprising. Nor is the fact that regional newspapers are as important as the newspapers published in the capital. The latter including *Le Monde* and *Le Figaro*, though internationally known, are ironically not really national newspapers as we understand them in the UK; they are rather Paris newspapers which are read nationally. They also have smaller circulations than the British national dailies. With a decline in newspaper readers, in Paris especially, came the sell out of France's famous socialist newspaper, *Libération*, born out of the student revolt of 1968 and founded by Jean-Paul Sartre who was the first editor. *Libétion* run as a journalists' collective until 1996, was forced to sell out to big business in 1996 and become a newspaper 'like any other'. Another sign of the times perhaps, is that the biggest selling newspaper in all of France is the sports rag *L'Equipe*.

France had no equivalent of the UK tabloid press until the 1994 arrival of *Infos du Monde*, France's first sensational tabloid that runs bizarre stories gleaned from around France; judging by its successful circulation figures (getting on for a quarter of a million a week), there is an appetite for such things. Some of the best known newspapers in France are:

La Tribune Desfossés: second most popular financial daily after *Le Figaro*.

Le Canard Enchaîné: infamous satirical/scandal rag.

Le Figaro: politically right wing, includes a lot of business and economic coverage.

Le Parisien: Paris daily which also has a provincial edition.

France-Soir: evening newspaper, mostly light news and chat.

Le Monde: founded at the end of the Second World War. Very serious, politically centre left.

Libération: former socialist newspaper founded by Sartre. Became mainstream after commercial sell-out in 1966.

UK Newspapers

For those addicted to the UK press, it is fairly easy to get hold of English newspapers like *The Times* on the day of publication, while the *International Herald Tribune* is published in Paris. Needless to say, British newspapers are expensive in France. An alternative is to subscribe to *The Times* before you move and get it at a reduced rate (see *useful address* below, or *The Guardian Weekly* which is a compilation in English, of the main articles from *The Guardian* and the *Washington Post* and *Le Monde*. Subscriptions from: The General Manager, The Guardian Weekly, 164 Deansgate, Manchester M60 2RR.

Useful Address

The Times: Subscriptions Department, P.O. Box 479, 1 Virginia Street, London E1 9XU; tel 0171-782 6118; fax 0171-782 6132. The Times is available early on the day of publication at 16 francs (Monday to Friday) or 18 francs (Saturday). Subscriptions are available from an approximate cost per copy of 6.93 francs and same day, hand delivery is available in Paris (postcodes 75, 92, 93 & 94). Next day mail delivery is available everywhere. Contact London: + 44 171 782 6118.

Regional press
In France, regional newspapers have large readerships, in some cases, only a few thousand fewer than the Paris dailies. One, *Ouest-France* has overtaken both regional and Parisian dailies with a circulation of 800,000 (double that of *Le Monde*) and has thirty-eight local editions covering the departments in western France. Generally however, the urban French seem to prefer their news in the form of current affairs and general information weeklies such as *L'Express Le Point Le Nouvel Observateur* and *Paris-Match*.

Magazines
While newspaper readership may be declining, the magazine market in France is buoyant. Such is the French love for magazines that there are no fewer than 4000 titles to choose from. A large part (1,300) are technical and professional magazines; about 500 (400 of which are for local publication) deal with general information and politics. Others which are big business include leisure titles dealing with special interests, (sports,hobbies, women's magazines). Purely society and people interest magazines are also popular :*L'Evénement du Jeudi, Voici Point de Vue* and *Galla* to name but a few.

Expatriate English Language Newspapers and Magazines
One of the best known general expatriate magazines is *Resident Abroad* (subscriptions: P O Box 387, Haywards Heath, RH16 3GF; tel 01444-445520). There are a handful of English-language newspapers published in France, for the British and American expatriate communities. One of the best known is probably *France-USA Contacts* (*FUSAC*, 3 rue La Rochelle, 75014 Paris; tel 1-45 38 56 57) a free, fortnightly newsletter which comprises mostly classified adverts for accommodation, jobs, services and a social calendar. It is distributed to all the regular ex-pat gathering places in the capital.

Two other anglophone newpapers are published monthly in the Dordogne: *The France Review* (subscriptions: Les Caulins d'En Haut, 47120 St Sernan de Duras. UK administration e-mail: francereview@star.co.uk or tel 01525 402818) is published by Richard Barker, while *The News* (SARL Brussac, BP 59, 24500 Eymet, France; tel + 33 5 53 23 84 30; fax + 33 5 53 22 41 91) owned by Clin Bond is its rival published a few miles away. It is difficult to imagine how two papers, both catering for the same small English-speaking community can survive; a merger was attempted but failed in 1993. A newsletter *Le Réseau Amical* (Jeffrey Design, 51, Maskelyne Ave, Bristol BS10 5DA; tel/fax 0117 942 1697) has useful articles on practical aspects of daily life in France. £6 buys you an annual subcription (4 issues) and membership of their network of home-owners in France which is invaluable for swopping information.

A glossy magazine *Boulevard France* is available on subscription from Mediatime France (68 rue des Archives 75003 Paris; tel + 33 1 44 78 82 82; fax + 33 1 44 78 82 83), or from WH Smith in Paris or news-stands in New York. The same company also publishes the magazine *Living in France*.

Books
French language publishing obviously does not have as wide an international market as that of English. Also, the range of books available in a French bookshop may seem limited if you are used to the multi-floor establishments of the bookstore chains in the UK. For instance gardening and DIY books, which command a lot of shelf space in the UK, are not big sellers in France. However, the strong literary tradition of France ensures that there is no shortage in the classical and historical departments. Books in France are very expensive by UK standards,

as they carry TVA (VAT). There are a number of English book shops in Paris including WH Smith and and Galignani in the rue de Rivoli. Another, Shakespeare and Company (see below) also operates as a writer's guest house and is a well known source of temporary employment.

If you are desperate to keep up with English-language publishing, you could take a list of UK publishers with you. All the major publishing houses have mail order departments and will send books abroad on request. Alternatively, you could join some bookclubs in the UK that cater for your tastes and that sell by mail order only. Make sure first, that they will send books abroad. 'The Good Book Guide' (24 Seward Street, London EC1V 3PB; tel 0171-490 0900; fax 0171-490 9909) produces a monthly magazine containing a wide-ranging selection of books, audios, CD-ROMs etc which can be mailed anywhere in the world and will send a complimentary copy of their magazine on request).

Paris Bookshops stocking English Publications

The Abbey Bookshop: 29 rue de la Parcheminerie, 75005 Paris; tel 01 46 33 16 24; fax 01 46 33 03 33.

The Australian Bookshop: 33 quai des Grands Augustins, 6th arrondissement, Paris; tel 01 43 29 08 6.

Galignani: 224 rue de Rivoli, 75001 Paris; tel 01 42 60 76 07. Nearest métro: Tuileries.

Shakespeare and Company: 37 rue de la Bûcherie, 75005, Paris; tel 01 43 26 96 50.

Tea and Tattered Pages: (second hand books and American cookies), 24 rue Mayet, 6th arrondissement, Paris; tel 01 40 65 94 35.

W H Smith: 248 rue de Rivoli, 75001 Paris; tel 01 44 77 88 99; fax 01 42 96 83 71; Minitel: 3615 Smith.

Post, Telephone and Minitel

The French postal service is run by The Ministry of the Post-Office and Telecommunications (P&T). Since the beginning of 1991 it has been separate from Telecommunications when the telephone service became France Télécom). The postal service is a public company and has done much in recent years to throw off its old-fashioned reputation for inefficiency by introducing new services, streamlining deliveries and carrying out a modernisation programme of all post offices.

Post offices (known as *la poste* or the *bureau de poste*) are found in all cities and towns and open 8am-7pm (with a lunch break in some areas) and 8am to noon on Saturdays. If only a stamp or two is needed it is more usual to buy these at a *tabac*. There are nearly 6,000 post offices in towns and an additional 4,260 in rural areas. In areas where there has been a rural exodus leaving mostly the elderly and infirm, the post office has adapted its services to take this into account. For instance the elderly or handicapped who need to pay bills can request a postman to call at their home. This is known as *SVP Facteur* (Postman please). In other cases, the postmaster may be a part-time job which can be doubled up with being a shopkeeper, garage-owner and so on.

It is not customary to use the regular postal service for urgent letters as this can take a few days to arrive in another part of France. Instead, there is an extra fast delivery service *Chronopost* (the equivalent of UK Special Delivery) which assures delivery throughout France by the next morning. There are special services for businesses including mailouts (*Téléimpression*) and express, local, national and international parcel delivery.

Always use the postcode on items sent within or to France: this is the five figure code written next to the city or town name. It is not necessary to write the département name in a French address, as one would write the county name in the UK, since the first two numbers of the code indicate this. In common with other European countries it is becoming more usual in France to place a nationality letter with the postcode e.g. M Martin, 35 rue Gambetta, F-31000 Toulouse.

Those who live in a remote area might have their post delivered to a box (boîte postale) rather than to their home and in this case the address may be a B.P. number. A temporary arrangement can also be made to have letters sent c/o Poste Restante at the nearest main post office (Poste Centrale). A small fee is charged and proof of identity is necessary when collecting mail.

The Post Office also operates financial services including *Comptes Cheques Postaux* (CCP) (Post office cheque accounts) and *Caisse Nationale d'Epargne* (CNE) (National Savings Bank).

Junk Mail

Junk mail is as much a problem in France as elsewhere. You should be able to stop a large part of it by communicating your wishes in writing to the *Syndicat des entreprises de vente par correspondance* (60 rue de la Boétie, 75008 Paris).

Telephone

As little as two decades ago the telephone system in France was very old fashioned and unreliable. Now thanks to an annual research and development budget of more than a billion dollars, it has been revolutionised by new technology under France Télécom and compares with any advanced system in Europe or North America. For telephone installation and billing arrangements see *Setting up Home*.

French telephone numbers were all simplified in October 1996 by making them all nine digit numbers where ever you are in France. This makes life easier for foreigners who were inevitably confused by the former system which involved using a long distance access code 16 (which no longer exists). To call Paris and the Paris region dial the nine-digit number which begins with 1. For all other calls within France you dial a zero before the nine digit number. To call another country from France dial 00 before the number for the country concerned, then the subcriber's area code minus the first zero, then the subscriber's number. To call mobile phone numbers, dial 6 before the eight-digit number. Numbers are usually separated full stops when written.

Cheap Rates: telephone calls in France are 50% cheaper on weekdays between 10.30pm-8am and at weekends from 2pm on Saturdays.

Telephone Cards: *Télécartes* can be bought in post offices, tabacs and newsagents. They come in units of 50 or 120 units and can be used in telephone booths displaying the blue bell sign.

Emergency & Information Numbers: Directory Enquiries 12, Fire 18, Operator/ telephone faults 13, Police 17. Dialling emergency numbers is free from private telephones but in payphones you need to insert one franc minimum or a télécarte to get the phone to work, even though your coin will be refunded/no charge will be made.

All the usual telephone services are provided in France, including operator, transfer charge calls and a voice-messaging service (3672 Memophone). However, many of these are also available with Minitel (see below).

Fax machines (known as fax, téléfax or télécopieur) were unknown in France before 1988, but a postal strike acted as a catalyst and enabled fax companies to exploit the panic of businesses and professionals. Since then, the fax has become as indispensable in France as elsewhere. If you do not wish to receive junk mail by fax, ask France Telecom to put you on their *liste safran* (yellow list). They will then no longer put your name on lists sold to mail order companies.

There are over 158,000 card-operated payphones in France. Cards (*télécartes*) can be bought in post offices, tabacs etc. In addition there are over 60,000 public telephones in bars, restaurants and other establishments. Most of these accept coins, or in some places the proprietor does. In large cities and airports you can find telephones that accept bankcards. Telephone users with an international lifestyle use a Pastel Card which enables them to call from anywhere in the world using a special code number which automatically debits their account. A voice mail service was introduced in 1995 which lets callers from public telephones leave messages for numbers that do not answer or are engaged.

After lagging behind, France is catching up fast with some other European countries in the use of radio-telephones (mobile phones). Currently the main supplier is the France Télécom subsidiary Radiocom 2000. Sales of mobiles have topped the million mark (700,000 of them are French Telecom subscribers). In 1992 FT kicked off with two commercial radio-telephone networks under the marque Itineris which now includes the Tatoo paging service and the professional paging (Alphapage).

With all these innovations it is difficult to feel nostalgic for the telephones (usually in public bars) that took *jetons* (tokens) and which hardly ever worked. Telephone calls can also be made from main post offices.

Further information on telecommunications in France can be obtained from the Centre Nationale d'Etudes des Télécommunications (38-40, rue du Général Leclerc, 92131 Issy-les-Moulineaux Cedex; +33 1-45 29 44 44; fax +33 1 49 26 03 52).

Ex-directory

For a fee, France Telecom will put you on their *liste rouge* (ex-directory list).

Minitel

Ten years before the World Wide Web the French had Minitel which was perhaps one of the most exciting developments in French telecommunications and the most successful and widespread system of its kind in the world. Basically, Minitel is a computer terminal which is linked to the videotex/teletext information sytem called Télétel through the telephone system. By using a Minitel terminal any telephone subscriber can access directory enquiries nationwide and about 25,000 public and professional services. The Minitel Guide of Services is a directory which lists all the services offered for a particular topic. It can also be accessed on the Minitel terminal. The first three minutes of use are free and then varying charges are made depending on the service. In some ways the system is similar to the UK's Prestel, with the difference that Minitel is designed for the general public not just the business world. The superiority of Minitel is best shown by the number of terminals that are in use: there are 6.5 million terminals in use in France, about half of them in private homes and the subscriber total (currently around 20 million users) continues to increase.

Minitel terminals, of different degrees of sophistication, can be installed when a telephone is connected and also subsequently. Use of the service is charged at a basic rate of FF61.60 (approximately £6) per hour and the terminal is rented from PTT at a current rate of approximately FF85 (£8.50) per month. An increasing list of services is available on Minitel. One can play board and video games on the system, you can also access directory enquiries services in English, German and Spanish, and it provides a bank of information on weather, road conditions etc. A private individual can book and pay by telepayment for airline, train or theatre tickets and read the pages of a favourite newspaper on the screen. However, the great advantage of Minitel is that it is a two-way system: money can be transferred between bank accounts, bills paid, and shopping ordered and paid for. As an alternative to the fax, Minitel also has a service called Minicom which enables subsribers to leave messages for each other in 'electronic mailboxes'.

However despite the visionary brilliance of Minitel which preceded commercial use of the internet by years, it is now showing signs of being eclipsed by the international appeal of the World Wide Web.

France Télécom has made Minitel available to anyone with an Internet connection (you can download emulation software from www.minitel.fr) and publishes a range of Minitel booklets in English including *A Selection of Minitel Services* and it is possible to access Minitel services from many European countries including Britain. For further details contact France Télécom, 30 St. James Street, London SW1A 1HB (tel 0171-343 2424).

In France, Minitel is the responsability of the Association Française de Télématique (15 rue de la banque, 75002 Paris; tel +33 1 49 26 03 04; fax +33 1 49 26 03 52).

Local Government

The Préfecture and Mairie

At this point it is as well to mention something about local government in France as it varies greatly from that in the UK and is peculiar to France. The first radical reforms of the system which had lasted, with a few non-integral reforms, since the Napoleonic era, took place under the Socialist government of 1981-86. Thus it can be seen that until quite recent times , a highly centralized system of government existed. Most decisions were made in Paris by the President and then handed down to and carried out by local officials in each département and region. Under this system départements enjoyed virtually no say in local affairs; they were subject to edicts which emanated from Paris. The chief official in each area (*le préfet*) operated from the Préfecture was merely the local political executor of central government. Each département had a préfet, préfecture and sous-préfectures, but the regions had no administrative, only a geographical significance. In the early 1980's however, the situation changed radically. Individual regions and départements were then given their own councils and assemblies, the prerogative to introduce certain laws and the freedom to raise funds and to spend these as they chose. As a result of these changes the préfet lost much of his authority and was rechristened *Commissionnaire de la Republique* while his powers devolved onto the locally elected councillors of the communes, departments and regions. However, in France such changes take a long time to work through and it could be many years before the original préfectural system diminishes into total redundancy.

The mairie, with the mayor (*le maire*) as head of the local *commune*, is equivalent to a town or parish council: this unit existed before the government reforms, although after them it gained a little more independence.

Despite this devolution, France is still a rather centralised country and by no means as federally organised as Germany or as locally devolved as Switzerland. Individual regions and départements do not have total independence and tend to present a unified national image in most cases. Territorial units with special status (i.e. greater autonomy) are the cities of Paris, Marseille and Lyons; Corsica, Mayotte and Saint-Pierre-et-Miquelon.

Where to Go

The reader will have noticed throughout this book that most matters of local importance or personal and domestic documentation are dealt with at the préfecture or mairie. This is in direct contrast to the UK where there is often a special centralized office for each matter e.g. the DVLA for motor vehicles, or city council planning department for planning consents etc. Thus there is usually no need to write off all over France to obtain the various documents required: one local body can deal with all matters. In small towns, one office and one official may handle everything. In most cases, all enquiries can be made at the local mairie. Many of these are not imposing buildings and if in doubt they can usually be recognised by the tricolour flying above the entrance (though this also applies to gendarmeries). Some only open part-time. If the matter is not one dealt with by the mairie they will happily refer the case to the préfecture which if you live in a remote area can be quite a distance.

Dealing with the Mairie or Préfecture

The reception received at either a mairie or préfecture will vary as greatly as you might expect. Some officials are extremely helpful, while others are positively hostile, and it can take a good deal of effort and charm to squeeze the information needed from this latter group. French bureaucracy is not especially complicated, but a good deal more formal than in the UK. Few local government officials will speak any English so be prepared! A small charge is sometimes levied for some of the services which the mairie and préfecture offer.

One of the problems with dealing with local authorities, as an expatriate, is that one may not have the documents which every French national has as a matter of course. Nationals will always have an identity card and, when a couple marry, a *Livre de Famille* is issued which records various details about them, their marriage and family. For this reason it is essential to keep every official French document which one is given and a supply of photocopies too: never part with the originals unless absolutely essential. In the case of British-issued documents keep an official French translation (this will already have been done to obtain the *carte de séjour* anyway). Whenever one visits the mairie or préfecture on some enquiry, it is as well to take the whole lot with you. It is also useful to keep contact with a friend in the UK who can track down any official documents you might need in your dealings with the authorities.

Incidentally, one also registers births, marriages and deaths at the local mairie. Most marriages in France take the form of civil ceremonies at the mairie as church weddings do not have any legal significance. A marriage in France is universally valid, even if neither party is French.

For further details on the local government in France see *Administration — Region, Department and Commune* and *Internal Organisation* in the *Introduction.*

Social Security and Unemployment Benefit

Claiming the UK Job Seeker's Allowance in France

One of the advantages of labour mobility within the EU is that it is possible for those who are currently unemployed and claiming benefit, or eligible to claim it, to have it paid in another EU country if planning to go there to look for work. You have to have been claiming UK unemployment benefit for at least four weeks prior to departure and you can arrange to have the benefit paid in France, at UK rates, for up to three months while you are looking for a job. In order to do this, you should inform the UK office through which you are claiming benefit, of your intention to seek work elsewhere in the EU. You will need to do this at least six weeks in advance of your departure. The leaflet UBL22 *Unemployment benefit for people going abroad or coming from abroad* contains an application form for transferring benefit.

Your local UB office will inform the Overseas Benefits Directorate of the DSS who will provide you with the form E303 which is the standard EU form authorising another member state to pay your benefit. When you go to France you should present the form to the authorities in the area where you intend to look for work. This will be at the local office of the national employment service A.N.P.E. (*Agence Nationale pour l'Emploi*), or the town hall (*mairie*) if there is no nearby ANPE. The DSS Overseas Office in the UK will give you advice on where to register abroad. As there may be delays in payments received abroad, even when the procedure is meticulously followed, it is advisable to have some emergency financial resources of your own to fall back on.

Please note that anyone tempted to chuck in their present job to go on the dole for the requisite number of weeks before departing for France will be disappointed: by making themselves voluntarily unemployed they render themselves ineligible for Unemployment Benefit for six months. Likewise if you go on holiday to France and then decide to stay on and look for work, you will not be able to arrange UK benefits to be paid in France. Even if you are eligible, you should note that not only does the benefit run out after three months but you would require a *carte de séjour* to stay in France after this period and this is unlikely to be granted if you do not have a job.

Social Security in the UK

Anyone who has been living and working in the UK will have been paying UK national insurance contributions which entitle the contributor to various social security benefits, including unemployment benefit and a state retirement pension. However, if you are about to embark on a job hunt in France your position does need careful consideration. If you do not intend ever to return to the UK, then there is unlikely to be a problem. However, if you are planning to return at a later date and you are not working, then it is as well to ensure that national insurance contributions are kept up, otherwise you may not be entitled to all the usual benefits.

If a UK national works in another EU country and then returns to the UK, the fact that contributions have been paid there should keep his or her UK contributions record up to date. However, if the individual has not worked in France that record may lapse, although you are usually given the option to pay off the shortfall within a certain time limit. The best policy is again to check and to clarify your position before leaving the UK with the International Office of the Overseas Benefits Directorate (Tyneview Park, Benton, Newcastle-upon-Tyne NE98 1BA; tel 0191-225 5251/225-5298) which is the office of the DSS that deals with UK benefits being paid overseas. You should also request a copy of leaflet SA29 *Your Social Security, Insurance Benefits and Health Care Rights in the European Community* (last edition dated April 1996) and the booklet *Community Provisions on Social Security* both from your local DSS, or from the Overseas Contributions Department (EU) of the the Contributions Agency in Newcastle (see above address);

Social Security in France

France has a highly developed system of social security (*sécurité sociale*) benefits. The important implications of this regarding health benefits are dealt with earlier in this chapter — see *The National Health System in France*. There are however, other sickness and invalidity benefits, rent allowances and pensions, etc. available.

Social security contributions in France are treated as a fund quite separate from the money raised by the government from income tax. This is one of the reasons that rates of income tax do not seem high by European standards but social security contributions are much more substantial than in say the UK. The size of these contributions has been a perennial problem for successive governments. In the run up to the single currency, the new French government is pledged to implement radical cuts in public spending in order to reduce taxes and welfare charges, which means there may be imminent changes to the generous level of benefits described here, the details of which were not available at the time of press.

Social security contributions are payable by both employees and employers as a percentage of the gross salary earned: those who are self-employed must also contribute. The employee's contribution (see below for amount) is deducted at source, so those working legitimately in France will automatically be included in the scheme, even before they have obtained a social security number (known as a *sécu*). In this respect the scheme is very much like the National Insurance contributions payable in the UK.

All those who pay into sécurité sociale and their dependants, are entitled to the benefits of the scheme. Those who are not working may join if they wish, although few do, presumably because if they can afford not to work they do not require the benefits, or prefer to use private insurance schemes. Retired people are entitled to the medical benefits free of charge, (but not unemployment benefits).

In order to qualify for the full range of benefits on offer the claimant must have worked for at least three months in France or 520 working hours within the last 12 months and contributed to sécurité sociale. The benefits available include the following: medical insurance, unemployment benefit, sick pay, retirement pension, death grant, maternity benefit, housing benefit (for low income/employees or families), family allowance and industrial accident insurance. If you have a *carte de séjour* and have had a low income for two years before applying, you can claim a substantial part of your rent (65-70%) from the French social security. You should apply for this at the CAF (*Caisse d'Allocations Familiales*). You will need a signed letter from your landlord stating the amount of your rent, a declaration of income for the calendar year preceding the year of benefit, and various other documents which the CAF will tell you about).

When claiming benefits, a UK national, resident in France claims just like any French national and is entitled to the same treatment. For example, the employment-based benefits can be claimed at the branch of the nationwide employment organisation, Agence Nationale pour l'Emploi (ANPE), or from the local mairie if there is no ANPE. Unemployment benefit is claimed from a separate organisation (see below).

Unemployment Insurance: Unemployment (*chômage*) insurance is financed by employee/employer contributions underpinned by a state fund. Benefits are paid out by ASSEDIC (*Associations pour l'emploi dans l'industrie et le commerce*) Associations for employment in industry and commerce.

Unlike the UK, where benefits tend to be paid at a flat rate, in France and many other EU countries they are usually paid as a percentage of the claimant's former salary, subject to a minimum and maximum. For example, unemployment benefit is usually paid at about 40% of the salary last earned, sick pay is paid at 50% of salary. The industrial accident insurance meets all the medical and rehabilitation costs involved with any industrial accident, and provides a pension to the injured and their dependants.

In most cases the levels of benefits paid by sécurité sociale are considered adequate but modest. A great many employees take out private insurance schemes to top up the state benefits. This is particularly true in the case of health benefits (see *Health Insurance and Hospitals* earlier in this chapter) and pensions (see *Pensions* in the *Retirement* chapter). As a consequence many trades and professions have special 'top-up' insurance schemes (*mutuelles*) which employees can join: details can be obtained from the employer or relevant trade union once you have started work.

The basic level of employee national insurance contribution in France is currently approximately 19-24% of the gross salary. These contributions are deducted at source by the employer and typical employee contributions are made up of the following: 5.9% health insurances, 7.6% pension (*la retraite vieillesse*), 2.79-3.37% unemployment benefits. In addition there is normally a contribution of about 2% for an extra pension fund (*la retraite complémentaire*). The last contribution may vary in amount from one employer to another. Further details of social security payments and benefits and how to make/claim them may be found in the *Employment* chapter.

Income Support

In Britain, anyone coming from an EU country can claim income support in Britain whether they have worked there or not. In France, eligibility for the equivalent, *Revenu Minimum d'Insertion* (RMI), of 2,253 francs (about £250) per month for a single person and 3,379 francs (about £370) for a couple, is limited to those aged over 25 who have lived in France for three years.

Crime and the Police

Crime

France has a crime rate similar to that of other highly developed   European countries. However, the national crime pattern shows some uniquely French aspects as it tends to centre on particular urban districts, leaving the rest of France (especially rural areas) with contrastingly low crime rates.

Much crime tends to be petty, including burglary and purse snatching: car theft and break-ins are rife in many areas. The authorities in Paris are very conscious of the threat posed by terrorism, although the unwanted accolade of the most terrorist-bombed nation varies from year to year and other European nations including Britain and Spain have a similar problem.

In common with almost all capital cities with a constant throng of tourists, Paris has a high crime rate, as does the Côte d'Azur, particularly and unsurprisingly, of theft and burglary. Marseille is renowned as a centre of crime, including drugs and gangland activities.

A recent breakdown of crime figures shows that 65.5% of all crimes committed in France involved theft.

Having said this, there are rural areas of France that are virtually crime free and this can be one of the attractions of living in such areas. It is not unusual for people not to lock their homes or cars out in the deep countryside, although, at the same time, this is not to be recommended.

As in Britain, the authorities in France claim that crime rates have fallen overall. However, recent statistics suggest that both violent crime (excluding murder) and drug usage (but strangely, not drug trafficking) are on the increase.

France has 181 penal establishments and a prison population of about 58,000 of which only 4.2% are women.

The Penal Code and Judicial Courts

In 1994, after twenty years' preparation, France's penal code was completely revised. Until that time it was largely based on the Napoleonic Code laid down 183 years previously. The contemporary Criminal Code takes into account modern offences including sexual harassment and ecological terrorism and introduces an offence of crime against humanity (used to bring the case against ex-SS officer Klaus Barbie). Under the new code, vagabondage is no longer an offence, although this does not stop the mayors of important tourist towns passing by-laws against begging, which are in return promptly declared unconstitutional. There are also new laws to protect homosexuals. However, as well as the politically correct aspects, there are more conservative ones including 30-year prison sentences without parole for child murderers and stiffer sentences for drug-trafficking. The latter offence is one which nearly all the Britons held in French jails are there for. The most non politically correct change however is probably the new plea of 'legitimate self-defence of property' which has upset left-wing groups. This means that generally speaking, it is not illegal to booby-trap privately owned premises. Indeed some proprietors even emblazon the property with warning signs to this effect. However, before you rush out to consult ex-members of the military on how to lay a minefield around your property, you should be aware that if an intruder should be wounded, maimed or killed while trespassing on a booby-trapped premises, the property owner will almost certainly be prosecuted according to the seriousness of the injury inflicted. However, the law takes a less harsh view if the property owner takes the more dangerous course of trying to apprehend personally the intruder on his or her property and in the course of doing so kills them inadvertently (i.e. in the course of direct fighting). This is usually regarded as legitimate self-defence and generally carries no penalty. The terms actually used are that the householder is entitled to use 'reasonable force', but at the time of press there do not seem to be any cases where a proprietor has been charged with using unreasonable force. It is fairly common in France for those living in remote locations to keep firearms in the home. Permits for such firearms generally entitle the holder to keep the firearm within the home but not to carry it around outside. It is also against the law to carry knives. Obviously, there are different rules for hunting equipment.

There is also an article of the penal code (which has been in force since the 1970s), which makes it an offence for witnesses of a violent crime or mugging, not to try to intervene to help. If it is not possible to drive off the attackers, the witness should at least call for help. The same applies if a person sees someone in obvious need of medical help, it is an offence not to summon a doctor or the appropriate emergency services.

All police in France carry sidearms, truncheons and handcuffs and in their case they can argue any force they wish to employ is reasonable force as many witnesses of arrests can verify.

The Judiciary and Courts

There has long been doubt about the independence of the French judiciary, not least because the Justice Ministry is responsible for appointing state prosecutors and for telling them when to instigate judicial enquiries. This means that when the enquiries involve political corruption (as has been the case in recent times), the party in power is inclined to appoint tame judges who will do as they are told, or who share their views.

At the time of press, reforms are underway, not least measures to reinforce the presumption of innocence and stop trial by media, although pessimists fear this will simply muzzle the press when they try to bring corruption stories to light.

In France the judicial system is slow and cumbersome. For instance it can take minor civil disputes five months to come to court while those accused of more serious offences can wait up to three years to have their cases heard. The European Court of Human Rights has condemned French judges no fewer than 14 times for failing to come to a decision within a reasonable time. Part of the problem lies in the lack of magistrates: there are only 600 more magistrates in France than there were at the turn of century (when the population was much smaller) making a current total of about 6000), meanwhile the number of cases with which they have to deal has rocketed. There is no equivalent of the British lay magistrate in France.

There are several types of French civil and criminal courts:

Civil Courts

Courts	Deals with
Tribunaux d'instance	Small claims, rent etc. and civil cases up to Ff30,000 (£3,250)
Tribunaux de commerce	Disputes between merchants or anything to do with commercial acts. Are presided over by lay commercial judges (*juges consulaires*)
Conseils de prud'hommes	Labour conciliation tribunals. Deals with issues involving labour and apprenticeship contracts
Tribunaux paritaires des baux ruraux	cases involving agrarian landlord-and-tenant disputes
Tribunaux des affaires de Sécurité Sociale	disputes with the various social security agencies over payments for illness, pensions etc.
Tribunaux de grande instance	civil cases not heard in special courts including divorce, adoption etc. and some criminal cases.

Criminal Courts

Tribunaux de police	petty offences involving 1-2 days' imprisonment or fines ranging from Ff20 to Fr 6,000.
Tribunaux correctionnels	more serious offences punishable by imprisonment of up to 5 years (longer for drug-trafficking)
Cours d'assises	serious criminal offences composed of a presiding judge and two assessors (professional judges) and nine jurors. Decisions from the assizes courts may not be appealed against; only points of law.

For appeals there are 27 *cours d'appel*. The supreme court of appeal (*Cour de Cassation*), has the power to quash or annul sentences but does not consider the facts of the case, only whether the law has been correctly applied by the *tribunaux* and the *cours d'appel*. It will thus only exercise its power of annulment if it is deemed the law has been wrongly administered.

Police

French police are generally well equipped (and well-armed) to tackle the crime problem: they are strict, efficient and have far-reaching legal powers . Until recently French police had a reputation for ruthlessness and although this reputation has improved of late, they are generally not regarded as a user-friendly force and few people tend to ask them for help except in cases of absolute necessity.

Towns and cities have their own police (*police municipale/corps urbain*) who deal mainly with petty crime, traffic control and offences and road accidents. French police used to wear a military-style pillbox, peaked cap (*képi*), also worn by *gendarmes*, but this was abandoned some years ago in favour of contemporary blouson jackets and ordinary peaked caps for men and a trilby type hat for women. Police nationale deal with crime on a much larger and more serious scale, crossing city and departmental boundaries. Other divisions in the police force include the Compagnie Républicaine de la Sécurité or CRS (essentially riot police but often drafted to other less risky duties, such as patrolling the Côte d'Azur in summer). A special police division also patrols frontiers, acting in a customs capacity at land, sea and air frontiers.

A popular misconception seems to be that all French police (*agents de police*) are *gendarmes*. As their name (rough translation is 'armed men') would suggest, The gendarmarie nationale is a paramilitary police force and comes under the control of the Ministry of Defence. It may be the only police force evident in many quiet country areas. The Gendarmarie Nationale also patrols roads and undertakes other specialist duties including motorcycle escorts and sea patrols.

It is helpful to find out which force is actually required before contacting the police on a routine matter. Dialling '17' will connect you with the appropriate police service (which arranges ambulances) in an emergency: dial '18' for the fire and rescue services.

Women's Interests

Although much of the feminist hype and diatribe of the seventies and eighties has died down, in France as elsewhere there are still plenty of active groups concerned with women's issues at local level. A well-known centre in Paris, the Maison des Femmes, (8 Cite Prost, 11e; tel 1-43 48 24 91) has a network of contacts in other cities, hosts meetings and produces the magazine *Paris Féministe*.

Useful Addresses
Alliance des Femmes pour la Démocratie: 5 rue de Lille, 75007 Paris; tel 1 45 48 83 80; fax 1 42 22 62 73.
Association des Femmes Journalistes, AFJ: Maison de l'Europe, 35 rue des Francs-Bourgeois, 75004 Paris; fax 1 42 64 91 08.
Bibliotéque Marguerite-Durand, BMD: 79 rue Nationale, 75013 Paris; tel 01-45 70 80 30. Library/archive for the history of women in France and abroad. Important collection of feminist documents, lettres, manuscripts etc. Open Tuesday to Saturday inclusive from 2-6pm.
Centre National d'Information et de Documentation des Femmes et des Familles (CNIDFF): 7 rue du Jura, 75013 Paris; tel 01 43 31 17 12 13; fax 01 43 31 15 81.

Provides information on women rights, employment, professional and daily life. Can help with training schemes, enterprise creation, marriage counselling, health, sexuality and family advice. There are 160 branches CIFF-CIDF throughout the French provinces. Publications: *Nouv'elles* (quarterly), and *CIDF INFO* (monthly) containing legal and practical advice.

Choisir la Cause des Femmes: 102 rue Saint-Dominique, 75007 Paris. Defends the rights of all women to contraception and abortion, struggles against violence perpetrated on women, and campaigns for parity of representation for women in all elected assemblies.

Ligue du Droit des Femmes, LDF: Permanence téléphonique (24-hours); tel 1 45 85 11 37. Administration of the Centre d'Accueil Flora-Tristan for battered women, 142, ave de Verdun, 92320 Châtillon; tel 1 47 36 96 48.

Observatoire de la Parité entre les Femmes et les Hommes: 31 rue Le Peletier, 75009 Paris; tel 01 47 70 41 58; fax 01 42 46 99 69.

Union Féminine Civique et Sociale, UFCS: 6 rue Béranger, 75003 Paris; tel 1 44 54 50 54; fax 1 44 54 50 66. Feminist association, training organisation, organisation for the protection of the environment, consumer organisation, civic association. Publication: *Dialoguer* (quarterly).

Specialist Libraries

Librarie des Femmes: 74 rue de Seine, 75006 Paris; tel 1 43 29 50 75.

La Fourmi Ailée: 8 rue du Fouarre, 75005 Paris; tel 1 43 29 40 99.

Pets

A maximum of three domestic animals can be taken to France at one time, provided that they are at least three months old. However, the existence of rabies on the Continent, although mostly affecting wild animals, does mean that certain procedures must be followed.

Firstly, an anti-rabies certificate will be required by customs, or alternatively a health certificate issued no later than five days before departure: both certificates must be signed by a vet registered with the Ministry of Agriculture, Fisheries and Food (for further details see chapter *Setting up Home*). It is advisable to have the animal vaccinated against rabies before leaving the UK because dogs must otherwise be vaccinated on arrival. They are also obliged to have an annual booster thereafter. Rabies vaccination is not compulsory for felines, but if you are moving to an area where rabies is endemic it it advisable to have it done anyway.

As in other European countries it is usual for dogs to have an identity number tattooed inside one of their ears. This is performed by a vet and costs in the region of 300 francs. The idea is to prevent rabies certificates being used for more than one animal. The numbers are lodged on a central computer controlled by the Société Protectrice des Animaux (SPA) who can be contacted if the dog goes missing. This is also the only sure way of identifying your pet if it is lost as there is no system of dog licensing.

There seems adequate evidence that the French are just as fond of their pets as the British are deemed to be. However there are a few differences in attitude towards dogs in particular which will strike the British. For instance it is not uncommon in smart restaurants to see women guests (and occasionally men) arrive with underarm pooches which may even be provided with food, and sometimes a plate by the restaurateur. It is compulsory for dogs to be kept on leads in public parks and gardens and failure to comply results in an instant fine. In some parks dogs are banned completely though the rules in selected parks are being relaxed slightly.

Dogs

Humankind's best friend is much in evidence in France with there being a no less a hierarchy of pooches there, as exists in the UK. The French equivalent of Crufts is held outdoors at Longchamps during the summer. Generally it is more relaxed and informal than Crufts and is a popular day out with French people who like to bring their own not-so-pedigree canines along for the walkies. The French have an appealing selection of mongrels, often very shaggy and of completely indeterminate ancestry. The smaller more endearing ones tend to be family pets. There is a larger, more sinister version that accompanies beggars and is attached (if at all) to its owner by a dirty bit of string. The pitbull, so notorious in the UK is as much in a class of its own in France as in the UK. Defined as a dangerous dog (not least because of the human company it keeps), the pitbull is required to wear a muzzle in public and (in Paris at least) be listed on a police register. It is rumoured that drug dealers and other criminals go about their evil business accompanied by this canine (à la Bill Sykes) as the canine equivalent of the dangerous weapon that they are not allowed to carry.

French Attitudes Towards Animals

The French are less squeamish and sentimental than the British about animals generally. Animal rights groups do exist (mainly it seems fronted by Brigitte Bardot), but they are not as strongly supported or as zealous as in the UK.

There has been a revival of bullfighting (even though 70% of French people say they disapprove of it), centred on Nîmes in the South of France. Nîmes has an ancient tradition of the art (it is not considered a sport), but 20 years ago, interest seemed all but extinguished. However, owing to a revival of regional traditions generally and the right wing mayor of Nîmes in particular, the art was literally infused with new blood. Nowadays, there are three *ferias* (festivals) of bull-fighting a year and it has become positively trendy to attend (i.e. Parisians go). The old aficionados however tut-tut under their grizzled locks, and declare the revival is a watered-down version of the full-blooded original: the bulls have their horns blunted and are selected from weak specimens so the dice are loaded in favour of the matador (generally chosen for his eye-appeal, rather than his skill) and if he meets his come-uppance, its not by goring but because the bull runs away, or declines to become antagonised.

Importing Pets to the UK

Remember that if a pet is taken to or acquired in France, it cannot be be imported into the UK without undergoing a period of quarantine in order to guard against rabies. For further information contact the UK Ministry of Agriculture, Fisheries and Food (Hook Rise South, Tolworth, Surbiton, Surrey KT6 7NF; tel 0181-337 6611).

Religion

Catholics

France is primarily a Roman Catholic country. Despite its influence throughout French history, the Church is now neither as strict nor as strong as in the past and as in other highly-developed western European countries there has been a steady decline in the number of practisers. In 1993, 78% of French people considered themselves Catholics. Although the Church now tends to keep its distance from French politics (the French state was officially secularised in 1905), this did not stop its clerics dabbling in left-wing politics on social issues just after the Second World War. As a result there are many spiritual and charitable organisations that continue to be dynamic today. Some of the best known are *Le Secours Catholique* or *Caritas France*, created after the Second World War has an estimated 68,000 volunteers. Another, *Les Chiffoniers d'Emmaüs* founded by Abbé Pierre, is an international charity that helps the underprivileged and aims at the eradication of poverty.

The priesthood has suffered a dramatic decline in recruits. There are estimated to be barely a 100 new recruits to the priesthood annually compared with about 650 per year in the 1960s. The priesthood is thus an ageing body of shepherds and their flock is meagre; it is estimated that about 14% of the population regularly attend Mass. To satisfy the need for some kind of religion, albeit more relevant than the established one, there are many unofficial religious groups that meet in private homes. These tend to receive less publicity than mainstream rebels such as the Lefebvre faction of the Catholic church that continues to celebrate Mass in Latin. Lefebvre himself now resides in Switzerland where he ordains his own followers who wish to become priests.

The Catholic Church continues to exercise its influence in education. There are are 9,750 Catholic schools, including 6,000 primary establishments. Also, 1,700 *collèges* (first stage of secondary education) and 1,100 *lycées* (second stage secondary schools). Between them Catholic schools have about two million pupils or 17% of the school age population. And, the church does not evince feebleness is in upholding the right to state aid for Catholic schools which are separate from the rest of the French education system.

Regular attendance at church is sparse nowadays (especially among those aged 18 to 25) and, as in the UK, most people frequent church for christenings, weddings and burials only. In France a civil wedding ceremony must be held to validate a marriage legally and this is performed at the mairie. A church ceremony is optional and has no legal significance: some couples choose to have both, whereas others settle for a civil ceremony.

The Other Religions

A mere 1.7% of the French population (about 950,000) are Protestant. The three regions with the highest concentration of Protestants are Paris, Alsace-Lorraine and the south of the country. The predominant faction is the Calvanist Reformed Church (450,000 members). The only women priests in France are to be found in this church. Other Protestants include: Lutherans (270,000) most of whom are in Alsace-Lorraine, and the remainder are a mixture of Evangelicals, Adventists, Pentecostalists etc.

There are between 550,000 and 750,000 Jews in France representing a religion which has been present in France since the first century A.D. The largest populations are to be found in Paris, Marseille and Alsace. About 60,000 Jews have emigrated to Israel from France.

The largest of the other religions in France is Islam which has about four million practitioners on French soil. Many of them are French immigrants who arrived in bulk in the 1950s and 60s. They represent several factions of Islam including Sunnis of Maghrebian, i.e. north African origin; Turkish Islam which incorporates both

Sunnis and Shiites, and most recently, African Islam which has marabouts (religious leaders) for the various brotherhoods it tends to form.

Public Holidays

France does not have an excessive number of public holidays, but they are taken seriously with all shops etc. firmly closed on the appropriate day (not the nearest Monday to the public holiday as in the UK). However, apart from banks, which sometimes have lengthy closures, such events do not tend to extend into long weekends as in the UK, although this is an increasing trend. The main public holidays in France are:

1 January	New Year's Day
Easter Monday	Varies, as UK
1 May	Labour Day
8 May	Victory in Europe Day
Ascension Day	Varies
Whitsun (Pentecôte)	Varies
14 July	Bastille Day
15 August	Assumption
1 November	All Saints' Day
11 November	Remembrance Day
25 December	Christmas Day

Additionally, various regions and localities have their own festivals and carnival days which may not officially be public holidays but when most facilities will be closed. For example, Alsace-Lorraine celebrates St Stephen's Day on 26 December each year.

Time

The 24 hour clock system is used for all times in France. For example, shop opening hours are given as 09.00 à 17.30 (9.00am to 5.30pm) or train times as 20.20 (8.20pm) or 00.15 (12.15am).

France follows Continental European Time (CET) as do most EU countries with the exception of Greece, the UK and Eire. Summer time lasts from the last Sunday in March at 2am to the last Sunday in September at 3am, when clocks are advanced one hour. Consequently France is one hour ahead of the UK for most of the year, whether the UK is operating to Greenwich Mean Time (GMT) or British Summer Time (BST). However, clocks in the UK are changed later in the autumn than in France so for a time, in September and October, the two countries are actually sychronized: there are currently proposals to synchronize the times throughout the EU.

CONVERSION CHART

LENGTH (N.B. 12 inches=1 foot, 10 mm=1 cm, 100 cm=1 metre)

inches	1	2	3	4	5	6	9	12		
cm	2.5	5	7.5	10	12.5	15.2	23	30		
cm	1	2	3	5	10	20	25	50	75	100
inches	0.4	0.8	1.2	2	4	8	10	20	30	39

WEIGHT (N.B. 14 lb=1 stone, 2240 lb=1 ton, 1,000 kg=1 metric tonne)

lb	1	2	3	5	10	14	44	100	2240
kg	0.45	0.9	1.4	2.3	4.5	6.4	20	45	1016
kg	1	2	3	5	10	25	50	100	1000
lb	2.2	4.4	6.6	11	22	55	110	220	2204

DISTANCE

mile	1	5	10	20	30	40	50	75	100	150
km	1.6	8	16	32	48	64	80	120	161	241
km	1	5	10	20	30	40	50	100	150	200
mile	0.6	3.1	6.2	12	19	25	31	62	93	124

VOLUME

gallon (UK)	1	2	3	4	5	10	12	15	20	25
litre	4.5	9	13.6	18	23	45	56	68	91	114
litre	1	2	3	5	10	20	40	50	75	100
gallon (UK)	0.2	0.4	0.7	1.1	2.2	4.4	8.8	11	16.5	22

CLOTHES

UK	8	10	12	14	16	18	20			
Europe	36	38	40	42	44	46	48			

SHOES

UK	3	4	5	6	7	8	9	10	11	12
Europe	36	37	38	39	40	41/42	43	44	45	46

Metrication

France uses the metric system in all respects: the standards of measurement are often spelt as in the UK and are thus instantly recognizable. Temperature is always measured in celsius.

In the long run it is much easier to learn and think in metric rather than to always try to convert from metric to imperial. To facilitate this process a metric conversion table (including clothes and shoe size conversions is) given below.

In all cases measurements are quoted as a decimal and not a fraction; for example, on road signs, 'Toulon 12.7 km'.

Retirement

France has been popular with British visitors since the nineteenth century, but it has been the development of mass tourism in the latter part of the twentieth century that has made French life and culture accessible to many more people than before. As a result of this contact, recent decades have seen certain regions of that country experience a surge of popularity as a prospective area for retirement. Many people buy holiday homes when they are still living in the UK with the expectation of retiring to France when the time comes. Until recently, Spain had the largest colony of expatriate over 60s, but rising prices and complications with property purchase and sales left many people there disillusioned, if not hard put to make ends meet. France, may never be as popular as Spain was at its peak with those looking for a warm retirement spot, but it maintains a steady level of interest thanks to low property prices in many areas, less sharply rising prices generally and the beauty and diversity of the rural regions. Furthermore, many parts of France are becoming increasingly accessible thanks to new road and rail links.

Both the dream and the practical aspects of retiring to France can present an attractive proposition, and if carefully planned, also a viable one. If you are discriminating about the area and location you choose, there will be all the benefits of Spain, such as good weather and a substantial expatriate population of a similar age group, with the added benefits of novelty, a new culture and a different way of life. Additionally, although property prices vary greatly between different parts of the country (and even within them), it is possible to buy a property to retire to in France at a lower price than the equivalent in Spain. Finally, although many parts of this book apply equally to those wishing to retire and to work in France, this chapter aims to draw attention to the procedures and decisions which apply specifically to those planning their retirement in France.

The Decision to Leave the UK

At the mention of retirement in France, most of us would probably conjure up idyllic images: of — waking up to warm, sunny mornings, breakfasting on café au lait and croissants, buying wonderfully fresh produce in the market, dining out in little bistros, and having the leisure to appreciate the changing of the seasons. However, it is essential for anyone contemplating such a move to consider the realities and in particular how they will cope pratically and emotionally. For instance, the prospective emigrant must be able to afford the move financially, and also be willing to improve the quality of his or her French, if not to learn from scratch a new language (see *Learning the Language* at the beginning of *Daily Life*). Energy and enthusiasm are required to move and set up home in a new country and make new friends there, and being prepared to leave your former home permanently, and thus to see much less of UK family and friends can be an emotional wrench. Many people who retire abroad have plenty of energy, enthusiasm and experience with which to make a success of the move and are perhaps more committed to the venture than many younger people. However, many decisions to move are born from a love of the country disovered through past holidays, work, cultural exchanges etc. As living permanently in a country is not the same as spending short periods there, it may be a good idea to consider a long 'try out' holiday, of say six months, in the area in which you are interested. Alternatively, you could buy a second home in France (if finances permit) and spend several months there annually over several years and finally, make a permanent move to France, selling your UK residence only when you feel certain that it is right choice for you. Seeing your favourite area of France at different seasons is also important as many parts of France are bustling and cheerful in summer, but deserted and desolate in winter.

There is a popular misconception that because property is cheaper in France than in the UK, that living costs generally are cheaper but this is not in fact the case: many things including meat, utilities and insurance are more expensive and many useful things including books and clothes carry VAT. Two of the few commodities which are obviously cheaper in France are wine and quality eating out.

It would give an unbalanced view however, not to mention some of the very real advantages which can be derived from a move to France at retirement age.

1. Property costs can be up to 50 per cent lower in some areas of France than for an equivalent property in the UK.
2. Current UK property prices should enable many people to sell their UK home, buy a French one and have money left over.
2. The quality of life offered is often calmer and of a higher standard in France than in the UK.
3. Some rural areas are virtually crime-free.
4. The climate in many regions is more temperate.
5. The challenge of adapting to a new culture and way of life may bring a renewed zest to the lives of older people.
6. You would not forfeit any UK earned pensions by a move to France as both company and/or state pensions can be paid there at the UK rate (further details later in this chapter).
7. You need not feel isolated or lonely if you are determined to speak French, as knowledge of the language will act as a key to making friends and coping with all aspects of daily life.
8. Family and friends who were previously 'irregular' in their visits may perhaps show a sudden (and presumably not unwelcome) enthusiasm for visiting you once you have moved to your retirement property in the Dordogne or Brittany.

Procedure for Obtaining a Residence Permit

The procedure for EU nationals wanting to retire to France is fairly straightforward and very similar to that detailed at the start of the book; that is, both retirees and those planning to work in France must obtain a *permit de séjour* (residence permit) in order to stay there longer than three months.

All applicants will have to produce some proof that they possess sufficient funds with which to support themselves for a minimum period of one year. Although the amount of money deemed acceptable is subject to the merits of each individual case, it is advisable to have at least the equivalent of £12,000 capital available. Although a smaller sum may be acceptable as a basis for obtaining the *permit de séjour*, this is probably the minimum amount on which one could live comfortably in France for one year. Although some retirees claim that as little as £8,000 is adequate this presumably means you grow all your own food, do not have a car and do not go out much. A current statement of your account or a letter from the bank confirming the amount of money placed with them will be required as proof of sufficient financial resources.

If you know that you are going to stay in France, you must apply for a *carte de séjour* within three months of taking up residence. It is not necessary to apply for the residence permit before you leave the UK. However, some of the documentation necessary for the *permit de séjour* which involves translating UK documents into French (see *Residence and Entry* chapter) may be more easily done before you leave the UK.

The application procedure for those of retirement status is exactly the same as that detailed in *Residence and Entry Regulations* with the obvious exception of not needing to produce an employment contract. The documentation giving proof of your income may also be required, probably in the form of an official French translation from a UK bank: if the money has already been transferred to France, a French bank statement should suffice. If all the documentation (see *Residence and Entry* chapter) is in order, then the préfecture will issue you with a receipt (valid for three months but extendable if issuing the *carte de séjour* takes longer), and then with a *carte de sejour*. Allow three or four months for this process to be completed, although it has been known to take longer; six months is not uncommon.

Special Considerations

At present the *carte de séjour* issued to those of retirement, or any other non-working status, is only valid for one year, after which time the card-holder must apply to renew it. Although this is a comparatively simple procedure, applicants may need to produce further evidence of their financial status: in other words, they will need to show a minimum capital lump sum that conforms to the minimum resources under Title VIII of the French Social Security Code (currently 71,525 francs for persons accompanied by their spouse). After several years a longer-term *carte de séjour* may be granted. Eventually, the process of continual assessment of applicants' funds may be abandoned altogether.

At present the procedure for those who do not exactly fit exactly into the categories for application is far from well defined. Thus, if any unusual circumstances apply to your situation, it will very much be a case of feeling your way through the procedure. If, for example, someone is working in the UK and buys a holiday home in France which is later to become a permanent residence, they should be able to holiday there freely for up to three months while still working, but once retired, a *carte de séjour* will be required for stays of over three months. If a husband works in France but his wife does not, then the latter can be covered by the *carte de séjour* that is granted to the former on the basis of his employment status. Chauvinistically, such a procedure may not apply in the the reverse situation. Those who initially choose to retire to France, but who later decide to take a job, perhaps part-time, or to start a business there, need to change their original *carte de séjour* at the time of coming to such a decision. Although there is no reason why you should not be able to do this easily and quickly, it is may cause confusion at the local *mairie* or *préfecture* if they have not been asked to do anything similar before and so may prove more complicated than originally expected.

Non-EU Nationals

The procedure for non-EU Nationals proposing to retire to France is broadly the same as outlined above. However, there is an element of discretion involved on the part of the French immigration authorities concerning applications from non-EU nationals which does not exist towards those from EU nations, providing that all their documentation is in order.

Possible Retirement Areas

Those who have already visited France may have some idea of where they would like to retire to, while those who have not should plan a preliminary visit before committing themselves to any specific region. Many factors are involved in the property buyer's choice. Climate, scenery and available facilities are three key factors — all of which will be considered in the following guide. While many people planning a retirement purposely choose a quiet area, the holiday and resort regions of France are also very popular. However, those interested in the latter should consider what these areas will be like in winter, and also remember that property in holiday areas is inevitably more expensive than elsewhere. Whilst there are a good many expatriates and retired expatriates in France, however, there is no one area (like Jávea in Spain, for example) which has become a haven dedicated to the needs of a specific group in a 'Little England'. The nearest equivalent in France would probably be the Dordogne. The following guide, a mini-analysis of the areas of France traditionally popular with British retirement buyers, is intended to facilitate the choice of where to live once the decision to move has been made.

Aquitaine. South-west France. This area includes the attractive Dordogne river valley and, a little further east, the popular Lot département. Bordeaux is a major city in the region but most other areas are quiet and rural.

Languedoc. Although geographically positioned in the south of France, Languedoc is in many ways the quieter and slightly less fashionable, and thus less expensive, part of the Midi. It is possible to live quite near to the Spanish border (around Perpignan) and hence to enjoy the benefits of both France and Spain: Barcelona is approximately 100 miles/160km away.

Provence and the Côte d'Azur. These regions are traditionally what is understood as being the south of France, running from Marseille to the Italian border: the further east one goes the more fashionable the resorts become. This region is very popular for retirement, due to year round good weather. However, property is very expensive in both areas while the the Côte d'Azur is still the most upmarket area of France.

Poitou, Charentes. This is an attractive area in western France with a coastline to the Atlantic, and subsequently a popular spot with holidaymakers in summer, but quiet in winter. Property prices increase towards the coast; La Rochelle is an especially attractive resort.

Pays de la Loire. The area surrounding the Loire river is so large that it is usually considered as two regions of France — the Loire Valley and the Loire-West. The east of the Loire is convenient for Paris while the west offers access to the Atlantic coast and Brittany. However, as approximately 30% of the total population of the Pays de la Loire are under the age of 20 it may not be the ideal retirement spot for those who are not especially enthusiastic about the younger generation. On the plus side however, Nantes, the main town has a retired population of 48,000 and makes special provisions for its senior citizens over the age of 65, including letting them use public transport free of charge. There are at least 80 clubs in the city aimed at the retired. You would need to speak French to get the most out of such an abundance of mature conviviality though.

Brittany, Normandy and Nord-Pas-de-Calais. All three regions have attracted a lot of interest from retirement buyers in recent years due to the comparatively low property prices available and because of their accessibility to the UK. Brittany, famed for its unspoilt countryside, has become more popular as the region's accessibility to other parts of France has improved with the opening of both a motorway in the late 1970's, and a two-hour TGV connection between Paris and Rennes in 1989). Alongside these developments, however, Brittany has managed to retain its own very strong sense of individual identity, and its people, proud of their Celtic origins, have perpetuated many cultural traditions to which they are deeply attached.

Although Normandy has a rate of unemployment considerably above the national average, it also offers the lowest rate of local taxation per head outside the Paris region. The former will not affect those intending to retire to France, and the latter one will only to be to their advantage. The attractions of Normandy continue to grow when you consider the wealth of history if has to offer: Mont-St-Michel, the Bayeux tapestry, the sites of the D-Day landings and the eerie stillness of the vast cemeteries from both World Wars. Although many of Normandy's historic towns were devastated in the Second World War, extensive renovation and modernisation has not destroyed the essential character which the area retains. A final point to remember is that Normandy ranks fourth amongst French regions in terms of tourism and the seafront includes some of the most fashionable resorts along the north coast; depending on one's viewpoint this may act either as an added incentive or as possible disadvantage to the area. Inland there is much attractive countryside, especially in lower Normandy.

Nord-pas-de-Calais is one of the smallest regions in France but possesses the greatest population density outside the Paris area. The region includes some of the least inspiring scenery to be found throughout the country, much of it is flat and the Nord is virtually one long industrial conurbation. However, having said that, the main industrial city of Lille has experienced something of a renaissance in recent years and is far from dull. Furthermore, property prices are low (perhaps with reason). It is predicted that the arrival of the Channel Tunnel will substantially boost the economy and general affluence of the area.

Note that in all three regions the weather is similar to that in the UK, and although some towns may be very busy in the summer, others are quite remote, and all areas are generally much quieter during the winter months.

Choosing and Buying a Home for Retirement

After the region of France has been decided upon, you must then choose a property which is within your financial scope and which, unlike a holiday house, is suitable for year-round living. Current levels of property prices in France may well put those considering retirement, who have a house to sell in the UK, in an enviable position. However, there are obviously areas of France where prices are higher than in the UK, especially the Côte d'Azur and Provence. Before making a final decision it is important to consider the running costs and upkeep of the house in question: it may be, for example, that an apartment which is part of a copropriété (see *Setting Up Home*) can help solve some of the budgeting and maintenance cost problems for those who are retired. Accessibility is also an important point as some parts of France are very remote. Proximity to health services and other facilities is important, especially for those who do not now, or may not in the future, own a car. Note that very low prices in France almost always indicate that a property is isolated. Is a garden required? Cultivated gardens are by no means usual in France: this may be a positive attraction for those of us without green fingers, but a real disadvantage for keen gardeners.

Do not forget to consider and to allow financially for the state of the property you wish to buy. Again, low prices usually indicate dilapidation and sometimes dereliction. To some, renovation may be the perfect retirement pursuit, but it will inevitably have many unfamiliar aspects and thus be more difficult to pursue than in the UK. After considering these basic points there will still be a very wide range of properties from which to choose: a large château or manor house, a farm or farm cottage (*fermette*), a town house or an apartment? The possibility of buying property with business potential exists throughout France: you might consider buying a block of apartments and live in one while renting out the others, or convert a manor house to bed and breakfast accommodation. France offers all these options.

You are unlikely to find much in the way of sheltered housing or retirement developments in France, as is the trend in the UK and also in Spain. The reason for this is that proportionally, the ageing part of the population is not large although this is changing and is a problem for the future.

After taking advice on the range of properties available from an estate agent and having undertaken several inspection trips before buying, the final decision can be made. The actual purchase of the property is acheived through the procedures described in *Setting up Home*. A word of warning — do not be tempted to become too involved with the purchase procedure as a retirement hobby in itself; the time and patience required are invariably not worth it. It is better to leave it to the professionals while maintaining a keen and detailed interest in all the processes entailed.

UK State Pensions

There is no reason why a move to France should affect the provision or rate of state pension for the vast majority of British people. Whether or not it works to your advantage will depend on the current costs of living in France or currency fluctuations which are unpredictable. At the time of press, Britain's position on joining a single European currency remains one of 'wait and see'. If the UK remains outside the proposed currency union, it is hard not to envisage that it would be affected in some way by the value of the Euro; although the nature and extent of the sterling's reaction is as yet unpredictable.

If a pension is paid in France but sourced from the UK it is index-linked and will be uprated in line with levels in the UK. This is unlike the situation for British pensioners in some other countries, notably Canada and Australia where UK pensioners receive pensions frozen at the level when first claimed. This is one major advantage of retiring to an EU country.

Both those who have yet to claim and those who are already claiming a state pension should contact the DSS, International section in Newcastle-upon-Tyne NE98 1YX (tel 0191-218 7269 and ask for the Overseas Department) for details of payment arrangements for UK state pensions. For those who do not plan to spend periods longer than three months at any one time in France, the easiest course of action is to leave the state pension to mount up in the UK and to cash it in on returning. In the case of a longer or permanent stay in France the pension can still be paid to a UK bank account or to an agent or friend in the UK; alternatively it is possible to have the pension paid in France, usually on a monthly or quarterly basis by filling in form E121 issued by the DSS in Newcastle-upon-Tyne.

As stated, a UK state pension will be paid at UK rates and also in UK currency as long as any contributions still due are paid up: consider this point carefully in the case of early retirement.

The level of pension for UK emigrants in France bears no relation to French pension rates and increases. For information on French pensions see below.

UK Personal Pension Plans:
Those with personal pension plans should contact the company or financial consultant concerned for details of how the money can be paid in France. Usually the money will be forwarded in sterling, but some of the larger personal pension plan insurers can send foreign currency cheques, though an annual fee will be charged. One will need to ascertain the most financially advantageous way for receiving payment of the pension. If it cannot be paid in France you may need to maintain a UK bank account and stand the cost of currency exchange yourself.

You should note that contributions to a UK personal pension fund are not accepted if the person is not earning a UK income. Expatriates are however able to invest in offshore pension plans run from offshore finance centres such as the Isle of Man and the Channel Islands of Guernsey and Jersey. There would be no UK tax demands on the interest on such pensions which would be paid in full, but they would almost certainly attract tax in the country where they were being paid.

French Pensions

For many years France has had the reputation of treating its retired people more than fairly. For instance the retirement age in France is 60 years (in Italy it is still 65 and in the UK 65 for men and 60 for women) and French pensions are comparatively generous. Whereas in the UK pensions are paid at a basic flat rate (currently £56.10 per week) in France, rather like SERPS, the pension is earnings related. For instance under the Socialists the average pension amounted to 50% of the pensioner's average salary based on the average of their ten highest earning years up to a maximum of 149,820 francs. Under this men received 6,613 (about £718) and women 3,504 francs (about £380); i.e. considerably more than their British counterparts. The problem for the new government is that this high rate of pension payment is unsustainable in the current economic climate. The system relies on those in work paying into the Caisse de Retraite (state retirement fund) now, to fund those who are elderly now. The problems are that not only is umemployment rising, but the population is also getting top-heavy with older people, which is a problem for Europe generally as it hurtles towards the next millennium. Currently the French pension fund is running at an annual deficit of 20 billion francs. So far the government has been wary in tackling the problem head on, but has tampered with the length of time people must work in order to be entitled to a pension which will be raised from 37.5 years to 40 after the year 2003 and will also be calculated on the 20 highest earning years thus reducing the final total

The most radical reform of the French pension scheme is the introduction of private pension schemes (see below),which were almost unheard of prior to a new law passed in June 1997. The new goverment is determined on this innovation, not least because it will produce much needed capital for the Paris bourse.

For those French pensioners (usually farmers and women) who fall below the *Minimum Vieillesse* there are additional benefits which are means tested. In France there is also a legal obligation for children to contribute towards the upkeep of parents and grandparents unless they can provide proof that this is not financially possible.

1997 French Law on Private Pensions

In June 1997, France took the first major step towards allowing company pension plans for all. Company schemes existed before then, but only on a very restricted basis. The idea of the new law is to make private pensions accessible to many more people and to relieve the state of the burden of providing state pensions which it would be unable to sustain at the current level indefinitely. Such plans have been available in the UK for years, but until now have not been allowed in France. These plans will also be eligible for tax relief as in the UK. From 1998 it will also be possible, after the company pensions have taken root, to buy private pensions in France on the open market from a pension plan provider as in the UK. A private pension plan is known in France as a PER (*Plan Epargne de Retrait*).

If you are planning to retire in France, but are still working in the UK it makes sense to create a pension fund based on French-based funds and to receive the income in French francs in order to avoid possible currency fluctuations. There are several companies offering independent financial advice and tailored packages for expatriates in France; one such is Siddalls International (Parc Innolin, 3 rue de Golf, 33700 Bordeaux-Mérignac; tel +33 5 56 34 75 51; fax +33 5 56 34 75 52; UK tel 01329 288641).

Finance

Anyone considering retiring to a foreign country should take specialist financial advice regarding their own situation. Most people in a position to retire overseas have an amount of capital to invest, or will have when they sell their home, and it is essential to take good advice on how and where this may best be done. Moreover, those who intend to maintain connections with both the UK and France need to take advice on how their taxation affairs can be arranged to their own greatest advantage. Unless professional advice suggests otherwise there is no reason why one should not continue with bank accounts or investments already established in the UK, as in most cases it is possible to earn interest on deposits paid without deduction of tax where you are non-resident.

Taxation

The matter of taxation is inextricably linked with investment considerations. Reasonably impartial advice can be obtained from the UK Inland Revenue who should be able to advise you on what constitutes income to which they have no entitlement. They will in any case probably be easier to deal with than their French equivalent. Those in need of taxation advice should contact the Inland Revenue Office with which they last dealt, or alternatively the Inland Revenue's information office (Citygate House, 39-45 Finsbury Park, London EC2A 1HH; tel 0171-588 4226) — both of these are able to advise.

For those who intend to move permanently to France and to sever all financial connection with the UK (except for any pensions etc.) the situation may be quite straight forward in that they will be liable for French income tax. Note also that someone becomes liable for French income tax just by owning a property in France, even if not resident there. Non-residents must register their French property with the Centre des Impôts des Non-Résidents (9 rue d'Uzès, 75084 Paris) and will be charged tax based on an estimated letting value. This does not necessarily mean, however, that one will pay any, or much more, tax.

A more complex situation arises if one intends to divide one's time between the UK and France. In this case, it is advisable not to approach either the UK or the French tax authorities until specialist advice has been taken. It will be necessary to decide which income is taxed where and this will depend on where one is considered both resident and domiciled. Generally, one cannot totally escape UK taxes if more than 183 days are spent in the UK in the first year of possessing a residence abroad.

Finally, because the UK tax year runs from April to April and the French one from January to December there are advantages and disadvantages, from a tax point of view, in choosing a particular moving date. Whereas employees will not usually have much choice when they move, the retired person should make the most of the advantage of choosing a particular date.

In general, if their affairs are properly managed most people will not be substantially better or worse off under a French tax regime than a UK one: note, however, that in France there are tax allowances for the elderly and also for dependants.

Sécurité Sociale and French Pensions

Although the French social security system is covered in detail in *Daily Life*, the aim of this section is to outline the range of benefits available specifically to those in or approaching retirement.

Anyone who moves to France from the UK and is of retirement status is entitled to the health benefits of *sécurite sociale* mainly free of charge. This assumes, however, that you are entitled to, or claiming, a pension in the UK so, for example, someone who had retired before retirement age would not be covered. To claim free entitlement to sécurité sociale one must first complete form E121, available from the DSS in the UK (see above), and then register with sécurité sociale in France. You do this by going to the local branch of the Caisse Primaire d'Assurances Maladie (CPAM) in France and handing over the document sent to you by the UK DSS. You will then be given a *carte d'assure social* which should be carried with you at all times as it allows you among other things access to health care and hospital treatment, (although a financial contribution of about 25% is generally required — see *Daily Life*). For this contributory charge you can take out a supplemental insurance policy. These are sold by insurance companies all over France, but it is important to get several quotes and check the details what is covered carefully to ensure you are getting what you want. Another point to note is that the cover does not usually become active until up to three months after you have signed up for it. Alternatively, you can cover yourself with a UK based private healthcare plan; see pages 147 and 148.

Other benefits provided by the *carte d'assure social* include visits to doctors and dentists, glasses and medicines. For life-threatening conditions almost everything involved with your treatment and care is 100% free.

If a UK national moves to France whilst working and then later retires, he or she will thus be entitled to a French state pension rather than a UK one. However, this is dependent on the claimant having paid all outstanding National Insurance contributions before leaving the UK. The level of the French state pension provides a slightly better standard of living than its UK equivalent. However, the amount payable is still not large, and also varies according to the pensioner's age of retirement and the salary received in his or her last job. The main advantage of a French state pension is that it should, theoretically, always match the cost of living in France, whereas a UK pension payable in France could potentially fail to do this.

As discussed elsewhere, most employees in France pay into private insurance schemes which will top up their sécurité sociale benefits. Such schemes will not only comprise a great part of the patient's contribution to medical treatment (see section *Health Insurance and Hospitals*) but they will also increase the state pension payable. In many cases, the state pension added to the amount payable under a 'top-up' insurance scheme will give the retired person a pension of 100% of their past salary. However, note that such schemes must generally be started prior to retirement age (details obtainable from current employer). The few schemes available to those who have already retired, and which usually provide further medical benefits only, are likely to be very expensive.

Health

Health care is an important consideration when making a move to a new country in retirement. While many parts of southern France enjoy a mild climate which offers a positive health benefit it would be inadvisable to bet the preservation of your health on it. If you find yourself with the prospect of using French healthcare you can be assured that health facilities are generally good anywhere in France, and some excellent private hospitals exist for those who wish to pay for their own treatment. General practices, dental offices, clinics and hospitals which provide treatment at the sécurité sociale rate are generally reliable institutions. Additionally, if you have to see a specialist you will probably find the wait much shorter than in the UK. In general, all the medicines and procedures found in the UK are available in France, merely under different names.

The most likely problem, as already discussed, could be finding an English-speaking doctor. Therefore, unless your French is good you may feel more comfortable selecting a location where English speaking facilities are available, especially if you have a recurring medical condition (a list of English-speaking doctors is available from the local British Consulate). This may mean using private facilities, or alternatively, returning to the UK, with the extra expense which this involves. However, it is often quite practical to rely on sécurité sociale for medical care. Remember that under this system a patient's contribution of about 25% of the total treatment costs may have to be met. The cost of this, or the insurance to cover it, has to be budgeted for. As discussed above, those who have worked in France and paid into a private 'top-up' scheme, as most people do, have the bulk of this contribution covered: those who are retired and move to France, however, may not and should consider joining a French insurance scheme or a UK-based private healthcare plan as discussed above under *Sécurité Sociale and French Pensions*. For further details on the health system in France see *Health Insurance and Hospitals* in the *Daily Life* chapter.

Wills and Legal Considerations

Most people approaching retirement age have either already made, or intend to make, a will. Such a step assumes even greater importance and complexity if you intend to move abroad. If a will has not been made then take advice from a UK solicitor with experience of French law; even if a will has been made it must be reviewed before the move takes place.

Generally, the disposal of property held in France after death is governed by French law, *(droits de succession)* whether you are a resident of France or still a resident of the UK. As French law is quite different from Anglo-Saxon law in this respect in that a careful consideration of the options available for avoiding it should be made. A fuller explanation of the French inheritance laws can be found in the chapter *Setting up Home*. For possessions other than property one can elect that any disposal is governed by UK law whether one is a UK resident or a British citizen living as a French resident. If your will does not dictate that UK law be followed, then French law will automatically apply.

The main difference between French and Anglo-Saxon law is that in France, you are not allowed to dispose of your estate to whom you wish. There is a very strict code which governs to whom the estate may be left and in what proportion. It is sometimes possible to contravene this regulation, but it may result in greater taxes being payable on the inheritance.

In general, spouses under French law gain their inheritance rights under the French laws relating to marriage, not to those pertaining to inheritance itself. This recognises that a husband and a wife have both individual and communal possessions (e.g. a house would be a communal possession). On death, the surviving partner is entitled to all his or her individual possessions, but not necessarily in property. This is usually divided equally to any children. For example, if there are two children then each child will receive one half of the estate. In other words, a wife does not receive all her husband's estate on his death as is quite usual in the UK.

Many couples feel that their surviving spouse should receive all their own estate on their death and that children do not need a share in this. Fortunately, legal advisers can modify the effect of the French inheritance laws to more closely reflect the individual's own wishes. However, if individual arrangements are not made then, on the death of the estate-holder, the estate itself may be divided up contrary to the wishes of the deceased.

Death

This is something which inevitably affects us all, and although it may seem somewhat ironic to talk about the 'formalities' of death in France or any other country, these must be considered in advance. Initially, consider what the situation would be if your spouse should die after moving to France. It may well be that the survivor would want to return to the UK to be closer to family and friends: provision should be made for this at the outset, perhaps by arranging life assurance which will cover the costs of returning home. In a forced situation these costs could be much greater than those involved in the original move out.

Deaths in France must be certified by a doctor and registered within 24-hours at the mairie with the death certificate and the deceased's *carte de séjour*. It will be necessary to cancel the latter document and the surviving partner will usually be entitled to a *carte de séjour* in his or her own right, if they were previously covered by their spouse's application. A funeral cannot take place until the mairie gives its approval. If you do not know of a reliable funeral director who will take care of all the formalities, you can contact the *Association française d'information funéraire* (AFIF, 9 rue Chomel, 75007 Paris) which represents the funeral trade in France. They can also be accessed on Minitel (36.15 AFIF) for costings as well as other details. Note that as France is predominantly a Catholic country, burial facilities for other faiths are comparatively rare; the nearest British Counsulate will provide the address of a Protestant church or synagogue. Cremations, although less usual in France than in the UK, are becoming more more common; a request previously signed by the deceased or by the person dealing with the ceremonies is required for cremation.

It frequently happens, despite the expense of such an undertaking, that a spouse and family prefer their deceased relative to be buried or cremated back in the UK. If this is the case, then the British Consulate should be contacted as soon as possible for information and guidance on the appropriate way to carry out this procedure.

Daily Life, Hobbies and Interests

One of the most important reasons for retiring to France is so that you can build a new lifestyle and embark on an exciting, new challenge at this stage in life which the French call *le troisième âge*. France certainly offers this opportunity, but is near enough to the UK to make visits with family and friends quite practical and to allay any initial homesickness. Culturally, however, the two countries could be continents rather than one short stretch of water or tunnel apart, and it is often just this difference which attracts culture-starved Francophiles to the country.

Most people retiring to France tend to opt for a fairly quiet lifestyle, either in rural countryside or close to scenic parts of the coast. Such areas can, however, be very remote, especially through the winter, and it is often necessary to organise your own activities and entertainments, if you are to avoid becoming a recluse for six months of the year. Proportionally, the percentage of those aged 60+ is growing in France as in other Western economies. The over 60s can expect a healthy and active participation in the life of a community. If you are not French, or do not speak the language you will find it harder to meet people of your own age; although this may be considered an advantage by some. Of the 11.3 million people aged 60+ in France, more than a quarter live alone. The French dislike of formally organised social events and entertainments exists among the older generation and necessitates an adventurous social attitude among new arrivals to the community. The over 60s in France have a role in the community; many belong to associations that organise everything from prison visits to an counselling service for small businesses or school support groups. Thus it is difficult for a foreigner to get involved.

It is therefore important to have a variety of hobbies and interests which you can carry on with in France. For example, France has an ideal climate for gardening, although French people are only just beginning to take advantage of it; gardening not being a national pursuit in France as it is in the UK. Sports facilities are good, and golf, tennis and riding are widespread. This may also be the ideal time to take up a new pastime, such as painting or walking, to take full advantage of new and scenic surroundings. As far as reading is concerned, it may be difficult to obtain your favourite books in English even in a country which is so near to the UK, but, on the other hand, this should act as a further incentive to perfect your command of both written and spoken French. The French are very keen on continuing education and many universities offer courses aimed at older people or you can study with the University of the Third Age.

France is an ideal country for travelling and sightseeing — there is so much history and culture that you could make this one of your main interests. Very good facilities for camping and also caravanning exist and most public transport, museums, historic sites and leisure facilities offer very generous discounts (often 50%) for retired people. As mentioned earlier, food and wine are major and absorbing interests for all French people and one would certainly be missing out by not participating in this national preoccupation.

Having said all this, it is not essential that retirement years should be completely crammed with hobbies and interests in France. In most cases it is quite practical to take a job, perhaps part-time or on a consultancy basis, or to start a small business in France. This option is considered in the chapters *Employment* and *Starting a Business* and applies equally to those under and over retirement age. However, remember to check the position as regards the *carte de séjour* first as this will need to be replaced and amended to take account of your change in status.

SECTION II

Working in France

Employment

Business and Industry Report

Regional Employment Guide

Starting a Business

Employment

For anyone who is not yet old enough (or rich enough) to retire, finding a job will be the most important part of going to live in another country. Working overseas, temporarily or permanently, can be a way of furthering your career by getting valuable experience, or a means of fulfilling an ambition to live abroad: this chapter aims to cover both situations.

Since the arrival of the European single market, there has been nothing to prevent any UK national, in possession of skills and experience in demand, from working in France. The Treaty of Rome, which heralded the common market, guaranteed the free movement of labour and services in the countries of the EU. However it was not until comparatively recently that a system was devised to recognise the qualifications obtained in one EU country and used in another. Moving between EU countries is now easier from an administrative point of view than it was in the past. Initially, directives for the mutual recognition of qualifications were dealt with individually, for instance architects in 1985 and general medical practitioners (GPs) in 1986. It is estimated that of the 600,000 GPs in the Union only a small number, about 2,000 have taken advantage of the directive to work abroad.

In 1990, another directive ruled that all remaining professional qualifications not yet covered by EU directives should be left to the discretion of individual national governments as to whether to allow nationals from another EU country to use them with or without a period of probation, or having to take a further examination before practising. In general, qualifications obtained in one member country are now recognised in another.

Residence and Work Regulations

EU Nationals

Any EU national, regardless of skills and qualifications, can go to look for a suitable job in France. Once a job is found then that person can apply for a residence permit (*carte de séjour*) and ultimately, if they so wished, settle permanently there. For more details, see *Residence and Entry Regulations* chapter.

Non-EU Nationals

It is more difficult for nationals of non-EU countries to find work in France. For instance, Americans will find it difficult to find employment. What is more they must have arranged employment in advance of entry into France and have had their job arrangements approved by the French Ministry of Labour and/or their employer has to apply for approval to the Office des Migrations Internationales (44, rue Bargue, 75732 Paris) and have a pre-arranged, long-stay visa for workers. Things can be much simpler if the applicant already has *carte de résident* and has lived in France for ten years. Other exceptions are spouses of French citizens and students who have studied in France for two years and who have at least one parent who is a four-year resident of France. Also non-EU students are permitted to do some part-time work such as au pair or similar temporary jobs if they have a definite job offer. The network of Centres d'Information et de Documentation

Jeunesse (CIDJs) has some useful leaflets including: *Séjour et emploi des étrangers* (No 5.5701) and *Séjour et emploi des étudiants étrangers* (5.574).

Needless to say, the regulations can also be negotiated more smoothly if the applicant has a desirable skill, or has been offered employment by a French company, or the French subsidiary of the company employing them. Without any of the above advantages, it could be an uphill struggle to first convince an employer to employ them rather than any other candidate from within the country or other EU countries. Even if this proves feasible, they will not be entitled automatically to the right of residence and it is now more difficult for non-EU citizens to move their dependants to France (see *Residence and Entry* chapter).

Useful Addresses for Americans

Council on International Educational Exchange (CIEE): (205 East 42nd St, New York, NY10017; 1-888-COUNCIL). American college students with a working knowledge of French (usually two years' study) can look for a job in France and work for up to three months on an *authorisation provisoire de travail* by applying through the CIEE.

Council on International Educational Exchange: 1 Place d l'Odéon, Paris 75006; tel + 33 1 44 41 74 69. Eligible American students already in Paris can get support from the CIEE in Paris. For instance they can supply a list of potential employers compiled from those who have employed Americans in the past. Most of those using this scheme work in Paris and the suburbs. The French Embassy, (Cultural Services, 972 5th Avenue, New York, NY 10021; tel 212-439 1400), has an information sheet *Employment in France for Students*.

Accommodation and Residence Regulations

The way in which residence regulations are structured in France means that it is highly likely you will have to coordinate finding a job with finding a home. You will not be granted a residence permit without first producing proof of having found both a job and accommodation. It will be hard to find a job without first having a permanent address and equally difficult to buy or rent a home without first having a job offer, as repaying a mortgage will require an income, and a landlord may also require reference from an employer. Thus, something of a Catch 22 situation is created; a situation which the authorities in some parts of France, and other countries, have used as a means to practice an unofficial system of labour control. Probably the best attitude to take towards the situation, unless you are lucky enough to have a job lined up, is to recognise that the home and job which you first take in France may not be ideal but are a necessary stepping stone. Thus once established with both a home and job it will be possible to set about finding better alternatives.

Unemployment

The recession which began in the early nineties has had repercussions in France no less severe in France than in other major industrial nations. Unemployment (*le chômage*) topped the three million mark in 1993 and   is now running at 12.8% (3.28 million), and its reduction, especially amongst the under 25's is a priority concern for the government elected in 1997. At present, the level of unemployment is one of the highest amongst the highly industrialised EU nations. The forecast is that the current levels of unemployment will begin to fall now that the economy appears to be turning round and because phasing in of the 35-hour week will help to create new jobs.

This is a far cry from the optimistic years of 1988-1990 when France's economic growth was running at 4%. Unemployment is most prevalent among young people: one in five of the labour force under 25 is without a job. Likewise, those made redundant at age 50 or older, find it extremely difficult to find steady re-employment, unless they have a high level of prized skills, or are able to become self-employed. France's government is tackling the problem of youth unemployment by creating more CES (*contrats emploi-solidarité*) places which are temporary work schemes aimed at young people. The other measure is the provision of government subsidies to double the number of industrial apprenticeships on offer to 400,000. However these are merely very expensive government stopgap measures, as industry employers cannot forsee being able to take on apprentices permanently.

Demand for Foreign Staff

With so many French unemployed, foreigners looking for jobs in France, will have to concentrate on areas where there is a demand for bilingualism and other marketable skills. Even before the recession France was never the easiest country for foreigners to find work in because of the wealth of well-qualified people to take professional jobs, and also plenty of blue-collar and unskilled workers. It has long been one of the very few major countries to have a self-sufficient labour supply. However, the common market has created new opportunities, particularly for foreign employees, many of which are outlined in this chapter. For those looking for temporary and short term jobs, the reality is that now, more than ever job finding has to be well-planned and systematically carried out. This applies even to temporary jobs found on spec. For instance it is no good looking for a job in Paris in July and August when all the small businesses are closed. However, it would be worth visiting potential employers in the Alps during the summer to fix up a job for the skiing season. There are also possibilities for self-employment, even in times of recession, some skills including nursing, and services from hairdressing to financial advising will always be in demand.

French business and industry works very much to its own standards and specifications. Unlike many countries it does not always set out to follow the standards that are set by the USA. Nonetheless, over the last ten years, France has entered foreign markets, realising that to succeed it must produce products for international tastes and not just for Gallic ones. Perhaps due to this recent international bias in industry, French employers are now willing to recruit internationally, providing opportunities in industry for British professionals.

The French economy, though in a trough, still has a strong currency thanks to the *franc-fort* (strong franc) policy of recent government. It thus has all the potential to recover its dynamism. It will be helped by the country's continuing strong position within the EU and by the notable French ability to promote its own interests through EU policies. Those who start planning their employment in France now will be ready to take advantage when the economy begins its next upswing.

Working Conditions

Many British people who holiday in France are immediately taken with the lifestyle and the air of affluence. However working there is quite a different proposition and it is useful to consider what France is like as a country to work in. As recently as the early 1980's, France attracted few foreign workers. Most industries were in a poor state, and rates of pay were abysmally low. Industrial relations were also notoriously bad and employees enjoyed very little job security.

The France of the late 1990's offers a very different situation: high-tech industries are at the forefront of their field, and salaries in these, and the majority of other industries, have soared. Legislative reforms from 1983-86 have resulted in not only relatively good industrial relations, and professional equality between men and women but also high rates of remuneration for employees many of whom are as well off as their German counterparts, and, in many cases considerably better off than their UK ones. France therefore attracts both skilled workers and executives who, perhaps, once considered only Germany, Japan and the USA as the world leaders of industry.

The number of weekly hours worked per person is considerably less than in the UK — it is reckoned that only 10% of the French work force works more than 40 hours a week (compared with 47% in the UK); in addition, in France 72% of the workforce takes more than five weeks' holiday a year, compared with 22% in Britain.

The most radical change in working conditions in France for many years is the introduction of the 35-hour working week, expected to be fully implemented by 1 July 2000. This will be initiated by a parliamentary bill in 1998 offering employers (of more than ten staff) financial incentives to cut the working week. Additionally, employees will have a disincentive to work longer hours in the form of a taxation surcharge from 1998 onwards. The aim of these measures is to tackle France's unemployment problem by creating new jobs.

Thus France has very competitive terms for workers (though not so for employers). The free market economy is also one which receives close guidance and enthusiastic support from the state which proved quite successful throughout the 1980's. The way in which business is conducted may at times, especially in the south, seem casual to a British observer, but it has nonetheless produced results.

The potential shown by French industry in recent years should serve to remind foreigners that the country is attractive not only on the basis of its scenery, weather, food and culture but also on the basis of the opportunities to work in a dynamic environment with good conditions of employment.

The Employment Prospects

Obviously, once the economy starts to grow again, jobs will be generally easier to find in France. However, in some industries there is always a demand for particular skills and experience. France is particularly strong in most areas of advanced technology. This includes all aspects of electronics, computing, and high technology manufacture. Tourism is, and always has been, one of the largest and most successful French industries. Nice alone has eight million tourists a year, over half of them French. France has not traditionally been a world leader in the professional services industries; this is, however, one area which is now developing and where expertise is required: insurance, banking and advertising are all going through a period of expansion. It is not just French banks that can offer employment to foreigners; foreign banks from other EU countries can now provide their services outside their country of origin, through branches throughout the EU without the need to obtain special licences. However the most radical reforms are likely to be in the banking sector and in financial services particularly those connected with the stockmarket which is bustling with employees of newly-created securities subsidiaries and in the areas of pensions and insurance.

Overall, despite the slump, employment prospects still look better in France than in the UK where there has been a move towards an all-service industrial base, France has not taken this course and is home to many leading manufacturing industries, for example, motor vehicles, aerospace and defence equipment which, though they are hard hit at present will show their customary talent for adaptability, innovation and the ability to create new markets.

The common assumption that the main demands for employment are in modern industries is not necessarily correct. Although some of the traditional industries, e.g. steel production have died out, others have been, or are constantly being, modernised e.g. wine production and agriculture — France is largely self supporting in foodstuffs as well as being a major exporter of them.

France offers potential employment to a wide range of skills and abilities and expertise. Thus, while a scientist or a computer designer may well find numerous job opportunities in France, there is no reason why, for example, a plumber or a hairdresser should not also have access to an equal number of job opportunities; this is the very nature of the EU freedom of movement of labour provision. In whatever area you choose to work, however, the value of a knowledge of the French language cannot be overestimated . Details of ways of learning it, may be found in the section *Learning the Language* in *Daily Life*).

Evaluation of Skills

At this stage, it is wise to decide on a target job. This means assessing the kind of job for which you are most suited and examining the feasibility of doing it in France. It is not always a good idea to to start a completely new career when moving to a new country. Instead, it is safer to continue in a field in which you have built up expertise. Anyone considering executive and professional positions may want to take advice from a professional career consultant while those with a skill or trade should seek preliminary advice from their trade association in the UK.

French employers are anxious to recruit anyone who has a particular skill or ability which will ultimately further the interests of their company or organisation. This applies across the board from the most advanced technology projects to companies looking for sales representatives with a track record. French employers recognise all such skills and they are prepared to pay generously for them. The proven skills criterion also applies to much more mundane jobs. The majority of French workers, even those in quite basic jobs, have undertaken some form of apprenticeship or specialist training to qualify them for their position and they are known as *ouvriers qualifiés*; you should apply for positions for which you have appropriate qualifications or training.

If you are not sure how your qualifications correspond to French ones, the UK National Recognition Information Centre (UK NARIC) will advise you. The service is free of charge to students. For more information on UK NARIC, see below.

EC Professional Qualifications Directives

The EC Directive on the mutual recognition of professional qualifications (89/48/EEC) was notified to Member States in January 1989. This Directive (usually referred to as the first diploma directive), dealt with professional qualifications awarded after at least three years of higher education (e.g. doctors, dentists, pharmacists, architects, accountants, lawyers etc.). The second diploma directive (draft directive issued 19 December 1991) dealt with all qualifications that take less than three years to obtain (i.e. all the professions not covered by the first Directive) and was adopted in the summer of 1992. Another definition of the second diploma directive is all professional qualifications which are subject to a regulatory body in the state where they were obtained from now on should be acceptable in any other EU state. This directive, when fully implemented will enable those practising in the so-called regulated professions in their home state, to have their qualifications accepted in all the other member states for the purposes of employment or self-employment. The second directive extends the system and procedures existing before the summer of 1992 (see transitional directives below) and includes: qualifications achieved after post-secondary level education involving course of 1-3 years (defined as diplomas); awards made on completion of a course following a minimum school leaving age qualification (defined as certificates); and work experience. The member states implemented the second diploma directive in 1994. This mutual recognition of qualifications may in some instances be subject to certain conditions such as proficiency in the language of the state where the professional intends to practise and length of experience. A copy of the First Directive is contained in the booklet, *The Single Market, Europe Open for Professionals, EC Professional Qualifications Directive* obtainable from the DTI (Kingsgate House, 66-67 Victoria Street, London SW1E 6SW; tel 0171-215 5000). Further details of the qualifications covered by the second diploma directive (everything from hairdressing to insurance broking) can be obtained from the same address.

Prospective job seekers are therefore advised to consult the association relevant to their profession for the exact conditions for acceptance in France. You can do this at one of the 40 European Documentation Centres (EDCs) in the UK. To find the address of your nearest one, contact the Commission of the EC, Information Centre, 8 Storey's Gate, London SW1P 3AT; tel 0171-973 1992.

Although some professionals such as doctors and dentists have been able to practise in any EU state for several years, other professions have proved a stumbling block. In France, the problem of recognising British ski instructor qualifications, which the French consider not as comprehensive as their own, has been solved with the introduction of the equivalence. A further exam which must however be taken in France. (see below).

Certificates of Experience: member states, other than the one in which qualifications referred to in the second directive, were attained, may require evidence of one or more years of professional experience. In order to do this the home state can issue a Certificate of Experience. In Britain, those wishing to practise their trade or profession in another EU state can contact the Certificates of Experience Department of the Association of British Chambers of Commerce in Coventry (tel 01203-695688; fax 01203 695844), requesting an application form for a European Community Certificate of Experience (form EC2/GN). The form will be accompanied by a copy of the Directive (see above) applicable to the job. The applicant should check whether he or she meets the terms of the Directive before completing the application form. To be eligible for a certificate you must normally (but not exclusively) have had managerial or self-employed experience for a number of years in the job concerned. The DTI charges £80 for a certificate and a smaller fee for an update/revision. The charge is to cover the costs of checking and authenticating the information submitted by the applicant.

The DTI in London (0171-215 4648) produces a booklet *Europe Open for Professionals* which is regularly updated and is obtainable both from them and the Association of British Chambers of Commerce in Coventry.

UK National Academic Recognition Information Centre (NARIC) provides information on the comparability of overseas qualifications and can be contacted at ECTIS 2000 Ltd (Oriel House, Oriel Road, Cheltenham Glos GL50 1XP; tel 01242 260010; fax 01242 258600; e-mail: 106736.2043@compuserve.com), runs an enquiry service which provides information and advice on the comparability of international and UK qualifications.

Sources of Jobs

Newspapers
UK Newspapers and Directories
The combined effects of the Single Market and the implementation of the EC Professional Qualifications Directives (see above) are unlikely to trigger a flood of trans-continental job recruitment, but mobility has certainly become practicable for an increasing number of EU nationals. It is therefore likely that UK newspapers will carry a growing number of job advertisements from other member states including France. Most British newspapers including, *The Times, The Financial Times, The Guardian* and *The European* carry regular job adverts from other European countries. Every Thursday, the Appointments section in *The Times* provides a comprehensive list of opportunities throughout the market place both in Britain and overseas. The *Times Educational Supplement* (published Fridays) and the Education pages of the Tuesday edition of the *Guardian*, carry prolific advertisements for teaching English abroad. The *Guardian* also has a Europe supplement on Fridays, which includes a job section. A specialist fortnightly newspaper *Overseas Jobs Express* (available on subscription (PO Box 22, Brighton BN1 6HX) contains articles from a range of working travellers and a substantial jobs section under headings including: Education/TEFL, Hotel and Catering, Information Technology and Trade. Recent issues offered the following jobs in France: bilingual secretary, hotel staff, computer technicians and au pair/nanny.

Alternatively, a wide range of casual jobs, including secretarial, agricultural, tourism and domestic work, are advertised in the directory *Summer Jobs Abroad* while *Teaching English Abroad* lists schools worldwide which employ English language teachers each year and *Working in Ski Resorts Europe & North America* includes all the main French resorts and tells you how and where to get jobs in them. These publications are available from Vacation Work, 9 Park End Street, Oxford OX1 1HJ; tel 01865-241978; fax 01865-790885.

International and European Newspapers
International newspapers are a relatively new development in newspaper publishing; these publications circulate editions across several national boundaries and usually carry a modest amount of job advertising. Again, the number of adverts carried and the number of such publications is likely to increase in the near future. Presently, the newspapers to consult include the *The Wall Street Journal, Financial Times, The International Herald Tribune* and *The European*. As well as employers advertising in these papers, individuals can place their own adverts for any kind of job, although bilingual secretaries and assistants, marketing managers and other professionally qualified people seeking to relocate abroad are in the greatest demand. Obviously advertising rates vary, but will be several £s per line, per insertion. For details contact the classified advertising department at the addresses listed below.

The European: Classified Advertising Department, European Liaison, The European, Orbit House, 5 New Fetter Lane, London EC4A 1AP. The European, published weekly in the UK on Thursdays and distributed in every EU country on Fridays. The paper was bought back from limbo by the Barclay Brothers after the Maxwell fiasco and claims a cirulation figure of 18,115 in France.
The Financial Times:, 1 Southwark Bridge, London SE1 9HL; tel 0171-873-3000; in

France—FT Europe Ltd. Centre d'Affaires, Le Louvre, 168 rue de Rivoli, 75008 Paris; tel 1-53 76 82 56; fax 1-53 76 82 76. The FT is printed in English in the UK, Germany, France, The USA and Japan and distributed worldwide. International appointments appear on Thursdays in all editions.

International Herald Tribune: 63 Long Acre , London WC2E 9JH; tel 0171-836 4802; The IHT has a circulation in France of 39,000 and international recruitment appears on Thursdays.

Wall Street Journal: The International Press Centre, 76 Shoe Lane, London EC4; tel 0171-334 0008 — European edition published in Brussels : Wall Street Journal Europe, Bld. Brand Whitlock 87, 1200 Bruxelles; tel +32 27 41 12 11. The recruitment section which covers appointments and business opportunities worldwide and appears on Tuesdays.

French Newspapers

You can both place adverts in French newspapers as well as use them as a source of possible jobs. Keeping an eye on the jobs advertised in French newspapers may be helpful but obviously the majority of posts are aimed at French nationals. The potential for finding a job increases substantially if you are already in France, speak French and have marketable skills and a track record. For jobs in Paris, the main newpapers to consult are *Le Monde* especially the monthly supplement called *Campus* which contains job vacancies and general labour market information; *Le Figaro* (especially the pink Monday supplement) and *France Soir*. *Carrières et Emplois* which comes out on Wednesdays combines the week's job offers from both *France Soir* and *Le Figaro*. Another publication worth consulting is the weekly journal *L'Express*. For regional jobs consult the regional newspapers in the area where you will be based. For more information on the French press generally, see the *Daily Life* chapter, *Media* section.

Of course, because of the delay in the distribution of foreign newpapers in the UK, you can be at a disadvantage replying to adverts. If you can consult French newspapers on the spot while in France so much the better. Minitel is another possibility for up-to-date access.

Some French newspapers, including *Le Monde* and *Le Figaro* can be obtained in major city newsagents in the UK on the day of publication. Alternatively, try major city reference libraries.

Useful Addresses

Le Figaro: 25 av. Matignon, Paris 8; tel 1-40 75 20 00.
France Soir: 65 rue de Bercy, Paris 12th; 1-44 82 87 00.
Le Monde: 13 rue Falguière, Paris 15th; tel 1-40 65 25 25.

Other major newspapers and the main regional ones are listed in the *Media* section of the *Daily Life* chapter.

British Professional and Trade Publications

Professional journals and magazines are another possible source of job vacancies abroad, from British companies wishing to set up offices elsewhere in Europe and foreign firms advertising for staff e.g. *The Architects' Journal, The Architectural Review, Accountancy, Administrator, Brewing & Distilling International* and *The Bookseller* to name but a few. Anyone in the air transport industry should consult *Flight International* while those employed in the catering trade could try *Caterer and Hotel Keeper* and agricultural workers *Farmers Weekly*. Although published in the UK, some of these magazines are considered world authorities in their field and have a correspondingly wide international readership.

An exhaustive list of trade magazines can be found in media directories, for example *Benn's Media* and *Writers' and Artists' Yearbook* both of which are available in major UK reference libraries.

Professional Associations

UK professional associations are a useful contact point for their members with regard to practising elsewhere in the Community. During the negotiations involved in finalising the EU mutual recognition of qualifications directives, many professional associations negotiated with their counterparts in other member states and can therefore be helpful in providing contacts.

Details of all professional associations may be found in the directory *Trade Associations and Professional Bodies of the UK* available at most UK reference libraries. It is also worth trying to contact the French equivalent of UK professional associations: the UK body should be able to provide the address. Alternatively you can consult your trade union for information, as they may have links, however tenuous, with their counterpart organization in France. A list of addresses of the more mainstream professional organisations is given below.

Useful Addresses

Architects Registration Council for the United Kingdom: 73 Hallam Street, London W1N 6EE; tel 0171-580 5861.

Association of Professional Music Therapists: c/o Diana Ashbridge, Chestnut Cottage, 38 Pierce Lane, Fulbourn, Cambs, CB1 5DL; tel 01223-880377; 01223-881679.

Biochemical Society: 7 Warwick Court, Holborn, London WC1R 5DP.

British Computer Society: 1 Sandford Street, Swindon SN1 1HJ; tel 01793-417417.

British Medical Association: BMA House, Tavistock Square, London WC1H 9JP; tel switchboard 0171-387 4499; fax for international department: 0171-383 6644. The BMA's International Department gives extensive help and advice to its members wishing to work elsewhere in Europe, and to incoming doctors from other countries.

British Dietetic Association: 7th Floor Elizabeth House, 22 Suffolk Street, Queensway, Birmingham B1 1LS; tel 0121 643 5483.

Chartered Institute of Bankers: 10 Lombard Street, London EC3Y 9AS.

Chartered Institute of Building Services Engineers: 222 Balham High Road, London SW12 9BS; tel 0181 675 5211; fax 0181 675 5449.

Chartered Institute of Building: Englemere Kings Ride, Ascot, Berks SL5 8BJ; tel 01344 23355; fax 01344 875346.

Chartered Institute of Housing: Octavia House, Westwood Business Park, Westward Way, Coventry CV4 8JP. The CIH may be able to help individual members further by putting them in touch with key people/organisations in the EU.

College of Radiographers: 2 Carriage Row, 183 Eversholt Street, London NW1 1BU; tel 0171-391 4500.

College of Speech Therapists: Harold Poster House, 6 Lechmee Road, London NW2 5BU; tel 0181-459 8521.

Department of Education and Science: Elizabeth House, York Road, London SE1 7PH.

Faculty of Advocates: Parliament House, 11 Parliament Square, Edinburgh EH1 1RF; tel 0131-226 5071. Does not have a formal information service which helps members to find jobs abroad but it does maintain close links with other European Bars.

General Council of the Bar: 11 South Square Gray's Inn, London WC1R 5EL.

General Dental Council: 37 Wimpole Street, London W1M 8DQ; tel 0171-486 2171; fax 0171-224 3294.

General Optical Council: 41 Harley Street, London W1N 2DJ; tel 0171-580 3898; fax 0171-436 3525; e-mail: optical@global.net.com.uk

Institute of Actuaries: Napier House, 4 Worcester Street, Gloucester Green, Oxford OX1 2AW; 01865-794144; fax 01865-794094.

Institute of Biology: 20-22 Queensberry Place, London SW7 2DZ; tel 0171-581 8333; fax 0171 823 9409. Can give members advice/contacts in Europe.

Institute of British Foundrymen: Bordersley Hall, Alvchurch, Birmingham B48 7QA; tel 01527-596100; fax 01527-596102.

Institute of Chartered Accountants in England & Wales: Chartered Accounts' Hall, P O Box 433, Moorgate Place, London EC2P 2BJ; tel 0171-920 8100; fax 0171 920 0547. Is able to offer members advice on working within the EU. The institute also has an office in Brussels which may be contacted by its members on a freephone number 0500 893369.

Institute of Chartered Foresters: 7A Colne Street, Edinburgh EH3 6AA; tel 0131-225 2705.

Institute of Chartered Secretaries and Administrators: 16 Park Crescent, London W1N 4AH; tel 0171-580 4741; fax 0171-323 1132.

Institute of Chartered Shipbrokers: 24 St Mary Axe, London EC3A 8DE.

Institute of Civil Engineers: 1 Great Ceorge Street, Westminster, London SW1P 3AA; tel 0171-222 7722; (web: http://www.ice.org.uk). Also has an international recruitment agency: Thomas Telford Recruitment Consultancy (0171-987 6999; ext. 2441).

Institute of Marine Engineers: The Memorial Building, 76 Mark Lane, London EC3R 7JN; tel 0171-481 8493; fax 0171-488 1854; (Internet: http://www.engc.org.uk/imare). Provides its members with contacts and information through its network of branches throughout Europe.

Institute of Mining and Metallurgy: 44 Portland Place, London W1N.

The Institution of Electrical Engineers: Michael Faraday House, Six Hills Way, Stevenage, Herts SG1 2AY; International department tel 01438-767272; fax 01438-742856. Helps members who wish to travel or work abroad with details of the IEE representative in their new location who will then help them to find employment etc. Sometimes a job seeker company is used to help members find jobs abroad.

Institution of Gas Engineers: 17 Grosvenor Crescent, London SW1X 7ES.

Library Association: 7 Ridgmount Street, London WC1E 7AE; tel 0171-636 7543; fax 0171 436 7218.

Chartered Institute of Marketing (CIM): Moor Hall, Cookham, Maidenhead, Berks SL6 9QH; tel 01628-427500; fax 01628 427499; e-mai: marketing@cim.co.uk (website: http://www.cim.co.uk).

Pharmaceutical Society of Northern Ireland: 73 University Street, Belfast BT7 1HL.

The Registrar and Chief Executive, United Kingdom Central Council for Nursing, Midwifery and Health Visiting: 23 Portland Place, London W1N 3AF; tel 0171-637 7181.

Royal Aeronautical Society: 4 Hamilton Place, London W1V OBQ; fax only 071-243 2546.

Royal College of Veterinary Surgeons: Belgravia House, 62-64 Horseferry Road, London SW1P 2AF; tel 0171-222 2001; fax 0171-222 2004.

Royal Pharmaceutical Society of Great Britain: 1 Lambeth High Street, London SE1 7JN; tel 0171-735 9141; fax 0171-735 7629.

Royal Town Planning Institute: 26 Portland Place, London W1N 4BE; 0171-636 9107; fax 0171-323 1582.

Specialist French Publications

There is a range of French specialist publications aimed at jobseekers in France. *Courrier Cadres* is published by APEC (*Association pour l'Emploi des Cadres*, 8 rue Duret, 75783 Paris) which is a national organisation funded by employers and trade unions for the placement of managers and executives. This publication, is for those with Bac +4 or the UK/US equivalent (see *Higher Education* in the *Daily Life* chapter) and is open to foreign job seekers.

For the hotel and catering trade the French publication *L'Hotellerie* (published at 5 rue Antoine Bourdelle, 75015 Paris) is published weekly and has a large job section while *L'Usine Nouvelle* is for jobs in industry.

L'Etudiant (27 rue du Chemin Vert, 75543 Paris Cedex 11) publishes a magazine of that name with job opportunities for the summer vacation. The same publisher also produces *Le Guide des Entreprises Qui Recrutent*. The French graduate directory is *GO Guide des Opportunités* (Editions Formations-Carrières; 28 rue de la Trémoille, 75008 Paris) whose companion volume *Mémogenda* contains about 1,500 addresses of useful addresses including employers, the French government employment organisations and a range of recruitment consultants.

Employment Organisations

EURES

EURES (short for European Employment Services) is a computerised, pan-European job information network accessible through job centres which have a specially trained Euro Adviser. Through them, you can find out about jobs available in France. There are 42 Euro Advisers in France and a list of them can be obtained from the Pigalle ANPE (Agence Nationale pour L'emploi) in Paris (see below). Alternatively, you can access the EURES network from job centres in the UK. Job seekers can use EURES to find out about job vacancies in any member state plus some national background information including living and working conditions and taxation and social security. Advertising vacancies on the EURES network is free for employers, and all types of jobs from unskilled to executive and professional posts appear on the network (a total of about 5000 vacancies are listed at any one time). It may soon be possible for job-seekers as well as employers to advertise themselves on EURES.

Useful Addresses

ANPE International: 69 rue Pigalle, 75009 Paris; tel +33 (0) 1 44 53 16 16; fax +33 1 48 74 42 53; can supply a list of French Euro Advisers.

Overseas Placing Unit: Level 4, Skills House, 3-7 Holy Green, Off the Moor, Sheffield S1 4AQ; tel 0114 2596051. Central office in the UK for EURES network. EURES is also accessible through local UK Jobcentres.

UK-based Employment Organisations

There are some employment agencies in the UK which specialise in finding overseas jobs for clients. In many cases these agencies deal with a specific sector e.g. electronics, secretarial, medical, etc.; they tend to recruit only qualified and experienced staff, and deal mainly with regions of the world, e.g. the Middle East where there is still a shortage of home-grown specialists, rather than Europe. Most agencies are retained and paid by employers to fill specific vacancies and do not search on behalf of employees using them. An exception would be agencies, including Drake International (see below) which recruits bilingual staff, mainly secretaries and p.a.'s but also receptionists, customer services employees, administrators, interpreters and translators, for France.

Details of employment agency members of the national organisation, the Federation of Recruitment and Employment Services Ltd. (FRES) can be obtained direct from their London address (see below). Those interested should ask for the Overseas Agency List and enclose an A4, self-addressed envelope and a fee of £3.

Useful Addresses

CEPEC: Lilly House, 13 Hanover Square, London W1R 9HD; tel 0171-629 2266. A large UK management outplacement and consultancy which publishes the CEPEC Recruitment Guide, a directory of some 400 recruitment agencies and search consultants in the United Kingdom. The regularly revised *CEPEC Recruitment Guide* is available in reference libraries or from the above address for £37 including postage and packing.

CLC Language Services: Buckingham House, Buckingham Street, London WC2 6BU (0171-499 3365). Offers opportunities for Europeans and North Americans (where valid work permits apply) to work in EU countries at all levels from junior secretary to senior sales executive. Sectors include: sales, marketing and market research, banking, import-export, translating, interpreting, management consultancy, pharmaceutical, media sales and general commerce for secretaries.

Drake International: is based in London but for jobs in Paris contact their Paris office at 5 rue Keppler, 75016 Paris; tel + 33 1 47 20 42 54.

Federation of Recruitment and Employment Services Ltd: 36-38 Mortimer Street, London W1N 7RB; 0171-323 4300.

Sheila Burgess International: 4 Cromwell Place, London SW7 2JE; tel 0171-584 6446; fax 0171-584 1824. Also has a Paris Office: 62, rue St. Lazare: tel 1-44 63 02 57; fax 1-44 63 02 59. In business over ten years. Specialises in multi-lingual secretaries and personal assistants.

French Employment Organisations

Commercial Employment Agencies. legal restrictions mean that French private employment agencies, as in Germany, are prohibited as such and function only as temporary employment bureaux (*agences de travail temporaire/agence d'intérim*) and most are chains with branches in several cities. The addresses of some major ones in Paris are listed under *Temporary Work*.

The French National Employment Service

The Agence Nationale pour l'Emploi (ANPE), is the national government job service of France and as such has the monopoly on placements. All job offers in France have to be notified to the local ANPE office of which there are more than 600 throughout France, the various branches of the ANPE collect vacancies from employers and try to fill these positions with suitable applicants. It is estimated that 25% of job offers are made through the ANPE. Although most offices run a general drop in or Minitel employment service, some specialise in particular areas of employment such as hotel and catering, or tourism. For instance ANPE (12 rue Claude-Genoux, BP 133, 73208 Albertville) runs a special department for hotels and thermal institutions in the French Alps. In Paris where there are dozens of ANPE branches, ANPE also deal with *demandes d'emploi* (jobs wanted). For example, ANPE (12 rue Blanche, 75436 Paris; tel 1-42 85 44 00), posted jobs wanted advertisements in *Fig-Eco* (a supplement of *Le Figaro*) for a journalist, graphic designer and a bilingual secretary.   Yet other ANPEs are known as *antennes saisonnières* which are open during the summer or winter only. For example in the Alps there are extra winter bureaux (*antennes saisonnières hiver*)open from October/November to the end of February in most of the main resorts. In Annecy there is a year round bureau (ANPE, 8 bis rue de Rumilly, 74000 Annecy; tel 4-50 51 00 42). For further details of winter bureaux see *Temporary Work, Ski Resorts*.

The ANPE also has a specialised service for those with higher qualifications (but not necessarily graduates) seeking managerial posts. These are dealt with by the 18 or so ANPE *points cadres* located around France and there is a weekly guide of executive vacancies called *Atout Cadres* from the same organisation.

Useful Addresses (ANPE points cadres)

Alsace: Espace Cadre, 8 rue Adolphe Seyboth, 67000 Strasbourg; tel +33 3-88 15 46 60; fax +33 3-88 15 46 69.

Aquitaine: Ale Bordeaux Cadres, 1 Terrasse Front du Médoc, Tour 2000, 33076 Bordeaux Cedex; tel +33 5 56 90 85 10; fax +33 5-56 99 21 31.

Marseille: Marseille Cadres, 7-9 rue Jean Mermoz - 13272 Marseille Cedex 08; tel +33 4-91 81 73 82; fax +33-4 91 81 73 70.

Midi-Pyrenees: Espace Cadres, 6A Place Occitane, 31000 Toulouse; tel +33 5-61 12 59 59/ fax +33 5-61 12 59 79.

Orleans: Espace Cadre *ANPE:* 31 Avenue de Paris 45000 Orleans; tel +33 2 38 77 86 92/fax +33 2 38 77 86 99.

Nord/Pas-de-Calais: Lille Cadres, 15 Place aux Bleuets, BP 305, 59026 Lille Cedex; tel +33-3 20 51 00 19; fax +33 3-20 13 35 98.

Rhônes Alpes: Espace Cadres, 89 rue General Mangin, 38100 Grenoble; tel +33 4-76 40 76 72; fax +33 4-76 33 81 61.

Rhônes Alpes: Espace Cadres Villeurbanne, 7 rue Louis Guerin, 69100 Villeurbanne; tel +33 4-72 69 09 20; fax +33 4-72 43 09 21.

EU nationals from outside France are entitled to use the ANPE on equal terms with France nationals. In practice, ANPE's are primarily devoted to finding jobs for French nationals and have proved notoriously unhelpful to foreign job seekers, although this is something which varies very much from region to region. Needless to say the greater your ability to communicate in French the better your chances generally of a positive response.

Offices do not usually deal with individuals by letter so you will have to apply in person or through Minitel (see page 173). ANPEs are listed in the French yellow pages for each area under the classification *Administrations du Travail et de l'Emploi*. A list of ANPE's throughout France is available from the main office at ANPE, 4 rue Galilée, 93198 Noisy-le-Grande Cedex (tel: 1-49 31 74 00) which also operates EURES (see above).

Embassies and Consulates

Embassies and consulates will not assist members of the public to find jobs. Not only are they unable to deal with the amount of administration involved, but they are not keen to encourage foreign workers to take jobs away from nationals. However, they can be the source of some contact addresses. It may be worth contacting them by post, or in person, to see if they can assist. Most of them produce a few typed pages of information for foreigners about living and working in France. The French Consulates issue a free, leaflet on employment in France and the British representations in France generally have some information sheets for British subjects resident in France.

Chambers of Commerce

Chambers of Commerce exist to serve the interests of businesses trading in both France and the UK, they do not operate as employment agencies. However they may be able to offer background information which can be helpful in the job-hunting process; moreover, the French Consulate does propose the appropriate national chamber of commerce as a source of local information.

Perhaps the best way in which the national Chambers of Commerce can assist is by providing the names and addresses of member companies. Many of these companies are large organisations which may well have current or prospective vacancies. Thus, it is worth enquiring on the off chance that there is a job available at the time at which you apply.

The Chambers of Commerce in the UK and France have separate yearbooks which list member companies and give much useful information: contact these direct for further details and prices.

In addition to the national Chambers of Commerce there are local and regional branches all over France, in virtually every city and town. Many of these enthusiastically support local industries and companies and, on request, will supply details of them. It is unlikely, however, that they will know of actual, current vacancies, although information you can obtain from them could be a good pointer as to which areas to look at and which companies to approach. The addresses of the main Chambers of Commerce in each French region are listed later on in this chapter.

Useful Addresses

Chambre de Commerce Française de Grande-Bretagne: 197 Knightsbridge, London SW7 1RB; tel 0171-304 7021; fax 0171-304 7034; e-mail: bclub@ ccfgb.co.uk produces several useful publications including: *Setting up a Business in France* (£16), *Buying and Selling Residential Property in France* (£8), and *Living as a British Expatriate in France* (£11).

Franco-British Chamber of Commerce & Industry: 31 rue Boissy d'Anglas, 75008 Paris; tel 1-53 30 81 32; fax 1-53 30 81 35.

Assemblée Permanente des Chambres de Commerce et d'Industrie: 45 avenue d'Iéna, 75016 Paris (tel 1-47 23 01 11).

Placing Employment Wanted Adverts

When seeking a job overseas it is not always sufficient to rely solely on advertised jobs as a source of prospective employment. It can often be more successful to attract the attention of potential employers who may have a vacancy. Many employers are impressed by those who take the initiative to make a direct application, and, of course, in some cases it is possible that an employer may need just the service which you are offering.

One of the easiest ways of canvassing potential employers is to place a job request (*demande d'emploi*) in the French press. This is done in much the same way as you might place an 'Employment Wanted' advertisement in the UK. Obviously, the advertisement should be written in French and a telephone/fax number for replies provided if possible. You can place advertisements directly with a French newspaper but in the UK it is easier to use an advertisement agency. The weekly *European* newspaper has a special deal 'European Job Search' whereby you place an advert (for which there is a standard charge of £50 plus VAT), advertising your skills and languages and requesting employment in another European country.

It is also possible to advertise through Minitel.

Useful Addresses
European Classified Ads., Orbit House, 5 New Fetter Lane, London EC4A 1AP; tel: 0171 418 7883; fax 0171-713 1835. The European has a special self-advertisement deal for those looking for work abroad called European Job Search (see above). The European is published on Thursdays.
Mercury Publicity Ltd: International Headquarters, 16 John Street, Holborn, London WC1N 2DL; tel 0171-831 6631. Takes advertising for *Le Figaro* and *France Soir* and French regional newspapers. Recommends advertising in *Figaro Economie* a *Figaro* supplement that appears on Mondays.

Company/Organisation Transfers

The alternative to finding work in France by applying direct or in person, is to find a position within a company or organisation in the UK which offers the possibility of being transferred to France. Currently, few companies will guarantee staff that they will be posted to a specific country after a certain period. However, both the request and the practice are becoming more common as companies take advantage of the single European market for goods and services by expanding their operations elsewhere in the EU. Ideally, it could be envisaged that eventually companies will post staff as readily from Reading to Rennes as they do now from, say, London to Bristol.

Non-commercial international organisations also provide opportunities for transfers abroad.

The following types of companies and organisations can offer the option of working in France:

French Companies Operating in the UK. Over the last decade, a number of French companies have entered the UK market, often quite aggressively. For example, many food producers and distributors e.g. Yoplaît and also financial institutions e.g. Crédit Lyonnais and the Société Générale Merchant Bank. However, check first that the company you target is a French company. For example, French car manufacturers are very active in the UK market but the importing companies are essentially British, not French.
British Companies Operating in France. Despite criticism that UK companies have been slow to enter the French market, a number of British companies are now actively involved in France, including such household names as Marks & Spencer, Tesco, Glaxo, Wimpey, United Biscuits, Courtaulds, KP Foods, BP and ICI. Many more UK companies including smaller ones are following the lead provided, by the big companies. In the finance area, many British banks such as Hambros, Barclays, Abbey National, Woolwich etc. already have a significant presence in France. Altogether about 1,800 British companies have set up in France.
International Companies. There are an increasing number of multinational companies whose branches and subsidiaries are found all round the world and these can offer possible employment prospects. For example, Nestlé is essentially a Swiss company but also has major involvements in both the UK and France. Many addresses of companies of a similar status can be obtained through the

respective Chambers of Commerce as discussed earlier. The company names may be different in each country and often a certain amount of detective work is necessary to discover the extent of a particular company's operation in the UK and France and the consequent potential for later being posted elsewhere. A useful publication in this respect is *Who Owns Whom*, which is available in main reference libraries and provides the names of British companies with French subsidiaries.

Few companies will recruit exclusively with a transfer in mind, but you can always discuss your aims at interview; senior staff will be in a much stronger position to dictate their requirements.

Worldwide Organisations: Alternatively, there are jobs with world organisations, such as the United Nations, UNESCO, the World Bank, UNICEF etc. all of which have offices in Paris. Transfers within worldwide organisations are available for those with suitable qualifications. Further details are given under *Permanent Work*. Where a posting abroad is actually made, it will normally include many financial increments and perks; salaries are often negotiated at the highest international rates, higher than either the UK or French equivalents. Fringe benefits may include relocation assistance, subsidised mortgages, accommodation, school fees, health insurance and pension plans, etc.

Methods of Application

On Spec Written Applications

You may wish to compile an address book of companies likely to have a use for your particular skills and/or qualifications. Any reference library is a good starting point for compiling such a book. Possible sources of addresses include the Chamber of Commerce Yearbooks, the French yellow pages and various professional and industrial directories.

The main drawback of this method is that it can be a very arbitrary, not to mention lengthy, procedure and can cost a fortune in postage. It will be necessary to compile a great many letters in order to gain even a few leads; the acknowledgement rate may only be 1% or 2% of all letters sent and positive replies even less. Probably the best system is to maintain a rolling list: write a set number of letters each week and regularly replace the addresses used with new ones.

Unless you have a personal contact, letters of application should be addressed 'For the Attention of the Head of Personnel' (*A L'Attention du Chef du Personnel*), or the Head of Department (*Chef de Service*) or in the case of a multinational, Head of International Human Resources, and if you can discover their name by means of a quick telephone call, so much the better. Include a c.v. with your letter. If necessary both letter and c.v. should be professionally translated into French. A professional agency such as The Institute of Translation and Interpreting (377 City Road, London EC1V 1NA ; tel 0171-713 7600; fax 0171-713 7650; e-mail: iti@compuserve.com) will charge in the region of £70 for one thousand words, but obviously costs vary depending on what is involved. In view of the high cost of professional translations, it is worth checking other possibilities, e.g. local colleges of further education, or universities for this purpose. The best and most convenient method of preparing such letters is by word processor, photocopied circulars tend to receive a much lower response.

Note that such letters need not be restricted to companies, you can also send copies to recruitment agencies (*cabinets de recrutement*) and search consultants (*cabinets de chasseurs de têtes*) whose advertisements appear regularly in main French newspapers, weekly news magazines and trade publications. You can also send them to international recruitment agencies in the UK.

A directory of some of France's largest organisations and most important companies is provided at the end of this chapter and can be referred to as a starting point from which to begin targeting potential employers. You can also attend trade fairs in your own country or in France in order to collect the addresses and particulars of potential employers.

Personal Visits

Anyone who is in France looking for a job may want to make enquiries in person as to the availability of employment. This involves not only responding to jobs advertised but also canvassing potential employers on the spot. Usually an exhausting business entailing much wear and tear to shoe leather and the human spirit, it may still be possible to obtain a job offer this way. After all, all you need is one positive response so this technique is worth a try.

Before making an approach to a potential employer decide how you can best sell your skills, talents or experience. For example, those looking for casual work in the tourist industry could suggest that as native English-speakers they can improve the service that, for example, a hotelier or restaurateur offers to English-speaking customers.

When making impromptu personal visits to potential employers, ensure that you have a stock of c.v.'s with you to leave with the personnel department and that you give a contact telephone number. If you hear nothing for a few days it is advisable to follow up your visit with a telephone call. Of course, you may be lucky enough to be telephoned by the employer, or in exceptional cases, offered a job on the spot.

Form, Content & Style of Written Applications

In the vast majority of cases, no matter how one finds out about a job, it will be necessary to write a letter of application. This applies at all levels, except, perhaps, for unskilled work or casual employment. Unless an advertisement clearly states that a personal or telephone application is required, a letter is the best choice. The letter will normally have to be written in French and it is quite in order to have a professional translation made. On the other hand, it is not advisable to suggest that one's command of the language is substantially better than it is.

In many ways the process of doing business in France is relaxed and informal. This does not apply, however, to job applications. French employers require that a certain etiquette is maintained and impressions gained from correspondence are very important. In particular, the letter should be hand written, and tailored to the company/type of job for which you are applying, and appear individually prepared. The temptation to pour out reams of personal history should be resisted as the full dynamism and drive of your personality should be revealed at interview, and not at the application stage. The letter should be formal and respectful in style, clearly state your reasons for application and the relevance of your qualifications and experience to the employment available. Abbreviations should be avoided, as should jokes which may not be understood. For further guidance on writing business letters in French consult *How to Address Overseas Business Letters* by Derek Allen (Foulsham).

Curriculum Vitae

The basic essential of any application is the curriculum vitae CV or *Etat Civil*. The CV should contain concise information and should if possible be no more than one page (two pages maximum), and the information should create the best possible impression. For this reason, many people entrust the preparation and presentation of their CV to a company that specialises in this kind of service. They can be found by looking in the Yellow Pages under Employment Agencies. The cost is usually about £25 for a one-page graduate CV. Alternatively refer to the publication *The Right Way to Write Your Own CV* by John Clarke (Paper Fronts) and *CVs and Written Applications* by Judy Skeats and *Finding Work in France* (£4.99) published by Careers Europe and available from your local careers office.

Note that for a potential French employer the c.v. should be modified to remove any abbreviations and explain any qualifications, etc. which could confuse a foreign reader. A c.v. should be on A4 paper and it is acceptable to send out photocopies or print outs of this (unlike the letter of application which should appear personalised). Generally, it is better to provide a succinct CV that you may consider too short, rather than one which is comprehensive but which the employer will think overlong. You could then add in your letter of application that if any further information is required you will be happy to supply it. Do not send any certificates or documents with an enquiry or application as these stand little chance of being returned. If they are requested or if you feel they would help, then send photocopies only.

Interview Procedure

If you are offered an interview, remember that first impressions and appearances are crucial. Unless the job was advertised in the UK the interview is unlikely to be held in the UK. Check in advance that the travel costs will be covered, otherwise you will have to decide if the cost of the trip is justified. French employers tend not to offer interviews lightly, so the invitation to attend one is a positive sign. Those selected for interview tend to have been already shortlisted, which is different to the UK procedure, where all those whose initial applications appear appropriate may be interviewed and then those on the shortlist re-interviewed.

The importance of the first impressions cannot be stressed enough. As one expert put it, ' The interview begins the moment you walk through the door' so it will be up to you to create the right ones based on your knowledge of the company to date. The interview may be with just one person or with a panel. However, whatever the number of interviewers, this is likely to be a formal meeting as a casual approach to interviewing is unpopular and considered an American approach by the French.

Obviously an interview in France will be as much a test of language ability as job ability. This applies for more basic jobs as well as for executive positions. In particular, try to find out the correct pronunciation of names and titles beforehand. In general, 'Monsieur' and 'Madame' are sufficient forms of address, without the addition of a surname, and certainly first names should not be used. Remember to use the more formal 'vous' form of address throughout the interview unless, which is unlikely, an interviewer addresses you in the 'tu' form. Finally, note that handshaking is the norm throughout France; i.e. you shake hands both on arrival and departure.

Try to obtain some background information on the company before the interview and to show any knowledge you have acquired through this research during the interview. It is also a good idea to show a committed interest in all aspects not only of the job, but also an admiration for France generally. After the interview, a short note of thanks, written in French, is appropriate.

Temporary Work

This section deals with seasonal jobs for instance in agriculture, childcare, tourism, as well as a variety of possibilities temping through agencies. Temping is something which many people might have to do before they find a long-term post. Teaching English as a foreign language is dealt with under *Permanent Work* although temporary posts, are also available in this field.

Agriculture

Although the number of people engaged in agriculture for a living is declining in France, there are still more livelihoods tied up with the land than in other, highly developed European countries. The recent rise in unemployment is bound to reduce the possibilities for casual farm work for foreigners, but there are thousands of temporary agricultural jobs throughout the year and so this should thus be considered a major source of temporary work. Some harvests are traditionally the preserve of itinerant workers from other Mediterranean countries: grape picking (*les vendanges*) is often done by Spanish, Portuguese and Moroccan teams who return to the same vineyards year after year. However, the necessity of human pickers has in many areas given way to the mechanical pickers.

Nearly every region of France has its agricultural specialities and the vineyards reach from the salt marshes of the Camargue in the south, north to the Loire and Champagne; there are luscious fruits including melons and peaches produced by the Mediterranean climate of Languedoc and apples and plums in the more temperate Dordogne. Other regions where the land is remarkably productive include the great Rhône valley which is a fruit and vegetable region; while the south-west around Bordeaux is where maize growing is concentrated. The Loire Valley, the Paris Basin, Brittany and Normandy are other areas with high volumes of agricultural produce. These are just some of the possibilities for harvest work which can begin as early as mid-May in the south of France for strawberries to late October for grapepicking. Conditions of work vary, but many workers are expected to provide their own accommodation and food so a tent is essential. Jobs are found most easily by visiting the local ANPE or by going round knocking on doors. It is altogether an easier task if you have your own transport.

One potentially useful organisation (apart from the CDIJs and ANPEs) is the French organic farm organisation *Nature et Progrès*. The address from which you can obtain a list of organic farms in France (price 50 francs), that take working guests in exchange for free board and lodging is 1 Avenue Général de Gaulle, 84130 Le Pontet (tel +33 4-90 31 00 42). The guide is entitled *Les Bonnes Adresses de la Bio* and lists French organic farms by *département* and their requirements for temporary workers. Nature et Progrès changes address frequently, so if you are coming from the UK you can also contact WWOOF (Willing Workers on Organic Farms) by sending a s.a.e. to 19 Bradford Road, Lewes, Sussex BN7 1RB. Membership costs £10 a year and includes a bi-monthly newsletter with adverts for help in the UK and abroad.

For those with a professional interest in farming, the International Farm Experience Programme (YFC Centre, National Agricultural Centre, Kenilworth,

Warwickshire CV8 2LG) arranges courses combining language tuition and work experience on farms for five months beginning in February and July. Five weeks at a language school are followed by four months on a farm. Free board and lodging throughout the language course and wages at local rates while on the farm are provided. Applicants must be aged 18-26 and have at least two years of practical farming experience. Travel costs and insurance are subsidised.

Sésame (formerly the Centre de Documentation et d'Information Rurale), a Paris agency (9 Square Gabriel Fauré, 75017 Paris; tel 1-40 54 07 08, fax 1-40 54 06 39) arranges for agricultural *stagiares* (trainees) to work on farms around France but they do not deal with seasonal agricultural work. Applicants with access to Minitel can contact Sésame using the code (36-15 ESAME), or by post enclosing an IRC if from abroad.

Au Pair and Nannying

Despite its potential drawbacks (awful parents, abominable children and sexploitation), being an au pair/nanny/mother's help, officially known in France as *stagiare aide-familiale* is probably still the best way of learning the language and getting to know the country and is a good starting point for going to live and work there on a longer-term basis later. In Paris particularly there is no problem finding posts: there are dozens of agencies in France as in the UK; also CIJ offices, and sometimes ANPEs have lists of families looking for live-in helpers. By arranging a job on the spot you get a chance to meet the family, inspect the accommodation and its proximity to amenities (isolation in the suburbs is not ideal), and more importantly the children (and vice versa) before committing yourself for the usual minimum of six months.

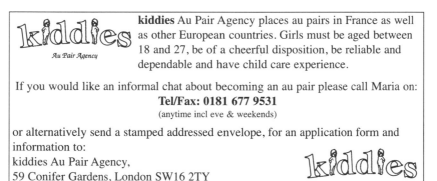

kiddies Au Pair Agency places au pairs in France as well as other European countries. Girls must be aged between 18 and 27, be of a cheerful disposition, be reliable and dependable and have child care experience.

Au Pair Agency

If you would like an informal chat about becoming an au pair please call Maria on:
Tel/Fax: 0181 677 9531
(anytime incl eve & weekends)

or alternatively send a stamped addressed envelope, for an application form and information to:
kiddies Au Pair Agency,
59 Conifer Gardens, London SW16 2TY

The job of au pair is governed by regulations. Working hours are a 5½ per day, Monday to Saturday with one full day off and no more than three nights babysitting per week. Although few au pairs actually manage to keep these hours, if the family is a good one and takes a genuine interest in the au pair and includes them in family life, it can still work out extremely well for both parties. Anyone who really wants to concentrate on their studies in French should ask to be a demi-pair. This entails only 12 hours work per week in return for room and board but not pocket money. Au pair work should include only light household duties and normal childcare. An au pair is not obliged to care for children with special needs or disabilities. Free meals and single accommodation should be provided even outside normal duty hours. An au pair should attend a language course as this is considered one of the main objectives of the arrangement. The salary is tied into the SMIC (see *Aspects of Employment*) and is currently about 1,600 francs per month.

There are also regulations for the family employing you: by law, they are obliged to pay monthly social security contributions to the local URSSAF office to cover the cost of emergency or routine medical treatment. Au Pairs in or near Paris should expect to be given a *carte orange* travel pass) which is valid for most public transport and costs about 275 francs (about £30) a month.

It is also possible to find families who will offer a more informal arrangement such as several evenings of babysitting a week in return for board and lodging. For addresses of baby-sitting agencies in Paris you might be able to sign up with — see below.

Although the majority of French families will expect their child helper to be female, the concept of the male au pair is spreading, so males should not be put off from answering advertisements if they are good with children. You should also put up your own: one male au pair got his job by putting a job wanted notice on the upstairs notice board of the British Church (just off the rue de Faubourg St Honoré in Paris).

Au Pair Agencies

Note that agencies in France charge both applicants and families for their services; in the case of applicants charges can be as high as 700 francs.

Accueil Familial des Jeunes Etrangérs (AFJE): 23 rue du Cherche-Midi, 75006 Paris; tel 1-42 22 50 34; fax 1-45 44 60 48.

Alliance Culturelle Internationale (A.C.I.), 4 Av. Félix Faure, 06000 Nice; tel 4-93 13 44 13; fax 4-93 92 58.

Butterfly et Papillon, 5 Av. de Genève, 74000 Annecy; tel 4-50 46 08 33/4-50 67 01 33.

Anglo Continental Au Pairs: 21 Amesbury Crescent, Hove, East Sussex BN3 5RD; tel/fax 01273-705959.

Contacts: 55 rue Nationale, 37000 Tours; tel 2-47 20 20 57; fax 2-47 20 68 92.

Euro Pair Services: 13 rue Vavin, 75006 Paris; tel 1-43 29 80 01; fax 1-43 29 80 37.

Inter-Séjours: 179 rue de Courcelles, 75017 Paris; tel 1-47 63 06 81; fax 1-40 54 89 41.

Kiddies au Pair: 59 Conifer Gardens, Streatham, London SW16 2TY; tel 0181-677 9531; fax 0181-677 9531. Short and long-term placements around France.

Séjours Internationaux Linguistiques et Culturels (SILC): 32 Rempart de l'Est, 16022 Angoulême Cedex; tel 5-45 97 41 00; fax 5-45 94 20 63. E-mail: nadine.g@silc.asso.fr

Soames International: B P 28 77302 Fontainebleau; tel 1-64 78 37 98; fax 1-64 45 91 75.

Baby Sitting Agencies

Allo Maman Poule: 7 Villa Murat, 75016 Paris; tel 1-45 20 96 96.

Babysitting Service: 18 rue Tronchet, Paris 8th; tel 1-46 3751 24.

Business & Industry

Private Employment Agencies

As already stated, French regulations stipulate that commercial employment agencies in France only deal with temporary work. They can offer a range of work in offices, shops and industry and you have to register with them in person.

Agencies advertise in newspapers and weekly reviews and others may be found by looking in the pages jaunes under *agences d'intérim/personnel intérimaire/ travail temporaire.* There are dozens listed in the several directories for the Paris region.

Note that employment agencies are required by law to request a social security number (*un sécu*) which means that you can only get employment through them if you have already worked legally in France. Some working travellers claim that they have managed to get on an agency's books without one, especially in Paris. You may also have to show your *carte de séjour.*

For office temping jobs you will obviously need to be fluent in French. However, if you are not, there are other possibilities familiar to those with experience of similar agencies in the UK: market research (*entreprises en recherche de marché*) for international companies, leaflet distribution (*distributeurs en publicité*), door-to-door seller (*vendeur porte á porte*), all of which usually require less adept French, probably the ability to learn a specialised terminology or a salesperson's or researcher's patter off by heart. If your French is not up to even these jobs then you could try others where French is hardly required at all: domestic or office cleaner for contract cleaning firms (*entreprises de nettoyage*), house removals (*démenagement*), or night security (*surveillance de nuit/agent de surveillance*). For the last you can contact specifically: SICLI Securité Télésurveillance, 12 rue de l'Isly, Paris.

The Union Nationale des Entreprises de Travail Temporaires (UNETT, 22 rue de l'Arcade, 75008 Paris; tel 1-42 68 06 44; fax 1-42 65 90 31) can provide lists of temporary work agencies throughout France categorised by the sector in which they operate.

Private Employment Agencies
Britt: 10 Blvd des Capucines, 75002 Paris; tel 1-47 42 06 12.
Elite International: 10 rue de Louvois, 75002 Paris; tel 1-42 86 94 82.
Eric Soutou: 21 Avenue de l'Opéra, 75001 Paris; tel 1-42 61 42 61.
Hôtesse Secretaires: 12 rue Chabanais, 75002 Paris; tel 1-42 96 34 80.
Interim 6: 71 rue Bugeaud, 69006 Lyon; tel 4-78 24 31 51.
IPB Travail Temporaire: 14 rue Général Audran, Cedex, 92041, Paris La Défense; tel 1-49 04 85 00.
Manpower: Manpower France Head Office, 9 rue Jacques Bingen, 75017 Paris; tel 1-44 15 40 40.
Manpower (for Executives): Manpower Paris Cadres (Rive Gauche), 148 Bld. du Montparnasse, Paris 75014. tel 1-45 38 74 74.
3T Inter Européenne: 106 Avenue Jean Moulin, 78170 La Celle Saint Cloud; tel Paris 1-30 82 53 00).

Teaching English
Although this category of work is dealt with in greater detail under *Permanent Work* (see below), English teaching can also be considered a useful source of temporary employment. Once scornful of the mere suggestion of a need to speak English, the French have realised that for business and particularly for science and technology they cannot do without it. Hence the plethora of English language institutes, particularly in Paris and big cities. Many companies provide their employees with free language courses and thus business people provide the main source of clients. Although the majority of schools prefer people to work for a year or longer contract, some companies, notably Berlitz have a high turnover of staff

in their dozen or so Paris schools owing to the pressure many staff find themselves under. Probably preferable, and usually much more enjoyable, is offering private language tuition. The going rate is around £10 an hour. Advertisements offering tuition can be placed on notice boards (*panneaux*) in colleges, supermarkets, schools, and if possible in places where business clients are likely to see them, for instance on noticeboards in company premises though you may have to dress smartly and persuade security staff to let you do this. It is also possible to exchange language tuition in return for a room and keep. Another possibility is telephone teaching, but because it is so convenient and fun it is difficult to get such a post. The pay rates are about the same as for private language tuition.

Tourism

As one of the great tourist destinations of Europe, France has no shortage of related temporary work to offer in many categories. This section covers most of them including Euro Disney, hotels and catering, holiday centres and campsites, ski resorts and holiday boats. Of course work in tourism need not be temporary; those interested in making a career in tourism will find that most big companies e.g. Club Med have career development opportunities.

EuroDisney: (The Casting Centre, Euro Disney SCA, POB 110, 77777 Marne La Vallée, Cedex 4 (tel 1-49 31 19 99). Despite initial financial catastrophes which made pundits predict the folding of EuroDisney by 1994, it celebrated its fifth birthday in 1997. The enormous complex that comprises Disneyland Paris, 30km east of Paris, has nearly 6000 hotel rooms, and an entertainment centre as well as the huge theme park. Overall about 12,000 employees service the complex during peak season on a mixture of long-term and short term contracts. Seasonal positions are from March to October with a minimum availability of July to September. 'Cast Members' (Disneyspeak for staff) must all have a minimum of conversational French and preferably a third European language. The majority of jobs are in food and beverage, housekeeping, merchandising and custodial departments, though one of the best is as a disney character in costume. Further details in the UK from the Disneyland Paris Casting Department, Beaumont House, Kensington Village, Avonmore Road, London W14 8TS (0171-605 2961) or in France from the address above. Under the nationality quota that operates at EuroDisney, fewer than 2,000 workers will be British. The minimum period of work in summer is two months, and your ability to speak French will be tested at interview. Monthly gross wages start at about 6,407 francs (about £696). Deductions for social security are about 1,000 francs. There is some staff housing on site but not enough to go round. If you are allocated staff accommodation expect further deductions in the region of 2000 francs. Other staff get assistance in finding accommodation and a 50% reimbursement of commuting costs. In the case of temporary staff, travel costs to and from Paris are reimbursed on contract completion.

Campsites and Holiday Centres:
One of the favourite French pastimes seems to be camping, especially en famille. At the last count there were over 11,000 campsites in France about two thousand of which were small, basic, privately-run sites owned by families, farmers and even the odd British expatriate. Campsites are graded according to the facilities provided and there is an official rating system. At the top end, four star sites have a range of amenities from tennis courts to indoor recreation areas. Some of the larger sites are run by holiday companies and are popular with the British, Dutch, Germans etc.

A number of British companies also run sites in France and employ summer staff as campsite couriers who welcome the holiday-makers on arrival, clean the mobile homes on changeover day and carry out general maintenance duties. Although many companies recruit students and those having a gap year between school and university, it is possible for older people to be recruited. One company at least, (NSS Riviera Holidays of Hull), states a preference for mature, active couples aged 40+ with a pension or private income prepared to work a spring, summer or autumn for nil payment but with many perks including no charge accommodation and facilities, plenty of free time and help with ferry crossing and insurance.

Outdoor activity centres in France may be commercially run, or *Colonies de Vacances* (summer camps for children or families), run by the French government or French non-profit organisations. There is a non-profit association called UCPA which runs over 50 adult activity centres which need a range of staff including qualified sports instructors, bar and catering staff, nurses and possibly even language teachers. British companies like Discover and PGL operate summer activity camps for children and are another possible source of temporary work.

Note that of these jobs, only those with French-run campsites and centres are likely to help you integrate with the French, but all may give you the time to look around and arrange something more permanent.

Useful Addresses

Campsite Operators

Canvas Holidays: 12 Abbey Park Place, Dunfermline, Fife KY12 7PD; tel 01383-644018. April to the end of September. About £80 per week.

Carisma Holidays: Bethel House, Heronsgate, Chorleywood WD3 5BB; tel 01923-284235. Mid-May to the end of September. £70-£85 per week plus tips.

Chateau de L'Eperviere: 71240 Gigny-sur-Saone, Bourgogne Sud; tel 3-85 44 83 23; fax 3-85 44 74 20. Needs a joiner, plumber and a manual labourer for a maximum of six months from early in April to late September. Must speak French and have a driving licence.

NSS Riviera Holidays: 199 Marlborough Avenue, Hull HU5 3LG. Prefer older couples aged 45+ who are active, to work in a complex of 30 chalets, cottages and mobile homes on a 4-star holiday village between St. Tropez and Cannes doing DIY to a high standard 3 days a week in return for free board and lodging, electricity and gas and other perks.

Trans Sure Ltd. c/o Cour du Château, 44430 Le Loroux-Bottereau; tel +33 2-40 03 74 72. LGV Drivers required to work in Europe for the UK camping industry. The job involves loading and delivering camping equipment from central depots to campsites at the beginning of the season. The equipment is then picked up and returned to the depots at the end of the season. Often hard work but very sociable. Wages are £30 a day (usually five days a week). Accommodation provided when not working. Outward and return travel paid for if needed. Periods of work from March 15 to May 15 and September 10 to October 30. Applicants need Class 1 or 3 LGV licences, and at least one year's driving experience. Contact Jamie Ramsden.

Vendée Loisirs Vacances: 78 ave Abbé Thibaud, 85690 Notre Dame de Monts, France (tel 251-59-06-37; fax 251 59-78-00).

Holiday Centres

Acorn Venture Ltd. 137 Worcester Road, Hagley, Stourbridge DY9 ONW; tel

01562-882151. Needs instructors with relevant qualifications and a qualified nurse.

Carisma Holidays: Bethel House, Heronsgate, Chorleywood WD3 5BB; tel 01923-284235. Site Managers, Full season (12 May to 24 September) to work on beach sites in France.

Centre d'Echanges Internationaux: 104 rue de Vaugirard, 75006 Paris. Employs youth leaders from March to September to teach sports, dancing, music, crafts etc. in international holiday centres. Applicants must speak French.

Centre de Vacances d'Aulon: 65440 Guchen. Children's holiday camp needs assistant group leaders to work with children aged six to 12 years and 13 to 17. £105 to £115 per month according to ability. Free board and lodging.

Centre de Voile l'Aber-Wrac'h, Boite Postale 4, 29870 Landeda; tel 2-98 04 90 64; fax 2-98 04 97 22. Sailing instructors and sailing camp leaders for Brittany sailing centre during July and August. Pay is £87 weekly plus board and lodging. Must be qualified.

Discover: Hobo Travel Ltd. Timbers, Oxted Road, Godstone, Surrey RH9 8AD; tel: 01883-744392; fax 01883-744913. Adventure training and personal developement courses based in the Cevennes, southern France.

Haven Europe: 1 Park Lane, P O Box 216, Hemel Hempstead HP2 4GJ. Needs general staff to work in one of three French holiday villages owned and run by Haven: receptionists, bar staff, qualified lifeguards, entertainment staff, grounds/maintenance and accommodation/facilities cleaners. April to October. Fluency in French needed for those with direct customer contact.

PGL Travel: Alton Court, Penyard Lane, Ross-on-Wye, Herefordshire HR9 5GL; tel 01989-767833. PGL runs adventure holiday centres throughout France: the Ardèche, the Alps, the Mediterranean coast etc. and needs domestic staff, leaders, instructors, nurses and drivers between March and the end of September. Staff get pocket money and full board.

UCPA:(Head Office) 62 rue de la Glacier, 75640 Paris 13; tel 1-43 36 05 20. Chain of over 55 centres set up nearly 30 years ago. They are operated on a seasonal basis: some have both a summer and winter season, but most are for summer only. Each centre caters for two to three hundred adults and employs 12-20 instructors, plus catering staff.

VFB Holidays Ltd.: (Normandy House, High Street, Cheltenham GL50 3HW; tel 01242-235515. Organises family activity holidays at various centres in France including the Alps and the Auvergne. Employs representatives (who also help with the activities) for two months from end of June to September. Applicants should be bilingual English/French and have a background in Physical Education activities and a first aid qualification. Recruitment takes place in January for the following season.

Hotels and Restaurants
Probably one of the easiest types of temporary work to get, especially on the spot if you choose a thriving tourist region in high season. Most people get jobs by asking in person. Wages are at the SMIC rate. It is possible to arrange work in advance from the UK, either by writing to hotels direct (proprietors' names and addresses can be obtained from a tourist guide), or through the handful of agencies like UK Overseas Handling (see below). Alternatively, *The Directory of Summer Jobs Abroad* (Vacation Work, Oxford) is an annual publication with lists of employers and their precise terms and requirements.

Useful Addresses:
CLEI (The European and International Placements Centre, 103 Avenue Hereiot,

56000, Vannes, Brittany; tel +33 2-97 40 56 56; fax +33 2-97 40 56 57. This company has links with a catering training college in Vannes and one of the services it offers is 'the reception in France of young foreign professionals in hotel and restaurant training. It can also help those who wish to work in commerce, service and industry.

Horizon HPL: Signet House, 49/51 Farringdon Road, London EC1M 3JB; tel 0181-404 9192; fax 0171-404 9194; in France: 22/26 rue du Sergent Bauchat, 75012 Paris; tel 1-40 01 07 07; fax 1-40 01 07 28. Horizon is a French/British linguistic training organisation that can place candidates in hotels and companies throughout France for linguistic and professional experience. Candidates should be EU nationals, have basic French and be motivated to learn in a new environments. A follow-up is organised during the stay in order to ensure progress. Recruitment all year. Stays from three months.

Ski Resorts:
There are various possibilities for those looking for temporary work in the Alps. You can either work for the French, in which case you will need to speak the language. You will also receive a reasonable wage based on the French statutory minimum known as the SMIC. The disadvantage is that in some cases you would have to find your own accommodation. Alternatively, you can work for a British company, receive only pocket money and free board and lodging, look after British punters and learn virtually nothing about the French, but a lot about skiing. The types of job available working for the French include all types of hotel, catering and bar jobs, night club coat check, night watchman, cleaners, letting agency receptionists for self-catering apartments and ski shop assistants. There has been a problem with British ski instructor qualifications being accepted in France, unless British qualified instructors pass a very competitive French exam the *equivalence* which involves a slalom against the clock. Even so with too little work all the time for all the instructors, work is by no means guaranteed.

If you hold professional qualifications in hotel catering or tourism, you could try the A.N.P.E. in Albertville (12 rue Claude-Genoux BP 133, 73208 Albertville; tel: 4-79 37 87 80; fax: 4-79 32 72 03) which has a centralised placement service for vacancies in: Morzine, Avoriaz, La Clusaz, Chamonix, Megève, St.-Jean-de-Maurienne, Bourg-St.-Maurice, Les Arcs, Tignes, Val d'Isère, Les Deux Alpes, Courchevel, Méribel, Chamrousse and L'Alpe d'Huez. Vacancies can also be found through MINITEL 36.14 Alpes. If you are in France and have access to a Minitel terminal you could try registering your application directly. In theory, you will be informed directly of vacancies suitable for your qualifications. The Albertville A.N.P.E. also operates in the summer as well for a different selection of resorts including thermal spas like Thonon-les-Bains and Aix-les-Bains.

AGENCES LOCALES POUR L'EMPLOI (French Work Bureaux)
Opening periods may vary, except year round offices.

Haute-Savoie
Chamonix: 30 Allée Louis Lachenal, 74400 Chamonix; tel 04 50 55 88 00; fax 04 50 55 86 79. Open all year.
Megève: 28, Place de l'Eglise, 74120 Megèved; tel 04 50 58 78 61; fax 04 50 91 98 56. Open approx 21 October to end of March.
Morzine: Ancienne Poste, 74110 Morzine; tel 04 50 79 21 99; fax 04 50 79 25 34. Open from 1 October to end of February.
Taninges: Ave. Thézière, 74440 Taninges; tel 04 50 34 33 94; fax 04 50 89 44 42. Open mornings all year.

Thônes: Place Avet, 74230 Thônes; tel 04 50 32 18 31; fax 04 50 02 19 83. Open from mid-November to end of March.

Isère

l'Alpe d'Huez: Place J Paganon, 38750 L'Alpe d'Huez; tel 04 76 80 69 07. Open from 7 October to the end of December.

Les Deux Alpes: Mairie de Mont de Lans, BP 12 — Centre Administratif, 48 Avenue de la Muzelle, 388860 Les Deux Alpes; tel 04 76 79 50 94; fax 04 76 79 25 15. Open from 7 October to the end of December.

Villard du Lans: Place P Chabert, 38250 Villard de Lans; tel 04 76 95 57 62; fax (Radio Locale) 04 76 95 90 28. Open all year.

ANTENNES A3 SAISON HIVER (Seasonal Work Bureaux)

Opening dates may vary from year to year

Savoie

Bourg Saint Maurice, Le Sainfoin, rue Jean Moulin, 73700 Bourg St. Maurice; tel 04 79 07 25 34; fax 04 79 07 58 93. Open from the beginning of June to the end of March.

Courchevel: Le Forum, rue du Plantray, 73120 Courchevel; tel 04 79 08 00 48; fax 04 79 08 10 28.

Les Menuires: Maison des Saisonniers, 73440 Les Ménuires; tel 04 79 00 71 32. Open from the beginning of October to mid-December.

Méribel: Office du Tourisme, 73550 Méribel; tel 04 79 00 51 75. Open from the beginning of October to mid-December.

Modane: 34 ave Jean Jaurès, 73500 Modane; tel 04 79 05 21 91; fax 04 79 05 17 76. Open from the beginning of November to Christmas Eve.

La Plagne: Office du Tourisme, B.P. 52, 73214 La Plagne Cedex; tel 04 79 09 01 14. Open from the beginning of October to mid-December.

Tignes: Office du Tourisme, 73320 Tignes; tel 04 79 06 42 08. Open from the beginning of October to mid-December.

Val d'Isère: Les Richardes, 73150 Val d'Isère; tel 04 79 06 11 80. Open from the beginning of October to the end of March.

A useful publication is Vacation Work's *Working in Ski Resorts Europe and North America* which describes all the main French resorts and how, when and where to get jobs in them. British tour operators who go to France are also listed in this publication as are their precise requirements.

Other Sources of Ski Jobs

Club Mediterranée: 25 rue Vivienne, 7502 Paris: UK office: 106-108 Brompton Road, London SW3 1JJ; tel 0171-581 5454. Apart from its holiday villages worldwide Club Med operate ski resort hotels in l'Alpe d'Huez, Les Arcs, Avoriaz, Chamonix, Les Menuires, La Plagne, Superbagnères, Tignes, Val Claret and Val d'Isère. You have to have worked for them in summer first and the minimum contract is 6 months. Club Med also employs about 1,000 ski instructors.

Domaines du Soleil; 48 rue des Acacias, 75017 Paris; tel 1-44 09 22 01; fax 1-44 09 22 02. Property agent that specialises in resort apartments in holiday places including ski resorts. Needs seasonal helpers to look after clients in the resorts.

Pierre et Vacances: La Grande Arche, Paroi Nord, Cédex 61, 92054, Paris-la-Défense; tel 1-41 26 20 00; fax 1 41 26 25 72. Pierre et Vacances real estate and holiday company has hotels and self-catering apartments in most French ski resorts. They employ resort representatives from different EU countries. Applicants must be fluent in French.

Snow-Fun: B.P. 287, 73150 Val d'Isère, France. tel 4-79 41 11 82; fax 4-79 41 11 80. Snow Fun is a French company with a chain of six ski shops and two ski schools in Val d'Isèere which between them employ 100 staff (40 in the shops and 60 ski instructors).

Sogim: Résidence Les Hauts de la Vanoise, 72440 Val Thorens; tel 4-79 00 02 76; fax 4-79 00 09 92. Estate agent that lets apartments in ski resorts and employs seasonal workers December-April to deal with clients in the resort.

Students Abroad/Global Nannies: 3 Kneller Road, New Malden, Surrey KT3 5ND; tel 0181-330 0777; fax 0181-330 0345. Au pair/au pair plus/nanny jobs in French alpine ski resorts from December until the end of April. Applicants must enjoy winter sports, speak basic French and have previous childcare experience. Ski resort jobs go quickly so early application essential.

UK Overseas Handling (UKOH) International Recruitment: in France: P.O. Box 46, 73602 Moûtiers, Cedex France; in the UK: P O Box 4083, Brentwood CM15 9HJ. UKOH recruits for large and small British self-drive companies operating in the Trois Vallées, Tignes, Val d'Isère, La Plagne and Les Arcs, as well as for a French company called Eurogroup which owns and operates hotels, restaurants and nightclubs in Méribel, Courchevel and Val d'Isère. Applicants must speak very good French. Salaries range from £220 per month if working part time, up to £650 for full time work, plus food and lodging.

Applicants should be nationals of an EU country; gap students and those looking for a career in tourism are welcomed. Employees need to speak very good French, be bright, flexible, keen and prepared for hard work: most jobs require experience and for all enthusiasm is vital. Applications to the above address.

Voluntary Work

Those who can afford not only to offer their services free, but also in many cases pay a small daily fee for board and lodging (though occasionally this is provided at no cost), will find a wide range of opportunities available. This is a good way to make French contacts and improve your French, but not usually a way to support yourself once you are in France except in certain instances: for example, if you happen to be a qualified archaeologist or stone mason etc. who joins a summer camp and then manages to stay on a remuneration basis to work on a long-term project. There is a free leaflet *Chantiers de Travail Volontaire* (Voluntary Work Camps) available from the CIDJ (see below) which lists most of the organisations in France offering this kind of work. Many are connected with the preservation and maintenance of France's architectural and historical heritage, but social programmes are also a possibility.

Addresses of Voluntary Work Organisations:

APARE: Campus Européens du Patrimoine, 41 cours Jean Jaurés, 84000 Avignon; tel 4-90 85 36 72; fax 4-90 86 82 19. A European wide organisation for the preservation of cultural heritage. Organises a mixture of academic and practical 'campuses'. Employs volunteers to take part in over 20 summer work camps in Provence, mainly restoring ancient buildings. About 30 hours work a week in the mornings. Work camps last three weeks. The fee of 650 francs per week includes board and lodging and the minimum age is 14, 16 or 18 years, depending on the project.

Associations des Paralyses de France: 17 Boulevard August-Blanqui, 75013 Paris; (tel 01 40 78 69 00; fax 01 40 78 69 73). Employs assistants to work in holiday centres for handicapped adults for 15-21 days during summer. Pocket money, board, accommodation and expenses are provided. Applicants should be able to speak a little French. Applications to APF Evasion at the above address.

Chantiers d'Etudes Medievales: 4 rue du Tonnelet Rouge, 67000 Strasbourg; tel 3-88 37 17 20. Takes volunteers to work on archaeological digs and the restoration of monuments: each scheme normally involves an international team of 20-30 people working for six hours daily, six days a week. Camps last fifteen days and occur from the end of July to mid-September. The charge for basic board and accommodation is £55-£65 weekly.

Institut d'Histoire: Université du Mans, Avenue O. Messiaen, Le Mans, 72017 France; tel 2-43 83 31 64; fax 2-43 83 31 44. Takes volunteers to assist on archaeological digs. Work is for eight hours daily, five days a week. Board and lodging are free. A knowledge of French or English is required and the minimum period of work is three weeks in July.

Jeunesse et Reconstruction: 10 rue de Trevise, Paris 9. Requires volunteers for projects all over France. Type of work varies depending on the camp but may include constructing community centres or digging drains in wet areas. Board and lodging are free. About seven hours work per day, five days weekly. Volunteers are international. Those who commit themselves for three months receive pocket money.

Rempart: 1 rue des Guillemites, 75004 Paris; tel 1-42 71 96 55; fax 1-42 71 73 00; Minitell 3616 REMPART. Rempart needs volunteers to work on about 140 archaeological sites all over France. Wide range of projects includes, chapels, abbeys, ancient villages and Gallo-Roman sites. Board and accommodation normally cost £3/£4 daily: some camps are free. Many craft skills required including masonry, carpentry and interior decorating. Plenty of free time for recreational activities. Some camps take families. A knowledge of French is desirable.

La Sabranenque: Centre International, rue de la Tour de L'Oume, 30290 Saint Victor la Coste; tel 4-66 50 05 05. Restoration organisation that needs helpers to work on villages, sites and simple monuments using traditional building methods. Two weeks minimum between 1 June and 30 August.

Solidarités Jeunesse: 38 rue du Faubourg Saint-Denis, 75010 Paris; tel 1-48 00 09 05; fax 1-42 46 49 32. Organises long-term (minimum six or nine months; maximum 12 months) voluntary work with disadvantaged adults and children and young people from rural areas. Volunteers' work varies depending on the project and may include some of the following: help with leading work camps, joining in activities, helping with renovations of buildings, vegetable growing, animal husbandry, organising training sessions and collective life. Ages for volunteers are 18-25 and return travel is reimbursed. Free board and lodging are provided.

Training & Work Experience Schemes

One of the problems for those leaving school or university is that when they begin to look for work, they find that they are up against those with a proven track record, who understandably find greater favour with employers than those with no experience in the work place. The EU has come up with various schemes for young people aimed at giving them an advantage with regard to European job opportunities. The most ambitious of these schemes is Leonardo. Yet other work experience programmes are run by private agencies or individuals.

HORIZON HPL: Paris Office: 22-26 rue de Sergent Beauchat, 75012 Paris; fax + 33 1 40 01 07 28. Horizon is a private French/British organisation that organises work experience placements in hotels and businesses for those who wish to improve their languages. Work placements of three or six months are combined with French tuition in Paris. Horizon charges fees for 'enrolment and acceptance' of £240-£300 and for tuition and training while in France. Hotel Trainees get accommodation and wages.

SOCRATES: (c/o Central Bureau for Educational Visits & Exchanges, 10 Spring Gardens, London SW1 2BN; tel 0171-389 4004; fax 0171-389 4426). Socrates is an inter-EU group of schemes including Erasmus, Leonardo and Lingua which enable young people to undergo short term training or work experience, or in the case of Erasmus, study, in another EU country. The aim is to prepare them for their working life. The various strands of this set of schemes are aimed at different ages from 16 upwards and most programmes are for a period of three weeks or three months but there are also possibilities for longer placements of up to a year.

Comenius: aimed at schools and school staff. Options include European in-service training courses and activities for educational staff.

Erasmus: options include university students and academic staff to study/teach at a university in another EU country.

Leonardo: options include vocational training and placements in other EU countries of among others: students, graduates and those on an advanced course of vocational training that is not degree level and young workers and apprentices. Among other strands of Leonardo is are the intensive work experience placements in another EU country. Work placements last three weeks to 12 months in another EU country. There is a separate strand, Youthstart, for young people under 20 years in particular the unemployed and unqualified.

Lingua: set up in 1990, Lingua is aimed at, among others, foreign language teachers. Under the scheme teachers can spend time in the country whose language they propose to teach. Lingua funds scholarships and exchange visits for students and teachers of modern languages.*Lingua*: options include : language teacher training and assistantships for future language teachers.

ProEuropa: Europa House, Sharpham Drive, Totnes, TQ9 5HE; tel 01803-864526. ProEuropa is linked to the Leonardo scheme and arranges work experience abroad for those aged 18-27. Work placements tend to be in the Colmar (Alsace) or Bordeaux regions. Participants have to pay £75 towards travel and insurance costs and take £500 spending money to cover food etc. Accommodation is provided free. The scheme includes a month's language tuition before you go and a basic knowledge of French is required for initial eligibility. Placements usually last 12 weeks.

Bursaries for Socrates-Erasmus intended to help with costs are available depending on the location and length of the placement: contact the UK Erasmus-Socrates Student Grants Council, R&D Building, The University, Canterbury, Kent CT2 PD (tel 01227-762712).

Centres d'Information Jeunesse (CIJs)

There are about 30 CIJs in France which are a useful source of information particularly for foreign students. Although it is by no means their main function, they can help people find jobs, particularly seasonal agricultural work and other part-time and temporary possibilities for the summer and winter. In addition they can provide leaflets on the regulations that affect foreign students. If you wish to have information about these in advance, you should send four International Reply Coupons to their Paris office: Centre d'Information et de Documentation Jeunesse (CIDJ), 101, Quai Branly, 75740 Paris Cedex 15 (tel 1-44 49 12 00). They will not however deal with job applications by post. For these you must call in person. Some CIJs just display vacancies on notice-boards in their offices, while others have a more formal system run in conjunction with the local ANPE.

There are CIJs in Amiens, Bastia (Corsica), Besançon, Bordeaux, Caen, Cergy Pontoise, Dijon, Evry, Grenoble, Lille, Limoges, Lyon, Marseille, Melun, Montpellier, Nancy, Nantes, Nice, Orléans, Poitiers, Reims, Rennes, Rouen, Strasbourg, Toulouse and Versailles.

The CIJ in Marseille (4 rue de la Visitation, 13248 Marseille Cedex 04 (tel 4-91 49 91 55) is particularly useful for agricultural jobs and for *animateurs* (children's summer camp monitors), while the Nice CIJ has plenty of catering jobs. Mother's help jobs are also available through some CIJs.

Permanent Work

The details and information at the beginning of this chapter will be useful reading for those looking for long term and permanent work in France. This section deals with individual areas of work such as teaching English as a foreign language, information technology, bilingual secretarial work and working for the institutions of the European community.

Computers/Information Technology

Those who work in computing and can speak another European language are almost always able to find jobs in the EU. British computer science graduates are also highly thought of and many get jobs by approaching recruitment agencies that specialise in computer personnel (see below)

Apart from specialised jobs in the computer field, those with computer expertise could consider working as an IT trainer. Many companies offer their staff on-going voluntary training schemes of which the most popular are English (see below) and computer studies. If you have any experience in this field and speak good French, you could try contacting companies direct.

Useful Addresses & Publications

Computer Contractor/Computing: Two magazines published by VNU Business Publications, 32-34 Broadwick Street, London W1A 2HG; tel 0171-316 9000. Both carry regular job adverts from companies like Computer Futures and MBA who can place computer personnel in France.

Computer Futures: Contract Services, 2 Foubert's Place, Regent St. London W1V 2AD; tel 0171-446 6666; fax 0171 446 0095; website: http://www.compfutures.co.uk. A leading supplier of IT contractors worldwide. Ring for an appraisal of the demand for your skills.

DUX International: Riverbank House, Putney Bridge Approach, London SW6 3JD; tel 071-371 9191; fax 071-371 7409. Specialises in computer vacancies in Europe.

Freelance Informer: a fortnightly magazine published by Reed Business Information (0181-652 3999). Carries a large number of international recruitment adverts.

Hewlett Packard: Service Recrutement, 38053 Grenoble, Cedex 09, France. Worldwide R&D, Marketing and Strategy centre for PC division.

JCC Limited: Alban Row 27-31 Verulam Road, St. Albans, Herts. AL1 1NX; tel 01727-836361. Agency that regularly recruits computer personnel for France.

Hunterskil: Project House, 110-113 Tottenham Ct. Road, London W1P 1BX; tel

0171-383 3888; fax 0171-387 2048. Specialises in IT recruitment for software and communications projects in France.

InterEurope Projects Services: 12 St George's Business Park, Alstone Lane, Cheltenham, Glos. GL51 8HF; tel 01242-523973. Occasionally offers jobs for computer professionals and translators in France.

Unilog DRG: 97 Blvd. Pereire, 75017 Paris; tel 1-40 68 40 00. French IT company that employs graduates with or without computer science qualifications as long as they are motivated to acquire computing expertise. Applications must be in French and addressed to the recruitment department.

Secretarial
Useful Addresses:

Boyce Bilingual: 5-7 John Prince's Street, London W1M 9HD; tel 0171-491 9800; fax 0171-491 4893. Recruit secretaries and other bilingual office staff.

Insead: Direction des Resources Humaines, Service Recruitment et Accueil, Blvd. de Constance, 77305 Fontainebleau, Cedex, France. Recruitment and training institution that specialises in placing bilingual/polyglot secretarial staff.

Sheila Burgess International Recruitment Consultants: 4 Cromwell Place London SW7; tel 0171 584 6446; in France: 62 rue St. Lazare, 75009 Paris; tel 1-44 63 02 57; fax 1-44 63 02 59. Specialises in bilingual secretarial/PA personnel for permanent positions with international companies in Paris. Clients includes international companies and firms and EU bodies and international organisations. Please note jobs are not temporary or of a short term nature.

TEFL and Teaching
There is a continuing demand for English language tuition in France, particularly from the business sector. Larger French companies, are encouraged to set aside part of their annual budget for staff training under the *Droit de Formation Continue.* The most popular *formations* are English and computer studies. In some cases American English is considered more useful and so there are opportunities also for American TESOL (Teaching English to Speakers of Other Languages), teachers. Although the work permit regulations are more complex for non-EU citizens (see *Residence and Entry* chapter), if there is a demand for a teacher in American English, it should not prove difficult to obtain one for a specific job.

Teaching jobs in France sometimes appear in British newspapers and the relevant journals: regular standbys in this respect are *The Guardian's Education Section* which appears on Tuesdays and *The Times Educational Supplement* published on Fridays. More specifically, the monthly 'trade' newspaper *EL Gazette* (Dilke House, 1 Malet Street, Bloomsbury, London WC1E 7JA) is available on subscription (£23.50 per annum in the UK) or £1.50 a single issue and is a useful source of job possibilities. A comprehensive guide covering all the practicalities of TEFL teaching with listings of schools and their requirements worldwide is *Teaching English Abroad* (Vacation Work Publications, tel 01865-241978).

For qualified American TEFL teachers the *TESOL Placement Bulletin* from TESOL (1600 Cameron Street, Suite 300, Alexandria VA 22314-2751) is published six times annually and is sent to TESOL members who register for the Placement Service (cost $21 in the USA). Another relevant North American publication is *The International Educator* (POB 513, Cummaquid, MA 02637, USA and 101 Pope's Lane, London W5 4NS) which concentrates on jobs in international, English-medium schools, most of which follow either an American curriculum or the International Baccalaureate (IB).

You should note when applying for teaching jobs that there is considerable variation between schools. They may or may not help you find accommodation, you have to be flexible about working hours and the contracts last from nine months to two years. Shorter contracts are also available at some schools. In some cases you will need your own transport, for instance if teaching is carried out at business premises or on a one-to-one basis in clients' own homes. All these details, and the conditions of employment should be gone into with the school concerned before you accept a job. However careful you are though, it seems to be the opinion of the majority of those who have taught English abroad that language schools tend to regard their teaching staff as expendable, often overworking them and expecting complete flexibility (i.e. to take on extra classes at the drop of a hat). Consequently, there is usually a fairly rapid staff turnover as staff find they cannot take the stress on a permanent basis. However, despite the potential drawbacks, English teaching can provide a reasonable way to live and and work in France. All you need is a good education, preferably to degree level, excellent communication skills and preferably one of the recognised English teaching qualifications. It is also one of the best possible ways to meet a wide variety of French people and there is considerable job satisfaction to be had from watching your class or students improve. If you decide to take up Teaching as a Foreign Language (TEFL) as a career after establishing yourself in one city or another, you could consider opening your own language institute (see *Setting up a Business* chapter).

One of the improvements for teachers of English in France in recent years is that their conditions of employment have become regulated. This means that for salaried teachers, formal contracts and the regulation benefits, sick pay, etc. have to be provided by the employers. (see
Aspects of Employment below). Legislation also applies to wages which are now set at F8000 monthly.

For details of many courses and possible TEFL qualifications, consult *Teaching English Abroad* (see above). You can also obtain a free list of the main (RSA/UCLES) courses with their addresses only, from the British Council (Information Centre, Medlock Street, Manchester M15 4PR (0161-957 7755) which also distributes and information pack *How to Become a Teacher of English Abroad*.

If you are applying on the spot, you will find language schools listed in the French yellow pages under *Enseignements Privé de Langues* or *Ecoles de Langues*.

EU Lingua Scheme: The Lingua scheme is aimed at promoting language teaching of all the languages in the EU as a foreign language. It also enables teachers of foreign languages to train and study in the country whose language they are teaching which now In its first year of operation (1991) 516 teachers from the EU received grants. Now thousands of teachers take part in the scheme annually. France is very popular country in which to be a Lingua scheme participant. For further details of the Lingua scheme, see *Training Schemes* above.

Addresses of Language Schools
Inlingua 109 rue de l'Université, 75007 Paris; tel 1-45 51 46 60; fax 1-47 05 66 05.
Inlingua is an international chain of language teaching schools of which there are 29 in France. A minimum of two years' teaching experience and fluent French is required. You can approach the schools direct. Further details in the UK can be obtained from inlingua Teacher Training and Recruitment (Rodney Lodge, Rodney Road, Cheltenham, Glos GL50 1XY; tel 01242-253171.
Audio English: 44 Allée de Tourny, 33000 Bordeaux; tel: 5-56 44 54 05. Applicants must have a BA or equivalent and good French. The minimum contract is 10 months. Minimum pupil age: 6 years. The director is Monsieur Labat.
British Institute (University of London): 11 rue Constantine, 75340 Paris Cedex 07.

High level TEFL qualification required and at least five years' teaching experience.

Business English Service and Translation:, 24 Blvd. Béeranger, 37000 Tours; tel 2-47 05 55 33; fax 2-47 64 40 27. Applicants must have a BA, RSA certificate or good teaching experience. Contracts for 9 months to 2 years.

Centre d'Etude des Langues: Z.I. du Brockus, B.P. 278, 62504 St. Omer. tel: 3-21 93 78 45. Minimum contract 9 months. Adult and child classes.

Cybele Langues: 7 rue Artois, 75008 Paris; tel 1-42 89 18 26; fax 42 89 25 21. Takes British teachers and other anglophones (American, Australian Canadian) if they have working papers. Applicants should have a BA and at least 2 years' teaching experience in a school. Students are all business people.

Demos Langues: 33 Cours de la Liberté, 69003 Lyon; tel 4-78 60 15 60; fax -78 62 25 18. Also at 4 Place Schuman, 38000 Grenoble, and 20 rue de l'Arcade, 75008 Paris; tel 1-44 94 16 32. Takes British and American teachers with a BA and 1 year's experience in TEFL, or RSA certificate. Contracts for an academic year or January to June. Students are mainly adults with a wide range of ages.

Fontainebleau Langues & Communication: 15 rue Saint-Honoré, B.P. 27, 77300 Fontainebleau; tel 1-64 22 48 96; fax 64 22 51 94. Applicants must have TEFL training (i.e. RSA certificate) and be dynamic). Minimum contract one year. Some teaching takes place at business premises so own transport a necessity.

Working for EU Institutions

The majority of the European Commission's 15,000 staff are employed in in Brussels and Luxembourg. Although The European Parliament sits in Strasbourg once a month, but the staff there are mainly on loan from Brussels.

There are civil servants in France that are employed by the EC (European Commission) but their numbers are relatively small and such jobs are not available on spec.

Miscellaneous Useful Publications & Addresses

Association Pour l'Emploi des Cadres: (APEC) 51 Blvd. Brune, 75689 Paris Cedex 14; tel 1-40 52 20 00; fax 1-45 39 88 85. A private organisation financed by subscriptions from private companies which specialises in managerial staff employment.

Bilinguagroup: 49 Maddox Street, London W1R 9LA; tel 0171-493 6446. Recruits all types of bilingual staff including secretarial, legal and executive.

International Jobs (A Guide for UK and Overseas Students) and *Working in Europe:* booklets, both distributed by the University of London Careers Advisory Service (50 Gordon Square, London WC1H OPQ; tel: 0171-554 4500) at a cost of £1.50 each including postage and packing. Useful information on multinationals who often recruit in Britain.

Solicitors in the Single Market: (£22.90) & *Free Movement of Lawyers* (£80), both available from the Law Society Shop, 227 The Strand, London WC2.

Working in the European Community: (Hobsons). Includes employment possibilities, placement agents and general advice on the mobility of graduates. At the time of writing a new edition was in preparation.

Aspects of Employment

Salaries

French salaries compare favourably in both world and European terms and most people moving from the UK to an equivalent job position in France, at whatever level, can expect to receive a higher salary there. The following table shows how salary levels and living costs in some major countries compare to those in the UK. Note that both salaries and living costs will be higher in the capital cities.

	Salaries	Living costs
France	30%-50% more than UK	5%-10% less
Germany	50%-60% more than UK	10%-15% more
USA	80%-250% more than UK	20%-30% less
Italy	50% more than UK	20%-25% more
Scandinavia	40%-55% more than UK	up to 50% more
Switzerland	100%-250% more than UK	up to 30% more
Benelux	30%-45% more than UK	up to 5% more
Japan	80%-100% more than UK	35%-50% more

Although the chart above makes French salaries seem attractive by UK standards, they will be less so to people from other industrially advanced countries. This certainly applies to executive and professional jobs, and therefore reduces some of the competition from other foreigners. There are however drawbacks in that if you add together social security deductions, income tax and a high level of indirect taxation, the burden of tax overall is probably higher than in the UK. However this is offset, particularly in the case of executives by a generous range of company benefits and schemes from which may be derived fiscal or financial benefits (see *Benefits* below). It is generally the self-employed who are worse off in France as they do not have access to the range of benefits and perks and are likely to pay considerably more tax than in the UK. This may account in part for the popularity of the French pastime of tax avoidance.

Most salaried jobs are covered by collective bargaining agreements (*conventions collectives*) between employers' and employees' bodies nationally or regionally. This effectively means that wage rates for different jobs are fixed, but it also means that wages tend to keep pace with the cost of living generally. Employers must, by law, offer at least the minimum wages which have been negotiated. One of the points to note about French salaries, as with many other countries, is that there is a greater differential than in the UK between unskilled or semi-skilled and professional jobs. Thus, although in France, a senior manager could earn up to double a UK salary, a clerk or factory worker would receive only about 30% more.

Unlike the UK, France has minimum wage legislation which is an advantage for anyone considering taking up unskilled or casual work. This is known as the Salaire Minimum Interprofessionel de Croissance, usually referred to as *le SMIC*. This rate increases periodically, as it is indexed to the cost of living. Currently the rate is about 6,656 francs (July 1 1997) per month (169 hours).

It is worth noting that employees, by definition, are salaried staff rather than wage earners; even if paid hourly, one will usually receive one's earnings on a monthly basis, not weekly as is still common practice in the UK. The traditional way of paying wages in France (which still occasionally occurs), was fortnightly.

Social Security Contributions

French *sécurité sociale* contributions are compulsory for employees and the self-employed. Often referred to colloquially as *la sécu*, contributions cover a comprehensive range of cradle to grave benefits including sickness and maternity, unemployment, work injury and old age benefits. The generosity of these benefits does not come cheap and contributions are correspondingly high — often fifty to

60% of gross pay, the lion's share of which (about 40%) comes from the employer. The self-employed are responsible for their whole contribution and the cost is fairly punitive.

The national body in charge of social security is the *Caisse National d'Assurance Maladie*. On a local level, you deal with the *Caisse Primaire d'Assurance Maladie*.

If you are working in France as part of a company posting, or as a self-employed person, you can continue paying UK national insurance contributions for a maximum of up to two years after which it is obligatory to pay French *sécurité sociale*. The advantage of continuing to pay UK social security contributions for as long as possible is that they are much cheaper than in France. For further details see *Health Insurance Contributions* and *Social Security in the UK* and *Social Security in France* in the *Daily Life* chapter.

Benefits and Perks

As already mentioned, there is a tendency for French salary figures to greatly under-represent the bottom line or actual financial package offered. It is thus usual to expect various benefits and perks to be included in a salary as a matter of course. Often, senior and middle management receive a bonus, perhaps linked to the profits of their company, of 10% or even 20% of their salary. The vast majority of employees, even those in the most mundane jobs, receive an extra month's salary at Christmas; this is known as the 13th month (*13'eme mois*) payment. Some organisations also give a 14th month bonus prior to the summer holiday period. Additionally, profit-sharing schemes (*Participation des salariés aux résultats de l'entreprise*), which also entitle one to various tax benefits, are becoming more common in France as are company investment securities schemes (*plan d'épargne d'entreprise*) whereby the company holds an investment portfolio on behalf of its employees. Another possibility sometimes offered is share option schemes (*options sur actions*).

Having a company car, is regarded as an important company benefit in the UK, but is far less common in France. The most usually offered benefits are private health plans (*mutuelles*) either contributory or wholly paid by the employer, which top up the amount of health insurance above that provided by the state. Such benefits are of real value when one considers that sécurité sociale pays a maximum of 75% towards non-emergency hospital treatment. Other benefits may include everything from all expenses paid holidays to rent free accommodation.

Working Hours, Overtime, Holidays

The regulations governing working conditions in France are set down in the Employment Charter (*Code de Travail*). At the time of press, the French working week is in the process of being reduced to 35 hours, which is intended to be fully implemented by 2000. This is a core strategy of the current government (elected in 1997) to deal with France's serious unemployment as the reduction in hours will create new jobs — an estimated 42,000 in 1998 and increasing as the measure takes effect.

Unless you are executive (*cadre*) level, or have negotiated a contract that says otherwise, there is an obligation for the employer to pay overtime (*heures supplémentaires*). In some industries, employers and unions have negotiated longer working weeks (i.e. up to 44 hours) without overtime, but the average number of hours worked over a year cannot exceed 39 hours per week. Employees can be asked, but not compelled, to do overtime of up to 130 hours per year, although with collective agreements this figure can be increased. The maximum number of hours per week permitted over 12 consecutive weeks is 48. In practice, the majority of French workers of all grades regularly work in excess of 39 hours weekly. It is anticipated that the introduction of a 35-hour week to increase the number of jobs, will necessitate the introduction of higher taxes on overtime to deter employees from working longer hours.

The normal working day is from 8.30am to 6.30pm Monday to Friday with a long lunch break. Executives and managers in Paris and the big cities often finish work later around 7.30 or 8pm, and in the south earlier, but the long lunch break of up to two hours, is generally sacrosanct. In Paris lunch is generally from 1pm or 2pm whereas in the provinces it is more likely to be from midday or 12.30pm. Saturday morning used to be included in the working week, but this is now rare.

Flexi-time (*horaire mobilé/horaire flexible*) is used in many companies. Generally there is block time (*temps bloqué/heures de présence obligatoire*), usually 8.30 to 11.30am and from 13.30 to 16.00pm when all employees are required to be present. Outside these hours employees may make up their hours according to choice and convenience.

By law, all employees are entitled to five weeks paid holiday per year, plus 11 different public holidays — in some jobs more may be offered. It is usual for some companies, especially factories, to close down during July or August so total flexibility as to holiday dates may not always be possible.

Trade Unions and Conditions of Work

The power of the trade unions (*syndicats*) in France has declined since the decade of the seventies when labour disputes and strikes were the norm. Since then the membership of the largest and most influential union, the CGT (see below) fell from over two and a half million to one million and thirty thousand in January 1991. One of the reasons for the unions' decline is recent legislation which has encouraged, even forced employer and employees, with or without unions, to talk and negotiate wages and working conditions. This has helped to avoid many of the traditional problems between workers and management. Despite this reduction of influence it is estimated that around four million French wage-earners are unionized in a veritable alphabet jungle of acronymically named unions, which in turn are grouped in confederations. Unions tend to be strongest in the older, traditional industries and hold little sway in the new, high technology ones. They also usually operate on a regional basis rather than nationally with the exception of the notorious French lorry drivers' union. Some of the main unions you are likely to come across are:

Confédération Générale du Travail (CGT). The largest trade union and traditionally controlled by Communists, the CGT's main territories are the two largest cities, Paris and Marseille. Its main support is found amongst heavy industries, mining, docks, electricity, newspaper printing and railways.

Confédération Générale du Travail-Force Ouvrière (CGT-FO); 198, ave du Maine, 75680, Paris Cedex 14; tel 01 45 39 22 03. With an estimated membership of 420,000 the CGT-FO should not be confused with the CGT from which it split in 1948. The CGT-FO, often just referred to as *Force Ouvrière* is affiliated to the International Confederation of Free Trade Unions (ICFTU) and the European Trade Union Confederation (ETUC). Traditionally, the bulk of its support came from nationalized industries and the civil service.

Confédération Française Démocratique du Travail (CFDT); 4 blvd. de la Villette, 75955 Paris, Cedex 19; tel 01 43 03 80 00. The CFDT came into being in 1964 when the majority of the members of the *Confédération des Travailleurs Chrétiens*

(CFTC) wanted to emphasise their secularism by changing the union's name. It has about 680,000 current members from among strictly white collar employees, particularly in the chemical, gas and metallurgy industries.

Confédération Française des Travailleurs Chrétiens (CFTG); 13 rue des Ecluses Saint-Martin, 75483 Paris Cedex 10; tel 01 42 40 02 02. Founded in 1919, the CFTG is an offshoot of the CFDT—it broke away in order to promote the idea of Christian Unionism based on Catholic doctrine and the notion of the Church and State working in harmony and recognising the problems of the working class. It has a nationwide membership of about 250,000 (including 60,000 pensioners) representing a variety of industries.

Confédération General des Cadres (CGC); 30 rue de Gramont, 75002 Paris; tel 01 42 61 81 76. Founded in 1944, the CGE has about 180,000 members. Originally a military term for officers of the army, *cadres* has come to mean any type of executive or manager. CGC adherents include engineers, workshop supervisors and technicians as well as sales representatives and agents.

The Conseil National du Patronat Français (CNPF); 31 avenue Pierre-Ier-de-Serbie, 75116 Paris; tel 01 40 69 96 00. This is one of the employers' unions (*syndicats patronaux*) and was formed in 1946 at the instigation of the government. It represents the majority of firms (except SMEs which have their own union, the CGPME (see below). The CNPF represents employers in their dealings with the state. The CNPF has a strong influence on the economic and social policies of its membership which is drawn from the ranks of business, industry and banking.

Confédération Générale des Petites et Moyennes Entreprises (CGPME); 10 terrasse Bellini, 92806 Puteaux Cedex; tel 01 47 62 73 73. The CGPME split away from the CNPF in 1948. Comprising 400 or so federations it brings together some 80% of the professional classes found in SME's in industry, trade and services and 256 inter-professional structures found in the departements and regions. Membership totals about one and a half million firms.

Fédération de l'Education Nationale (FEN); 48 rue la Bruyère, 75002 Paris; tel 01 42 61 81 76. Founded in 1928 it was part of the CGT but left to become independent in 1948. Currently the umbrella organisation for about 50 teaching unions it has a membership of about 180,000.

With the decline of working class consciousness which led directly to the creation of trade unions and gave them momentum, has come a decline in militancy and consequently memberships have fallen. More recently there has been a trend towards the formation of representative committees (*coordinations*) and autonomous unions which focus on specific sectorial demands such as teachers, nurses and students. Representative committees however, still need the power of the trade unions behind them to enhance their chances of a satisfactory outcome to disputes.

Companies with more than ten employees are entitled by law to appoint representatives or employees' councils. These bodies are entitled to certain information from the management of a company which must also consult them on certain matters relating to pay and working conditions. The councils, of course, do not have legal powers to change management decisions but this is still an arrangement which has helped to avoid disputes.

Contracts of Employment

If you are offered a job and decide to accept the pay and conditions offered, it is a legal requirement to sign a contract of employment (*contrat de travail*). There are a number of different types of contract all of which have varying implications. There are however two main types:

Fixed Term Contract (Contrat à durée déterminée): Fixed term contracts must be in writing and the date for termination must be given in the contract. This contract can be for temporary employment if for a specific purpose but fixed term generally means for a maximum period of 24 months. The contract may be renewed twice, but not for a period exceeding the original contract or 24 months total. There is no minimum period for the contract.

Indefinite term contract (Contrat à Durée indéterminée) This is the usual type of contract for permanent employees. Unlike the contrat á durée déterminée, it does not have to be in writing. However, it is obviously sensible to insist on having it in writing for future reference. Most indefinite term contracts include a trial period, usually three months, after which the contract becomes binding on both parties.

A contract of employment should detail, at the very least, the job title, duties and responsibilities, hours of work, rate of pay and terms of dismissal inolved in the position. A contract can sometimes be very complex; French business people often have a very detailed understanding of the law. Even if one's French is good, it may be advisable to engage professional help in understanding a contract. One of the most important stipulations of French employment law is that an employee can only be dismissed or made redundant in very specific circumstances (see below).

If a contract has run to its full course, the employee is entitled to an end of contract bonus (*indemnité de fin de contrat*) which amounts to five per cent of the salary plus any other bonuses granted by the employer. An *indemnité de fin de contrat* is not payable in the case of seasonal or temporary work.

Rights of Temporary & Seasonal Workers

There are separate contracts for seasonal workers (*saisonniers*) and temporary employees (*travailleurs temporaires*), but these afford few rights to employees while embroiling employers in the social security system.

Employers who want to take on part-time home helps/au pairs etc. have to pay employee social security contributions. Once employment has been formalised, employers have to observe the complex rules of dismissal which is why many families employ home-helps and baby-sitters on an informal cash-in-hand or exchange for room and board basis.

A contract of employment must be presented when applying for a residence permit, (*carte de séjour*), in France. It may also be required on other occasions e.g. pay slips are not sufficient proof of holding a job, a contract of employment, obviously, is.

France does have a sizable black market workforce who work without any form of employment contract and consequently without the benefit of sécurité sociale or the substantial legal protection to which all employees are entitled. The size of this workforce is not as great as in, for example, Italy, but is more extensive than in the UK, and it is not uncommon for people to be asked to work 'unofficially' in seasonal jobs such as tourism or agriculture.

Termination of a Contract

If you have a *contract à durée déterminée*, i.e. with a date of termination, it can only be terminated before that date if specific circumstances arise. If one of the parties has committed a *faute grave* (serious fault), or through (*force majeure*), events or circumstances occur which are beyond the control of either party. For various reasons the regulations governing termination and dismissal are very formal and precise and non-observance of the step-by-step rules for dismissing employees can lead to the dismissal being invalid.

Termination by the Employer: If the employer terminates the contract prematurely, compensation payable amounts to the total remuneration due until the contract expires. If the employee is dimissed for *une cause réelle et sérieuse* the employer must summon the employee, by registered letter (*lettre recommandée*) to attend a formal meeting during which the reasons for dismissal will be clearly stated. Within 24 hours the employer must send a further registered letter notifying the employee of his or her final decision and the reasons. If the employer fails to take these steps, the dismissal will not be valid.

Termination by the Employee: If however, the employee defaults on the contract or commits another *faute grave*, he or she will have to compensate the employer. If the employee simply wishes to terminate the contract, notice should be given in writing and sent by registered mail, and no reason need be given. The amount of notice depends on the category of job: factory workers have to give a week's notice, white collar workers usually have to give a month while senior employees (*cadres*) are expected to give two or three month's notice. An employee who has not committed any *faute grave* is entitled to an *indemnité compensatrice de congé payés* (payment in lieu of holiday entitlement due up to the time of leaving).
Force Majeure (the occurence of events beyond the control of either party), absolves either party of the obligation to pay compensation.

Serious Dispute with the Employer: in the event of there being a serious dispute between employee and employer you can contact the Prud'homme organisation in Paris (27 rue Louis Blanc, 75010) set up to help employees whose interests have been threatened and to protect their legal rights. If they decide you have a case it can take about six months to come to court. You will need a lawyer and in a straightforward case this can cost in the region of 4000-6000 francs. If you win, you can expect to be awarded a sum of money depending on the facts of the case.

French Pensions

The French pension system is more generous that the UK's although the government is considering reforms which reflect the changing situation and the new austerity in France. At present the retirement age is 60 for men and women (lower than the EU average of 65 years). Under the socialist government, anyone retiring at this age who had worked for 37½ years earned a state pension of 50% of their annual salary in their ten highest earning years, with a ceiling of 149,820 francs. The average French pension is about 6,613 francs for men and 3,504 for women. The French pension system depends on those who are working paying into a state fund, the Caisse de Retraite which in turn supports those on a pension. Despite this the pension system runs up an annual deficit of 20 billion francs. The French government is pondering several solutions to the problem, one of which is to raise the retirement age, another to encourage the creation of commercial private pension schemes which do not yet exist in France. Already, French pensioners are slightly less well off as the government has increased the number of years that need to be worked before claiming pensions to 40 years, as from the year 2003. In addition the calculation of the pension will henceforward be based on the 20 highest paid years, thereby slightly reducing the overall amount.

Restrictions on UK Managed Pension Funds

This is potentially a great problem for those moving from Britain to another EU country to live and work, particularly if they have already worked in the UK. The problem concerns managed pension funds and how to carry on making contributions when you have left the country where you started one. At present, if you have a UK managed pension fund, you cannot continue to make contributions once you have left the UK. So far the EU Commission has not come up with any solution as the countries concerned cannot agree to allow pension funds companies to operate freely across community borders. Thus while EU citizens are guaranteed freedom of mobility, their pension funds are hedged around with restrictions when in fact it should be permissable to start a pension fund in one country and then transfer it with you wherever you move in the EU. People from the UK who have gone to work elsewhere in the EU for the same company, have found that not only are they not permitted to continue contributions to their occupational pension fund back in the UK, but they may be legally bound to contribute to another country's state pension fund and may even end up paying tax on their employer's contributions which will be classed as 'benefit in kind'. At the time of press, it would appear that there is legislation in process to make private pension funds movable around the EU.

Women in Work

The number of women now working in France has increased sharply in recent years to over 40% of the workforce. However, this trend applies to women in their 20s and 30's. Fewer French women older than forty tend to have jobs and of those that do, a great many work part-time (*travail à mi-temps*), as in the UK. Another similarity with the UK is that certain areas, e.g. teaching, nursing and service industries are still predominantly staffed by females. It is slightly more difficult, for women to find an entry into traditionally male-dominated jobs in France than in the UK, although this situation has been changing since a law concerned with the professional equality of men and women, La Loi Rondy sur l'égalité profession-nelle, came into effect in June 1983. This ensures, amongst other things, that the career progress of women executives is not hindered by chauvinism. Companies of three hundred personnel or more are required to produce an annual report comparing the situations of male and female employees, in order for a check to be made on the relative progress of men and women of similar professional expertise. However, it is generally agreed that fewer French women have ambitions to reach the top of their profession than their UK and US counterparts.

Women intending to build a career in France will probably find the notion of sexual and professional equality much more accepted in Paris, known for its international outlook, than in the provinces. The high technology centres of Lyon and Grenoble are also said to favour sexual equality in professional hierarchies.

Despite extensive regulations in force to develop equal opportunities in France and also to ensure equal rates of pay between men and women performing the same career role, many women do not receive equal pay, although the gap is narrowing fast and France is making a concerted effort in this respect, unlike many other countries.

French companies are generally quite progressive in providing crèche and other child care facilities which allow flexibility in hours for working mothers.

Maternity Benefits, Parental Leave and Employment Rights

French maternity benefits are extremely generous which is sometimes held up as a reason for French employers not to promote women to positions of power and responsibility, i.e. because women are likely to cost them more in benefits than a male employee. Pregnancy (*la grossesse*) is profitable for many families since the social security system positively encourages it. Women are entitled to sixteen weeks maternity leave: 6 weeks prior to the birth and ten weeks post delivery at 90% of their normal salary. If more leave is advised by a doctor then this must also be allowed at full salary. For the second and third children, maternity leave is increased to eight weeks before and 18 weeks after the birth. Other maternity benefits are related to the term of employment.

Both parents are entitled to an additional year of unpaid parental leave (*congé parental*) after which the employer is obliged to re-employ them in their former job at the same salary, or a higher one if wage/price index increases have occured in the interval. Fathers are also entitled to three months unpaid paternity leave. All the above rights are also applicable in the case of adoption.

French Labour Relations

Throughout the 1980's a much more balanced and satisfactory relationship developed between employers and employees. This was in large part due to the periods of power enjoyed by both socialist and right-wing governments, who managed to introduce legislation favourable to both workers and employers. In addition, some state industries have been privatised which has helped present the state and the law as a mediator rather than just an employer.

Of course, labour disputes and strikes still occur, but current legislation is designed to channel employees and employers into negotiations thus providing greater potential for defusing disputes. Generally, French employers are now more sympathetic to their employees' demands for a good standard of living and more willing to share the financial success of their companies. At the same time, employees have become more aware of the need for quality, competitiveness and the financial success of the company for which they work, especially if they have a stake in it.

French employers tend to resemble those found in the USA in that they demand a very high standard of competence and are also often impatient and intolerant of mistakes. For these reasons most modern French companies are both efficient and motivated. Employers are often willing to consider new ideas from their employees, and, in the case of a foreign employee, much headway could be made by suggesting alternative practices or helping to develop a market, where appropriate, in the new country. Most employers will expect a certain degree of determination and initiative from their employees, confounding, to some extent, the traditional image of a relaxed business atmosphere though this is still favoured in the south of the country.

Promotion

At one time the system of employee progress up the promotional ladder was almost rigidly predetermined in the majority of French businesses. It was extremely difficult to advance one's career at a faster rate than that dictated by the company for which one worked and employees tended to stay within one organisation, rather than switch to a competing firm in seach of better prospects. Nowadays, most companies prefer to single out employees who show particular ability and reward them financially and with promotion rather than watch them take their talents elsewhere. This is a trend which has brought about the evolution of the French equivalent of yuppies. The current situation is therefore beneficial to the able, and there is an awareness amongst employers that fast lane promotion should be allowed when merited.

The promotion disadvantages for foreign employees are therefore likely to be caused by other factors. One possible problem which foreign employees may encounter when working within a French company is that their level and breadth of education is different to their French counterparts. In some ways it may exceed the other, in others it may fall short. Many senior French business people, for example, have trained in the legal profession, even though they may never have had any intention of pursuing a legal career.

Another possible problem for anyone working in France who is poached by a rival firm or simply wishes to transfer for career reasons is that they may have to sign a *clause de non-concurrence* to prevent them from divulging the business secrets of one company to another. This occurs particularly in the sphere of high technology. Such clauses are enforceable under French law and one should be aware of them, as it is a serious offence to be convicted of breach of confidentiality.

Despite all protestations to the contrary, the Gallic version of the old boy network is still a force to be reckoned with in France. Consequently it can be difficult for the foreign executive to make headway without an appropriate infrastructure of contacts and friends.

European Business Studies: One possible solution to the problem of discrepancies in education and business background is to take a postgraduate course at the College of Europe in Bruges. Applicants require a BA and courses are in administration, economics or law. A number of scholarships are awarded each year through the cultural department of the Belgian Embassy in London.

Guide to Regional Sources of Employment

In the *Introduction* to this book, the main cities and regions of France were discussed with a view to residence. In this section the same major cities and regions are covered, but this time with a view to indicating the main possible sources of employment.

The information provided will give some idea of the industries which are dominant and the types of jobs which are most readily available in each area. In each case, several sources of further information on the region in question are given. The press listing is for the regional newspaper in that area which may be a source of jobs and information; other local newspapers may also be useful. The Chamber of Commerce may be able to provide information as discussed earlier in this chapter and the listing usually gives the address of the largest branch in that region — there will be others in adjacent towns

ALSACE
Main City: Strasbourg
Regional Newspaper: *Dernierères Nouvelles d'Alsace*
Chamber of Commerce: Chambre de Commerce du Bas-Rhin, 10 Place Guteberg, 67081 Strasbourg Cedex; tel 03 88 75 26 26; fax 03 88 61 53 54.
Industry/Other Comments: Strasbourg itself is a major administrative centre for the EU and seat of the European Parliament. It also has a very important university and is an academic and financial centre. Outside Strasbourg the main industries include mining, minerals, heavy engineering, automotive, textiles and brewing and wine production. Mulhouse is a heavy industry area.

AQUITAINE
Main City: Bordeaux.
Regional Newspaper: *Sud Ouest*, Paris papers also relevant.
Chamber of Commerce: CRCI Aquitaine, 185, cours du Médoc, B.P. 143, 33042 Bordeaux Cedex; tel 05 56 11 94 94; fax 05 56 11 94 95.
Industry/Other Comments. Aerospace, aeronautics, electronics, agri-foodstuffs and wood pulp are Bordeaux's main industries. It is also a base for high technology manufacturing of various kinds. Bordeaux is also an important port, both for imports and exports. Outside Bordeaux a small amount of tourism exists especially on the coast (e.g Biarritz, St. Jean-de-Luz, Arcachon). Wine production is a major industry on which Bordeaux will continue to thrive thanks to its great name vineyards and the new ' Wine City' project.

AUVERGNE
Main City: Clermont-Ferrand.
Regional Newspaper: *Progrès de Lyon.*
Chamber of Commerce: CRCI, Aéroport de Clermont-Ferrand/Aulnat, B.P.25, 63510 Aulnat; tel 04 73 60 46 46; fax 04 73 90 89 22.
Industry/Other Comments. Clermont-Ferrand is an important academic town and also has a wide range of light manufacturing industries in addition to the major industrial presence of the Michelin tyre company. Other than Clermont-Ferrand, St Etienne is a major, heavy industrial and mining town in the old style. The rest of the region is largely agricultural centred on beef cattle and cheese production. The area includes various spa towns, such as Vichy, where some, mainly domestic, tourism exists.

BRETAGNE (BRITTANY)
Main City: Rennes.
Regional Newspaper: *Ouest France.*
Chamber of Commerce: CRCI Bretagne, 1 rue du Général Guillaudot, 35044 Rennes Cedex; tel 02 99 26 41 41; fax 02 99 63 35 28. (Also has an office in UK: Brittany Chamber of Commerce, 8 Creed Lane, London EC4V 5BR.)
Industry/Other Comments. Rennes is the industrial hub of the region and companies there are involved in printing and publishing, motor and automotive manufacture and telecommunications. Rennes is also an academic and administrative city, and as such is a centre for research and development of all kinds. The port of Brest has recently developed industries in engineering and electronics. The Brittany region is otherwise supported predominantly by agriculture including fruit and vegetables similar to those grown in south-west Britain, and is also France's most important area for pig production. Tourism is a major industry but the season generally lasts between May and October only.

BOURGOGNE (BURGUNDY)
Main City: Dijon.
Regional Newspaper: see Paris press.
Chamber of Commerce: CRCI Bourgogne, place des Nations Unies, B.P. 209 21006 Dijon Cedex; tel 03 80 60 40 20; fax 03 80 60 40 21.
Industry/Other Comments. Well known for wine and food production, Burgundy has a reputation for mass production of many of its wines, unlike many areas of France. Traditionally the region's prosperity came from heavy industry, now declined, leaving food, wines and agriculture of greater economic importance. Still

prominent industries include iron and steel, engineering, glass, ceramics, motor manufacture. Mâcon and Bourg-en-Bresse are more industrial than Dijon. Tourism, based on the region's gastronomy and architectural heritage, is also fairly important.

CHAMPAGNE-ARDENNE
Main Cities: Châlons-sur-Marne, Reims.
Regional Newspaper: see Paris press.
Chamber of Commerce: CRCI champagne-Ardenne, 10 rue de Chastillon, BP 537, 51011 Chalons-en-Champagne Cedex; tel 03-2669 33 40; fax 03 26 69 33.
Industry/Other Comments. The new autoroute from Calais to Dijon will benefit the region and underline its growing importance. Traditionally the area had much heavy engineering, steelworks, mining, textiles etc. which are gradually being replaced by new industries including electronics and agri-foodstuff production. Agriculture, primarily cereal crops, continues to be an important industry, although the region's riches derive directly from champagne, an industry in its own right, centered on Epernay.

LA CORSE (CORSICA)
Main Cities: Ajaccio and Bastia.
Regional Newspaper: *Corsican*.
Chamber of Commerce: CCI d'Ajaccio et de la Corse du Sud, Quai l'Herminier, B.P 253, 20179 Ajaccio Cedex; tel 04 95 5155 66, and CCI de Bastia et de la Haute-Corse, Nouveau Port, BP223, 20293 Bastia Cedex; tel 04 95 54 44 44; fax 04 95 54 44 45.
Industry/Other Comments. Corsica, although technically part of metropolitan France is industrially and commercially as separate as it is geographically. It has a small population, owing to emigration, no heavy industry and only limited agriculture, mainly vineyards and sheep. The island is however famed for its magnificent coastline and tourism, mainly domestic, is the main source of revenue.

CÔTE D'AZUR
Main City: Nice.
Regional Newspaper: *Nice Matin*; also Paris press.
Chamber of Commerce: Chambre de Commerce et d'Industrie, 20 boulevard Carabacel, BP 1259, 06005 Nice Cedex 1; tel 04 93 13 73 00; fax 04 93 13 73 13, Nice.
Industry/Other Comments. Nice and its environs are world famous for their fashionable resorts, and tourism is the most high-profile industry, together with the convention and conference trade. However, other high-tech industries also exist here, including electronics and computing, telecommunications and marine industries. Sophia Antipolis near Nice, is one of the most important high-tech centres of France. More non-tourist industry is to be found at Cannes and Menton: Grasse is the perfume centre of France with a large number of factories dedicated to its production.
The principality of Monaco is quite separate commercially from mainland France and exists mainly on the many forms of the tourist and entertainment trade for which it caters. A useful contact is the Chambre Economique, 2 avenue Prince Albert, Monte Carlo.

FRANCHE-COMTE

Main City: Besançon.
Regional Newspaper: *L'Est.*
Chamber of Commerce: CRCI Franche-Comté, Valparc - Z.A.C. de Valentin, 25043 Besançon Cedex; tel 03- 81 47 42 00; fax 03 81 80 70 94.
Industry/Other Comments. This region has a higher percentage of its population working in industry than any other region of France. Principal industries are light and heavy engineering, light assembly, textiles, mining and minerals. Appropriately enough perhaps for an area that borders Switzerland, Besançon is the clockmaking centre of France and is famed for high precision engineering. Montbéliard-Sochaux is the base of the Peugeot car company and other parts of the region produce small amounts of cheese, woodwork and artisanal products. In addition, the area attracts a modest number of tourists and Besançon is said to be one of the best places to learn French.

LANGUEDOC

Main City: Montpellier.
Regional Newspaper: *Midi Libre*
Chamber of Commerce: CRCI Languedoc-Roussillon, 254 rue Michel Teule, Z.A.C. d'Alco, BP 6076, 34030 Montpellier Cedex 1; tel 04 67 61 81 00; fax 04 67 61 81 10.
Industry/Other Comments. Languedoc is one of the newest and fastest economically developing areas in France, it also has an important academic and research centre in the old university city of Montpellier. Prominent industries, in both the city and the rest of the region, include computers, electronics, medical equipment and research, telecommunications. Other main cities, Perpignan and Nîmes are similarly high technology-based and as a result of the above-mentioned economic boom, construction is also a major industry. In the summer, tourism provides a useful boost to the economy along the now highly developed coastal stretches while wine production and agriculture (Mediterranean fruit and vegetables) predominate inland.

LIMOUSIN

Main City: Limoges.
Regional Newspaper: *Sud Ouest* (Bordeaux) and *La Dépêche* (Toulouse).
Chamber of Commerce: CRCI Limousin-Poitou-Charentes, Blvd des Arcades, 87038 Limoges Cedex; tel 05-55 04 40 00; fax 05 55 0 40 40.
Industry/Other Comments. In many ways Limousin encapsulates rural France at its most tranquil, the main industry being agriculture, mostly small-scale cattle farming. Agri-foodstuffs and leather products are also important. Additionally, there are local, cottage industries in metalwork, glass etc. while Limoges porcelain is known worldwide and is probably the region's most famous industry. The regional authorities are trying to open up the region commercially and encourage tourism.

LOIRE-VALLEY/CENTRAL

Main City: Orléans.
Regional Newspaper: see Paris press.
Chamber of Commerce: CRCI Centre, 6 rue Pierre et Marie Curie - Z.A. d'Ingré, B.P. 109 45142 Saint Jean de la Ruelle, Cedex; tel 02 38 26 26 26; fax 02 38 43 00

39; and CCI du Loiret, 23 place du Martroi, 45044 Orléans, Cedex 1; tel 02 38 77 77 77; fax 02 38 53 09 78.

Industry/Other Comments: The Loire valley, in effect a sub-region of the Loire region, is now an important commuter area serving Paris, as well as a popular tourist centre. Other main industries are agriculture and, food manufacture and processing.

LOIRE-WEST

Main City: Nantes
Regional Newspaper: *Ouest France* and *Presse Océan*
Chamber of Commerce: Chambre Régionale de Commerce et d'Industrie Pays-de-la-Loire, 16 quai Arnest Renaud, Centre de Salorges, quai Ernest Renaud, B P 90517 44105 Nantes Cedex 4; tel 02 40 44 63 00; fax 02 40 44 63 20.

Industry/Other Comments. The industrial hub of the whole Loire region is the Nantes-Saint Lazare port complex, one of the largest in France. Nantes is linked to Paris by high speed train (TGV) which takes 2 hours. The region's industries include electronics, engineering, garment and footwear manufacture. Other regional industries are traditional, including food processing, maritime industries, fishery, agriculture and wine production. New industries are also being established in research and development services and telecommunications.

LORRAINE

Main Cities: Metz, Nancy.
Regional Newspaper: *L'Est Républicain.*
Chamber of Commerce: Chambre de Commerce et d'Industrie, 10 Viaduc J.F. Kennedy, C.S. 4231, 54042 Nancy Cedex; tel 03 83 90 13 13; fax 03 83 28 88 33.

Industry/Other Comments. The wealth of this region once derived from old heavy industries connected with iron, steel and coal production but these, to a large extent, have ceased to exist. The region is now undergoing a period of industrial reconstruction and conversion as can be seen from the diversity of its commercial enterprises. Nancy is an important academic city, as well as being an administrative, business and commercial centre. Other industries in the city include finance, banking, electronics and computers. The region, as opposed to the city, is important for agriculture, food processing and textiles.

NORD-PAS-DE-CALAIS

Main City: Lille.
Regional Newspaper: La Voix du Nord.
Chamber of Commerce: CRCI Nord-Pas-de-Calais, Palais de la Bourse, 59800 Lille; tel 03 0 63 79 79; fax 03 20 20 13 02 00.

Industry/Other Comments. This region is one whose importance was traditionally based on heavy industry including mining and steel production, which have declined considerably in recent years, and have been replaced with some high-tech businesses. Major industries include heavy engineering, mining and mineral exploitation, electronics, transport and distribution and energy industries. The area is currently experiencing a   development boom as a result of government incentives for inward investment and the increased opportunities afforded by the Channel Tunnel and the TGV high speed link to Paris, Lille, Brussels etc. More than 400 international companies are already established in the region including British companies Whessoe, BP, Courtaulds, K.P. Foods and P&O.

NORMANDIE (NORMANDY)
Main City: Rouen.
Regional Newspaper: *Paris-Normandie*; also Paris press.
Chamber of Commerce: CRCI Haute-Normandie, 9 rue Robert Schuman, 76000 Rouen; tel 02 36 88 44 42; fax 02 35 88 06 52 and CRCI Basse-Normandie, 21 place de la République, 14052 Caen Cedex; tel 02 31 38 31 38; fax 02 31 85 76 41.
Industry/Other Comments. Rouen and the Seine valley comprise a heavy, industrial area with two major ports: Le Havre and Rouen. Industries include heavy engineering, metal industries, motor manufacture, chemicals, petrochemicals, pharmaceuticals, plastics. New industries include electronics and telecommunications. Normandy is how ever largely rural and agricultural (livestock, dairy products and fruit), and also, through the summer months, an important tourist region. Paris is easily accessible.

PARIS/ILE DE FRANCE
Main City: Paris.
Regional Newspapers: Paris press — see section on newspapers in *Daily Life*.
Chamber of Commerce: Chambre de Commerce et d'Industrie Paris, 27 avenue de Friedland, 75382 Paris Cedex 08; tel 01 42 89 70 00; fax 01-42 89 78 68.
Industry/Other Comments. Needless to say, most industrial and commercial sectors are represented in Paris and its hinterland which contain some 18% of the total population of France. Unusually, some heavy industry (notably motor manufacturing) still exists, in the capital itself. Paris is the seat of all the machinery of government and its higher functionaries and is one of the most famous tourist cities in the world. International organisations including UNESCO and OECD also have their seats there. The hinterland is important for agriculture and is a very fertile area. Important business and commercial areas outside central Paris are La Défense to the west and Quai de Bercy in the south east. As in London, some of the outer suburbs of Paris are business and commercial centres in their own right, for example, the new town of Marne-la-Vallée to the east.

PICARDIE (PICARDY)
Main City: Amiens.
Regional Newspaper: *La Voix du Nord*.
Chamber of Commerce: CRCI, 36 rue des Otages, 80037 Amiens Cedex 1; tel 03 22 82 80 80; fax 03 22 91 29 04.
Industry/Other Comments. Some heavy industry, generally iron and steel based, exist throughout the region alongside chemical, tyre manufacturing, engineering and textile industries. Agriculture and food production (cereals and industrial crops) are also important and there have been developments in the agri-foodstuffs industry. Tourism is also expanding.

POITOU-CHARENTES
Main City: Poitiers.
Regional Newspaper: *Sud Ouest* and *Ouest France*.
Chamber of Commerce: CRCI Limousin-Poitou-Charentes, Blvd des Arcades, 87038 Limoges Cedex; tel 05 55 04 40 00; fax 05 55 04 40 40; and CCI de la Vienne, 47 rue du Marché, BP 229, 86006 Poitiers Cedex; tel 05 49 60 98 00; fax 05 49 41 65 72.
Industry/Other Comments. Tourism is undoubtedly a growing industry throughout the region although fisheries and agriculture (especially beef production) presently

provide most jobs. Poitiers is a localised business and commercial centre while La Rochelle is one of France's leading resorts. The region is also the centre of brandy production, around Cognac.

PROVENCE
Main City: Marseille.
Regional Newspaper: Paris newspapers apply but also see *Le Provençal* and *Le Méridional*.
Chamber of Commerce: CRCI Provence Alpes Côtes d'Azur Corse, 8 rue Neuve Saint-Martin, B.P. 1880, 13222 Marseille Cedex 01; tel 04 91 14 42 00; fax 04 91 14 42 45.
Industry/Other Comments. Marseille is traditionally a heavy industrial area, most of which still exists, albeit on a smaller scale than before. Other industries include chemicals, oil, textiles, pharmaceuticals, heavy engineering, iron, steel and shipyards. Marseille and Toulon are major merchant port and distribution centres involved in maritime and shipping services and research. New growth industries in Marseille include electronics, computing, aerospace and light, high techology manufacturing. The rest of Provence is largely agricultural, growing Mediterranean produce: both the coast and the Alps are important tourist areas.

PYRENEES
Main City:Toulouse.
Regional Newspaper: *Dépêche du Midi.*
Chamber of Commerce: Chambre de Commerce et d'Industrie, 5 rue Dieudonné Costes, B P 32, 31707 Blagnac Cedex; tel 95 62 74 20 00; fax 05 62 74 20 20; and CCI de Toulouse, 2 rue d'Alsace-Lorraine, BP 606 31002 Toulouse Cedex; tel 05 61 33 65 00; fax 05 61 55 41 26;
Industry/Other Comments. Toulouse is very much a boom city economically and all its industries are high technology, including aeronautics, aerospace, aviation, electronics, data processing, computers and robotics.. Toulouse also boasts many academic and research facilities as well as government offices. The Pyrénées area generally tends towards traditional agriculture and wine production and is very much in contrast to its thrusting capital city.

RHÔNE-ALPES
Main City: Lyon.
Regional Newspaper: *Progrès de Lyon*; also Paris press.
Chamber of Commerce: CRCI Rhône-Alpes, 75 cours Albert Thomas - 6e Avenue. 69447 Lyon Cedex 03; tel 04 72 11 43 43; fax 04 72 11 43 62.
Industry/Other Comments. Lyon is France's second city as far as commerce, rather than industry, is concerned. It is also a major administrative and academic centre. The Lyon conurbation is France's second largest manufacturing and services area. Many industries in or near Lyon are new or rejuvenated, including computing, electronics and communications, although traditional industries also exist, based on the River Rhone: for instance textiles, chemicals, petrochemicals and motor manufacture and automotive companies. Despite the heavy industry in Lyon, the area also has some agriculture and wine growing.

SAVOY & DAUPHINY
Main City: Grenoble.
Regional Newspaper: *Dauphiné Libéré* and Lyon press.

Chamber of Commerce: Delegation Tourisme-Montagne de la CRCI, 1 place André Malraux, B.P 297, 38016 Grenoble Cedex; tel 04 76 28 28 00; fax 04 76 46 75 19.

Industry/Other Comments. Grenoble is one of the booming new French techno-cities. Its industries are almost all high technology and include computing, electronics and telecommunications. The area is also the centre of the substantial French nuclear industry and Grenoble is an important academic, scientific and research centre which boasts a famous university. Traditional industries include engineering, mining/minerals and textiles. A substantial tourist industry exists with the region all year round, although principally in winter as most of the French Alpine resorts are to be found here.

Directory of Major Employers

The following addresses and telephone numbers refer to major employers in France and the respective industries in which they are involved are also given.

Aérospatiale: 37 boulevard de Montmorency, 75016 Paris (tel 1-42 24 24 24). Aerospace, aeronautics.

Air France: Compagnie Nationale, 45 rue de Paris, 95747 Roissy Charles de Gaulle Cedex; tel 1-41 56 78 00.

L'Air Liquide: 75 quai d'Orsay, 75321 Paris Cedex 07; (tel 1-40 62 55 55). Chemicals.

Alcatel Alsthom: (formerly CGE), 54 rue de la Boétie, 75008 Paris; tel 1-40 76 10 10. Electrical equipment, telecommunications.

Béghin Say: rue Joseph Béghin, 59239 Thumeries (tel 3-20 62 44 00). Food.

Bouygues: 1 avenue Eugène Freyssinet, 78280 Guyancourt; (tel 1-30 60 23 11). Construction.

BP: 8 rue des Gémeaux, 95866 Cergy Pointoise Cedex; tel 1-34 22 40 00. Oil, chemicals.

BSN: 9 rue de Téhéran, 75008 Paris (tel 1-42 56 44 00). Food.

Carréfour: 5 avenue Poincaré, B.P. 419, 75769 Paris Cedex 16; tel: 1-53 70 19 00. Retail.

Casino: 96 avenue Aristide Briand, 92220 Bagneux; tel 1-46 65 38 38. Distribution.

CEA Industrie: 60 Avenue Général Leclerc, B.P. 6, 92265 Fontenay aux Roses; tel 1-46 54 70 80. Nuclear power.

Compagnie Française Philips: Direction et Services Centraux Administratifs, 2 rue Benoît Malon, BP 313, 92156 Suresnes Cedex; tel 1-47 28 10 00. Electrical.

Compagnie Générale des Eaux: 52 rue d'Anjou, 75384 Paris Cedex 08; tel 1-49 24 37 76.

Docks de France Ouest: ZI du Menneton, Avenue Charles Bedaux, B P 1805, 37018 Tours Cedex; tel 2-47 77 77 77.

Dumez GTM: 57 avenue Jules Quentin, 92022 Nanterre Cedex; tel 1-41 91 40 00. Construction.

Dumez TP: 32 avenue Pablo Picasso, 92022 Nanterre Cedex; tel 01 46 95 40 00.

EDF: 2 rue Louis Murat, 75008 Paris. (tel 1-40 42 22 22). Electricity supply.

Elf Aquitaine: Tour Elf La Défense 6 2, place de la Coupole, Paris la Défense, 92078 Courbevoie Cedex; tel 1-47 44 45 46. Oil, petrochemicals.

ESSO-SAF: 1 blvd Victor, 75015 Paris; tel 1 40 60 66 60/72. Petrochemicals.

Euromarché: 4 quai de Bercy, 94220 Charenton le Pont (tel 1-43 53 75 00). Distribution.

FIAT Lease Industries: Siège Social; Fait Auto France SA, 80 quai Michelet, 92532 Levallois Cedex; tel 1-44 21 93 50.

France Télécom: Direction Générale, 6 Place d'Alleray, 75015 Paris Cedex 15; (tel 1-44 44 22 22). Telephone utilities.

Gaz de France: 23 rue Philibert Delorme, 75840 Paris Cedex 17; tel 1-47 54 20 20. Gas utility.

Hachette: 43 Quai de Grenelle, 75015 Paris; (tel 1-43 92 30 00). Publishing.

IBM France: 76 Quai Râpée, 75012 Paris; tel 1-40 01 50 00. Office systems and computing.

Imetel: 33 avenue du Maine, Tour Mairie, 75015 Paris; (tel 1-45 38 48 48).

Lafargues Aluminates: 28 rue Emile Menier, 75016 Paris (tel 1-53 70 3 00.). Construction and materials.

Michelin: place des Carmes, 63040 Dechaux (tel 4-73 30 42 21). Tyres, publishing.

Office Commercial de Publicité (OCP): 21 rue Mademoiselle, 75015 Paris; tel 1-44 19 60 75. Distribution.

L'Oréal: 14 rue Royale, 75008 Paris (tel 1-40 20 60 00). Cosmetics, pharmaceuticals.

Péchiney: Immeuble Balzac, 10 Place Vosges, La Défense 5; 92048 Paris la Défense Cedex; tel 1-46 91 46 91.

La Poste (PTT): Cabinet du Directeur, 6 Blvd de la Marne, 76035 Rouen, Cedex; (tel 02 35 08 70 70). Postal services.

Le Printemps: 102 rue de Provence, 75009 Paris (tel 1-42 82 50 00). Retail, distribution.

Promodès France: 123 rue Jules Guesde, 92300 Levallois Perret; tel 1-47 15 64 00. Distribution.

PSA (Peugeot-Citroën): 75 avenue de la Grande Armée, 75016 Paris (tel 1-40 65 55 11). Cars, commercial vehicles, engineering.

Renault (Poteries): 18410 Argent sur Sauldre (tel 02-48 73 63 71). Cars, commercial vehicles.

Rhône-Poulenc: 25 quai Paul Doumer, 92408 Courbevoie Cedex; (tel 1-47 68 12 34). Chemicals.

Saint Gobain: Les Miroirs, 92096 La Défense Cedex; (tel 1-47 62 30 00). Glass and other industrials.

Schneider: 64 rue Carnot, 92150 Suresnes; (tel 1-47 28 67 00). Electronics.

Shell France: 89 blvd Franklin Roosevelt, 92564 Rueil Malmaison Cedex; (tel 1-47 14 71 00). Petrochemicals.

Système-U Expansion: Alimentation Générale, 7 chemin de la Moselle, 57160 Scy-Chazelles; (tel 3-87 30 15 09; 3-87 33 11 77). Distribution.

Thomson-CSF: 173 Boulevard Haussmann, 75008 Paris; (tel 1-53 77 80 00). Electronics.

Total: Siège Social, Tour Total, 24 Cour Michelet, La Défense 10, Puteaux, 92069 Paris la Défense Cedex; (tel 1-41 35 40 00). Oil.

Usinor-Sacilor: Direction Générale du Groupe, Immeuble Pacific, TSA 10001/13 crs Valmy; 92070 Paris la Défense Cedex; tel 1-41 25 60 10. Steel.

British Companies and Organisations Offering Employment in France to UK Graduates

Bankers Trust Company: 1 Appold St. Broadgate, London EC2 2HE; tel 0171-982 2500. International Merchant Bank. Normally recruits from universities. Applicants for Paris should be bilingual.

Barclays Bank: P O Box 256, Fleetway House, 25 Farringdon Street, London EC4; tel 0171 489 1995. Special recruitment programme in the UK offers opportunity to transfer abroad.

Beazer: Templeford Hall, Sandy, Bedfordshire SG19 2BD. Construction. Apply to UK office; tel 01234 767644.

Booz Allen & Hamilton International (UK) Ltd. 7 Savoy Court, The Strand, London WC2R OEZ; tel 0171-393 3333. Business analysts and consultants. Normally recruits graduates pre-MBA.

Boston Consulting Group: Devonshire House, Mayfair Place, London W1X 5FH; 0171-753 5353. Management consultants.

British Council: 10 Spring Gardens, London SW1A 2BN; tel 0171-930 8466. Promotes all aspects of British culture abroad. Enquiries to UK office or British Council offices in France.

Clifford Chance: 200 Aldersgate Street, London EC1A 4JJ; tel 0171-282 7000. International lawyers.

Coats Viyella plc: Head Office, 28 Savile Row, London W1X 2DD; tel 0171-292 9200. Contact for graduate recruitment: Mrs. Ann Field.

DNV: Palace House, 3 Cathedral Street, London SE1 9DE; tel 0171 357 6080. Consulting engineers, maritime services and risk and environmental assessment. Recruits engineers worldwide and has offices all round France.

Dow Corning: Cardiff Road, Barry, South Glamorgan CF6 TYL; tel 01446 732350. Manufacture of silicone chemicals. Can recruit in France, but apply to UK office if in UK.

First Choice Holidays: Olivier House, 18 Marine Parade, Brighton, East Sussex BN2 1TL; tel 01273-677777. Leading tour operator with opening abroad and in France in winter and summer.

Four Square: (Division of Mars GB Ltd.): Armstrong Road, Basingstoke, Hants. RG24 ONU; 01256-471500. Automated Drinks Systems. Has an office in France. Has recruited UK graduates for sales and marketing in France.

Friendly Hotels plc: Premier House, 112-114 Station Road, Edgware, Middx HA8 7BG; tel 0181-233 2001. Hotel group with main interests in the UK expanding interests in Europe including France where it has several hotels including one in Caen. May be worth trying if you are prepared to work for them in the UK first.

Freshfields: 65 Fleet Street, London EC4Y 1HS; tel 0171-936 4000. Lawyers. Contact UK office in first instance for details of associate offices in France. Paris office tel + 33 1-44 56 44 56.

GEC Alsthom, T & D Power Electronics Systems, PO Box 27, Stafford ST17 4LN; 01785-256221. Recruits electrical/mechanical engineers for France.

ICI: Group Personnel, PO Box 6, Shire Park, Bessemer Road, Welwyn Garden City AL7 1HD; tel 01707 320827.

Inlingua Teacher Training and Recruitment (Rodney Lodge, Rodney Road, Cheltenham, Glos GL50 1XY; tel 01242 253171; Runs 250 Language Schools worldwide.

International House: 106 Piccadilly, London W1V 9FL; 0171-491 0959. Runs 95 English Language Schools in 20 countries and internationally recognised training courses for TEFL teachers.

Kimberley Clark Ltd.: New Hythe Lane, Larkfield, Aylesford, Kent ME20 6RX; tel 01622-616000. Soft tissue and allied products. The company has a policy of making transfers to France and other European Union countries available to all the workforce.

Marks & Spencer plc: Michael House, 47-57 Baker Street, London W1A 1DN; tel 0171-935 4422.

MEMEC (Memory & Electronic Components) plc. 17 Thame Park Road, Thame, Oxon; tel 01844-261919. Marketing, selling, distribution, support & repair of advanced technology products.

Pitman Professional English Centres: Pitman Central College, 154 Southampton Road, London WC1B 5AX; Recruitment tel 0171-278 7462.

SGS-Thomson Microelectronics Ltd.: Planar House, Parkway, Globe Park, Marlow, Bucks. SL7 1YL. Semi-conductors.

Slaughter & May: 35 Basinghall Street, London EC2V 5DB. Lawyers.

Tioxide UK Ltd.: Billingham, Cleveland, TS23 1PS; 01642-370300. Chemical, mechanical engineering. Office in Calais.

Trowers & Hamlins: 6 New Square, Lincolns Inn, London WC2A 3RP; tel 0171-600 1200. Lawyers. Temporary postings in France.

Wiggins Teape: P.O. Box 88, Gateway House, Basing View, Basingstoke, Hants. RG21 2EE; tel 01256 724724. Paper manufacturers. Technical, engineering staff for France.

French Offices of British and US Companies

Automotive Products France: 177 rue Fauvelles, 92404 Courbevoie.

Barclays Bank: 21 rue Lafitte, 75009 Paris; tel + 33 1 44 79 79 79; fax + 33 1 44 79 72 52; and 45 blvd Haussmann, Paris; tel 1-55 27 55 27.

British Airways: Immeuble Kupka A, 18 rue Hoche, La Défense Cedex, 75009 Paris; tel + 33 1 46 53 73 24.

British Steel France: 3 allée des Barbonniers, 92692 Gennevilliers Cedex.

British Telecom France SA: Immeuble Jean Monnet, 92061 Paris-la-Défense Cedex.

British Tourist Authority: 63 rue Pierre Charron, 75008 Paris.

Charterhouse SA: 47 Avenue George V, 75008 Paris.

Commercial Union Assurance: 100 rue de Courcelles, 75017 Paris; tel 00 33 144 01 90 00.

Cooper France SA: 15 rue Sorins, 92000 Nanterre.

Courtaulds Fibres SA: Pont du Leu, 62231 Coquelles.

DHL International: BP 50252 rue de la Belle Etoile, 2.1. de patinet II, 95957 Roissy.

Financial Times: FT Europe Ltd. Centre d'Affaires, Le Louvre, 168 rue de Rivoli, 75008 Paris; tel 1-53 76 82 56; fax 1-53 76 82 76.

GEC-Alsthom National Headquarters: 38 Ave. Kleber, 75795 Paris, Cedex 16; tel + 33 1 47 55 20 00. Anglo-French. High speed trains and generating equipment.

Gestetner SA: 71 rue Cammille Groult, 94400 Vitry-sur-Seine.

Guardian Royal Exchange: 42 rue des Mathurins, 75008 Paris.

Hambros France Ltd.: 16 Place Vendôme, 75001 Paris; tel + 33 1 42 60 57 17; fax + 33 1 42 86 90 19. Merchant bank.

ICI France SA: 2 avc Louis Armand, 92607 Asnièrcs Ccdcx.

ICL France SA: 24 avenue de l'Europe, 78140 Velizy-Villacoublay.

International Herald Tribune: 181 av. Charles de Gaulle, 92521 Neuilly; tel + 33 141 43 93 00.

JCB France: (Rochester UK), B P 671, 3 rue de Vignolle, 95200 Sarcelles Cedex.

Johnson Matthey & CIE: 13 rue de la Perdrix ZI, 93290 Tremblay-en-France.

Laboratoires Glaxo Wellcome: 43 rue Vineuse, B.P. 166 16, 75016 Paris.

Laboratoires Fisons SA: Tour PFA — la Défense 10, 92076 Paris-la-Défense Cedex 43.

Legal & General Assurance: 58 rue Victoire, 75009 Paris.

Legal & General Bank (France): 58 rue de la Victoire, 75440 Paris Cedex 09; tel

75440 Paris Cedex 09; tel +331 48 74 35 72; fax +33 1 45 26 65 60. Private investment bank.

Lloyds Bank SA: 15 avenue d'Iéna, 75783 Paris Cedex 16; tel +33 1 44 43 42 32; fax +33 1 44 43 42 05.

Lucas France SA: 11 rue Lord Byron, 75008 Paris.

Marks & Spencer (France) SA: 6-8 rue des Mathurins, BP 252-09 75424 Paris; tel +33 1 44 53 50 00.

Midland Bank SA: 20 bis Avenue Rapp, 75332 Paris Cedex 07; tel +33 1 44 42 70 00; fax +33 1 44 42 71 36.

Powell Duffryn Compagnie Française: 35 avenue de l'Europe, 78143 Vélizy-Villacoublay Cedex.

Nat West Markets France: National Westminster Bank SA, 13 rue d'Uzès, 75002 Paris; tel +33 1 42 33 51 54; fax +33 1 40 26 08 64. Merchant bank.

Rank Video Services France: 1 rue Edouard Denis Baldus, 71100 Chalon-sur-Saône.

Rank-Xerox SA: 3 rue Bellini, 92806 Puteaux.

Reckitt & Coleman: 15 rue Ampère, 91301 Massy Cedex.

Rowntree Mackintosh SA : Noisiel, Marne-la-Vallée, 77422 Torcy.

SAFAD (Alfred Dunhill): 15 rue de la Paix, 75002 Paris.

Securicor France SA: 12 Avenue des Cocquelicots, 94380 Bonneuil-sur-Marne.

WH Smith & Son SA: 248 rue de Rivoli, 75001 Paris.

Standard Chartered Bank Ltd.: 4 rue Ventadour, 75001 Paris.

Tesco Stores Ltd.: Head Office, Delamere Road, Cheshunt; tel 01992 632222. In December 1992, Tesco took over the French supermarket group Etablissements Catteau which has about 90 stores in north-west France including the grocery chain Cedico and two hypermarkets (HyperCedico) near Calais.

Thorn EMI Computer Software (Feltham), 101-109 rue Jean Jaurès, 92300 Levallois-Perret.

Trusthouse Hotels: 23 place Vendôme, 75001 Paris.

Weatherall Green & Smith: 64 rue de la Boétie, 75008 Paris.

Wimpey: 72-78 Grande rue, 92310 Sèvres.

Other American companies:
Details of American companies which operate in France can be obtained by purchasing the *The Guide to doing Business in France* published by the American Chamber of Commerce in France (21 avenue George V, 75008 Paris; tel 01-40 73 89 90; fax 01 47 20 18 62).

Other Possibilities: The French Cognac company, Hennessy, based in Cognac, employs some bilingual English staff and a dozen or so summer guides to show coach parties and tourists round the Hennessy production premises.

Useful Publications

International Employment Gazette: 1525 Wade Hampton Blvd. Greenville, SC 29609. Toll free US tel 1-800 882 91 88. American subscription magazine with details of professional jobs worldwide with a European section.

Working and Retiring Abroad — A Financial Guide: (Tolley) by Robert Maas of Blackstone Franks and Co. Very detailed handbook by an expatriate tax expert.

Starting a Business

Until recently, the majority of people taking up residence in France did so for career reasons, or to retire there. However, these are by no means the only options available; for some, the intention of starting or buying a business in France is the main cause of their moving there.

Operating a business abroad is not necessarily the preserve of established business people or multinational companies. In addition to the traditional large-scale opportunities, recent administrative developments within the EU have made a point of encouraging small and medium-sized businesses and individuals, to set up enterprises in other EU states. Apart from manufacturing, business ventures can take almost any form: running small shops, art courses, letting agencies, providing bed and breakfasts, building and plumbing services are just some already in existence. Other professional services, from farming and landscape gardening to running bars and franchises also offer potential livings.

Inevitably, the cultural differences between France and the UK complicate an already nerve-racking undertaking for someone determined on setting up a new business in France. Such a venture is risky enough in the UK alone, where 50% of all new companies go to the wall within their first year of existence. In France, however, the failure rate is less discouraging at about 30%. Although the statistics may offer better odds for the survival of small businesses in France , this should not belie the extra difficulties caused by unfamiliarity with foreign business procedures and a lack of personal contacts, the absence of which could prove serious drawbacks. One solution is to look for a French business partner or company with compatible interests, at least initially. It may also help to side-step some of the convoluted bureaucratic processes involved in creating a business from scratch. If this is not possible then you may need to consult a *centre de gestion* a partnership of accountants and other professional business advisors whose expertise lies in launching new businesses and providing financial and other services. Controls on foreign investment in France were eliminated early in 1996 and tax legislation for foreign businesses is competitive.

Despite the fact that there are hundreds of thousands of small businesses (*fonds de commerce*) in France, the French are regarded as far less of a nation of entrepreneurs than the British when it comes to the small business sector. Small businesses tend to have been established for several generations and to be run along traditional lines. However, in the boom year of 1988 an impressive 13% of the working population created their own commercial enterprises and there remain plenty of gaps in the market for small, specialised businesses to fill. Additionally, the forecast improvement in the economic climate of France for 1998 and beyond, may well provide opportunities and flourishing conditions for small, private enterprises.

European Monetary Union 1999

At the time of going to press, the full implications of the arrival of European Monetary Union and the introduction of the euro (the single European currency) on 1 January 1999 were just being assessed. From that date financial transactions in countries signed up for EMU can be in the new currency, though this will not be compulsory until the euro notes and coins replace national currencies by 1 July 2002 at the latest. Euro notes and coins will be introduced overnight in 2002. Until this time the franc will exist alongside the euro and be fixed on it. According to discussions in progress at the time of press, British businesses will almost certainly be able to deal in Euros from 1 January 1999, even though it appears at the time of press that Britain will not be joining the single European currency at that date. The practical considerations for businesses in France following the introduction of the new single currency include switching to euros for accounts and audits and where applicable, issuing share certificates in euros. It is predicted by various economists that EMU will result in historically low interest rates in most European countries.

Financial and Linguistic Considerations

Anyone intending to start, or buy, a business in France should initially consider what kind of scale it will be on, the level of personal investment and whether outside finance will be required. For instance even a very modest business would probably require a minimum sum of £30,000 cash to buy, or £50,000 cash to start, and twice these amounts is preferable. If you need additional finance from a bank then you will need to draw up a very detailed business plan which should include items such as whether the business will be run from your own premises or leased ones, whether you are starting from scratch or acquiring an existing business, what legal form the business will take and what activities it will engage in. Lastly, and perhaps most difficult, a projection of profitability will be required.

Other basic requirements for running a business in France are: to be fluent in the language, or a willingness to become so; expertise and experience of a popular profession or trade, e.g. farming, catering, interior decoration or hairdressing etc. Also, familiarity with French business practices, the country itself and previous business know-how, although not essential, would be a great advantage.

Residence Regulations

EU nationals are entitled to move to France to set up, or to buy, a business without any prior authorisation. The regulations for those wishing to take up residence in France in order to buy or start a business are broadly the same as for those wishing to take up employment, and may be referred to in the *Residence and Entry Regulations* chapter.

Non-EU nationals may, however, require a visa and should consult the French Consulate about this. Generally, non-EU nationals are expected to make a more substantial business investment in order to gain admittance to France, whereas EU nationals are usually accepted no matter what the scale of their proposed business activities. Non-EU Nationals will also need to obtain a special foreign merchant's permit (*carte de commerçant étranger*) which can take up to six months to obtain. Having said this, it is advisable for EU-Nationals to coordinate the purchase or setting up of a business with obtaining the *carte de séjour*. No financial commitments of any sort should be made until you are reasonably certain that this will be granted.

When applying for the residence permit, evidence must be produced that the applicant intends to set up in business. Business registration (*immatriculation au registre du commerce*) is in any case compulsory and involves registering with the local Chambre de Commerce (or Chambre des Métiers if you are a self-employed tradesperson). Farmers should register with the Chambre d'Agriculture. One can find the appropriate address from the local library, mairie or the Assemblée Permanente des Chambres de Commerce et d'Industrie (APCCI).

Each of the above-mentioned bodies will require proof that the applicant is in, or about to set up a business. They will then issue a certificate which can be presented to the mairie or préfecture with the application for a *carte de séjour*: the latter will require renewal after 12 months, as in the case of an employee. This procedure should be followed by anyone who is self-employed, or who runs a company which they own but of which they are also an employee. Whatever entity the company takes e.g. an SA, SARl or SCI (see *Business Structures* below), the legal, financial and registration formalities involved can usually be dealt with in a few weeks. Those who initially start or buy a business but who later take a job, or vice versa, must be sure to change their *carte de séjour*. If one wishes to set up a business in France but not actually to become a resident there, then enquiries should be made to the French Consulate, as it may be necessary to seek approval from the Ministry of Finance. Such a procedure is not necessary for businesses based outside France merely doing business with France.

Finally, note that in France a distinction exists between businesses and trades (*métiers*). A shop, for example, is a business, but a plumber or builder is a tradesperson, even if he or she works from a shop.

Procedures Involved in Buying/ Creating a Business

Creating a New Business

Starting a new business will almost certainly require more capital than buying one, and consequently constitutes a greater risk. If you have to take out a loan, you will have to have a well thought out business plan. It is also advisable to ensure you have enough capital to keep the business going until it turns a profit which may be several years. However, once you have built up a successful business there is a potential financial gain from selling it on.

Anyone aspiring to this kind of venture will need a sound knowledge of business management in general, and to have pinpointed the type of business for which there is already a demand which has not yet been saturated. Finding a gap in the French market which you feel you can fill is another entrepreneurial possibility. Such a 'gap' is likely to be a product or service from home which does not exist in the host country. Again, there is an element of risk involved as the French are traditionally resistant to new products or new ways of doing things. Consequently, any new idea needs to be good. Remember however, that even with a good idea, the break-even point will probably take longer to reach than in the UK: in France it may take four years to return any profit.

Buying an Existing Business

Buying an exisiting business can be a cheaper and less risky venture than starting one from scratch. It also results in less preparatory paperwork as you do not need to generate all the basic company documents. Generally, the cost of buying small enterprises is much less in France than in the UK: property and land are also cheaper. Thus, many people wanting to buy a business have found they can do so in France, whereas a similar type of business in the UK would be totally beyond their reach.

One problem with buying in France is that there is often not a wide choice of businesses for sale in any given area, as family enterprises tend to remain within the family or to be sold by word of mouth, rather than to be advertised. The French organisation Centrale Immobilière des Commerçants et des Entreprises (CICE), PSTIC, Centre de l'Horloge, 2 Sq. de la Penthière, 49000 Angers; tel 2-41 48 56 56; fax 2-41 48 51 00, publishes a quarterly magazine giving listings of all types of small businesses for sale everywhere in France. The magazine costs 25 francs an issue, or 240 francs for a year's subscription within Europe. It is also available on subscription outside the EU.

Another fact to bear in mind is that many small businesses exist at subsistence level, rather than generating a rising profit. This tends to be because a typical proprietor sees his or her business as a way of life, rather than a streamlined system geared to making profit. This type of concern may suit those from the UK who are looking for a sideline or semi-retirement business, but obviously not those who have a more financially ambitious idea of business. This is not to say that the concept of getting rich quick through a timely business enterprise is unknown in France; just that it is not a generally anticipated consequence of commerce as it seems to be in the UK.

Those looking at advertisements of businesses for sale will see that some give the price for *fonds* and some for *fonds et murs*. This is because the French make a distinction between the physical property (*les murs*) and the business including goodwill, the trading name, and other tangible and intangible assets which comprise *les fonds* or *les fonds de commerce*. This means that buying an existing business normally involves two transactions: buying the business (*fonds*) which includes the goodwill, the clientele, the fittings and fixtures. Purchase of the existing stock is normally negotiated separately. The premises may either be bought outright, or rented. The former involves a similar procedure as for residential property (see *Setting up Home*). The main difference between the two is that the fees involved, which cover the notarial charges, expenses and taxes, etc. may be rather greater for a business. These can be in excess of 20% of the purchase price: always ask for a quotation beforehand. Renting is often a cheaper alternative under a commercial lease, *le bail commercial* (see below).

Starting a Business

Obviously, the final decision whether to create, or whether to buy a business will depend on financial considerations rather than personal inclinations. However, if you are contemplating starting a business of a type already present in France it is advisable to look at as many similar businesses as possible and find out as much about running costs and tax and other charges as you can and compare them with the UK. You will also need to carry out a thorough feasibility study which might include: taking into account the number of similar businesses in the area, the size of the local population or expected itinerant business and thus whether the area can support another business of a similar kind. If you employ people to work for you, you will have to fulfill stringent legal and financial obligations under France's complicated and burdensome employment laws. Even if you rent premises rather than buy them, and work on your own, you can pay up to 65% of your income in social security charges, which is why many French people claim they are working part-time.

Raising Finance

To start or buy any French business an amount of ready cash is almost certainly required. Many people find they are able to raise this capital by selling their UK home, as even after buying a French one of similar standard there is, at current property prices, likely to be a surplus which can be used for business purposes.

If necessary a loan can be raised from a financial institution. UK High Street banks are unlikely to be able to provide finance for the purchase or creation of a small business in France if the prospective owner intends to move to France permanently: a situation which may well change in the future. However, most French banks will consider applications for finance from those wishing to set up business in France and can be approached initially through their UK offices who may assist in setting up a loan with their relevant branch in France, or at least provide an introduction.

The terms on which a bank provides finance for buying or starting a business abroad are broadly similar to those you would expect in the UK. You have to demonstrate some business ability, have a well thought out business plan and be able to offer some security. It is unlikely that a bank will provide a sum in excess of the amount which you are able to inject in cash: such a loan would usually need to be repaid over a period of between five and seven years.

One alternative worth considering as a means of raising business finance is to mortgage any property you buy which is also sufficient to provide business start-up or purchase capital. This allows for a longer repayment period and removes the need to make a case out for your proposition.

Incentives

It may be worth investigating the financial incentives provided in France for the purpose of encouraging investment of all types. Some are suitable for single traders while others, such as EU regional aid programmes and those run by the French Industrial Development Board DATAR (see below) are geared to small and medium-sized businesses engaged in industrial production:

1.*Interest Subsidy:* Craftspeople/traders with evidence of trading or a qualification can apply for subsidised loans where part of the interest will be paid by the state.

2.*Tax Incentives:* It is possible to claim temporary tax exemption or reductions from local and regional authorities and the state. For instance new companies, whatever their business entity, if they are engaged in individual, commercial or craft activity can have 100% tax exemption on profits for the first two years, 75% for the third year, 50% for the fourth and 25% for the fifth year. However, there is a list of activities excluded from this exemption, among which are agriculture, finance, insurance, management and real estate rental.

Business licence taxes (*taxes professionelles*) are waived for the first year of any business, after which exemptions may be possible at the discretion of the local authorities. Businesses with a turnover of less than 500 million francs apply to the Préfecture. The maximum permitted period of tax exemption is five years.

For businesses with a turnover above 500 million francs, the French Government provides financial support through DATAR for certain types of businesses, and for businesses in specific areas which have been designated privileged investment zones. The latter are located in Bassin Minier and Sambre Avesnois in the north of France. Enterprises established before May 14 1998 which create a minimum of ten jobs can may enjoy a tax credit of 22 per cent for years from the creation of the company. Firms approved for establishment in these zones will have the tax credit deducted from corporate income tax for ten years. Other tax and welfare exemptions apply to companies setting up operations in special rural zones before December 12 2001. Details of the support available and the conditions which apply are available from DATAR (see below) or the from Ministry of Agriculture.

DATAR

The French Government provides support for new business and industry very enthusiastically. This includes investment and business ventures from overseas countries and within Europe, France is one of the leading countries for attracting such ventures.

The development of business and industry is under the overall control of a special development governmental organization called DATAR (Délégation à l'Aménagement du Territoire et à l'Action Régionale). This organization has offices in various foreign cities, including London (21-24 Grosvenor Place, London SW1X 7HU; tel 0171-823 1895; fax 0171-235 8453), which can provide extensive information on the processes involved in doing business in France. DATAR produces periodic reports concerned with actually doing business in France, the French system of taxation, tax incentives, company law and other business-related subjects. These publications are primarily focused at those who intend to buy or start up a business in France and can be obtained from the organisation's UK address.

The agency can also advise on grants and incentives for which owners of new businesses in France may be eligible, as well as providing details of contacts in particular regions and industries of France who will be able to provide further assistance. DATAR also has offices in the areas of France which have been identified as requiring special attention and have subsequently been designated enterprise zones by the French government: such areas include Lille, Nantes, Rouen and Clermont-Ferrand.

Chambers of Commerce exist in all French towns of a reasonable size and should be any prospective entrepreneur's first port of call. Also contact the regional development association, Agence Régionale de Dévelopement, which also exists throughout France. Both of these institutions are able to help and advise on business start-up and purchase procedure.

Finding a Business

In theory there is no reason why buying a business in France should be any more complicated than buying one anywhere else. However, very few foreigners have bought businesses there in the past, and business creation has tended to be the more popular alternative.

Businesses for sale can be found through both specialist business agents and estate agents. The easiest way to locate these is through the French Yellow Pages available at major city libraries in the UK, under *Immobiliers*. Major French newspapers also include some some business for sale advertisements: these newspapers are listed region by region in *Daily Life*. Although some preliminary research and investigation can be done from outside France, in order to prepare any sort of valid shortlist it is essential to visit the country for at least one inspection trip.

In order to establish the feasibility of any business it is advisable to build up a detailed knowledge of the trade or area in question. In particular, you should take into account location, local competition, previous results and profits etc, very much as you would expect to do anywhere. A survey of small businesses carried out in the latter 1980s, a time at which the French economy was just begining to move away from state control) showed that the most popular region for private enterprise was Paris (28%) and then the Rhône-Alpes (12%). This survey showed that over 47% of private entrepreneurs were in services, 36% in industry and commerce and 9% in cottage industries. Finally, 48% of these entrepreneurs were aged thirty to forty and 27% aged twenty to thirty.

For those considering the purchase of any business connected with tourism or leisure (as many expatriate businesses tend to be) it is particularly important to see how the business varies seasonally as in some areas businesses survive on the income generated by summer tourism, while others have year-round tourism potential.

The French publication *Acheter ou Vendre un Commerce* published by Centrale Immobiliere des Commerçants et des Entreprises CICE, see address above), is an invaluable specialist publication for those wishing to buy a business in France. British publications which may contain some businesses for sale adverts include *Living France* (01234-240954) and *French Property News*. In addition many of the UK-based estate agents that deal in French property generally have some small businesses on their books, often as part of a residential property.

Useful Addresses:

ABCD Entreprise: 4 Quai de Bercy, 94227 Charenton; tel 1-43 53 75 00. Can help with all aspects of starting business, from acquisition to office and secretarial services.

Agence Noel Jacques: 2 Place du Marchix, 22100 Dinan (Côtes-d'Armor); tel 2-96 85 30 45; fax 2-96 85 40 96. Has access to a national network of contacts for buying businesses. Specialists in hotels, bars, restaurants, cafés. Can help with all aspects, legal, financial etc. of setting up commercial ventures.

Network France: 12 Castle Street, Cambridge CB3 OAJ; tel 01223-464441; fax 01223-356410. Can locate businesses of various types (Hotels, restaurants, bed and breakfast, bars, farms and others) all over France through a network of local agents.

Getting Legal and Financial Advice

It is advisable to obtain an independent valuation of the business to ensure that the price being requested is fair and reasonable. When buying in France it is essential to take professional advice both on the viability of the business and the purchase procedure. To do this it is advisable to retain an accountant, a lawyer and one's own estate agent or notaire as a consultant. The best way to find a lawyer with the appropriate experience is probably by personal recommendation if at all possible. Otherwise, contact several and be very probing about their credentials, particularly their experience of French procedures and laws. Obvious positive signs are that they have a French partner, (either a firm or an individual lawyer), and that they are knowledgeable about and and experienced in the relevant French legal procedures. Any reputable firm will be happy to go to lengths to reassure you about having appropriate credentials. Both French and British accountants and solicitors with appropriate experience can be found through adverts in the *Living France* magazine (01234-240954) and in the French Chamber of Commerce in Britain's publication *Setting up a Small Business in France* (see below for address).

Useful Addresses:

Cabinet Henderson: Accountants in France, Nastringues, 24230 Vélines, France; tel + 33 5-53 23 44 52; fax + 33 5-53 27 03 34. Bi-lingual accountants with experience of small to medium size British-owned businesses.

French Chamber of Commerce in Great Britain: Knightsbridge House, 197 Knightsbridge, London SW7 1RB; tel 0171-304 7021; fax 0171-304 7034; e-mail:bckyb@ccfgb.co.uk

Holman, Fenwick and Willan, Solicitors: Marlow House, Lloyds Avenue, London

EC3N 3AL; tel 0171-488 2300; fax 0171 481 0316; also office in Paris (tel 1-44 94 40 50). Solicitors experienced in business start-ups in France.

Jeffreys Henry: Chartered Accountants, Freepost, London EC1B 1BT. Has offices in Paris, Lille and Nice. Specialist tax and financial advisors to companies and individuals considering setting up business in France. Also offices in Paris, Lille and Nice.

Prettys Solicitors: Elm House, 25 Elm Street, Ipswich, Suffolk IP1 2AD; tel 01473-232121; fax 01473 230002 Group 3. Offers a bilingual business service in conjunction with *notaires* and *conseillers juridiques* on all aspects of setting up and operating a business in France.

Stephenson Harwood: 1, St. Paul's Churchyard, London EC4M 8SH; tel 017-329 4422. Legal advice for businesses in France. Also at Fidal, Les Hauts de Villiers, 2 bis, rue de Villiers, 92300 Levallois Perret; tel +33 1-46 39 46 46.

Templeton Associates: tel: 01225; 422282; tel/fax 01225-42287; e-mail: templeton@cableinet.co.uk
Advice on acquisitions and setting up a business in France.

Glossary of Terms and Abbreviations for Business Purchase

French	Abbrev.	English
affaire	aff.	business
carte de commerçant		trader's card
centre commercial	ctre.cial.	shopping mall
cession		sale/transfer of a business
Chambre des Métiers		chamber of trades
chiffre d'affaires	ca.	turnover
code du travail		labour laws
conseil juridique		legal consultant
courtier		broker
couverts	cvts.	seating capacity
droit au bail		right to lease
fonds de commerce		business + goodwill, lease, trade name & marks
franchisé		franchisee
franchiseur		franchisor
matériel complet	mat. pro.	office equipment
Registre du Commerce et Commercial & des Sociétés Companies		Companies Register
surface commercial	surf.ciale.	area of commercial premises

The Purchase Procedure

The purchase of a *fonds de commerce* should involve the drawing up of contracts for both parties (i.e. the buyer and the seller), by either a *notaire* or a legal consultant *conseil juridique*. The contract must include details such as the turnover,(*chiffres d'affaires/ca.*) and profit or loss of the business and the title to the property in which the business is conducted. French law also requires that two notices of sale should appear in the legal announcements pages of the *Bulletin Officiel des Annonces Civiles et Comerciales - BODACC* (Bulletin of Civil and Commercial Notices). This is to ensure that any creditors know of the the state of business and can therefore claim any outstanding dues. Creditors' claims are taken from the sale price which the buyer lodges with the notaire in a stakeholder account (*compte séquestre*).

Other procedures connected with purchase include the payment of transfer tax (*droits d'enregistrement*) which varies according to the estimated value of the business, but can amount to about 14% on a business with a transfer value exceeding 300,000 francs.

If the buyer is obtaining a business with existing employees, he or she must comply with French labour legislation which requires that the workforce will have been consulted prior to the sale.

Once the business has changed hands, the name and particulars of the new owner have to be entered in the Commercial and Companies Register (*Registre du Commerce et des Sociétés*).

Renting Commercial Property

It is quite common in France to have two options, when acquiring a business; either to purchase the property outright or to rent it. Renting the property is obviously cheaper, in the short term.

The protections afforded by law to domestic tenants may not apply to a commercial lease (*le bail commercial*). Thus, it is essential to take legal advice to ensure that the lease is satisfactory: such advice can be obtained from an independent estate agent or notary. However, as with domestic leases, business leases usually include a right to rent clause which is obviously essential to protect the future, and future value, of the business.

The law governing commercial leases says that the lease must be in writing, and a minimum of nine years duration, with a possibility for the tenant to terminate the lease at the end of each three-year period. (Quite often in advertisements for businesses for sale you see: *Bail: 3-6-9, reste 4 ans* or *6 ans, 7 ans* etc.); *reste* refers to the period remaining on the lease. However, if the business person or company requires a lease for a shorter duration, two-year leases, or a lease terminable by either party at any chosen moment (*convention d'occupation précaire*) are also possible, but there is no accompanying protective legislation or tenant right to renewal.

The rent may be subject to negotiation by both parties. Under present law a sliding scale clause may be inserted into the lease by which the rent can increase in conjunction with the quarterly index of the cost of housing instruction (*indice INSEE*) but if the rent increases or decreases by more than 25%, it is the market value, rather than the indexed sliding scale which prevails. Landlords can legally countermand this regulation by claiming that substantial improvements have increased the value of the building by more than 10% since the lease was signed in which case the rent may exceed the maximum increase imposed by the index.

Pas-de-Porte: Sometimes in advertisements you will see *pas-de-porte* mentioned. This is a lump sum, payable to the landlord when entering into a commercial lease. It is also possible for the landlord of a commercial property to demand a deposit of three to six months rent. When buying a *fonds de commerce* the buyer should check for restrictive clauses in the seller's lease. For instance it will probably be necessary to engage a notary to draw up the deed of transfer and the landlord will have to be present when the parties sign.

When a tenant wishes to renew the lease he should inform the landlord six months in advance. The rent will be reviewed and fixed according the indice INSEE, the market value, or some other private arrangement. The conditions for renewal are that the tenant must have been operating the business for a minimum of three years and be the owner of the business. These regulations apply to EU nationals only. Should the landlord not grant renewal, the tenant is entitled to compensation (*indemnité d'éviction*) on reasonable terms which may include the market value of the business and the cost of removal and relocation. However, if the tenant is the subject of an eviction order for non-payment of rent, change of use of premises or is in contravention of other terms of the lease, the landlord will not have to pay compensation.

Sub-letting is not permitted without the prior consent of the landlord. The sub-let should be formalised in writing and authorised by the landlord so that when the main lease terminates, the sub-letter can request a renewal.

Ideas and Procedures for New Businesses

Those who decide to start a small business from scratch will need a very good and sound business idea plus the flair and determination necessary to get it off the ground and most importantly, a proper marketing strategy and business plan. As mentioned, there are two routes to follow; one is to jump on the bandwagon of an existing French business idea that is proving lucrative, the other is to find a gap in the market that your business can fill. In either case research will need to be carried out in France itself. There is no reason why some British-flavoured businesses should not be exportable to France in the way that some French businesses have successfully been imported into Britain where you can now find authentic French boulangeries and patisseries for which there is a ready market in well chosen areas. It may therefore be possible to transmit some forms of UK establishments successfully to France.

Looking for a gap in the market can be a more risky, but ultimately perhaps, a more rewarding venture if the idea takes off. Try to find a business that is commonplace in the UK but rare or non-existent in France and which has a universal appeal. For example, there are few English-style pubs in France, and it is hard to find any foreign food; garden centres are rare, although the French are increasingly keen on gardening. In some cases, a hobby could translate into a French business, although one would need to be very knowledgeable in the chosen area, for example, there are very few antique shops in France. It may also be possible to transfer a current business or trade to France. For example, plumbers, builders, hairdressers, small garages etc. are needed in France, as in any other country. Other businesses can exploit traditional French tastes: for example running a snail or truffle farm. However unlikely it may sound, there are such British enterprises in France. Marmalade is another product the French cannot seem to get enough of, and there are possibilities for cottage industries to produce this and other typically British consumables.

The best way of approaching setting up a business is to identify an area of France which you like and look to see how your idea could adapt to that area. Regional and local differences may mean that an idea may work in some parts of France but not in others, thus necessitating some market research. Is there a demand for your product or service? What is the competition? Could you obtain supplies easily? Are staff available? What are the legal and licensing formalities involved, and what implications do these carry? Some ideas for potential businesses may be gathered from the following run-down on the types of business that have recently been started by foreigners moving into France.

Shops

From an administrative point of view, shops are one of the simplest businesses to start. In addition, the French particularly appreciate small shops offering quality goods and personal service, in spite of the large number of hypermarkets. These shops can range from being simple grocery stores to specialist shops, such as the enterprising surf shop which opened in Biarritz. There are also possibilities for mobile shops. Marmalade, tea and English bread (which makes better toast than the French version) are just some of the items for which the French have developed a liking. It is possible to sell from the mobile shop in markets on market day. You would obviously need to make regular trips back to Blighty to renew supplies.

There is a trend in France, similar to that in Spain, towards opening English-style shops (such as English bookshops, bakers, video-markets etc.) in areas with expatriate populations. This may be a continuing possibility, provided that the market in some areas is not already saturated. It is worth remembering however, that there are not as many year-round expatriates in France as there are in Spain so you would almost certainly have to cater for a partly French clientele as well.

Bars and Cafés Running a sociable watering hole in a seaside place or a pretty village is one of the more idealised business ideas; and applies to France no less than in other lands where the British have expatriated themselves in large numbers. Almost every French village already seems to have several bars and cafés. However, such enterprises are not necessarily large income providers and the clientele may be limited. For this reason, many people also consider opening a bar or café as a retirement business.

Moreover, setting up such an establishment is often not as simple as it appears. One drawback is that these businesses can involve long working hours, with little free time. In addition, competition is tough and the bureaucracy involved in obtaining a licence to sell alcohol is considerable, although this should not be a problem if one is buying a going concern.

Drinking establishments are defined under French law as *débit de boissons* and the licence required comes in four variations depending on the categories of beverages served:

1. For non-alcoholic beverages.
2. For 1 and also drinks no more than 3 per cent proof spirit.
3. For 1 and 2 and also drinks having an alcohol content of 18 per cent proof
4. For 1,2, and 3 and also all other liquors and spirits which are not prohibited by French law.

The procedure for opening, or acquiring a drinking establishment involves providing the local authorities (usually the mairie) with written notification of your intention, at least 3 weeks in advance.

Restaurants. There is always plenty of custom in France for good restaurants. Whether grand ones with table linen and uniformed waiting staff, or small informal bistros. However, something that all these establishments share is the serious attention to detail and the quality and presentation of the food. However, because of client expectations the restaurants in France, even basic, inexpensive restaurants must offer good food in order to survive. Since British cooking still tends to be regarded as something of a joke in France, any restaurant with a British owner needs to establish a reputation immediately for its accomplished chef and unique service.

As in the UK a distinction is made in law between restaurants and bars. Restaurants are regarded as places where drinks are served as an accompaniment to food and less stringent regulations are in force for eating, as opposed to drinking establishments.

Tea shops A way round the alcohol licence rigmarole might be to open a tea shop serving English-style bread, cakes, muffins and scones baked on the premises. There could be a lunch-time sandwich service and afternoon teas with a range of tea flavours.

Hotels. As with restaurants, good hotels in France (in any price range) are always popular and can be very profitable enterprises. It is essential to choose the location of the hotel with care, and to either have or gain experience of the trade before embarking on this kind of enterprise.

Probably the main advantage of entering this business is that hotels and properties for conversion can be purchased very cheaply. However this must be balanced against the notarial charges which are higher for hotels than for non-commercial property. Any establishment with more than 6 letting bedrooms is classed as a commercial hotel business and the notary charges 21% on top of the agreed purchase price. So a 16-roomed hotel for £100,000 may not be quite such a bargain after all. On a more modest level, there is also scope in France for guesthouses and bed-and-breakfast type accommodation, perhaps within one's own home (see below).

There are very strict regulations governing both hotel and restaurant premises, the majority of which are related to the protection of human life against the risk of fire and other emergencies which could result in panic. The formalities involved in setting up a hotel involve compliance with the classification standards, depending on what category (no star, one star, two star etc) you are intending to register in. The hotelier also has to complete a barrage of forms to be returned to the mairie to verify compliance with the required standards. The operator must register the establishment on the Commercial and Companies Register and submit to a departmental inspection before consent to open as a business is granted.

Providing Residential Activity Holidays/Holiday Accommodations

France's substantial tourist industry means that residential activity holidays (e.g. art courses, sports etc.) and holiday accommodation, particularly apartments or cottages, are in high demand. The business is usually seasonal and profits in most cases not high; but again the lower prices of property make the idea more viable.

Bed and Breakfasts: Usually advertised in much the same way as in the UK with handmade signs by the wayside reading *Chambres d'Hôtes*. No prior authorisation from the authorities is required but a provider must register with the *Registre du Commerce et des Sociétés* already mentioned.

If an evening meal is also provided a licence 3 (see drinking establishments above) is required in order to serve drinks with the meal.

Gîtes: This word has by now become familiar to many Britons, not least because some of the estimated 60,000 privately owned self-catering homes available in France are run by them. A gîte is a low price, rurally located, simple self-catering accommodation rented to holidaymakers. Brittany Ferries who took over the marketing for 1,200 properties formerly organised by the defunct *Gîte de France* organisation have exacting standards. Further information on 0990 360 360).

To qualify as a Gîte Rural, holiday rental properties should be registered with the National Organisation of Gîtes, Gîtes de France. The requirements are for certain standards of decoration and equipment to be maintained, that the property must be available to rent for at least three months a year and that the owners live close by. The advantage to be gained is that a gîte rural qualifies for a lower rate of tax to be paid by the owner than either bed and breakfast or guesthouse accommodation. Also that by appearing in the Gîte Organisation's handbook, publicity is laid on and there is a reasonable chance of a steady influx of customers, though this generally only happens in the most popular holiday regions.

Short Lets of Furnished Property. Many people with a holiday home in France help pay for it by letting it out for short periods, a few weeks or months at a time, to holiday makers. No prior authorisation is needed, but the owner must pay a small businesses income tax (*Impôt sur les bénéfices industriaux et commerciaux* BIC) unless it is their main residence, or part of it, for not more than 5,000 francs.

Those who choose to invest in alpine property will be able to let it out in both winter and summer. The potential for winter letting in fashionable French ski resorts like Val d'Isère, Méribel and Courchevel is prodigious as tour operators usually want to secure suitable accommodation on five-year contracts. Private-owners with prime and well-positioned property on the slopes can recoup a year's running costs from a three-week let around February half-term. Alternatively, purpose-built studios in a popular resort such as Les Menuires, can be let to young travellers who are notching up a season working in a ski resort. Some of those who have invested in alpine property also manage to run their own skiing packages included catered chalet accommodation, from what is essentially their own holiday home.

The renting of unfurnished property is much more strictly regulated and leases are not normally for less than three years. For further details, see the chapter *Setting up Home.*

Sports. Sporting activity is not yet as popular in France as in the UK. Nevertheless, it is a growing industry which carries strong business potential for those with qualifications or experience. Possible openings include sports, squash and golf clubs, tennis and fitness centres and riding schools. Fortunately, with the exception of water sports centres and ski schools, there is not a great deal of commercial competition in this field at present.

Franchising. Anyone who is tempted by the idea of running their own business, but who is deterred by the high failure rate, may consider taking on a franchise. Under this system, a company authorises the franchiser to sell that company's goods or services in a particular area, usually exclusively. Franchising is well known in the United States and Britain, and was introduced into France in the 1980s; by 1986 there were around 500 companies offering franchises, and twenty thousand franchisers.

Franchising brings with it several advantages. Normally in the first year of business, many small concerns experience difficulties while establishing a reputation and building up a clientele. With a franchise, the franchiser is selling a name that already has a reputation, and whose products are in demand through national advertising. The company offering the franchise will also help the franchiser obtain, equip and stock the premises, and will handle the accounting. In exchange, the franchiser pays royalties which are proportional to the sales.

Companies offering franchises in France include André, Pronuptia, Descamps, Kis, McDonalds and Yves Rocher. Since franchise terms vary amongst companies, and some may not be favourable, it is advisable for anyone considering this option to go into the details extremely carefully.

Farming & Wine-growing. Farming of various types has been one of the most popular business activities for foreigners moving to France in recent years: approximately 600 farms were sold to European farmers from outside France in 1988 alone. This is mainly due to the comparatively low cost of both land and property in France. A number of farmers from the UK have found that they can buy (or rent) in France, whereas this would be prohibitively expensive in the UK. A further attraction is that farming is one business where UK methods and techniques can be duplicated in France, such techniques often being more advanced than those used in France itself.

The French government is generally keen to encourage foreigners to farm in France. It may grant financial aid to farmers under 35 or to those in possession of a diploma recognized by the French Ministry of Agriculture. Those who plan to farm in less popular or depopulated regions may also be eligible for help with farm modernization and other financial incentives from government agencies. For instance in 1995, the regional government of the Limousin region in central France advertised in British publications for farmers to go there to replace the indigenous farmers who had drifted away to better paid work in the cities. They were offering up to £100,000 in loans at 2.5% interest. About 50 British farmers took up the offer, but some were dismayed by the hostile attitude of the locals. So be warned: farming is not for the faint hearted, and a knowledge of French is pretty much essential if you are to make friends. To qualify for such incentives experience in the work is essential. Further information for farmers and details of possible grants can be obtained from the Association Départementale pour l'Aménagement des Structures des Exploitations Agricoles ADASEA (see address below).

Wine-growing by the British in France has a long and mostly honourable history as the names of some of the top-notch Bordeaux château remind us. At one end there are the multinational and tycoon investors like Pearson and George Walker and in the middle are the owner-grower viticulteurs Britanniques the likes of which run châteax Méaume, du Seuil (Graves) and Bauduc (Entre-Deux-Mers) as well as others. At the other end are those who send their crop to the local *cave cooperative* to be turned into the local plonk. To buy a fully-fledged château vineyard does not come cheap. Buying a chateau and turning it into a château labelled wine comes even less cheap since you have the outlay on equipment such as a wine press and metal tanks and barrels. You would need an expert consultant to assess the potential of the land for producing a good wine; this would include soil content and its suitability. The micro-climate is also crucial, particularly the likelihood of frosts. Not least would be the status of your own skills (or lack of them) as a wine maker. It is possible to study oenology at a French university and become an apprentice; it is possible to teach yourself the basic principles. A combination of the two and some practical experience is the ideal (apart of course, from growing up in the business).

Property dealing. In the chapter *Setting up Home* the procedures for the acquisition of property in France and the possible advantages were discussed in relation to whether the property was for permanent or holiday use. Another possibility exists — that of speculating in French property. This is largely possible because of the disparity in prices between the countries.

A few expatriates have moved into this business by buying, renovating and then reselling properties. This is usually done direct into the UK market, as holiday property, to reach the higher prices that are usual for such property. A business in property renovation would require higher than average capital (because of financial liability for taxes and debts), as well as some experience in the purchase and conveyancing procedure, and building works. This might be obtained from initially purchasing and restoring one's own property.

Once you have gained experience, and have bought another property through a notaire, he or she will be able to help you set up a real estate company (*société civile immobilière*, or SCI). (See business entities below).

Exporting

The DTI and the British Embassy and Consulates General in France recently held a range of promotional activities which included the sectors listed below, and suggested that export activities could be carried out via a representative (importer, commission agent or stockist/distributor), selling through a manufacturer of complementary products with an established network, setting up a branch office or subsidiary or by establishing a company in France.:

Automotive components
Boats and boating equipment
Environmental goods and services
Food and drink
Garden supplies
Medical supplies
Tabletop goods for the hospitality industry

Useful Addresses:

The following can provide advice, details of the regulations, legal services, and in some cases, provide grants for individual businesses.

Agence Nationale pour la Création et le Développement (ANCD): 14 rue de l'Ambre, 75014 Paris; tel 1-42 18 58 58; fax 1-42 18 58 00.

Agence Nationale pour la Création d'Entreprise (ANCE): 14 rue Delambre, Paris 14th; tel 1-42 18 58 58. Has a library and Minitel/Internet service which the public can use. Can also advise on who to contact for a particular business project. Knowledge of French useful when dealing with this organisation.

Business Development Network International: 4 Ave des Jonchères, 78121 Crespières; tel 1-30 54 94 66; fax 1-30 54 94 67. Holds meetings for small businesses; has a network of about 400 small companies, consultants, entrepreneurs and start-ups. English/French. Meetings are in Paris only.

Centre National pour l'Aménagement des Structures des Exploitations (CNASEA): 7 rue Ernest Renan, BP 1, 92136 Issy Les Moulineaux Cedex; tel 1-46 48 40 00; fax 1-46 48 74 11. Information and advice for farmers. Also agricultural grants.

Centre d'Etudes du Commerce et de la Distribution (CECOD): 18 rue de Calais, 75009 Paris; tel 1-40 69 38 47; fax 1-42 80 43 94. Commercial research.

Conseil National des Professions de l'Automobile (CNPA): 50 rue Rouget de L'Isle, 92158 Suresnes Cedex; tel 1-40 99 55 00; fax 1-47 28 44 15. Information about regulations for automobile repairers and traders.

Crea Conseil: 41 rue St-Augustin, Paris 12th; tel 1-47 42 25 70; specialised agency which will complete the necessary legal formalities and advise on financial matters and services for businesses in Paris.

*DATAR:*The French Industrial Development Board, 21-24 Grosvenor Place, London SW1X 7HU (tel 0171-823 1895).

Délégation à l'Aménagement du Territoire et à l'Action Régionale (DATAR): 1 avenue Charles-Floquet, 75007 Paris (tel 1-40 65 12 34; fax 1-40 65 12 40).

Fédération Nationale des Sociétés d'Aménagement Foncier et d'Etablissement Rural (FNSAFER): 3 rue de Turin, 75008 Paris; tel 1-44 69 86 00. Information about

SAFER, the French land commission agency which can both exercise a premptive right to buy agricultural land for sale but also sells land. There is a special section called *Terres d'Europe* (tel 1-44 69 86 10), which deals with foreigners.

Federation Nationale de l'Industrie Hôtelière (FNIH): 22 rue Anjou, 75008 Paris; tel 1-44 94 19 94; fax 1-47 42 15 20. Provides information on regulations governing the hotel industry.

Invest in France: 28 rue du Docteur Finlay, 75015 Paris; tel + 33 1-44 37 05 80; fax + 33 01 44 37 05 90; internet: http://www.investinfrance.org

Tax Relief and Grants on Rentable Property.

If the intention is to buy a property and then let it there are a number of important considerations in addition to those mentioned above. These mainly concern the treatment of income for tax purposes and the availability of grants.

If you declare the rental income in the UK, then you will have to pay tax to the Inland Revenue. The tax rate depends on your own tax rate, but the main point is the allowance given for overseas investment. At the time of writing, each individual tax inspector has discretion as to whether you can claim interest paid on a loan as an 'expense'. There are virtually no other allowances given in the UK.

However, if you declare the income in France, you have to pay 5.5% TVA on the gross amount, and you are then allowed a number of allowances under French law. These include:

Interest on a French Franc loan taken in France. Depreciation at the rate of 4% of the value of the property per annum.

Management charges. Charged by an agent handling the rental, or to cover your costs in advertising, etc. These can be 10% for country property and 15% for town property.

Maintenance and cleaning costs. May include repairs to the property; you may even be able to claim for inspection trips to the property.

If you are claiming French allowances you will almost certainly need a French accountant to complete the returns for you and pay the income into your French bank account. It also makes even more sense to have a French franc loan. You can however earn up to 5,000 francs per annum from short-term letting of rooms without being liable for French taxes.

If you intend converting barns, stables, etc. into gîtes or letting units, you may be eligible for a grant of some kind. This would come from the département, region, state, or even the EU. The mayor of the commune is all-powerful, and it is he or she who will decide whether or not to give planning permission. The mairie will also point you in the direction of the right person for a grant. The Gîtes de France organisation is currently giving grants of 40% of the cost of renovation; but you are tied to them for letting for ten years.

In specific regions of France, it is even possible to obtain discounts on mortgage interest on renovation. You can also qualify for another grant if you are creating employment in the area. At present there are about 250 different grants available.

The Cost of Buying a Business

The following list provides some examples of the type of businesses for sale in France. Prices, converted into pounds sterling at the rate of exchange current at the time of going to press, are for the business and freehold, excluding stock unless stated.

Business	Area	Price
Bar/Rest./Snacks	village centre, Haute-Pyrenees	£88,000
Bar only	small village, Charente	£60,000
Grocery shop in a small village, with 1 bed accomm.	Picardy	£28,500
Boulangerie	Rouen suburbs, primary position	£84,000
Bicycle/sports hire (Seasonal business only) kiosk & stock)	Languedoc	£9,200
Café-Bar (Business and property on lease, prime position)	Languedoc	£62,350

Useful Addresses:
The following are relocation agents with expertise in organising business relocations from the UK to France:
PMI: 12 Marsh Lane, Leonard Stanley, Stonehouse, Glos., GL10 3NJ; tel 01453-823535; fax 01453-828923.
Raymond Lowe Associates: 44 Brunswick Road, Shoreham-by-Sea, West Sussex, BN43 5WB; fax 01273-454790.

Business Structures and Registration

As in the UK, there are various legal entities which a business can form though there is perhaps a greater diversity of types in France, with strict rules applying to the operation of each type of business.

Bureau de Liaison/*Bureau de Représentation:* A liaison office is the minimal type of business foray. It essentially provides a shop window for foreign companies to communicate with potential customers but is not a business entity in the sense of having a legal relationship with customers or third parties. It may carry out assessments of the market and promotional activities. The main obligations of a bureau de liaison are to conform with French regulations on publicity and advertising materials. Any company dealing in comestibles should note that foreign foodstuffs may not be advertised on French television. Liaison offices must be registered with the Register of Companies.

Entreprise Individuelle: This is a popular form of business for the self employed with a modest turnover, who do not engage in any large financial activities, since in the event of problems, personal liability is unlimited. It is suitable for a sole trader and requires no start-up capital. There are three types of *entreprises individuelles*: *profession libérales* (e.g. doctors, accountants, lawyers etc., *Commerçants individuels* (shopkeepers and other traders) and *artisans* (craftspeople). Note that members of some trades and professions must hold qualifications which are recognised in France and all are obliged to attend a short 'business management course'. In some areas this just means a day enjoying the hospitality of the local mayor. Social security deductions are very high in France for the self-employed and represent about 35% of total earnings before taxes are deducted.

They are also compulsory regardless of a lack of profit, or if losses are being incurred which is not uncommon in the first couple of years of business.

Société à Responsabilité Limitée *(S.A.R.L.)*. This is the most common form of limited liability company and is suitable for small and medium-sized businesses. However the extra costs in annual social security payments and business taxes can be extortionate, even if only a handful of staff are employed, see *Employing Staff* below. A SARL may be formed with between two and fifty shareholders of which a three-quarters majority is needed to alter the company's constitution and expand or decrease the capital. Shareholders may be of any nationality, and the company must possess a minimum capital of 50,000 francs. A SARL may have one or two managers *(gérants)* categorised as salaried employees for tax and social security purposes. An annual audit by a statutory auditor *(commissaire aux comptes)* is not required unless turnover and/or employee numbers exceed certain limits. An AGM must be held to approve the financial statements before the end of the financial year.

Société par actions simplifié — SAS: the SAS is a simplified version of the SA introduced in 1994 in response to a need for a more flexible structure to facilitate cooperation between businesses. The corporate share capital of the shareholders must be a minimum of 1.5 million francs (or the foreign currency equivalent). The SAS cannot issue shares publicly.

Entreprise Unipersonelle à Responsabilité Limitée (E.U.R.L): Is another limited liability entity and is basically a SARL adapted to a sole person with the same amount of start up capital.

Société Anonyme (SA): An SA, is appropriate for larger, more prestigious concerns and is the French equivalent of the UK plc. It requires more capital than a SARL, the minimum amount required being 250,000 francs, and includes more formalities than a SARL. An SA also demands a minimum seven shareholders and is run by a board of 3 to 12 directors *(conseil d'administration)* appointed for a maximum of six years and a *président directeur générale* (PDG).

If the start-up capital is subscribed in cash, only 25% needs to be paid up before incorporation and the balance within five years. Shares which are subscribed in kind must be entirely paid up and the contributions are subject to appraisal by the *Commissaire aux Apports* (Contributions Auditor) to assess their value. An SA must have an annual general assembly of shareholders and external auditors.

Partnerships: The laws of partnership in France are complicated as so many different forms exist. Expert advice is essential for those proposing any form of partnership. Some of the types are:
Société en nom Collectif (SNC): General Partnership which must have at least 2 members with no minimum capital restriction. The shareholders have joint and several unlimited liability for the company debts. For tax and social security purposes, the member shareholders are categorised as individual traders.
Société en Commandité Simple (SCS): The SCS is a limited partnership. There is also a *Societé en Commandité par Actions: (SCA)* This is a joint stock company whose active partners have unlimited liability and sleeping partners whose liability is limited to their stake in the company.
Société Civile: (SC) A Civil Company may only deal in civil (i.e. non commercial matters) which include, agriculture, building, and the professions. An SC has several forms and a minimum of two shareholders. For instance an SCI (*Société Civile Immobilière*) is a form commonly used for a real estate holding company, also for managing real estate, letting and property purchase. It is therefore useful

for groups of expatriates buying property together to form or join an SCI. In this form, the SCI is registered as the owner of the property or properties and it can be a useful way of by-passing French inheritance laws (see *Setting up Home*). In the SCI form it is similar to a partnership as individuals are taxed individually on their capital gains when they sell, gain income, or incur losses. An SCI cannot be used for commercial purposes but may be transmuted into a SARL. It is possible to create a SARL which rents the property from the SCI thus protecting the stakeholders and their property from personal liability in case of financial or tax problems. There are however tax liabilities involved in changing from an SCI to SARL (or indeed from any business entity to another) so it is advisable to take expert fiscal advice at the outset.

Succursale: Branch office. Another possibility for UK companies already in business in the UK is to open branch offices in France. These are not legally separate from the parent company and thus all business must be concluded with the parent company which is likewise responsible for any debts incurred by the branch office.

A branch office has more powers than a liaison office because it can conduct business in its own right (subject to the above). Note however, that for tax purposes it is treated as a separate entity from the parent company. It must therefore keep its own company books.

All SARLs, SAs, Commandités (partnerships) and other business entities must be registered with the Commercial Register and the Chamber of Commerce (see below).

If you are buying a business then its legal form will have important tax implications. For example, the purchase of a company involves extra purchase taxes and duties.

Procedure for Registering a Company

There are several important procedures for registering and incorporating businesses set up in France, which must be executed within two weeks of beginning operations there. It is advisable to initiate the procedures at the CFE (*centre de formalités des entreprises*), at the local chamber of commerce as soon as you arrive. The business must be registered on the Registre du Commerce et des Sociétés which will be done by the CFE locally with the *Greffe* (clerk) from the *Tribunal de Commerce* (commercial court). Failure to register within the time limit is subject to penalties.

As with all bureaucratic procedures a barrage of personal documents is required including a copy of a birth certificate issued within the last three months and an accompanying official translation. If a British company is being registered then a copy of the memorandum and articles of association (*les statuts*) with a professional French translation will be required. The company registration number allocated by the Registre de Commerce is then relayed to the company's French bank the tax office and social security offices and any other relevant authorities including the *Institut National des la Statistique et des Etudes Economiques (INSEE)* which will issue the company with a NAF, SIREN and/or SIRET number.

The CFE, which handles all the administration involved in registering new businesses is usually the local chamber of commerce and industry. For instance if the traders, merchants and other businesses come under the following categories:

Répertoire des Métiers (Trade Register) or *Les Groupements d'Intérêt Econo-miques* (Common Economic Interest Groups) and *Sociétés de fait* (de facto companies). There are however other CFE's :
Chambre des Métiers (Chamber of Trades) for craftspeople who are self-employed or with a firm.
Greffe du Tribunal du Commerce: (Clerk of the Commercial Court). For sales representatives.

Company Banking and Accounts

When opening an acccount you will need to be present in person and to provide proof of personal identity including a passport, birth certificate, translated memorandum and articles and certificate of incorporation. When setting up a company, the share capital will be held in a blocked account until the company registration formality has been completed. Other company banking facilities, loans, overdrafts etc. will have to be negotiated on an individual basis.

For company accounts, you will almost certainly require a French accountant to set up the books and accounting system as it varies from the British system. If the books do not conform to French auditing requirements they will have to be redone which for several years' accounts would be very expensive. The annual publication *Mémento Comptable* published by Editions Francis Lefebvre and written by Price Waterhouse is the main reference accounting manual.

Running a Business

Running a small business in France tends to be a more easy-going and relaxed affair than in the UK. Business procedures can be fairly informal, especially in the south where a Mediterranean attitude prevails. As already mentioned, running a business can become a way of life rather than a purely profit-driven exercise.

Small, privately-owned businesses, by their very nature, demand much hard work, long hours and little free time. Much emphasis is placed on offering a personalised service and a high level of customer care, since establishing a good reputation and relationship with the customers is vital for the survival of a business. Formal advertising and marketing tend to be less important, and beyond the financial range of most small businesses. Nevertheless, dealing with suppliers and other contacts will demand the full extent of one's persuasive skills and negotiating techniques.

However, the relaxed attitude described above does not extend as far as bureaucracy and officialdom are concerned. In addition, some types of businesses may find themselves up against the ever instrusive, and occasionally bizarre-seeming, regulations that emanate from Brussels. In France, accounting and other official procedures are often very complex and professional advice in matters such as taxation will be essential.

Employing/Dismissing Staff & Employer Contributions

Nearly all businesses employ staff, whether part- or full-time. This can be a good way of integrating into the local community. Employees are usually taken on for a three-month trial period. During this time employment may be terminated by either party without any notice being given. If the trial period proves successful, then a contract of employment will be drawn up. This should always be in writing and a copy retained for future reference along with any correspondence with the employee. The different types of contract are dealt with fully in the *Employment* chapter.

The local ANPE office will usually be pleased to help with staffing requirements and to advertise these free of charge. Remember that if any foreigners are to be employed in your business, they will require a contract of employment as soon as possible in order to obtain their *carte de séjour*. Whether a spouse, if employed in his or her partner's business, would gain a *carte de séjour* as a dependant or an employee, is something of a grey area. This should be checked out through the *préfecture de police* if applying for the permit in France, and through the French consulate if applying in the UK.

The rules which govern relations between employers and employees in France are embodied in the detailed statutory regulations known as the *Code du Travail* which among other things sets out minimum wages and working conditions, hours of work, amount of paid holiday allowed per year etc. Some sectors of industry have their own collective bargaining agreements (*conventions collectives*) forged between the labour force and managements which come into effect the moment employment is offered. For other sectors, there is a statutory minimum wage (SMIC), which is indexed to the cost of living.

The discharging of employees is governed by a strict set of procedures which if not followed may result in penalties for the employer and/or reinstatement of the employee. If the proposed dismissal results from the serious malconduct of the employee he or she must be summoned prior to the dismissal and the reasons for the notice given fully. Other procedures must also be followed further details of which are given in the *Employment* chapter. If employers wish to make staff redundant for economic reasons, then it is a lengthy process hedged about with restrictions. Among other things, the employer will have to pay compensation, *indeminité de licenciement* the amount of which is fixed by law.

Under the Code du Travail, employers must pay mandatory social security contributions for their employees. These contributions, together with payroll taxes add 60% to the payroll costs. The employer contributes 45% and the employee 15%. There are also supplementary pension schemes run by employers usually jointly with the unions. As the employer's social security contributions for employees are much higher than employee contributions they add considerably to the financial burden inflicted on small businesses.

Taxation

Businesses, no less than individuals incur a range of taxes. In general, sole proprietors and partnerships will be subject to taxation on their profits calculated similarly to corporation tax (*impôt sur les bénéfices des sociétés* or *IS*) and also Capital Gains tax (*taxe sur les plus-values*) if appropriate. However, most business expenses are recoverable against the eventual tax bill and for very small businesses a flat tax is negotiable.

In order to meet the Maastricht criteria for joining the Single European Currency (for which the deadline is 1 January 1999), French corporation and and capital gains tax were given hefty surcharges from 1997. Corporation tax for 1997 was levied at 41.6 per cent, (down to 39.9 per cent in 1998). Companies with a turn over of less than 50 million francs (i.e. 80% of the companies eligible for corporation tax in France) are exempt from these increases.

Companies, whether SAs or SARLs, are liable to Corporation Tax of up to

36.6% on profits, although there are exemptions and reductions for certain types of businesses and/or businesses in particular areas (see *Incentives* above). Since French controls on foreign investment were abolished in January 1996, France has been trying to woo foreign investors with competitive rates of taxation on corporate main offices, foreign executives and distribution facilities. Note that businesses are also liable for a higher rate of Capital Gains Tax than individuals.

All businesses must be registered with the local tax authorities and Sécurité Sociale. The Commercial Registrar does this automatically for SAs and SARLs. Businesses must register with the TVA (VAT) authorities and charge that tax on sales; the system works very much like that in the UK, except that there are three different rates: the low rate of 5.5% (comestibles, most pharmaceutical items, books and water), 22% for 'luxury' goods such as cars and perfume and a standard rate of 20.6% for everything else.

The main taxes someone acquiring a business would be liable to pay are:

Droits d'enregistrement: Transfer duties. Anyone buying a *fonds de commerce* with a transfer value greater than 100,000 francs is liable to transfer duties which can amount to more than 14% on a business with a value in excess of 300,000 francs.

One way of moderating the transfer tax is when a small company is subjected to a take-over, in which case the transfer duty is at a fixed rate of 4.8%.

Capital Gains Tax: capital gains tax is payable on share sales (*plus-values sur titres*) and if the business itself is sold. If the assets have been held for less than two years the rate is 34% which is reduced to 19% if they have been held for longer than two years.

The taxes liable for the operating period, depending on the type of business are:

Bénéfices industriels et commerciaux (BIC): Certain types of business and entrepreneurs are eligible to pay BIC (instead of corporation tax). These include: individuals, sole proprietors, partners of an EURL and partners in a partnership (*associés de sociétés*). The BIC is applied to profits at the same rates as for personal income tax. Whether or not it is more advantageous to opt for BIC or corporation tax depends on the level of taxable profits earned.

Bénéfices non commerciaux BNC: Professional Income. Professional income includes profits earned by individual professions: all types of legal and medical exponents, sportsmen and women, accountants etc. These individuals must calculate their net profit after all expenses.

Impot sur les bénéfices des sociétés IS: Corporation tax. Profits made by a company after deductions of expenses occurred are liable to corporation tax at 36.6% (compared with 31% in the UK) on both distributed profits and those retained in the business. All joint stock companies pay this tax. In the case of partnerships it is possible to opt for this tax but normally profit is divided up among the partners who are then taxed individually according to their share (see BIC above). This is also the case with joint ventures. In certain circumstances and for certain types of business corporation tax is waived completely or partly for up to five years.

Taxe Professionelle: Local business tax/business licence tax. This is another major business tax levied in France. The rate varies according to the region, as local authorities have some discretion in the level although there have been attempts to harmonise the rates. Typically it could be calculated at 18% of the salaries paid in the year before last plus the annual rental value of the fixed assets in the same year, whether owned or rented. However this tax is often subject to a temporary waiver under the many incentives offered to new businesses, particularly in areas of high unemployment. There is in any case, no tax for the first year of business. It would be advisable to establish an exemption at the outset before registering a business. Enquiries can be made to DATAR, the French Industrial Development Organisation.

Taxe sur la Valeur Ajoutée TVA: Value Added Tax. The principle of VAT is that each supplier has to charge VAT on sales (output) and the buyer then claims credits for VAT paid on goods and services (input), against output VAT. Since VAT is recoverable in the case of companies, it is the ultimate buyer or consumer who actually carries the tax burden. It has long been known that VAT is one of the principal sources of revenue for the French treasury as it is applicable to almost everything in France including books, heating, water etc. and is thus a sweeping form of indirect taxation on the public.

In France, VAT is imposed on all economic transactions: manufacturing, trading, agricultural activities, and services. Exempted are all salaried activities. Sales of goods are VAT liable where the goods are delivered in France and where the individual or entity providing the service has France as its place of business. There are specific rules for VAT liability on certain services: advertising, recruitment, research, patent transactions, know-how and trade marks and renting of machinery or equipment. All these services are VAT liable when the object of these services is located within France and the provider outside France. Otherwise, VAT is usually reclaimable on exports and the new single market VAT system has supposedly made redundant the lengthy, expensive border checks and provided a computerised VAT system (VRIES) to accelerate VAT returns.

Despite the single market agreement of a single standard minimum rate of VAT (15%), many countries, including Britain and France continue to levy VAT at a higher rate than this. Up to 1997 VAT was payable in the country where the products/services etc were sold; after that year this was reversed so that VAT is payable in the country where the goods originated.

The VAT form is known as a 'CA3' and must be completed and returned to the tax authority at monthly or quarterly intervals. Businesses within the EU must have an EU VAT registration number and a file a *déclaration d'échange de biens* (disclosure) of all goods bought from another EU country or sold to another EU country.

Other Business Taxes

There are a number of sundry business taxes mostly payable by companies with ten or more employees and which are calculated from the total salaries paid:

Taxe sur les Salaires: (Payroll Tax). Levied on employers not liable for VAT. The tax varies according to the annual salary of the employee.

Participation construction: Compulsory Construction Investment Tax. Levied at 0.65%.

Participation formation continue: Training tax. Levied at 1.2%

Taxe d'apprentissage: Apprentice tax. 0.6%.

Finally there are taxes on real estate (*taxes foncières*) which are calculated on the supposed rental value of developed and undeveloped land.

Accountancy Advice

Businesses must prepare accounts each year, and in the case of partnerships, SAs and SARLs these must be supplied to the Commercial Registrar; they must also follow a prescribed legal format.

Accountancy advice is readily available in all parts of France: one should approach several firms and engage the one which takes an interest in and seems equipped to advise on the business's accountancy requirements. Unfortunately, accountants (*experts comptables*) are not allowed to advertise, but listings can be found in the telephone directory.

One major difference between French accountancy and that practised in the UK is that accountancy and audits to prepare the accounts are separate functions. Therefore you will require an accountant to give accountancy and tax advice, but a separate firm of auditors to prepare the annual accounts. Although there are a few UK accountants with experience of French procedures, most business people choose a local French financial adviser. Alternatively, various international firms of accountants have offices in both countries, including Coopers & Lybrand Deloitte, and Price Waterhouse.

Useful Addresses:
International, and UK chartered accountants with French associates:

Cabinet Henderson; Accountants in France, Nastringues, 24230 Vélines, France; tel + 33 5-53 23 44 52; fax + 33 5-53 27 03 34. Bi-lingual accounts with experience of handling the tax affairs of small to medium size, British-owned businesses.

Dixon Wilson Chartered Accountants: Rotherwick House, 3 Thomas More Street, London E1 9YX; tel 0171-628 4321; fax 0171-702 9769; and in Paris: 4 rue de Logelbach, 75017 Paris; tel 1-47 64 05 45; fax 1-40 53 00 49. Specialists in dealing with the accountancy and tax requirements of British businesses which are establishing a presence in France.

Dukes Chartered Accountants: Appleton House, 139 King Street, London W6 9JG; tel 0181-846 9644; fax 0181-741 4373. Has associate office in Paris.

Jeffreys Henry: Chartered Accountants, Freepost, London EC1B 1BT. Offices in Paris, Lille and Nice; tel 0171-253 7064.

JPA International: JPA-Bourner Bullock, tel 0171-240 5821; in Paris + 33 1-40 72 23 33. Over a dozen offices in France.

Bentley Jennison Accountants: Suite 3, Bishton Court, Telford Town Centre, Telford TF3 4JE; 01952-200808; fax 01952-200959. Paris Associate: Conseil & Expertise, 21/23 Blvd. Richard Lenoir, 75011 Paris; tel + 33 1 49 29 55 10; fax + 33 1 4805 1932.

Legal Advice

The prospective businessman in France is almost certainly going to need specialist legal advice, both in the setting up or purchase of the business, and in future operations. This applies no matter how small or large the business is. French law originates from Napoleonic times and is very different to the Anglo-Saxon law of northern European countries.

There are some UK law practices who are specialists in French law, as well as some international law firms with offices in France which specialise in giving both legal and financial advice. However, small businesses can also consult a local French practice particularly if recommended by other clients; such firms are easy to find but your French will have to be good, otherwise you will need an interpreter as English-speaking French lawyers are fairly rare.

As in the UK, French lawyers tend to work together in practices made up of a handful of lawyers. Therefore one firm can deal with most matters, be it contract law, employment law or litigation, etc. Not all lawyers (*avocats*) are qualified to act in a court.

Note that the essential difference between lawyers and notaires is that the latter are usually only involved with the law as it relates to contract, and also property matters.

Useful Addresses:

Holman, Fenwick & Willan Solicitors: Marlow House, Lloyds Avenue, London EC3N 3AL, tel 0171-488 2300; fax 0171-481 03 16; In France: 3 rue de la Boétie, 75008 Paris; tel 1-44 94 40 50; fax 1-42 65 46 25.

Jane Hood-Williams: Downsons Solicitors and Notaries, 52, Rectory Road, West Bridgford, Nottingham; tel 0115-9816868; fax 0115-9455859.

Penningtons Solicitors: Bucklersbury House, 83 Cannon Street, London EC4N 8PE; 0171-457 3000; Paris office: 23 rue d'Anjou, Paris 75008; tel 1-44 51 59 70.

Lefevre Pelletier et Associés: 136 Avenue des Champs Elysées, 75008 Paris; tel +33 1 5393 3008; fax +33 1-53 93 30 30.

Templeton Associates: tel 01225-422282; tel/fax 01225 422287. Advice on aquisitions and setting up a business in France.

Business Insurance

French insurance commands a large market and is subject to legal regulatory control under the *Code des Assurances* and all insurance companies of whatever kind in France come under the scrutiny of the Direction Générale des Assurances. When choosing an insurance company, as in the UK, many companies deal with a broker specialising in their field. Insurance in France seems very expensive as it is subject to tax from 7% to 30% depending on the type of insurance. Owners and tenants of business premises will require insurance against property damage and the subsequent financial losses incurred, and against legal liability to another party.

In addition there are special policies for hotels, restaurants and bars. Insurance companies will be particularly concerned that proprietors of such establishments observe the rigorous safety standards and provisions for the security of the property of guests anywhere on the premises including the carpark. This is because in France proprietors are legally responsible for guests' property.

Anyone dealing in motor vehicle repairs or sales is under a legal obligation to protect the vehicles not only while on the premises but in their charge outside the premises, for instance when on tow etc.

It is compulsory for anyone operating in a professional capacity to be insured.

For builders, there is a ten year legal liability for work carried out. Owing to the extensive litigation possibilities to which this exposes the practitioner, it is advisable to find an acute and experienced insurance broker who can devise a very intricate insurance cover.

Useful Addresses

AGF Insurance: Commercial Division, Suite 2, 2nd Floor, London Underwriting Centre, 3 Minster Court, London EC3 7DD; tel 0171-617 4514.

Centre de Documentation et d'Information de l'Assurance (CDIA): 2 rue de la Chausée d'Antin, 75009 Paris; tel 1-42 46 13 13. General enquiries from the public about insurance in France must be in written form.

Direction Générale des Assurances (DGA): 54 rue de Chateaudun, 75009 Paris; tel 1-42 81 91 55.

Fédération Françaises des Sociétés d'Assurance (FFSA): 26 Blvd. Haussmann, 75009 Paris; tel 1-42 47 90 00; fax 1-42 47 93 11.

Miscellaneous

Registering Rights Over Industrial Property: Foreign business people should register their industrial property rights (i.e. patents) which can thereby be protected for exclusive exploitation for 20 years while Trade marks (marques) can be protected for ten years. This should be done at the Institut National de la Propriété Industrielle (INPI, 32 rue des Trois Fontanot, 92016 Nanterre Cedex; tel: 1-46 92 58 00.

Incorporation Fees: There are certain reasonably modest costs incurred for the registration of a company on the Commercial and Companies Register. These are in the region of £70 for a sole trader and and £120 for a limited liability entity. Additional fees are needed to cover the printing of legal announcements and tax on the start-up capital. The total would come to about £300 for a limited liability, plus any legal or accountancy fees.

Siège Social: Registered Office. It is obligatory for all French companies and branches of foreign companies to have a registered address that is not just a post box number, but a genuine office from which it can carry out commercial business. The address must be registered with Register of Companies at the same time as the business. In large towns and cities it is possible to find agencies that can provide a siège social and other facilities for smaller businesses.

Statuts: (Company statutes). These are the memorandum and articles of incorporation required by all French companies prior to registration. The should embody the details of the company including the form, name, siège social, aims, total capital, share value and restrictions on share transferability and the powers and limitations of named persons representing the company etc.

Doing Business with France Without Forming a Company

Apart from the Bureau de Liaison, all forms of company already mentioned incur French tax liability. Likewise the appointment of a dependant agent or a resident salesperson with authority to make contracts, or the establishment of premises will also lead to French tax liability. There are some methods of trading however, which do not normally lead to liability for taxation in France.

Distribution Agreement: Under such an agreement, a distributor is allowed a gross margin on sales by the company for which he/she is distributing in France.

Commercial Agent: This is a popular form of distribution agreement in France. The Commercial Agent is an independent contractor who courts orders from clients on behalf of the manufacturer. For this service the agent is paid commission, normally a percentage of the total sales. Note that under French law, undue termination of such an agreement with a commercial agent can result in a settlement for damages in favour of the agent who is deemed to have been unfairly treated and the amount can total twice the gross annual remuneration earned by the agent.

Commissionaire à la vente: Similar, but less formal than a commercial agent, in that the commissionaire à la vente orders from the the supplier on an ad hoc basis.

Franchises: A franchise agreement is where the franchisor agrees with the franchisee to allow him/her the right to run a franchise for the sale of goods or services to clients in return for an agreed system of remuneration.

Business Glossary

French	**English**
Acte de commerce	commercial act
Cession	sale/transfer of a business)
Commissaire aux apports	auditor for contributors
Compte séquestre	stakeholder account
Concessionnaire	distributor
Courtier	broker

Direction du Trésor	Treasury Directorate
Gérant	legal manager
Intérêts des prêts	Interest
Filiales	subsidiaries
Franchisé	franchisee
Franchiseur	franchisor
Huissier de justice	bailiff
Lettre de change	bill of exchange
Mandat	power of attorney; proxy
Moins-values	losses
Plus-values	capital gains
Redevances et honoraires	Royalties
Report des Pertes	losses
Retenues à la source	witholding taxes
Tacite reconduction	automatic renewal of a contract
Société-mère	parent company
Travailleur indépendant	self-employed person

Summary

Just as the French are eagerly taking up the business opportunities that are now available to them in other EU countries, France itself is already very much open to foreigners wishing to start or buy a business there. Although the French have never been very keen on foreign business people entering the French market and making profits for foreign companies, they are very enthusiastic and supportive of anyone wishing to invest in France with a French business or company. This does not mean, however, that setting up any business in France is easy. Inevitably, it will be a more difficult process than in the your own country. The rewards themselves may not be any greater than those which could be achieved in the UK, but the setting-up costs are frequently less.

The overall advice is to proceed very much in the same way as you would if you were starting or buying a business in the UK. Make use of all the support that is available and take expert professional advice in order to deal with the differences in French law and business practice.

Relevant Publications

Business Guide Supplements: published several times yearly by the American Chamber of Commerce in Brussels. The supplements are a useful reference to current EC legislation and policies and offers analyses of their impact on businesses. Can be ordered by telephoning +32 2 513 6892; fax +32 2 513 7928.

Directory of European Industrial & Trade Associations: published by CBD Research Ltd. 15 Wickham Road, Beckenham, Kent BR3 2JS; fax: 0181-650 0768. At £127, this is probably one to consult in a library.

Intrastat Classification Nomenclature (ICN): A 650 page guide for businesses doing interstate business in the EU and turning over more than £135,000 a year. It gives the vital EC code number for every possible item traded in the EU from artichokes to zips. Without such a code number, a business person will not be able to complete a Supplementary Statistical Declaration, SSD (in quadruplicate) which will make you liable to a fine (see VAT above).

Setting up a Small Business in France: (£16) published by the French Chamber of Commerce in Great Britain, 197 Knightsbridge, London SW7 1RB; tel 0171-304 7021; fax 0171 304 7034; e-mail: bclub@ccfgb.co.uk.

PIC International: 93 Av. Champs Elysées, 75008 Paris; tel 1-47 23 00 07. Magazine advertising all types of businesses for sale.

Other Sources of Help & Advice
The Department of Trade and Industry
The DTI (Ashdown House, 123 Victoria Street, London SW1E 6RB; helps potential Euro businesses with a range of free publications including *Guide to Sources of Advice* about setting up business in Europe, regulations and EU legislation affecting small businesses. The DTI also offers an information service and practical assistance to those wanting to set up in Europe. It also has a series of desks for individual countries. Call the main switch board on 0171-215 5000 and ask for the French desk.

French Government Tourist Office:
The Conference and Incentive Department of the French Tourist Office runs a location service, free of charge for organisers or businesses wanting to hold product launches anywhere in France.

Useful Contacts
The American Chamber of Commerce in Paris: 21 av George V, Paris 8th; tel 1-40 73 89 90; fax 1-47 20 18 62.

Assemblée des Chambres Françaises de Commerce et d'Industrie (ACFCI): 45 Avenue d'Iéna, 75016 Paris; tel 1-40 69 37 00. French Chambers of Commerce Network can supply a list of Chambers of Commerce of which there are 183 throughout France.

Assemblée Permanente des Chambres de Métiers: (Chambers of Trade Network), 12 Avenue Marceau, 75008 Paris; tel 1-44 43 10 00. Can be contacted for a national list of Chambre de Métiers.

Association of British Chambers of Commerce: tel 0171-222 1555.

The British Chamber of Commerce: 41 rue Turenne, Paris 3rd; tel 1-44 59 25 20.

Confederation of British Industry (CBI): tel 0171-379 7400.

Department of Trade & Industry (DTI): Business in Europe hotline: tel 0117 944 488.

European Commission: The European Commission has set up various EU wide business cooperation schemes including BC-NET, a network of business consultants and economic development agencies supported by the Commission. The task of the BC net is to assist and give advice to SMEs (Small and Medium-sized entreprises) in particular for their search for cross-border cooperation partners. BC-NET can carry out a confidential partner search. The other scheme is BRE designed to assist SMEs in finding a partner by publicising their needs in local publications, internet sites etc. Further details from: BC-NET Help Desk (tel +32 2 296 2808; fax +32 2 296 25 72) and BRE Help Desk (tel +32 2 295 91 17; fax +32 2 296 42 71). European Commission representation in Scotland: tel 0131 225 2058; Wales 01222 371631; Northern Ireland 01232 240708; Brussels switchboard +32 2-299 1111.

European Information Centres (EICs): provide information on European Union issues for to small and medium-size businesses. EICs have a continuous flow of information on Europe and have access to EU databases, including BC-Net (British Cooperation Network) which can assist companies looking for business partners in Europe. Not all services can be provided by all EICs and some charges may be made for some services. Some UK EICs: Belfast 01235-491031; Birmingham 0121-4550268; Bradford 01274-754262; Bristol 0117 973 7373; Burgess Hill 01444 259259; Cardiff 01222-229525; Exeter 01392 214 085; Leeds

0113 283 3126; Maidstone 01622 694109; Newcastle 0191 2610026; Norwich 0345 023114/01603 625977; Leicester 0116-255 9944; London (West End) 0171 734 6406; Manchester 0161-237 4000; Nottingham 0115 962 4624; Sheffield 0114 253 2126; Southampton 01703 832866; Stafford 01785 222300.

Export Market Information Centre (EMIC): Kingsgate House, 66-74 Victoria Street, London SW1E 6SW; tel 0171 215 54444/5. Further research on the French market can be undertaken at the EMI Centre including market reports, mail order catalogues, directories, development plans and commercial on-line databases.

Franco-British Chamber of Commerce & Industry: 31 rue Boissy d'Anglas, 75008 Paris; tel 1-53 30 81 32; fax 1-53 30 81 35.

Personal Case Histories

Paul Player and Moira Evans

Paul Player and Moira Evans had shared a passion for skiing for many years when they decided to give up their stressful lives (Paul worked as a Financial Advisor with a major High Street bank and Moira, a qualified accountant, worked as a business advisor for a large pharmaceutical company in the UK) and move to France to run chalet holidays in the Alps.

'Having stayed in many ski chalets ourselves, we had a good idea what we were looking for — we just needed to find it!'

They contacted a number of agents in the UK who specialised in selling French properties but had little success and found the agents to be out of touch with the market place 'one property we asked to view had been sold three years earlier'. They then decided to go and look for themselves and decided on the Morzine area as a starting point as it met their criteria: good skiing, summer trade, nice place to live and affordable.

'After being shown a number of very run down properties we were beginning to despair of finding anything suitable'. At that time there was less property available than is currently the case and the pound was relatively weak. By chance they passed an Agent's window displaying brand new properties and decided to investigate further, although originally they hadn't considered building a chalet. They were shown a number of building plots by the agent and immediately fell in love with one of the plots — it was a very sunny spot in a beautiful Savoyarde village with terrific mountain views. 'With some trepidation we signed for the land on New Year's Eve 1995'.

The agent found them a builder and they agreed on the design and specification for the chalet. 'We thought we had plenty of time as we didn't need the chalet until Christmas 1996, but we hadn't reckoned on French builders'. Although their contract with the builders specified completion by the end of October 1996 the chalet wasn't actually handed over until December 20th, and their first guests arrived on December 21st! 'Fortunately we had access to the chalet while the builders were still working on it, otherwise we would not have been ready for our guests'. With hindsight they realise that not being in France while building was in progress was a mistake as it wasn't possible to keep track of progress and 'chivvy' the builders when necessary, and would also have a very much more specific contract next time around.

'Purchasing our property and setting up our business was relatively straight forward, but this would have been much more difficult without the help of our French accountant and Sam Crabb Consultancy in France (01935 850274) in the UK'. They have now learned to find their way around the French systems themselves, but found help essential in the early days.

After the initial trauma of not knowing whether the chalet would be finished on time, and climbing a steep learning curve in their first season, the business is now flourishing with a very promising winter season ahead. Paul and Moira are also looking forward to the next season, after being very agreeably surprised by the extent of the activities that are available in the Alps in the summer, complemented by hot sunny days and stunning scenery.

For anyone contemplating purchasing a property or setting up a business in the Portes du Soleil area of the French Alps, Paul and Moira can provide accommodation in their luxury chalet, help you look for properties and give you the benefit of their experience of living and working in France. Alternatively, if you would just like an holiday, winter or summer, they can send you a brochure. You can contact them by telephone or fax on +33 4-50 79 50 27.

Roger Beresford

Roger Beresford, and his family spent a very enjoyable self-catering holiday on the Côte d'Azur and decided they would like to buy a house in France 'as an investment and for our enjoyment'. Realising that the price of property in that area was beyond his means he looked for an attractive region where property prices were moderate and settled on the Pyrénées Roussillon. At the time he bought a property there, Roger was employed by a bank which provided loans on favourable terms to employees.

By the time his family had grown up and had families of their own a larger house was required to accommodate them when they came to stay and Roger bought his second French home and had no problems with French red tape when importing furniture from the UK. He applied for a *carte de séjour* when he decided to retire to France. He bought a car in France since, as he puts it 'We have heard of people having awful (and costly) problems in getting UK cars registered in France'.

A former chartered secretary and member of the British computer society, Roger admits to understanding French well but is still working on his speaking skills by attending French lessons in Perpignan. His wife speaks French well. They have no problems socialising with the French; in fact as Roger says:

> *We have a far more active social life here than we ever had in England, but this may be because we now have more time. We try to spend more time with French people and tend to steer clear of expatriate socialising as coffee mornings are not really our scene. We also try to involve ourselves as much as possible in village life and find everyone most friendly and helpful.*

When asked what he liked most about living in France, Roger cited the climate, the scenery, the culture and the absence of 'whenever we hear it, the depressing English news'. However no paradise is perfect: 'The drivers go too fast and come too close and there is no cheddar cheese'.

Jackie and Barry Devereux

Jackie and Barry Devereux, who are in their forties, moved to France in 1991 where they run residential painting courses (Painting at Le Pigeonnier) from their home in the south of France. Jackie was an art and calligraphy teacher who taught at local colleges for many years, while Barry was an industrial photographer. They had originally planned on starting such a business in North Wales as long ago as 1983, but while the work was coming in they continued in their respective professions. When the recession bit in 1989, they were forced to abandon their plans and move to Peterborough. They thought about moving to Portugal or France because, as Jackie put it 'if we were going to be poor, we might as well be poor in a warm climate'. Neither of them spoke a word of any foreign language.

There was also, a sound practical reason for the move abroad. Jackie says 'we spotted a gap in the market when we realised that there was a growing demand for residential art courses abroad, but few organisations to satisfy it'.

Owing to the recession it took them nearly 18 months to sell their house in Peterborough (it had also lost a third of its value) and make the move. Almost immediately they arrived in France, they embarked on language courses lasting six months. Jackie went to Beziers for classes, first private, then in a group and finally, an elderly local couple 'adopted them' and spent one evening a week speaking with them in French. When they first moved to France, they lived in a caravan in the grounds of a friend's château. They finally bought a house with a three-acre vineyard which they have since turned into a park.

They are now 'living their dream' and although they will never be in the big business league, they are successful in their own terms with a loyal as well as expanding clientele.

We asked Jackie?

What do you think is essential to making a success of living and working in France?

Don't expect it to be easy living in another country; you have as many problems in daily life here as you would have in the UK. We think it is very important to get integrated into the local community, and it pays off. For instance we are regular customers of the local petrol station and during the French truckers' strike (of 1997) when petrol was being rationed, the owner rang us to say that if we were in difficulties, to let him know and he would help us. We know some expatriate types who keep themselves to themselves and insist on 'being British'. We make a joke about it; in any case Barry is a New Zealander. We have integrated so much that I now feel a little bit French, and when I go to the UK I feel like a foreigner.

What are advantages for you personally of living in France?

As an artist, you are treated differently. In the UK, art is considered as an easy option and not a real occupation. In France, being an artist is considered a true profession and consequently you are treated with respect.

What do you feel are the drawbacks of living in France?

The bureaucracy is much worse than anything you can imagine. There are serious paper pushers here, and you can never get a decision on anything as you are simply referred on to someone else. You waste an awful lot of time on this aspect of life. But the functionaries are not usually difficult to deal with, in fact they can be quite pleasant, charming even. But the way the operate could easily drive you mad; it helps if you are already a bit mad already.

Do you have any regrets about leaving the UK?

The biggest regret is not being near friends and family. When there is a crisis, you suddenly feel the distance between you and them. It is very important to have the wherewithal to pop back to them whenever there is a need or you want to be with them.

Vacation Work publish:

	Paperback	Hardback
The Directory of Summer Jobs Abroad	£8.99	£14.99
The Directory of Summer Jobs in Britain	£8.99	£14.99
Adventure Holidays	£7.99	£12.99
Work Your Way Around the World	£12.95	£16.99
Working in Tourism – The UK, Europe & Beyond	£10.99	£15.99
Kibbutz Volunteer	£8.99	£12.99
Working on Cruise Ships	£8.99	£12.99
Teaching English Abroad	£10.99	£15.99
The Au Pair & Nanny's Guide to Working Abroad	£9.99	£14.99
Working in Ski Resorts – Europe & North America	£10.99	–
Accounting Jobs Worldwide	£11.95	£16.95
Working with the Environment	£9.99	£15.99
Health Professionals Abroad	£9.99	£15.99
The Directory of Jobs & Careers Abroad	£11.95	£16.99
The International Directory of Voluntary Work	£9.99	£15.99
The Directory of Work & Study in Developing Countries	£8.99	£14.99
Live & Work in Russia & Eastern Europe	£10.99	£15.95
Live & Work in France	£10.99	£15.95
Live & Work in Australia & New Zealand	£10.99	£14.95
Live & Work in the USA & Canada	£10.99	£14.95
Live & Work in Germany	£10.99	£15.95
Live & Work in Belgium, The Netherlands & Luxembourg	£10.99	£15.95
Live & Work in Spain & Portugal	£10.99	£15.95
Live & Work in Italy	£10.99	£15.95
Live & Work in Scandinavia	£8.95	£14.95
Travellers Survival Kit: Lebanon	£9.99	–
Travellers Survival Kit: South Africa	£9.99	–
Travellers Survival Kit: India	£9.99	–
Travellers Survival Kit: Russia & the Republics	£9.95	–
Travellers Survival Kit: Western Europe	£8.95	–
Travellers Survival Kit: Eastern Europe	£9.95	–
Travellers Survival Kit: South America	£15.95	–
Travellers Survival Kit: Central America	£8.95	–
Travellers Survival Kit: Cuba	£10.99	–
Travellers Survival Kit: USA & Canada	£10.99	–
Travellers Survival Kit: Australia & New Zealand	£9.99	–
Hitch–hikers' Manual Britain	£3.95	–
Europe – a Manual for Hitch-hikers	£4.95	–

Distributors of:

Summer Jobs USA	£12.95	–
Internships (On-the-Job Training Opportunities in the USA)	£16.95	–
Sports Scholarships in the USA	£12.95	–
Making It in Japan	£8.95	–
Green Volunteers	£9.99	–

Vacation Work Publications, 9 Park End Street, Oxford OX1 1HJ
(Tel 01865–241978. Fax 01865–790885)